An Introductory Reader to the Writings of Jim Cummins

BILINGUAL EDUCATION AND BILINGUALISM
Series Editors: Professor Nancy H. Hornberger, *University of Pennsylvania, Philadelphia, USA* and Professor Colin Baker, *University of Wales, Bangor, Wales, UK*

Other Books in the Series
At War With Diversity: US Language Policy in an Age of Anxiety
    James Crawford
Bilingual Education and Social Change
    Rebecca Freeman
Curriculum Related Assessment, Cummins and Bilingual Children
    Tony Cline and Norah Frederickson (eds)
Dual Language Education
    Kathryn J. Lindholm-Leary
English in Europe: The Acquisition of a Third Language
    Jasone Cenoz and Ulrike Jessner (eds)
Foundations of Bilingual Education and Bilingualism
    Colin Baker
Language Minority Students in the Mainstream Classroom
    Angela L. Carrasquillo and Vivian Rodriguez
Languages in America: A Pluralist View
    Susan J. Dicker
Learning English at School: Identity, Social Relations and Classroom Practice
    Kelleen Toohey
Language, Power and Pedagogy: Bilingual Children in the Crossfire
    Jim Cummins
Language Revitalization Processes and Prospects
    Kendall A. King
Multicultural Children in the Early Years
    P. Woods, M. Boyle and N. Hubbard
Policy and Practice in Bilingual Education
    Ofelia García and Colin Baker (eds)
Reflections on Multiliterate Lives
    Diane Belcher and Ulla Connor (eds)
The Sociopolitics of English Language Teaching
    Joan Kelly Hall and William G. Eggington (eds)
Studies in Japanese Bilingualism
    Mary Goebel Noguchi and Sandra Fotos (eds)
Teaching and Learning in Multicultural Schools
    Elizabeth Coelho
Teaching Science to Language Minority Students
    Judith W. Rosenthal

Other Books of Interest
Beyond Bilingualism: Multilingualism and Multilingual Education
    Jasone Cenoz and Fred Genesee (eds)
The Care and Education of Young Bilinguals
    Colin Baker
Encyclopedia of Bilingualism and Bilingual Education
    Colin Baker and Sylvia Prys Jones

Please contact us for the latest book information:
Multilingual Matters, Frankfurt Lodge, Clevedon Hall,
Victoria Road, Clevedon, BS21 7HH, England
http://www.multilingual-matters.com

BILINGUAL EDUCATION AND BILINGUALISM 29
Series Editors: Nancy H. Hornberger and Colin Baker

An Introductory Reader to the Writings of Jim Cummins

Edited by

Colin Baker and Nancy H. Hornberger

MULTILINGUAL MATTERS LTD
Clevedon • Buffalo • Toronto • Sydney

Library of Congress Cataloging in Publication Data
Cummins, Jim [Selections. 2001]
An Introductory Reader to the Writings of Jim Cummins/Edited by Colin Baker and Nancy H. Hornberger.
Bilingual Education and Bilingualism: 29.
1. Education, Bilingual. 2. Bilingualism. 3. Language and education. I. Baker, Colin.
II. Hornberger, Nancy H. III. Title. IV. Series.
LC3701.C86 2001
370.117'5–dc21   2001030279

British Library Cataloguing in Publication Data
A catalogue entry for this book is available from the British Library.

ISBN 1-85359-476-8 (hbk)
ISBN 1-85359-475-X (pbk)

Multilingual Matters Ltd
UK: Frankfurt Lodge, Clevedon Hall, Victoria Road, Clevedon BS21 7HH.
USA: UTP, 2250 Military Road, Tonawanda, NY 14150, USA.
Canada: UTP, 5201 Dufferin Street, North York, Ontario M3H 5T8, Canada.
Australia: Footprint Books, Unit 4/92a Mona Vale Road, Mona Vale, NSW 2103, Australia.

Typeset by Wayside Books, Clevedon.
Printed and bound in Great Britain by Cambrian Printers Ltd.

Contents

Acknowledgements

The editors would like to thank Professor Jim Cummins and all the publishers who kindly granted permission to reproduce copyright material that is collected in this volume. The sources are listed listed below.

Section 1: The 1970s

A Theoretical Perspective on the Relationship between Bilingualism and Thought. *Working Papers on Bilingualism.* April 1973, pp. 2–10. By kind permission of the Ontario Institute for Studies in Education, Toronto.

The Influence of Bilingualism on Cognitive Growth: A Synthesis of Research Findings and Explanatory Hypotheses. *Working Papers on Bilingualism.* April 1976, pp. 1–43. By kind permission of the Ontario Institute for Studies in Education, Toronto.

Immersion Programmes: The Irish Experience. *International Review of Education.* 1978, Vol. 24, pp. 273–82. By kind permission of Kluwer Academic Publishers, The Netherlands.

Linguistic Interdependence and the Educational Development of Bilingual Children. *Review of Educational Research.* 1979, Vol. 49, pp. 222–51. By kind permission of the American Educational Research Association, Washington DC, USA.

Research Findings from French Immersion Programs across Canada: A Parent's Guide. 1979 [1983]. Canadian Parents for French, Ottawa, Ontario, Canada.

Section 2: The 1980s

The Entry and Exit Fallacy in Bilingual Education. *NABE Journal.* 1980, Vol. 4, pp. 25–60. By kind permission of NABE, Washington DC, USA.

Tests, Achievement, and Bilingual Students. *FOCUS.* February 1982, Number 9, pp. 1–7. By kind permission of the National Clearinghouse for Bilingual Education, George Washington University, Washington DC, USA.

Learning Difficulties in 'Immersion' Programmes. Chapter 7 of *Bilingualism and Special Education: Issues in Assessment and Pedagogy.* 1984. By kind permission of Multilingual Matters, Clevedon, UK.

Empowering Minority Students: A Framework for Intervention. *Harvard Educational Review.* 1986, Vol. 56, No. 1, pp. 18–36. By kind permission of the President and Fellows of Harvard College, Cambridge, MA, USA.

Psychological Assessment of Minority Students: Out of Context, Out of Focus, Out of Control. *Journal of Reading, Writing and Learning Disabilities International.* 1986, Vol. 2, pp. 9–20. By kind permission of Taylor & Francis Inc., Philadelphia, PA, USA.

From the Inner City to the Global Village: The Microcomputer as a Catalyst for Collaborative Learning and Cultural Interchange. *Language, Culture and Curriculum.* 1988, Vol. 1, pp. 1–14. By kind permission of Multilingual Matters, Clevedon, UK.

From Multicultural to Anti-racist Education: An Analysis of Programs and Policies in Ontario. In T. Skutnabb-Kangas and J. Cummins (eds) *Minority Education: From Shame to Struggle.* 1988, pp. 127–57. By kind permission of Multilingual Matters, Clevedon, UK.

The Role and Use of Educational Theory in Formulating Language Policy. *TESL Canada Journal.* 1988, Vol. 5, pp. 11–19. By kind permission of TESL Canada, Burnaby, BC, Canada.

Section 3: The 1990s

Heritage Language Teaching in Canadian Schools. *Journal of Curriculum Studies.* 1992, Vol. 24, pp. 281–6. By kind permission of Taylor & Francis Ltd, Abingdon, Oxford, UK.

Empowerment through Biliteracy. In J.V. Tinajero and A.F. Ada (eds) *The Power of Two Languages: Literacy and Biliteracy for Spanish-speaking Students.* 1992, pp. 1–17. By kind permission of the McGraw-Hill Companies, New York, USA.

Multicultural Education and Technology: Promise and Pitfalls. *Multicultural Education.* Spring 1996, pp. 4–11 (co-authored with D. Sayers). By kind permission of Caddo Gap Press, San Francisco, CA, USA.

Babel Babble: Reframing the Discourse of Diversity. Chapter 9 of *Negotiating Identities: Education for Empowerment in a Diverse Society.* 1996. By kind permission of the California Association for Bilingual Education, Los Angeles, CA, USA.

Cultural and Linguistic Diversity in Education: A Mainstream Issue? *Educational Review.* 1997, Vol. 49, No. 2, pp. 99–107. By kind permission of Taylor & Francis Ltd, Abingdon, Oxford, UK.

Alternative Paradigms in Bilingual Education Research: Does Theory Have a Place? *Educational Researcher.* 1999, Vol. 28, No. 7, pp. 26–32. By kind permission of the American Educational Research Association, Washington DC, USA.

Jim Cummins:
A Biographical Introduction[1]

On the 3rd July 1949, an Irishman was born in Dublin to a middle-class family, with a respectable banking official father, a devoutly religious mother and two brothers, one older, one to be born later. Although neither parents nor grandparents spoke Irish with any degree of fluency, the middle-born son, James Patrick Cummins, would within three decades become one of the world's greatest experts on minority languages.

We are all inescapably part-products of our families, schooling, local community and native country, and his roots have been one influence on both the direction of Jim Cummins' writing and his message. His early experiences of language in education, the sanctimony of rigid religion, and the pathos, potentiality and prosperity of emigration from Ireland to Canada each affected his lifelong mission.

The Irish Context

The psyche of the Irish people is bound up with a turbulent religious, economic and political history. The colonialism of the English led to repression and domination; famines and poverty led to massive emigration. Close to half of all the people born in Ireland from 1820 to the present have emigrated. Many emigrated to the United States and Canada to seek fame and fortune: Jim Cummins was one of the most successful.

Despite an uncharitable economy that brought famine and fleeing to other countries, many Irish immigrants into the United States and Canada, the United Kingdom and elsewhere in the world, continue to cherish the home country, valuing the Irish language and culture as symbols of a distinct and dramatic heritage. An Irish emigrant rarely forgets the emerald green fields, beautiful coastal scenery, small cottages and large churches, the sad and lively music from fiddle and pipe, the gaiety of the dance and song, and the taste of whiskey and stout that raise spirits amidst the darkest of days. But many emigrants also remember days when stern religious beliefs permeated if not dominated families and schools, when the relationships of priests and people were not always spiritually uplifting but sometimes involved deceiving power relationships.

If national profiles are momentarily allowed, there is a deep pride in being Irish, outwardly symbolized in the colorful intensity of melody and jig, and oral traditions and written text that envelope a delightful indigenous wit and merriment. Most Irish combine a charm, gentility and hospitality that belies a history of coercive colonialism, frequent famine and enforced emigration.

With immigration go the possibilities of assimilation or integration into a new country, but also the threat of rejection, ridicule and racism. For most immigrants there is instant powerlessness, immediate disparity of status, the expectation of being subordinate and inferior to longer-term residents. But immigration is ambivalent. With emigration and immigration also go fresh expectations and new optimism. There is the prospect of a fresh beginning, the chance of a prosperous future and the dream of a fuller enjoyment, equity and empowerment. For Jim Cummins, immigration became not only a personal experience but also a topic for an influential academic contribution. Indeed, no Irish emigrant has ever had such a major international influence on how people throughout the world see immigration, minority languages and minority language education.

Emigration and immigration are often bound up with the languages of the old and new country. Immigrants are faced with internal decisions and external pressures to lose or retain heritage languages and learn the language of the receiving country. The possibilities of bilingualism are often threatened by the subtractive pushes of majority language speakers towards accepting the domination of their language.

Irish emigrants to North America had the benefit of speaking English. Not all spoke Irish fluently – yet Irish people have traditionally given high symbolic value to their heritage language. The Irish language is an important emblem for many Irish emigrants representing a people who are proud of their roots and origins. After the Irish Free State was established in 1922, the Irish government was enthusiastic for the Irish language to be imposed on the nation as a symbol of unity and freedom from oppression. The government of Ireland invested significantly, although rarely effectively, in a wide variety of economic, social, cultural and educational initiatives to promote Irish. But the history of the Irish language this century has sometimes been that the oppressed became the oppressors, the conquered became those who wish to conquer the language life of the Irish population by a form of language planning that verged on being coercive. For example, up to the 1970s, those who failed to pass Irish in their school leaving certificate examination received no credit for any of the subjects they did pass and were essentially deemed not to have graduated from secondary school. Many Irish people of Jim Cummins' generation have family members and friends who experienced this fate.

Irish education has always been conscious that reproduction of the Irish language requires the strong assistance of schools. At its best, there has been a long tradition of dual language education, with children learning through the medium of Irish and English. There is a history of success in Irish bilingual education where both languages have been used to transmit curriculum content. In contrast, there is a history of relatively ineffective drip-feed Irish language lessons imposed on every child at each grade level. In such language learning, Irish has tended until recently to be taught formally and not for communicative fluency; as a subject and not for everyday communication; for examination purposes but not for usage; for symbolic purposes rather than for daily conversation.

But it is not language that once dominated Irish education. Rather, it was religion. Irish education has historically been dominated by Catholic catechisms and conformity, by Fathers and Nuns some of whom were kindly and godly, others more keen on humiliation rather than humility, indoctrination rather than induction, enslavement rather than enlightenment. Until recently, much Irish education was dominated by the Classics more than Science, Literature and Language rather than Technology, with Religion pervasive. Dogma was impelled; doubt was forbidden. Families seemingly collaborated with schools to ensure that sin and a simple faith was top of the agenda, with Catholic compliance essential for salvation.

The coerciveness of religion in Ireland has clashed in recent decades with postmodern society. New generations have challenged Catholic orthodoxy and insisted on open-mindedness. Younger generations have become critical of authority, challenging the power of the priest and pulpit, arguing for the social construction of knowledge instead of imposition of dogma. Rational consent and not rigid conformity, re-positioning and not reliance on authority have become the new order for thinking. Jim Cummins is part of that new order, and for language minorities has been a powerful persuader and advocate.

The Education of an Irish Scholar

Born into an English-speaking family, Jim Cummins first encountered Irish as a Dublin schoolboy at the age of four with Irish language learning lessons that were part of the regular school program for all children. At seven years of age, he first encountered bilingual education when he spent a successful year at an Irish Gaelscoil. Ahead of the Dual Language movement in the United States, the school taught 80% through the medium of Irish and 20% through the medium of English. The children in the school were mostly from English-speaking homes and the parents warmly supported the school's mission in Irish language revitalization. Jim Cummins picked up Irish fairly easily at that school and found that learning content through a second language was effective and efficient. An advocate for bilingual education was born in the experience of one year of elementary schooling.

The remainder of his schooling did not build linguistically on that one year in the Irish *Gaelscoil*. Unhappily, the Irish taught in subsequent schools was taught formally, almost as a foreign language, and Jim lost some fluency in Irish, although he passed his examinations for matriculation purposes. However, the young Dubliner showed considerable promise.

University days often mark a different relationship between language and power. In school, the discourse frequently aims to control and coalesce. At University, there is the chance of a discourse of criticism, collaboration, analysis and evaluation. The hierarchical control over curriculum content and ideas experienced during school days can be replaced by a more open expression of ideas, moving from a discourse of fear and submission to a discourse of counter-assertion, challenge and a collaborative construction of meaning.

At University College Dublin (UCD), Jim studied Psychology after a general foundational fresher year beginning in 1967. Psychology had just been placed on the UCD curriculum. The undergraduate shone at this new subject which became the discipline through which his early writings and research were conducted.

As a student, Jim Cummins showed the academic capacity to synthesize, memorize, and easily connect new knowledge from a variety of disciplines. In Ireland and the United Kingdom, less than 5% of students have historically obtained a first class honors degree classification, an award that marks them out for future excellence, leadership or fame. Jim Cummins graduated in 1970 with a first class honors BA degree. His great potential was evident in the award of a 'summa cum laude' (literally, 'with the highest praise') degree – but perhaps not to himself.

The seeds of emigration were sown in those undergraduate days. During both the second and third year of his university undergraduate career, Jim Cummins worked during the summer in Massachusetts, firstly as a children's camp counselor in a YMCA camp at Lynn (north of Boston) and the following year in a restaurant in Chatham on Cape Cod. This was his first experience of the United States, enjoyable enough to tempt further experiences abroad. This positive experience, plus the young 20-year-old having moved away from the fervent Catholic religion of his mother and schooling, made graduate study in North America attractive. He had also enjoyed traveling abroad, and found the experience of a different culture and country appetizing.

The seeds of emigration found germination in a chance encounter with one of the founding fathers of bilingualism and bilingual education. Jim Cummins recounts an incident that enthused his applying for a graduate program in North America. While taking a one-year Postgraduate Applied Psychology Diploma in Dublin (1970–71), Jim went to hear Wally Lambert speak in Dublin about the newly founded and successful French immersion programs in Canada. This was Jim's first encounter with bilingual education as an academic topic. He instantly became intrigued.

At the end of the talk, with the press waiting impatiently for an interview with Wally Lambert, a conversation occurred which changed the direction of a young graduate's career. In an unrushed, helpful and positive manner, Wally spent time encouraging Jim in the idea of doing a PhD in North America. This advice made a persuasive impression and became one catalyst in the formation of a scholar who would change the world's understanding of bilingualism and bilingual education.

In 1971, Jim applied to the Universities at Edmonton and McGill for a PhD place. While other North American universities were attractive, they required a $20 to $25 application fee. In the event, only Edmonton (in the form of Professor Metro Gulutsan) accepted Jim. He also had acquaintances who had been to Edmonton to study Economics. Given the history of Irish emigration, his parents were happy for him to pursue further studies abroad, although they assumed he would be back permanently to Ireland following the Graduate program.

Jim entered Canada as a 'landed immigrant' (rather than on a student visa) which opened up more possibilities of work. At the University of Alberta in Edmonton, Jim spent three years (1971–74) working on the relationship between bilingualism and cognition, and on bilingual education. He worked with Metro Gulutsan who was multilingual and a fervent activist in preserving the Ukrainian language and culture in Canada. As part of his role in the University of Alberta, the young Jim Cummins was required to assist Metro Gulutsan on a third-year undergraduate course on bilingualism, particularly assessing course work by students. This was a fast immersion in the topic that Jim had not covered in his own undergraduate or Diploma courses.

Apart from the successful PhD thesis, Jim Cummins worked with Metro Gulutsan to produce two papers (1974 and 1975), and this marked Jim's arrival on the publishing scene, particularly in the area of bilingualism and thinking. Such publications were written at a pivotal time in Canadian history. In the early 1970s, Canada was vigorously discussing its two solitudes, the place of French and English within the language and cultural mosaic of Canada, and the possibilities of bilingualism and biculturalism. Also in these early days, immigrant languages such as Ukrainian and Hebrew, plus the native Canadian languages, were beginning to be recognized as worthy of academic study and were becoming part of public discourse. Research on bilingualism had been underway for several decades, but as a more minor topic without a disciplinary foothold. The Canadian debates brought bilingualism and bilingual education into the press, public consciousness and pedagogy. Into the debate stepped a modest, quiet and highly talented Irishman. Unsuspecting of his future or the contribution he would make, Jim Cummins began to change the language and the direction of the debate in ways that are now firmly ingrained, largely accepted and internationally acclaimed.

In 1974, Dr Jim Cummins returned to Dublin, Ireland to become a Research Associate at the Education Research Centre in St Patrick's College. Here he became involved in surveys of schoolteachers and acquainted with language assessment procedures. Much of this research has remained unpublished. While at St Patrick's College, Jim met John Edwards (then at St Patrick's and now at the University of St Francis Xavier in Canada), who increased his awareness of new and blossoming areas of academic study: minority languages, bilingual education, language shift and rising political controversies.

During this two-year research period, Jim Cummins also discussed issues related to bilingual education with Irish revivalists, people who were strongly committed to affirmative action to revive the Irish language. One of the topics which frequently came up in these discussions was the status of John Macnamara's large-scale study of Irish-medium programs, published in his 1966 book *Bilingualism and Primary Education: A Study of Irish Experience* (Edinburgh: Edinburgh University Press). Macnamara had interpreted the data from his national survey as showing that bilingual education was relatively ineffective and that the use of the Irish language in school led to lower achievement. Finding alternative interpretations in the research data, and doubting the validity of Macnamara's conclusions, Jim published a critique together with new data from Irish-medium programs which he had collected. The paper 'Immersion programmes: The Irish experience' (1978) became an important harbinger of theoretical concepts to come.

Macnamara (1966) argued for a balance effect in languages. As one language increased, he argued, the other declined. This triggered off early ideas about separate underlying proficiency and common underlying proficiency in the young Dublin Research Associate, ideas that effectively demolished the balance notion. Jim also found that Macnamara had misinterpreted his data. Closer analysis would have shown that dual language use for content teaching in bilingual schools led to higher Irish achievement at no cost to achievement in other academic areas. Jim pointed out that Macnamara had confounded the effect of instruction through a weaker language with the effect of testing through a weaker language.

The Macnamara controversy was an early precursor in revealing that politics is never far away from discussions of bilingualism and bilingual education. Research on education and language soon becomes embroiled in political controversy, the discourse of power and prejudice, hypocrisy and hate, even the injection of smear and fear, as California in the late 1990s powerfully revealed in the Unz attack on bilingual education in Proposition 227.

The Canadian Academic

In 1976, Jim Cummins returned to Canada to become a Canadian as well as an Irishman. Apart from frequent international travel, it is Canada that has been his home ever since. During his graduate days at the University of Alberta, he married a Canadian and in 1974 they bore a daughter. The preference was for her to be educated in Canada in a non-religious educational setting, something which at that stage was rarely available in Ireland. In 1976, Jim became a Research Associate at the Centre for the Study of Mental Retardation at the University of Alberta. Here he renewed his association with Ukrainian bilingual education programs that sought to revitalize a language being stifled in Russia. Jim witnessed the effective activism of the Ukrainian community, an established community whose members were enthusiastic to avoid language and cultural loss.

In Alberta, at the invitation of the provincial francophone community organization, Cummins participated in a series of panel presentations in remote, traditionally francophone communities. These presentations were designed to inform both francophone and anglophone parents of the educational benefits of dual language programs in which both French and English first language students could participate. At that time, due to the small numbers of students in these communities, a bilingual program would be instituted only if both groups agreed to participate.

Jim Cummins' research during this period included investigating special needs education for bilingual children – a theme that has run through his career and produced an influential book in 1984 entitled *Bilingualism and Special Education: Issues in Assessment and Pedagogy*. During this period, Cummins learnt that working with communities, face to face, was important and carried high impact. No cloistered academic, he acquired the confidence to work with a wide spectrum of people: parents and politicians, administrators and activists, students and school staff. He found he could talk spontaneously with a depth of instant thinking that allowed effective answers. Emerging from psychology as his first and primary discipline, he was also accumulating a width of knowledge and understanding that could address a variety of interdisciplinary issues. Drawing solely from neither psychology nor sociology, linguistics nor politics, education nor modern languages, he can synthesize and integrate all these perspectives to communicate with communities and organizations, teachers and policy makers, academics and parents.

Also during this 1976 to 1978 period, Jim Cummins became involved with the Canadian 'Parents for French' movement. This has been an effective pressure group of parents campaigning for immersion education across Canada. For Jim, this was also community-based work from which he learnt that change and evolution in bilingual systems need the empowerment of the community and collaboration with parents and pivotal educationalists. During this time he wrote a short 'Parent's Guide to French Immersion' which received a large distribution in Canada and outside.

In the 1976 to 1978 period, Jim Cummins produced 14 research papers, some based on his PhD thesis which concerned bilingual and monolingual populations, and some based on collaboration with J. P. Das. In this early period, Jim Cummins not only was launched on the international publishing scene but also revealed an outstanding quality that has continued ever since: a willingness to address the full range of issues bearing on bilingualism and bilingual education, and not just the narrowly psychological ones. His early papers between 1974 and the end of that decade address topics including cognition, bilingual education, psychological theory, reading instruction, immersion education, reading difficulties, mother tongue maintenance, metalinguistic awareness, immigrant children, language proficiency, special needs children, the Ireland and Canada context and the relationship between anglophone and francophone communities in Canada. The ability to work in an interdisciplinary manner, synthesizing widely different themes, and also to write prolifically, was apparent in the late 1970s and has continued unabated ever since.

While at the University of Alberta Centre for the Study of Mental Retardation, Jim Cummins negotiated access to a plentiful reservoir of data from psychological assessments of children in a local school board. Out of this wealth of data, Jim uncovered considerable discrimination against bilingual children in the tests and assessments. He also found that most teachers and psychologists were largely unaware of either the extent or nature of this discrimination. In looking through more than 400 teacher referral forms and psychological assessments, Jim noticed that children often seemed to have attained fluency in English very rapidly, but this fluency was not matched by their performance either in the classroom or on formal tests. On this basis, he formulated a distinction between Basic Interpersonal Communicative Skills and Cognitive Academic Language Proficiency (BICS and CALP) that has become part of the language of bilingualism and bilingual education ever since.

In this late 1970s period, there are two other influences important to mention. First, Jim Cummins found by chance a report in Professor Gulutsan's files by Tove Skutnabb-Kangas and Pertti Toukomaa, 'Teaching Migrant Children Mother Tongue and Learning the Language of the Host Country in the Context of the Socio-cultural Situation of the Migrants Family' (Tampere, Finland: Tukimuksia Research Reports, 1976). As he acknowledged in his early writing, Jim found this important in that it mirrored, confirmed and extended his ideas on BICS and CALP and the Thresholds theory. Fascinated with this early influential report from Finland, Jim found someone in Tove Skutnabb-Kangas who was also pushing back the frontiers of knowledge about bilingualism and bilingual education.

Second, Jim visited the Ford Foundation in New York at their invitation. He made a vivid impression not only because of the youth and informality signaled by his jeans and long hair (his customary attire at the time), but also, and primarily, due to his vision about bilingualism. The Ford Foundation found a young man of immense ability and potential, with innovative ideas and creative solutions. This visit announced a new major player on the United States bilingualism and bilingual education scene and marked the beginning of Jim's involvement with US academics such as Lily Wong Fillmore and Rudolph Troike. This early visit led to Cummins' participation in the landmark series, *Bilingual Education: Current Perspectives*, published in 1976 and 1977 by the Center for Applied Linguistics with support from the Ford Foundation.

In 1978, Jim became a Visiting Professor at the Modern Language Centre, Department of Curriculum, the Ontario Institute for Studies in Education. Appointed by H. H. Stern, and then working under the wise and encouraging leadership of Merrill Swain, he has remained loyal to OISE ever since, despite attractive offers to move. In a collegial and supportive atmosphere, OISE has provided the intellectual and prestigious environment for a prolific writer and influential international contributor. Moving from Visiting Professor to Associate Instructor to Assistant Professor to Associate Professor and now as full Professor in the Modern Language Centre, there are few academics in Canada of such international distinction and eminency.

As with many highly creative people in academia, Jim has the ability to stand apart and be critical, and to accept periods of intellectual loneliness. Also, to say something so significant and original that others will instantly criticize from traditional perspectives and alternative paradigms requires a self-assurance and sense of rightness in what one is doing. Few, if any, critics have attacked the whole: just some of the components in isolation (see *Language, Power and Pedagogy: Bilingual Children in the Crossfire* (Clevedon: Multilingual Matters, 2000) – a remarkable feat in 30 years of prolific academic writing.

Children, Collaborators and Colleagues

Most educators learn much from their children, including about schooling. Jim Cummins not only experienced Canadian immersion education as an academic topic, but also through his children's experience. Reflections on his children's encounter with bilingual education has helped Jim to analyze the current pedagogical issues of immersion education. For example, is the introduction of English language and literacy at grade 4 for native English-speaking students in French immersion rather late? Is there too much concentration on correct grammar and correcting mistakes in French language teaching? Are there dogmas of immersion education that have become so strongly embedded in a successful system that there is currently a lack of instructional imagination or a progressive pedagogy? The experiences of his children in bilingual education have been a catalyst for posing such questions.

No academic is an island. While many academics, researchers and also importantly teachers and educational administrators have influenced Jim Cummins, there are six people needing particular mention.

In the early days, Tove Skutnabb-Kangas' writing was confirmation and elucidation of concepts he had developed in his early research. BICS and CALP, the Thresholds theory, but also early ideas about discrimination, social justice and the powerlessness of bilingual people resonated in Tove's work. In 1978, they met in Montreal and later Jim went to Scandinavia (Finland, Sweden and Denmark) to lecture and learn from the context from which Tove was writing. When lecturing in Scandinavia, he learnt to speak without a script at conferences, finding that his carefully prepared script was not always relevant to the audience. The ability to *ad lib* also reflects a confidence in depth of understanding, width of knowledge and sense of purpose. In 1988, with Tove Skutnabb-Kangas, he produced an edited book entitled *Minority Education: From Shame to Struggle* (Clevedon: Multilingual Matters) which became both celebrated and influential, moving debates from a solid theoretical and contextual basis to a spirited fight for equity and justice in the treatment of language minorities.

Second, Lily Wong Fillmore is a close friend and has provided strong support and encouragement since they first met in the late 1970s. Lily and Jim have taught a series of week-long summer courses together over the years, in various venues across the United States. Recently, they collaborated in materials development for teaching English as a second language. Both are authors of the Scott Foresman ESL program published in 1995. Lily's support, intellectual inspiration and uncompromising commitment to equity for bilingual students remain strong influences on Jim's work to this day.

Third, in the 1980s, working with the Californian State Education Department, Jim Cummins collaborated with Stephen Krashen and others in putting together a highly influential, policy-relevant theoretical framework for bilingual education in California and elsewhere. A soulmate was found. There are some important parallels between Jim Cummins and Stephen Krashen: both have made a considerable impact on educational practice and policy; both have sought to move from theory and a synthesis of research into addressed practising educators in their work; both have formulated their theoretical ideas explicitly with the intent of influencing both policy and classroom practice. Both have also experienced intense criticism from fellow academics of some aspects of their work but this criticism has not significantly diminished the continuing impact of their ideas in both academic and classroom contexts.

Fourth, Merrill Swain has been a close colleague of Jim Cummins at OISE since she invited him there in 1978. They collaborated on an important book published in 1986 entitled *Bilingualism in Education: Aspects of Theory, Research and Policy* (New York: Longman). When Jim was being attacked for his work on language proficiency, Merrill Swain joined him in replies and counter-argument and placed her considerable academic credibility behind Jim's arguments. As Head of the Modern Language Centre at OISE, Merrill Swain helped ensure the fertile conditions for Jim Cummins' contribution to international debates and policy making.

Fifth, in the 1980s, Alma Flor Ada was influenced by Paulo Friere and showed by word and deed how his views on education related to powerless bilingual minorities, particularly Latinos in the United States. Her advocacy for language minorities, her close collaboration at the community level in literacy projects, her championing of critical literacy and critical pedagogy have influenced Jim Cummins' writings, including recent publications. Their joint concern for social justice, equity and empowerment of minorities has begun to influence debates on how to transform relations between communities and schools.

Sixth, Dennis Sayers encouraged the entrance of Jim Cummins into debates about the use of information and communication technology (ICT) as a means of both empowering minority language children and creating internationalism. This has added new dimensions to the study of multilingualism and multiculturalism, language awareness and cultural diversity. They met in the summer of 1984 in Boston, and later produced a book called *Brave New Schools: Challenging Cultural Illiteracy through Global Learning Networks* (New York: St Martin's Press). Such a partnership fired Jim's imagination as ICT provided the means for developing critical language awareness among students, and for minority language students to explore issues of cultural identity, critical enquiry and knowledge generation.

Research and Publications

From 1980 through to the present, Jim Cummins has won many research grants that reveal two things in particular. First, funding is for him a means to an end and not an end in itself. Despite many research grants, Jim Cummins has placed moving the frontiers of knowledge and understanding at the top of his priority list. Indeed, he suggests that some of his most influential research has been unfunded. Second, the funding shows the enormous variety of Jim's interdisciplinary portfolio. Topics undertaken with research funding include: language proficiency, North American identity, evaluation of bilingual education, literacy development, the establishment of a National Heritage Language Resource Unit, use of the microcomputer, the assessment and placement of minority students, ESL students and school collaboration.

With considerable experience as well as conviction, Jim Cummins argues that writing is often more influential than research; synthesis and theory more influential than single research studies, although there are always links and harmonization. Also, Jim Cummins argues that to be influential, one has to work with teachers and educational administrators. Dialogue with teachers, and reflecting on that dialogue, is an important way of moving his areas of interest further and also enhancing policy, provision and practice in education. He manages to link the highest academic credibility with addressing the practical realities of teachers. Jim Cummins bridges the theory–practice gap in education by regularly involving himself in workshops with teachers, giving an average of 12 to 15 keynote/invited plenary presentations and more than 40 workshops annually. In such presentations, Jim provides the clarity and logic needed to combat, for example, the way the press treats immigration and bilingual education in the United States.

Another example of Jim's ability to move successfully from theory to the needs of practitioners, parents and the general public is the outstanding *Bilingualism and Minority Language Children* (Ontario: OISE, 1981) booklet that was written after Jim had settled in Toronto. Even today, this booklet is an outstanding model of effective communication of basic ideas, theories and solutions to problems. With graphics and clever analogies, it is a persuasive booklet about the value of bilingualism and bilingual education, and how misconceptions of bilingualism can be replaced by models and theories based on evidence.

Deep within the persona is the urge to create change within education. To do this, there has to be a sense of audience, a sense of how to communicate directly with teachers and administrators in ways they understand, which are context sensitive and socially appropriate. Such a stance means that repetitively winning large research funding, playing clever games with research data and statistical analyses, can never be top of the agenda. Establishing sound theoretical formulations and frameworks, and relating these to classroom practice, means that the written and the spoken word become important.

A brief glance at Jim Cummins' *curriculum vitae* (see pp. 342–360) shows that his publication outlets have been wide: books and journals, monographs and booklets, tests and curriculum programs, book chapters and book forewords, book reviews and popular articles in magazines. The sense of audience is far wider than that achieved by the typical academic, including parents, policy makers, politicians and the general public. This requires empathy with the audience, an ability to be non-threatening while also carrying a clear message adapted to the audience yet without losing sight of central themes.

While being sensitive and sympathetic to different international audiences, different contexts and possibilities, Jim Cummins has never been afraid to argue his case, even when controversial. Never abrasive nor confrontational, never part of a formal political movement or activist organization, he has argued a personal case but has always respected dialogue. He is ever tolerant of viewpoints from different cultures and creeds, and enthusiastic about diversity in language and culture. A key to understanding his basic philosophy is tolerance of minority viewpoints, anti-indoctrination, and anti-hypocrisy. It is probable that his experience of a very narrow form of pre-ecumenical Irish Catholic education in the 1950s and 1960s which taught dogma, intolerance of non-Catholic doctrine, and involved hypocrisy in religious and educational practice, led to a lifetime's reaction where tolerance of alternative beliefs, respecting the rights of those with different beliefs, avoiding intellectually stultifying dogmas, and bringing honesty and not hypocrisy to both policy and practice are foundational.

Jim notes that he stands by the basic ideas he formulated in his early work, although he would certainly express some aspects of them differently at this time. Over the years, there has certainly been a development, a progression in ideas, and both clarification and innovation, representing an expansion of theoretical concepts rather than any fundamental change. As the readings of this book show, the notion of BICS and CALP has evolved through stages into a more elaborate theoretical framework about language proficiency. Problematic terms such as 'semilingualism', used in early papers to refer to the academic consequences that result from the suppression of children's bilingualism in school, have been unambiguously repudiated. The embeddedness of academic language development, and schooling generally, in a nexus of societal power relations has been elaborated.

However, if there has been a major evolution it is in moving away from early interests in psychology, cognitive development, assessment and psychometrics to a growth in socio-political ideas. From the early days of a relatively individualistic perspective, there has grown a view of society and politics that is most fully expressed in his recent book *Language, Power and Pedagogy: Bilingual Children in the Crossfire* (Clevedon: Multilingual Matters, 2000). There is a realization that to effect change amongst policy makers and politicians, among teachers and school districts, both understanding the politics and addressing those politics is essential.

While such a socio-political concern is evident in recent writings, as readings in this book will portray, it is Jim's involvement with the California Association for Bilingual Education (CABE) that symbolizes his leadership in political activism. The involvement with CABE has meant valuable interaction with practitioners, with real classroom situations and real political issues. Such an involvement with practice demands cross-disciplinarity. Solutions to problems and moving education into a new century cannot occur in a disciplinary tunnel.

Also, working with the California State Education Department provided Jim Cummins with the stage and the audience to deliver his powerful script. Cooperating with California State Education Department administrators (who had often derived from the Peace Corps in the 1960s and 1970s) enabled him to express views about the role of theory, but also about equity, tolerance, empowerment, collaborative relationships and critical pedagogy. Proposition 227 in California and the hypocritical message of Ron Unz was confirmation for Jim Cummins of the increased and continued need for fighting intolerance, dogma, the language of fear, and the need for educational and social justice for those socially excluded and educationally damaged by anti-bilingual education politics.

Internationalism

While criticisms and controversy are the inevitable part of a life of an academic who has made such a major theoretical and practical contribution, validation of that contribution comes in three ways. First, only a very small minority of academics have been critical and as Jim Cummins' recent book entitled *Language, Power and Pedagogy: Bilingual Children in the Crossfire* (Clevedon: Multilingual Matters, 2000) reveals, many of these criticisms come through misunderstandings and misinterpretations, second-hand readings of his work. However, the great majority of authors, academics, researchers, organizations and administrations have accepted and used Jim Cummins' cross-disciplinary, prolific and influential ideas.

Second, there is the impact on teachers and practice, classrooms and schools that tends to be ignored by academics, is often hidden from view but is never silent in conversations with those who have attended Jim's workshops, lectures or have engaged in genial conversation with him. Any real evaluation of Jim Cummins' contribution has to accept that terms such as BICS and CALP are part of the professional language of many minority language teachers. His arguments about early exiting from bilingual education, language thresholds, and the number of years it takes to acquire sufficient language proficiency to cope in the curriculum, have made their way into the working vocabularies of countless thousands of teachers. Here is someone who has fed hungry classroom teachers, hungry for reasons to support their preference for bilingual education and bilingualism, their wish to deliver a more tolerant and equitable education that moves language from being a problem, even beyond being a right, to being a resource of importance to the individual and to communities and whole societies.

Third, no evaluation of Jim Cummins, even an interim one such as this, can avoid the internationalism of his work and influence. Beginning from the strengths of a comparative perspective deriving from his early experiences in research and advocacy with Irish speakers in Ireland and with Francophone, Anglophone, and Ukrainian communities in Canada, he has gone on to visit and consult with multilingual communities around the world. His *curriculum vitae* modestly lists lecturing at the University of the Aegean, Rhodes in Greece, at the Sophia University in Tokyo, in New Zealand and in the Basque Country and recent consultation on issues related to the education of the Muslim community in Thrace. Where minority languages and minority language education are studied throughout the world, Jim Cummins is a household name. All serious students of these areas will have read Jim Cummins. Where he visits, he not only reassures and legitimizes but also inspires and motivates. His considerable intellectual prowess means that he is a catalyst for change, an authority that lends credibility, but also infuses new ideas. With quiet persuasion goes considerable influence. Respect for his work is joined with admiration for his commitment. By gentle influence and not dogmatic preaching, he delivers an understanding of the international experience of bilingualism that ensures generalization of his message across continents.

Conclusion

Many Irish emigrated to Canada and the United States. Among the millions of immigrants, a few have become renowned. Included in that list is Jim Cummins. Asked if he was Irish or Canadian or a hyphenated version of those two, he replied that he was fully Irish and fully Canadian. There is probably no Irish person and a few Canadians within the fields of education and language who have achieved such international eminence, academic acclaim and practitioner impact.

Jim Cummins: born and schooled in Ireland; educated and enlightened in Canada; an advocate for tolerance, equity and justice for minority peoples throughout the world.

Notes

1. This chapter is based on an extended interview of Jim Cummins on 9th and 10th December 1999 by Nancy Hornberger and Colin Baker. The interview was tape-recorded with the kind permission of Jim Cummins. The writers are grateful to Bridget A. Goodman, Graduate School of Education, University of Pennsylvania, for her transcription of those tapes. The chapter is based on that interview but also contains an interpretation and evaluation of the contribution of Jim Cummins by the authors. A Canadian Studies Program Grant (605-02-1999/2000) to Colin Baker facilitated his work on this chapter. He wishes to express his appreciation to the Canadian High Commission for the grant.

Section One: The 1970s

At just 24 years of age, while at the University of Alberta, Jim Cummins published his first paper entitled 'A Theoretical Perspective on the Relationship between Bilingualism and Thought'. Placed in an Ontario Institute for Studies in Education publication *Working Papers on Bilingualism*, these papers marked an emerging interest in the 1970s in bilingualism and provided much initial stimulation for researchers and practitioners.

This first paper derives from Psychology, Jim Cummins' foundational discipline, with a discussion of the psychology of bilingual thinking, Macnamara's analysis of bilingualism and cognition, and Cummins' belief that bilinguals can have superior thinking abilities based on their dual linguistic systems.

There are several themes in this paper that are harbingers of Jim Cummins' contribution over the next three decades. For example, he argues that theoretical contributions on bilingualism are relatively few while empirical studies are comparatively more substantive. The last paper in this Reader (published in 1999) returns to the same theme of the importance of theory and the lack of interest in theory by researchers and particularly by policy makers; indeed this theme is constant in his work.

The second paper in this section was also published in the *OISE Working Papers on Bilingualism*. Published in April 1976, and writing from the Educational Research Centre, St Patrick's College, Dublin, the theme concerns the relationship between bilingualism and cognition. The opening paragraph ends with a sentence that has been influential ever since: 'there may be a threshold level of linguistic competence which a bilingual child must attain both in order to avoid cognitive deficits and allow the potentially beneficial aspects of becoming bilingual to influence his cognitive functioning'. The Thresholds Theory was born.

This paper aimed to resolve a contradiction that existed in the mid-1970s. Early research had shown bilinguals as having relatively lower performance levels on various cognitive measures compared with monolinguals. Yet the classic Peal and Lambert research (1962), along with early work on the metalinguistic advantages of bilinguals, revealed higher levels of cognitive performance by 'balanced bilinguals'. Jim Cummins' resolution of the contradiction was by the Thresholds Theory.

His detailed and careful review of the early research led him into providing three 'deep' explanations of the relationship between bilingualism and cognition: the experiential enrichment hypothesis, the codeswitching hypothesis and the objectification hypothesis. A reading of this section shows that Jim Cummins was interested from the beginning of his academic career in deep and comprehensive theoretical explanations of the relationship between language and cognition.

The third paper moves from Psychology, and from North American concerns of the 1970s, to Jim Cummins' native land: Ireland. Entitled 'Immersion programs: the Irish experience' and published in 1978 in the *International Review of Education*, Jim Cummins revealed his early interest in bilingual education. The Irish immersion schools had been used to illustrate the potential dangers of bilingual education in lowering academic performance. Jim Cummins reveals a much more positive picture providing evidence that children become bilingual at no cost to their first language. The paper also suggests that enthusiasm among teachers, support in the community and the home environment, are each important ingredients in the success of a bilingual program.

The fourth paper in this section is a classic. Entitled 'Linguistic Interdependence and the Educational Development of Bilingual Children' (1979), it has become one of the most cited and influential papers in the study of bilingualism. A central tenet is that a child's first language skills must become well developed to ensure that their academic and linguistic performance in the second language is maximized. Two theories are introduced. First, the Developmental Interdependence Theory suggests that growth in a second language is much dependent on a well-developed first language. Second, the Thresholds hypothesis proposes two thresholds a bilingual child has to pass to avoid the negative consequences of having two underdeveloped languages, and to obtain the thinking advantages of 'balanced bilinguals'. Those interested in critiques of these theories should consult Edelsky *et al*. (1983), Rivera (1984), Martin-Jones and Romaine (1986), Frederickson and Cline (1990), Edelsky (1991), Robson (1995), Wiley (1996) and MacSwan (2000). A detailed rebuttal can be found in Cummins (2000).

This paper does not stop with theoretical propositions but shows how each proposition has major implications for education. For example, for minority language children, effective education requires the home language to be well developed *and* used in school for academic learning in order to maximize both curriculum performance and efficiency in learning the second language (usually a majority language).

The fifth and final paper in this 1970s section was authored from his present institution, the Ontario Institute for Studies in Education. Originally written in 1979 and distributed by the Canadian Parents for French organization from 1983 onwards, it reveals a scholar who could move with ease from a lofty theory to the needs of a parent audience. Still a young academic, the paper reveals his vision that, to influence and change bilingual communities, writing must not only include contributions in learned journals and prestigious books. Scholarly writing also should relate to those who make decisions on a daily basis about bilingual children: parents and teachers.

In just five pages, Jim Cummins provides a strong argument for French immersion schooling by discussing achievement in French and English, achievement in other subjects of the curriculum, intellectual and emotional development, effects on intelligence and the importance of motivation and the home environment.

There is also another theme in this article. Jim Cummins shows his concern for less privileged children by discussing those with learning disabilities and how they can be empowered, academically and emotionally, by a bilingual schooling experience.

In conclusion, this 1970s section reveals that the early thinking of Jim Cummins already outlined the contours of his major contributions. Both his early theories and their policy implications have since developed and deepened. His ideas on the benefits of bilingualism, the Thresholds Theory, the educational advantages of bilingual education, interdependence in the development of two languages, and the centrality of theory alongside the crucial importance of dissemination were all launched in the 1970s, and refined but not rejected in the following two decades.

References

Cummins, J. (2000) *Language, Power and Pedagogy: Bilingual Children in the Crossfire.* Clevedon: Multilingual Matters.

Edelsky, C. (1991) *With Literacy and Justice for All: Rethinking the Social in Language and Education.* London: Falmer.

Edelsky, C. *et al.* (1983) Semilingualism and language deficit. *Applied Linguistics* 4 (1), 1–22.

Frederickson, N. and Cline, T. (1990) *Curriculum Related Assessment with Bilingual Children.* London: University College London.

MacSwan, J. (2000) The threshold hypothesis, semilingualism, and other contributions to a deficit view of linguistic minorities. *Hispanic Journal of Behavioral Sciences* 22 (1), 3–45.

Martin-Jones, M. and Romaine, S. (1986) Semilingualism: A half baked theory of communicative competence. *Applied Linguistics* 7 (1), 26–38.

Rivera, C. (ed.) (1984) *Language Proficiency and Academic Achievement.* Clevedon: Multilingual Matters.

Robson, A. (1995) The assessment of bilingual children. In M. K. Verma, K. P. Corrigan and S. Firth (eds) *Working with Bilingual Children.* Clevedon: Multilingual Matters.

Wiley, T. G. (1996) *Literacy and Language Diversity in the United States.* McHenry, IL: Center for Applied Linguistics and Delts Systems.

A Theoretical Perspective on the Relationship between Bilingualism and Thought

Theoretical analyses of the relationship between bilingualism and thought are relatively few. This is surprising in view of the substantial number of empirical studies on the effects of bilingualism on cognitive functioning. However, many of these studies have been carried out with inadequate theoretical guidelines. Typically, predictions have been derived only from the results of previous studies with little consideration of broader theoretical issues such as the relationship between language and thought. This neglect on the part of researchers has been partly due to the complexity of the issue and the lack of any clear consensus as to what are the interrelationships between language and thought.

However, in recent years, several separate lines of investigation have de-emphasized the role of language in cognitive functioning. The Piagetian school has consistently held that the development of the basic cognitive schemata owes little to language and this position has received strong empirical support from the investigations of Furth (1966) and Sinclair-de-Zwart (1969). Also, within the context of what Furth (1969) calls 'mediating representational knowing' imagistic mediation has taken over many of the functions once attributed to verbal mediation (Paivio, 1971).

It is against this background that the question of the effects of bilingualism on cognitive functioning must be posed. If language is less than crucial in cognitive development then surely one cannot expect that bilingualism will have any marked effects on cognitive development.

This is precisely the conclusion reached by Macnamara's (1970) theoretical analysis of bilingualism and thought. His analysis is aimed at showing that bilingualism is unlikely to have any causal effect on either intelligence or creativity. He points out

> The fears, or hopes, which caused people to study the relationship between bilingualism and I.Q. seem to spring from the general view that language either constitutes or creates intelligence. (1970: 34)

He subjects this linguistic determination to a *reductio ad absurdum* and shows how Ervin and Osgood models of compound and co-ordinate bilingualism depend on a similar view of the relationships between language and thought. Macnamara argues that linguistic functioning is to a great extent dependent on non-linguistic functioning of many sorts and supposedly linguistic universals are in fact universals of human intelligence. Against the background of his theoretical analysis of language and thought Macnamara concludes that

> … it seems unlikely that bilingualism should have any effect upon the development of the basic, common, cognitive structures. (1970: 33)

Macnamara's analysis poses serious problems for those who are carrying out research into the effects of bilingualism on cognition. It calls into question the whole purpose of investigating differences in cognitive functioning between bilinguals and unilinguals and the meaningfulness of any differences that happen to be found. Macnamara's analysis is both provocative and useful in that it should force the researcher to examine the broader theoretical context within which he is operating. If Macnamara's argument cannot be refuted then there is little purpose in carrying out research on this topic since the results will be theoretically meaningless.

The purpose of this paper is to attempt to bridge the gap between the theoretical and the empirical firstly by refuting Macnamara's analysis of why bilingualism is unlikely to affect cognitive functioning, and secondly, by placing research on the topic of bilingualism and cognition into a theoretical framework where the results can be meaningfully interpreted.

One feels intuitively that Macnamara's analysis must be faulty since researchers continue to report significant differences in cognitive functioning between bilinguals and unilinguals (e.g. Bain, 1973; Cummins & Gulutsan, 1973). The fact that the majority of the studies since the classic Peal and Lambert (1962) study arrive at conclusions which are remarkably consistent with each other adds to this conviction.

However, Macnamara's argument that bilingualism should have no large scale effect on intelligence or creativity is extremely strong. One way to by-pass it is to deny his claim that linguistic functioning is to a great extent dependent on non-linguistic functioning and does not play a crucial role in cognitive development. However, the present writer is in full agreement with this position. If one allows that language does not play a crucial role in the development of the basic cognitive structures surely Macnamara's conclusion that bilingualism is unlikely to do so either is inescapable.

I am going to argue that Macnamara's conclusion is not inescapable. His analysis is faulty, firstly, in that it fails to distinguish between the *specifically linguistic* effects of bilingualism or cognition and effects which are extrinsic to, or by-products of the fact that the bilingual has two verbal codes with which to represent the world. Secondly, the fact that language (in the unilingual situation) does not play a *causal* role in the development of cognitive structures does not necessarily mean that certain linguistic features of the bilingual situation will have no effect on the speed with which certain concepts are grasped in ontogenesis. In other words, the argument is that

(1) in addition to the primary linguistic difference between the bilingual and unilingual situations, there are potentially important non-linguistic differences which may facilitate or hinder mental development.

(2) while no large scale linguistic effects should be expected there are ways in which the bilingual's access to, and use of two linguistic codes might affect his mental development.

Linguistic and Non-linguistic Aspects of the Bilingual Situation

The bilingual's experience differs from the unilingual's not only by the fact that he has access to two verbal codes in comparison to the unilingual's one, but also by several factors which, although they derive from the primary linguistic difference, are not in themselves linguistic.

As an example of what I mean consider Furth's (1966) studies of the cognitive effects of deafness – similar to bilingualism in that both affect the way in which an individual represents his world. Furth found no cognitive deficiencies which could be attributed to the specifically linguistic factor (the fact that the deaf are linguistically deprived). He argues that most of the deficiencies which were found could be attributed to the fact that the deaf are deprived of normal social interaction rather than the linguistic deprivation is the causal factor in explaining the deaf child's intellectual lag. Furth uses this conclusion to support the Piagetian view that language is not the crucial element in the development of cognitive structures.

In a similar fashion it can be argued that there are two general ways in which bilingualism might affect cognitive growth – the specifically linguistic and the non-linguistic. Macnamara's (1970) analysis is deficient in that it fails to take any account of non-linguistic factors which may differentially influence the cognitive development of bilinguals and unilinguals. The distinction between linguistic and non-linguistic explanations has not been formally recognized up to now, although several investigators have proposed non-linguistic explanations to account for observed differences in the cognitive functioning of bilinguals and unilinguals.

Non-linguistic Explanations: This type of explanation involves accounting for the effects of bilingualism on cognition by reference to factors which are extrinsic to, or by-products of the fact that the bilingual has access to two verbal codes. This type of explanatory factor has been suggested by several investigators. For example, Liedke and Nelson (1968) suggest that the greater amount of social interaction which is presumably involved in learning two languages at an early age accounts for the higher level of concept formation which they found in their bilingual grade 1 group. Similarly, Peal and Lambert (1962) argue that the bilingual is exposed to a wider range of experiences due to his participation in two cultures.

A different type of non-linguistic variable has been suggested by both Peal and Lambert (1962) and Balkan (1970) to account for the bilingual's greater cognitive flexibility. They argue that the habit of switching languages and making use of two different perspectives develops in the bilingual a 'souplesse d'esprit' which will help him in tasks requiring preceptual or conceptual reorganization.

These explanations are 'non-linguistic' in that they do not emphasize the effects of the *specifically linguistic* variable (two verbal codes rather than one) on cognition. For example, the fact that the switching (in Peal and Lambert's and Balkan's explanations) is between two languages is not intrinsic to the explanation. The *causal* element is the switching of perspective rather than any specifically linguistic factor.

Linguistic Explanations: Several different types of linguistic explanations have been suggested to account for the observed superiority of bilinguals on tests of general reasoning and verbal intelligence. Peal and Lambert (1962), for example, have suggested that the overlap of French and English vocabulary could account for the bilingual's greater verbal ability and Lambert and Tucker (1972) suggest that transfer across and comparison of languages might have the same effect.

In order to explain the bilingual's superiority on tests of general reasoning or concept formation, Peal and Lambert (1962) follow Leopold (1949) in suggesting that because of his two languages the bilingual child may be forced to conceptualize things and events in terms of their general properties rather than relying on their linguistic symbols. Leopold (1949) observed that his bilingual child quickly learned to separate the sound of the word from the thing itself, and a recent study by Ianco-Worrall (1972) in South Africa has shown that bilingual children do in fact separate sound and meaning earlier than unilingual children.

This explanation is 'linguistic' in that the bilinguals' higher level of concept formation is explained as a *direct result* of the fact that they have two words for the same referent.

Similarly, many earlier studies made use of 'linguistic' explanations in that they attributed the bilinguals' lower level of verbal ability to inability to cope with two language systems.

Do these attempts at 'linguistic' explanations not contradict the fact that language should have no large-scale effects on the development of cognition? The key word here is 'large-scale'. No theorist denies that language plays an important role in mental development. What is denied (by the Piagetian school) is that language plays a *causal* role in the development of causal structures. Inhelder *et al.* (1966) express the Piagetian view as follows:

First, language training … operates to direct the child's interactions with the environment and thus to 'focus' on relevant dimensions of task situations. Second … language does aid in the storage and retrieval of relevant information. However, our evidence offers little if any support for the contention that language learning *per se* contributes to the *integration* and *coordination* of 'informational units' necessary for the achievement of the conservation concepts. (1966: 163)

It is certainly legitimate to ask 'If language (in the unilingual situation) helps the child focus on relevant dimensions of task situations, what will be the effect of access to two languages?' The effects of focusing on relevant aspects of the environment with two languages has been outlined by Leopold (1949) and Peal and Lambert (1962) and the accounts of these authors have been empirically supported by Ianco-Worrall (1972). Peal and Lambert's argument that it might lead to a higher level of concept formation seems very plausible.

Also, while Furth (1966) holds that language does not have any *large-scale* effects on cognitive development, he does not deny that the deaf are deficient in embodying concepts in language. Thus, while deafness will not prevent concept formation in general, it will hinder the representation of certain types of concept which are accessible and expressible mainly through the linguistic medium, e.g. the concept of democracy. In a similar fashion one can hypothesize that while language *per se* is not a causal element in the development of cognitive structures, the linguistic differences which distinguish bilinguals from unilinguals will lead to differences at the conceptual level.

What is the significance of this distinction between 'linguistic' and 'non-linguistic' explanations? By making this distinction explicit we should be enabled to think more clearly on the possible effects of bilingualism on cognitive development and relate our ideas to issues in the broader theoretical context. For example, it is clear that the 'language–thought' issue is not the only one relevant to the effects of bilingualism on cognition; the state of theory regarding the effects of social interaction on mental development is equally relevant. Thus, analyses such as Macnamara's, which are based on consideration of only one type of explanation can be seen as inadequate.

It is hoped that this analysis, by distinguishing the two fundamentally different ways in which bilingualism might affect cognitive functioning, will provide a more adequate theoretical context for the study of bilingualism and cognition than has existed hitherto.

References

Bain, B. C. (1973) Bilingualism and cognition: Toward a general theory. *Proceedings of the First Annual Conference on Bilingualism and the West.*

Balkan, L. (1970) *Les Effets du Bilinguisme Français–Anglais sur les Aptitudes Intellectuelles.* Bruxelles: Aimav.

Cummins, J. and Gulutsan, M. (1973) Some effects of bilingualism on cognitive functioning. *Proceedings of the First Annual Conference on Bilingualism and the West.*

Furth, H. G. (1966) *Thinking Without Language. Psychological Implications of Deafness.* New York: Free Press.

Furth, H. G. (1969) *Piaget and Knowledge.* Prentice-Hall.

Ianco-Worrall, A. D. (1972) Bilingualism and cognitive development. *Child Development* 43, 1390–1400.

Inhelder, B. *et al.* (1966) On cognitive development. *American Psychologist* 21, 160–4.

Lambert, W. E. and Tucker, G. R. (1972) *Bilingual Education of Children: The St. Lambert Experiment.* Rowley: Newbury House.

Leopold, W. F. (1949) *Speech Development of a Bilingual Child.* Evanston: Northwestern University Press.

Liedke, W. W. and Nelson, L. D. (1968) Concept formation and bilingualism. *Alberta Journal of Educational Research* 14 (4), 225–32.

Macnamara, J. (1970) Bilingualism and thought. In J. E. Alatis (ed.) *Monograph Series on Languages and Linguistics.* Georgetown University School of Languages and Linguistics.

Paivio, A. (1971) *Imagery and Verbal Processes.* New York: Holt, Rinehart Winston.

Peal, E. and Lambert, W. E. (1962) The relation of bilingualism to intelligence. *Psychological Monographs* 76, 546.

Sinclair-de-Zwart, H. (1969) Developmental psycholinguistics. In D. Elkin and J. H. Flavell (eds) *Studies in Cognitive Development* (pp. 315–36). New York: Oxford University Press.

The Influence of Bilingualism on Cognitive Growth: A Synthesis of Research Findings and Explanatory Hypotheses[1]

In recent years there has been a remarkable reversal of the research evidence regarding the influence of bilingualism on cognition. Investigations of the relationship between bilingualism and cognition conducted prior to the Peal and Lambert study in 1962 generally found that bilinguals performed at a lower level than unilinguals on measures of verbal intelligence (see reviews by Darcy, 1953; Jensen, 1962; Macnamara, 1966; Peal & Lambert, 1962). The results of the Peal and Lambert study and of the majority of subsequent investigations are in marked contrast to the results of earlier studies. These more recent studies indicate that at least in some bilingual learning situations, bilingualism can accelerate the development of non-verbal, and, indeed verbal abilities (Bain, 1974; Cummins & Gulutsan, 1974a; Liedke & Nelson, 1968; Peal & Lambert, 1962). There is also evidence that becoming bilingual facilitates aspects of cognitive flexibility (Balkan, 1970; Ben-Zeev, 1972; Ianco-Worrall, 1972). In addition, the research evidence points towards a positive association between divergent thinking skills and learning a second language in early childhood (Carringer, 1974; Cummins & Gulutsan, 1974a; Landry, 1974; Scott, 1973).

The present paper is concerned with the question of how do we resolve the contradiction between studies which have reported that bilingualism is associated with lower levels of cognitive performance and the more recent studies which have tended to suggest that bilingualism might accelerate aspects of cognitive growth? In order to establish a framework for the interpretation of these seemingly inconsistent findings it is necessary to review the relevant literature and examine those factors which differentiate these two sorts of studies. On the basis of this review, I shall suggest that the level of linguistic competence attained by a bilingual child may mediate the effects of his bilingual learning experiences on cognitive growth. Specifically, there may be a threshold level of linguistic competence which a bilingual child must attain both in order to avoid cognitive deficits and allow the potentially beneficial aspects of becoming bilingual to influence his cognitive functioning. Finally, I shall briefly review some of the factors which might positively influence the cognitive functioning of bilingual children who overcome difficulties in coping with two languages.

The Research Evidence

The introduction of standardized IQ tests in the early 1920s presented investigators with what appeared to be a straightforward means of discovering whether bilingualism affected intellectual abilities. However, as Peal and Lambert (1962) point out, many of the early studies which compared the IQ scores of unilinguals and bilinguals suffered from methodological defects in that they failed to control for confounding variables such as socio-economic status (SES), sex and the degree of the bilingual's knowledge of his two languages. The only clear trend that emerged from these studies was that bilinguals seemed to suffer from a language handicap when measured by verbal tests of intelligence (Darcy, 1953; Peal & Lambert, 1962). Peal and Lambert conclude their review of the literature as follows:

> In view of the weakness of the studies reviewed, the best general conclusion is that there is little evidence to suggest that bilinguals differ from monolinguals on non-verbal intelligence, but that there may be differences in verbal intelligence as measured by intelligence tests. (1962: 5)

Several studies conducted since the Peal and Lambert (1962) study add to the evidence that bilinguals may experience difficulties in expressing their intelligence through language. Macnamara (1966) reported that Irish primary school children, whose home language was English but who were instructed through the medium of Irish, were 11 months behind in problem arithmetic relative to other Irish children taught through the medium of English. The problem arithmetic test was expressed in sentences and presumably involved the mediation of language. No differences were evident between the groups on a mechanical arithmetic test whose problems were expressed in arithmetical symbols.

A recent study conducted by Tsushima and Hogan (1975) reported that grade four and five Japanese–English bilinguals performed at a significantly lower level than a unilingual control group on measures of verbal and academic skills. The bilingual and unilingual groups in this study were matched on non-verbal ability. The bilingual group was comprised of children whose mothers were born and raised in the United States. All of the parents of children in the unilingual group were born and raised in the United States. Tsushima and Hogan report that the bilingual children had been exposed to both English and Japanese in the home from infancy. However, no details are given of the bilinguals' relative competence in both languages, i.e. their degree of bilingualism.

A study conducted in Singapore (Torrance, Gowan, Wu & Aliotti, 1970) reported that children in grades three, four and five who were attending bilingual schools performed at a significantly lower level on the fluency and flexibility scales of the Torrance Tests of Creative Thinking (Figural Form A). However, the direction of the trend was reversed for originality and elaboration and differences in elaboration in favour of the bilingual group were significant. The trend for the superiority of the bilingual group on the originality and elaboration scales became stronger when corrections for fluency were made. The authors attribute the lower scores of the bilingual group on the fluency and flexibility scales to the influence of interference of associations in bilingualism. The results of this study are consistent with the results of a previous study in Singapore conducted by Gowan and Torrance (1965) who reported that Chinese, Malayan and Tamilese children between grades three and five, who were receiving instruction through their native language, performed at a significantly higher level on a non-verbal measure of ideational fluency than children who were receiving instruction through a second language (English). However, at the grade six level Chinese pupils receiving instruction in English did as well as Chinese pupils instructed through Chinese. This finding may be related to the fact that the sixth graders are likely to have attained a greater mastery of English than pupils in earlier grades. However, in neither of these studies in Singapore are details given of the degree of bilingualism of the bilingual pupils involved.

In summary, the results of a large number of studies indicate that, under some conditions, bilingualism, or rather the attempt to become bilingual, can adversely affect some cognitive processes. Negative effects have been reported most frequently in the areas of verbal and scholastic achievement and it thus seems reasonable to infer that many of the bilingual subjects in these studies failed to overcome difficulties in coping with two languages. It will be argued later that the positive cognitive consequences reported in many recent studies are a reflection of the fact that the bilingual subjects in these studies are likely to have overcome difficulties in coping with two languages.

The best known of these recent studies is that conducted by Peal and Lambert (1962) with French–English bilinguals in Montreal. Because several earlier studies had produced trivial results by attempting to measure the verbal intelligence of bilinguals through their weaker language, Peal and Lambert controlled for degree of bilingualism by using only bilinguals who had attained a relatively similar degree of competence in both languages, i.e. 'balanced' bilinguals. Within the context of previous studies Peal and Lambert's findings were startling to say the least. Not only did the group of balanced ten-year-old bilinguals show a higher level of non-verbal intelligence than the unilingual control group, they also performed at a higher level on measures of verbal intelligence – a complete reversal of previous findings. The contentious issue of whether or not the use of only balanced bilinguals in the Peal and Lambert study, and in subsequent studies, may have introduced a bias into the comparison of bilinguals and unilinguals (Macnamara, 1966), will be examined in a later section. For the moment, it is sufficient to note that the majority of more recent studies have taken precautions to ensure that the bilingual subjects have had a similar degree of competence in both languages and therefore, their results tell us nothing about the cognitive abilities of bilinguals who may have remained very much more dominant in one of their two languages.

The Peal and Lambert (1962) study was replicated in a Western Canadian setting by Cummins and Gulutsan (1974a) and similar results were reported. A group of balanced bilinguals was matched with a control group of unilinguals on SES, sex and age and was found to perform at a significantly higher level both on measures of verbal and non-verbal ability and on one measure of divergent thinking, i.e. verbal originality.

Two other studies carried out in Western Canada by Liedke and Nelson (1968) and by Bain (1974) also suggest that bilingualism might accelerate aspects of cognitive growth. In both these studies children who had become bilingual before coming to school showed higher levels of concept formation than control groups of unilinguals. The bilingual and unilingual groups in these two studies were matched on intelligence as well as on SES and sex.[2]

A study conducted in Switzerland by Balkan (1970) produced evidence to support the hypothesis that the attainment of balanced bilingualism might have a positive effect on 'cognitive flexibility'. Balkan matched balanced bilinguals and unilinguals on non-verbal intelligence and found that the bilingual group performed at a significantly higher level on two variables which he claimed measure 'cognitive flexibility'. One of these tests was similar to the Embedded Figures Test and involved an ability to restructure a perceptual situation (Figures Cachées). The other test required a sensitivity to the different meanings of words (Histoires). When Balkan separated his bilingual group into bilinguals who had learned both languages before the age of four and those who had become bilingual after the age of four, he found that the superiority of the early bilinguals over their matched unilingual counterparts was much more pronounced than that of the later bilinguals. The later bilinguals were only slightly superior to the control group on the measures of cognitive flexibility. This finding may be related to evidence summarized by Engle (1975: 311–2) that children in the early concrete operational period (approx. 6–8 years) experience more difficulty in learning a second language than do children at either a younger (before 6) or older (9–12) age level.

Other studies, carried out by Ben-Zeev in 1972 with Hebrew–English bilinguals and by Ianco-Worrall (1972) with Africaans–English bilinguals also support the hypothesis that bilingualism might positively influence aspects of cognitive flexibility. Ben-Zeev reported that her bilingual group had greater skill at auditory reorganization of verbal material, a more 'flexible manipulation of the linguistic code' and were more advanced in concrete operational thinking. Ianco-Worrall's (1972) study provides empirical support for Leopold's (1949) hypothesis that the simultaneous acquisition of two languages in early childhood accelerates the separation of sound and meaning or name and object. She found that, of the 4–6 year old bilinguals in her sample, 54% consistently chose to interpret similarity between words in terms of a semantic rather than an acoustic dimension, whereas practically none of the unilingual group showed similar choice behavior. The author concludes that

> ... bilinguals, brought up in a one-person, one-language environment, reach a stage in semantic development ... some 2–3 years earlier than their unilingual peers. A high percentage of these bilingual youngsters perceived relationship between words in terms of their symbolic rather than their acoustic properties ... (1972: 1398)

Although the majority of studies considered above have involved children who had become bilingual before coming to school, there is also evidence that exposure to an immersion or bilingual education program, in addition to promoting high levels of functional bilingualism, might positively affect some cognitive processes. The pilot class in the St. Lambert project, for example, have performed at a significantly higher level than the controls on measures of divergent thinking at the grades three, five and six levels (Bruck, Lambert & Tucker, 1973). Using data from the pilot and follow-up classes in the Lambert project, Scott (1973) has analysed the relation of divergent thinking to bilingualism. An analysis of covariance with Raven IQ scores and SES as covariates, showed significant differences in favour of the bilinguals on divergent thinking tests administered in the later grades of elementary school. In addition, the level of French speaking skills attained by children in the program was significantly predicted by their earlier (grade three) levels of divergent thinking. Scott argues from these results that bilingualism can both influence and be influenced by divergent thinking. In other words, the results are consistent with the interpretation that divergent thinking skills have been positively affected by the experimental program and also that they have acted as a causal agent in promoting functional bilingualism.

Further indications of a positive association between second language learning and divergent thinking come from studies conducted by Landry (1974) and by Carringer (1974). Landry reports that grade six children attending schools where a FLES program (i.e. between 20 and 45 minutes of second language instruction per day) was operative, scored significantly higher than a unilingual control group on both the verbal and figural parts of the Torrance Tests of Creative Thinking. Differences between FLES and non-FLES schools at the grade one and four levels were non-significant. Landry argues from these results that learning a second language in elementary school might increase divergent thinking skills.

Carringer's (1974) study, conducted in Mexico, found that 24 Spanish–English balanced bilinguals performed at a significantly higher level than 24 Spanish-speaking unilinguals on the verbal flexibility, verbal originality, figural fluency and figural originality scales of the Torrance Tests of Creative Thinking. These results, however, should be treated with caution since neither IQ nor SES appears to have been adequately controlled.

The Torrance *et al.* (1970) and Cummins and Gulutsan (1974a) studies, mentioned previously, suggest that bilingual learning experiences in the school may have a more positive effect on the 'originality' than on the 'fluency' or 'flexibility' aspects of divergent thinking. Torrance *et al.* reported lower levels of fluency and flexibility among bilingual children in Singapore but, when corrections for fluency were made, higher levels of originality and elaboration. Cummins and Gulutsan found highly significant (p <0.001) differences between balanced bilingual and unilingual groups on a measure of verbal originality but no differences on fluency or flexibility measures.

In a later analysis, Cummins (1975) compared the cognitive characteristics of balanced ($N = 12$) and non-balanced ($N = 11$) grade six children from English-speaking home backgrounds who were attending the French–English bilingual program in Edmonton, Canada. An analysis of covariance with SES as covariate showed no differences between the groups on verbal or non-verbal intelligence but significant differences (p <0.01), in favour of the balanced group, on the fluency and flexibility scales of a measure of verbal divergence. Differences between the groups on the originality scale approached significance (p <0.08). Two interpretations of these findings are possible: in the first place, since the balance scores for children from English-speaking homes are an index of French competence, it may be that verbal divergence is a correlate of ability to learn a second language in a bilingual program. This interpretation is consistent with Scott's (1973) finding that divergent thinking abilities significantly predicted later French-speaking skills of the experimental children in the St. Lambert project.

However, Scott's analysis also suggests that divergent thinking may have been influenced by the St. Lambert experimental program and the differences between balanced and non-balanced groups in the Cummins (1975) study can be interpreted in a similar way. If these differences have been caused by the bilingual program it is necessary to ask whether the program has positively influenced the divergent thinking skills of children who have attained balanced bilingual skills or negatively influenced the divergent thinking skills of those who have remained very much more dominant in English. In order to give an indication of whether the differences between balanced and non-balanced groups were due to the relative superiority of the balanced group or the relative inferiority of the non-balanced group, the divergent thinking performance of these two groups was compared with that of a unilingual group. The unilingual group ($N = 12$) was matched with both bilingual groups on verbal and non-verbal abilities and with the balanced group on SES. On the verbal fluency and flexibility scales the unilingual group scored at a similar level to the balanced group but substantially higher than the non-balanced group. On the verbal originality measure the unilingual group scored at a similar level to the non-balanced group but substantially lower than the balanced group. These differences approach but fail to reach statistical significance; nevertheless, they suggest that if divergent thinking skills have been influenced by the bilingual program the verbal fluency and flexibility skills of the non-balanced children may have been negatively affected and the verbal originality skills of the balanced children positively affected.[3] This interpretation parallels the findings of the Torrance *et al.* study and suggests the possibility that the lower levels of fluency and flexibility observed in the Torrance *et al.* study may be attributable only to those bilinguals who had failed to overcome difficulties in coping with two languages. By the same token, only those bilinguals who had overcome linguistic difficulties may have been at an advantage in originality and elaboration skills.

The findings of the Cummins (1975) study can be regarded only as suggestive due both to the small number of subjects involved and the fact that different interpretations of the results are possible. The reason these findings have been considered in detail is that they throw light on the cognitive characteristics of children who have attained only intermediate levels of bilingual skills. The findings suggest the hypothesis that the influence of bilingual learning experiences on cognitive functioning may be mediated by the level of competence which a bilingual child attains in the languages through which he must interact with his environment.

In summary, the findings of recent studies suggest that becoming bilingual, either as a result of home or school experiences, can positively influence aspects of cognitive functioning. There are indications in these studies that bilingual learning experiences in the school setting may be more capable of influencing divergent than convergent thinking skills. However, early or pre-school bilingualism does appear capable of accelerating the development of convergent skills.

These recent findings are clearly inconsistent with the findings of earlier studies. In order to resolve this inconsistency it is necessary to develop a conceptual framework within which similarities and differences between early and more recent studies can be specified.

A first step towards the development of such an interpretative framework is to abandon the expectation that research into the psychological consequences of bilingualism should produce completely consistent results. The search for consistent research results is based on a false premise – i.e. that there is but one single phenomenon or state called 'bilingualism' which ought to influence the mental lives of all bilinguals in much the same way. In fact, as Mackey (1971) points out, there is an enormous variety of bilingual learning situations, in each of which, different combinations of cognitive, attitudinal, social and educational factors are operative. Thus, the learning of two languages is likely to affect cognition in different ways depending on the age at which the languages are learned, whether they are learned separately or simultaneously, the opportunities for using both languages in the home, school and wider environment, the prestige of the two languages, the functions which the languages serve within a particular social context, etc. In short, each bilingual learning situation is unique and it is impossible to generalize from one bilingual learning situation to another. Consequently, the question for research is not what effects does 'bilingualism', *per se*, have on cognitive processes; rather, research should be directed towards identifying those conditions under which bilingual learning experiences are likely to retard or, alternatively, accelerate aspects of cognitive growth.

In this regard, the more recent studies which have reported positive cognitive consequences associated with bilingualism differ from many earlier studies both in methodology and in the socio-cultural contexts in which the studies were carried out. I shall consider these methodological and socio-cultural differences in turn and argue that, as a result of these differences, the bilingual subjects in recent studies are likely to have differed substantially from those of earlier studies in the level of linguistic competence attained as a result of their bilingual learning experiences.

Methodological Factors

The principal methodological difference between early and more recent studies concerns the procedures for choosing the bilingual sample. The majority of more recent studies, following Peal and Lambert (1962), have taken precautions to ensure that the bilingual subjects had developed a similar level of competence in both languages, i.e. were balanced bilinguals. Earlier studies, on the other hand, tended to use the bilingual subjects' competence in L1 and L2 as dependent variables and consequently, did not select only bilinguals who had developed balanced bilingual skills. The use of only balanced bilinguals in the Peal and Lambert study has been controversial (Macnamara, 1966) and needs to be considered in some detail. First, however, some of the methodological problems inherent in comparing the cognitive performance of bilingual and unilingual groups should be briefly pointed out.

In order to isolate the effects of linguality, bilingual and unilingual groups should be matched on any personal or background characteristic which might contribute to performance on the dependent variables. Peal and Lambert mention SES, sex and age as most important in this respect and point out that many earlier studies were methodologically deficient in that they failed to match bilingual and unilingual groups on these variables. In many studies which have used measures other than non-verbal intelligence as dependent variables (e.g. verbal ability, scholastic achievement, divergent thinking skills) bilingual and unilingual groups have also been matched on non-verbal intelligence. This 'cognitive matching' undoubtedly increases the degree to which non-linguistic variables are controlled. Studies which have used non-verbal intelligence as a dependent variable and consequently matched bilingual and unilingual groups only on SES, sex and age (e.g. Cummins & Gulutsan, 1974a; Peal & Lambert, 1962), are subject to the criticism that an index of SES, based on parental occupation, may not adequately control all relevant background differences between the groups. The studies of

Davé (1963) and Wolf (1966) have shown that such an index of SES is likely to account for only a relatively small proportion of differences in children's home environments. The inevitable margin for error in matching bilingual and uni-lingual groups argues for caution in accepting the results of any one study without confirmatory evidence from other studies which have used different approaches and which have been carried out in different bilingual learning situations.

The most controversial aspect of the Peal and Lambert study was their method of choosing the bilingual sample. Four measures were used to estimate the degree of French–English linguistic balance. These measures consisted of (1) a word association test in which the ratio of French–English word associations to stimulus words in each language was used to form a balance score; (2) a word detection test in which subjects had to find French and English words embedded in a series of letters; (3) the Peabody Picture Vocabulary Test which was used as a measure of oral English competence; (4) a subjective self-rating measure in which subjects rated their ability to speak, read, write and understand English. In cases where the different criteria were in disagreement Peal and Lambert gave more weight to the child's vocabulary score than to the other measures.

Macnamara (1966) has criticized Peal and Lambert's study on the grounds that their use of these measures in choosing the bilingual sample invalidates any linguistic comparison between bilingual and unilingual groups. He argues that

> ... it is extremely likely that in selecting for the bilingual group native French-speakers who had become balanced bilinguals, the authors selected children who on the whole were highly gifted and had a flair for language learning. So any linguistic comparison between these children and the monoglots was probably biased in favour of the former. (1966: 21)

Lambert and Anisfeld (1969), in a reply to Macnamara, have argued that the measures of linguistic balance did not bias the comparison in favour of the bilinguals. They make the point that these measures allowed children who had a low level of competence in both French and English to enter the bilingual sample and thus did not select only children with a flair for language learning.

Two inter-related issues in this controversy need to be distinguished. The first is whether or not any bias existed in the balance measures themselves. In other words, did these tests favour bilingual children who were more intelligent or verbally proficient? Secondly, is it, in principle, invalid to compare unilingual children with a selected group of balanced bilinguals, or, ought the bilingual sample be representative of all bilinguals – balanced and non-balanced?

Measures of linguistic balance are designed to measure a bilingual's relative degree of competence in L1 and L2. Performance on these measures may be correlated with intelligence or verbal proficiency, either because more intelligent children tend to become more balanced or, alternatively, because the attainment of balanced bilingualism may influence intellectual development. However, the tests themselves ought not to be loaded towards producing this result. In the word association test, for example, a 'balanced' bilingual may produce either a large number of words in each language or a small number. If only those individuals who produced a large number of words in each language were accepted as 'balanced bilinguals' then this measure would undoubtedly bias the comparison of bilingual and unilingual groups. However, the criterion of balance is the ratio of L1:L2 associations and the absolute number is irrelevant. Thus, there is no inherent tendency in this measure, or in other measures involving the ratio of L1:L2 performance, to select only those bilinguals who may have high levels of intelligence or verbal proficiency.

The problem in the Peal and Lambert study, however, is that, when the different balance measures were in disagreement, more weight was given to the Vocabulary score than to the others. The Vocabulary test was given only in English (L2) and thus a ratio of English:French vocabulary skills was not obtained for this measure. As Peal and Lambert themselves point out this may have led to the omission from the bilingual sample of some bilinguals who may have been balanced but whose vocabulary in both English and French may have been small. Thus, in the Peal and Lambert study the use of the English Vocabulary measure may have led to some degree of bias in the selection of the bilingual sample. The extent of the bias, if it existed, cannot be ascertained in the absence of data on the cognitive abilities of those bilingual children who were not included in the bilingual sample. The fact that subsequent studies have tended to corroborate the Peal and Lambert findings, combined with Lambert and Anisfeld's conviction that no bias existed, may indicate that the extent of the bias, if it did exist, was slight.

In studies subsequent to the Peal and Lambert study there is little evidence that the procedure used to select the bilingual samples in any way biased the comparison of bilinguals and unilinguals. Studies which used measures of balance invariably used the ratio of L1:L2 performance. In some studies (e.g. Balkan, 1970) all of the bilingual children who were tested easily met the criterion of balance and thus none were excluded from the bilingual sample. In several studies (Bain, 1974; Balkan, 1970; Ianco-Worrall, 1972; Liedke & Nelson, 1968; Scott, 1973) the matching of bilingual and unilingual groups on non-verbal IQ, as well as SES, sex and age, provided an additional safeguard against bias.

A recent study (Cummins, 1975) has examined the extent to which the use of measures of linguistic balance may have introduced a bias into the comparison of bilinguals and unilinguals. This study examined the relationship between cognitive performance and the attainment of balance for children from French-speaking homes, English-speaking homes and mixed French–English homes who were attending the bilingual program of the Separate School System in Edmonton, Canada. Within the French and Mixed groups, children who were more balanced in French and English skills tended to perform at a higher level

on both intelligence and divergent thinking tasks. However, only a small proportion of children in these groups failed to meet the criterion of balance. Only
four children (out of 29) from the French group and six (out of 30) from the
Mixed group were classified as non-balanced. The cognitive performance of
these non-balanced children tended to be only slightly worse than the performance of children classified as balanced in their respective groups. Thus, their
exclusion from the balanced sample in the Cummins and Gulutsan (1974a) study
is unlikely to have seriously affected the comparison of bilingual and unilingual
groups.

The cognitive characteristics of those children from English-speaking homes
who were classified as non-balanced ($N = 11$ out of 23) have been summarised
earlier. No differences were found between balanced and non-balanced children
on verbal and non-verbal abilities but there were large differences between the
groups on measures of verbal divergence. Our main interest here is whether this
finding may have been an artifact of the similarity between the word association
balance measure and the test of verbal divergence in which subjects were
required to list as many uses as they could think of for two common objects
(Utility Test). This possibility was rejected in view of the fact that the correlation
between Utility fluency and the ratio of French:English word associations was
non-significant ($r = -0.27$) and lower than the correlations between Utility
fluency and the other two balance measures (subjective self-rating balance ratio,
$r = -0.45$; teacher's rating of relative skills in French and English, $r = -0.35$).

The findings of the Cummins (1975) study have relevance for the second issue
in the controversy regarding the use of balanced bilinguals, i.e. whether or not it
is legitimate, in principle, to compare unilinguals with a sample of balanced
bilinguals to the exclusion of bilingual children who may have remained very
dominant in one of their two languages. It could be argued, for example, that a
relatively high level of intelligence or, possibly, language learning aptitude, is
necessary to become a balanced bilingual and, therefore, comparison of balanced
bilinguals and unilinguals on these traits, or traits related to them, is biased in
favour of the former. This argument, however, is inconsistent with the lack of
any differences in verbal and non-verbal intelligence between balanced and non-
balanced children from the English home background group in the Cummins
(1975) study. One could, of course, argue from the Cummins data and also from
Scott's (1973) findings that divergent thinking skills are related to the ability to
become functionally bilingual. This possibility is extremely interesting and the
exact relationships between second language learning and divergent thinking
skills will undoubtedly be more closely specified in future studies.

Another point is that the criterion of balance in recent studies which have used
tests of linguistic balance (e.g. Balkan, 1970; Cummins & Gulutsan, 1974a; Peal
& Lambert, 1962) has been quite lenient. As operationally defined in these
studies 'balance' does not imply complete equilinguality; the procedure is
designed only to eliminate those who are very much more dominant in one of

their two languages. In the word association balance measure, for example, a ratio of only 5:3 English:French or French:English words was necessary to meet the criterion of balance used in the Balkan (1970) and Cummins and Gulutsan (1974a) studies. In the Peal and Lambert study the criterion was even more lenient. Thus, a bilingual child who produced 30 English words and only 18 French words to the stimulus words would qualify as 'balanced' despite the fact that he is clearly more proficient in English. The point is that a high level of language learning aptitude or intelligence is unlikely to have been necessary to attain the criterion of balance in these studies since this criterion has been so lenient. The finding of no differences in verbal or non-verbal intelligence between balanced and non-balanced groups in the Cummins (1975) study supports this conclusion.

In summary, although the use of a Vocabulary test in selecting the balanced bilingual sample in the Peal and Lambert study may have introduced some degree of bias into the comparison of bilinguals and unilinguals, there is no evidence that the procedures used to select the bilingual samples in subsequent studies in any way biased the comparison of bilingual and unilingual samples.

The fact that recent studies which have reported positive cognitive consequences associated with bilingualism have involved balanced bilinguals, whereas the majority of earlier studies failed to control for degree of bilingualism, by itself provides only a partial picture of the linguistic competence of the bilingual subjects in these two types of studies. It tells us only that bilinguals who were very much more dominant in one of their two languages were not included in recent studies. It does not, however, tell us whether the L2 competence attained by the bilingual subjects in recent studies was attained at the expense of their competence in L1 (Macnamara's (1966) 'balance effect') or whether these bilingual subjects had a high level of competence in both their languages. In order to specify more precisely the differences in linguistic competence of the bilingual subjects in early and more recent studies, it is necessary to consider the social contexts in which these two types of studies have been carried out.

Bilingualism and Socio-cultural Factors

Paulston (1975) has noted that the socio-economic status of the students is the one overruling factor in distinguishing successful and unsuccessful bilingual education programs. She states that

> In every single study where monolingual children did as well as or better in L2 instruction than did native speakers, those children came from upper or middle class homes. (1975: 9)

Similarly, in the empirical studies reviewed above, those which reported that balanced bilingualism was associated with higher levels of cognitive performance tend to have compared the performance of bilinguals and unilinguals of relatively high SES. Many of the earlier studies, on the other hand, involved bilinguals who were of low SES. The reason for this was simply that in many countries bilingual communities tended to come from disadvantaged backgrounds (e.g. immigrant groups in the USA, rural children in Wales, etc.). A recently published report on bilingual–bicultural education in the USA has expressed this point:

> Those individuals who are commonly designated 'bilingual' (they are often not bilinguals but monolingual speakers of a language other than English) in this country are also those who, bearing the brunt of many forms of discrimination, tend to be of a low socioeconomic status such as Mexican Americans, Native Americans, Puerto Ricans, and many immigrant groups.
> (United States Commission on Civil Rights, 1975: 68)

Although it is not difficult to appreciate that the addition of a second language might well exacerbate the problems which lower SES children are reported to experience in coping with just one language (Bernstein, 1971; Edwards, 1975), the label 'SES' by itself, provides a very inadequate description of the societal conditions under which bilingual learning experiences can be expected to have either positive or negative cognitive consequences. One need only point to the successful replication of the St. Lambert experiment with working-class children in Montreal (Tucker, Lambert & d'Anglejan, 1973) to demonstrate that more than just SES is involved.

In a more general sociological context the distinction between the bilingualism of upper class children and of lower class children has been expressed in terms of 'elitist' and 'folk' bilingualism (Paulston, 1975). Elitist bilingualism is a matter of choice and has characterised the educated and upper classes of many societies throughout the centuries. This type of bilingualism has never been an educational problem. As Fishman (1967) puts it,

> ... where there has been a history of stable intra group bilingualism with real support from the educational system, there has been no history of retardation as a result, but rather a history of assets. Elitist bilingualism throughout world history has been of this kind. (1967: 82)

Folk bilingualism, on the other hand, is not a matter of choice but is the result of ethnic groups in contact and competition within a single state. This is the situation of many immigrant groups in North America who must become bilingual in order to survive. It is folk bilingualism which has, for the most part, been associated with negative cognitive and academic consequences, and there are many sociolinguistic factors which can be invoked to account, at least partially, for such findings. The attitudes of pupils and parents, the prestige of the bilingual's two languages, the functions which the languages serve within a particular social context, possible negative stereotyping and discrimination against minority language groups and many other factors are all likely to play an important role in explaining the negative effects associated with folk bilingualism.

However, from the point of view of the present paper, one problem with these socio-cultural factors in resolving contradictory research findings is that they are too distant from the actual process of cognitive development. Positive attitudes in the learner, for example, will undoubtedly contribute to the success with which he learns a second language, but they do not explain why learning a second language might positively influence aspects of cognitive functioning. Similarly, negative attitudes may help explain why an individual experiences difficulties in coping with two languages, but the negative attitudes are not the direct determinant of any cognitive difficulties that the individual might experience. In other words, there are intervening variables in the causal chain whose influence needs to be specified. Since these intervening variables seem likely to be related to the linguistic competence attained by bilingual children our main concern in considering socio-cultural factors is whether or not they can elucidate any differences in the level of linguistic competence attained by bilingual subjects in earlier as compared to more recent studies.

A distinction made by Lambert (1975) between 'additive' and 'subtractive' bilingualism is helpful in bridging the gap between socio-cultural factors and the actual process of cognitive development. In developing this distinction Lambert attaches special importance to one socio-cultural factor – i.e. the prestige or social relevance of the bilingual's two languages. He notes that in communities where studies have reported positive effects associated with bilingualism, the L2 has been a socially relevant language, the learning of which is unlikely to lead to replacement of the L1 (usually a prestigious or dominant language). However, for many ethnic minority groups the learning of L2 (usually the majority and more prestigious language) is very likely to lead to a gradual replacement of the L1. Lambert terms the former type of bilingualism 'additive' in that the learner is adding a new language to his repertory of skills. The latter type of bilingualism is termed 'subtractive' in that the bilingual's competence in his two languages at any point in time is likely to reflect some stage in the subtraction of the L1 and its replacement by the L2.

While the distinction between additive and subtractive bilingualism parallels the high SES, low SES and elitist–folk distinctions, it also carries implications for the bilingual's relative degree of competence in his two languages. Subtractive bilingualism, where L1 is being replaced by L2, implies that as a bilingual in a language minority group develops skills in L2, his competence in L1 will decrease. It seems likely that, under these circumstances, many bilingual children in subtractive bilingual learning situations may not develop native-like competence in either of their two languages. Thus, the concept of 'subtractive' bilingualism has affinities both to Macnamara's (1966) 'balance effect' hypothesis and to what Scandinavian researchers have described as semilingualism (Hansegard, 1968; Skutnabb-Kangas, 1975). The 'balance effect' hypothesis states that as a bilingual develops skills in one of his two languages, he pays for it by a decrease in competence in the other (Macnamara, 1966). While it has been demonstrated that this hypothesis does not hold in elitist or additive bilingual learning situations (e.g. the St. Lambert project), it does have relevance for the bilingualism of many language minority groups. Cummins and Gulutsan (1974b), for example, found evidence of a 'balance effect' in the linguistic competence of children from French-speaking home backgrounds attending a bilingual program in Edmonton, Canada. The French home language of these children was gradually being replaced by the majority language – English – and by grade six virtually all the children from French-speaking home backgrounds were somewhat dominant in English. The French children rated their competence in *both* English and French lower than other children in the program (from English and mixed French–English speaking homes) rated their competence in English. The French group also scored significantly lower than the other two groups on a measure of verbal ability (administered in English).

The concept of 'subtractive' bilingualism also implies a level of bilingual competence similar in some respects to what Scandinavian researchers have described as 'semilingualism'. The term 'semilingualism' refers to the linguistic competence, or lack of it, of individuals who have had contact with two languages since childhood without adequate training or stimulation in either. As a consequence, these individuals know two languages poorly and do not attain the same levels as native speakers in either language. Scandinavian researchers (e.g. Hansegard, 1968; Skutnabb-Kangas, 1975) have argued that this condition has negative emotional, cognitive, linguistic and scholastic consequences (see Paulston (1975) for a summary of Scandinavian research on 'semilingualism').

Since many of the early studies which reported negative cognitive consequences associated with bilingualism involved bilingual children from language minority groups, it seems likely that the L1 of many of the bilingual subjects in these studies was being replaced by L2. Consequently, many of these subjects may not have had native-like skills in either of their two languages. These bilingual subjects may very well have been balanced bilinguals, i.e. have had relatively equal competence in both languages. However, their L2 competence is likely to have been achieved at the expense of their L1 competence.

Recent studies which have reported that bilingualism might positively influence cognitive functioning have, as Lambert (1973) points out, been conducted in additive bilingual learning situations. There is evidence that in additive situations the L2 competence achieved by an individual is achieved at no cost to his competence in L1 (e.g. Cohen, 1975; Cummins & Gulutsan, 1974b; Lambert & Tucker, 1972, etc.). Therefore, the linguistic competence of the 'balanced' bilingual subjects in recent studies is likely to have differed considerably from the linguistic competence of 'balanced' bilingual subjects in earlier studies. In recent studies, the bilingual subjects are likely to have achieved a high level of L2 competence at no cost to their L1, whereas in earlier studies the bilingual subjects are likely to have paid for their L2 competence by a lowering of their L1 competence.

It must be remembered, however, that the bilingual subjects in recent studies may not be representative of all children who have undergone bilingual learning experiences in additive settings. In several of these studies bilinguals who have been very much more dominant in one of their two languages have been excluded from the bilingual sample. This raises the question of how the bilingual learning experiences of children who remain very dominant in their L1, yet are forced, at school or elsewhere, to function through their L2, will influence their cognitive growth. This question will be considered in the next section which examines the relationship between a bilingual's linguistic competence and his cognitive functioning.

Linguistic Competence and Cognitive Growth

The fact that the bilingual subjects in earlier and more recent studies are likely to have attained very different levels of linguistic competence suggests that the effects of bilingualism on cognitive growth may be mediated by the level of competence an individual attains in his two languages. In the initial stages of becoming bilingual (whether it is in the early years of life or as a result of school experiences), the child's cognitive system will inevitably experience some difficulty in coping with two forms of linguistic input. In some bilingual learning situations the initial difficulty is quickly overcome and the bilingual child rapidly learns both to understand and communicate in the second language at no cost to his native language. The research evidence reviewed earlier indicates that in cases such as this, where access to both languages is attained and maintained, bilingualism might positively influence the development of cognition. However, in bilingual learning situations where the child fails to overcome difficulties in coping with two languages the research evidence suggest that his bilingual learning experiences might have a negative effect on his cognitive functioning, at least in so far as this functioning involves language. Continued difficulties with language over a prolonged period of time are likely to mean that a bilingual child's interaction with an increasingly symbolic environment will not optimally promote his cognitive and academic progress.

If the level of competence which a bilingual child attains in L1 and L2 mediates the effects of his bilingual learning experiences on cognitive growth, then in immersion or bilingual education programs there may be a threshold level of L2 competence which pupils must attain both in order to avoid cognitive disadvantages and allow the potentially beneficial aspects of becoming bilingual to influence their cognitive functioning. Those aspects of bilingualism which might accelerate cognitive growth seem unlikely to come into effect until the child has attained a certain minimum or threshold level of competence in his second language. Similarly, if a child in an immersion program attains only a very low level of competence in his second language, his interaction with the environment through the medium of that language, both in terms of input and output, is likely to be impoverished. Not only will he fail to comprehend much of the content of schooling but he is also likely to experience difficulty in expressing his developing intelligence and operating (in a Piagetian sense) on the environment through his L2. One probable consequence of this is a decrease in intellectual and academic curiosity

It should be made clear at the outset that the threshold level of bilingual competence is an intervening rather than a basic causal variable in accounting for the cognitive growth of bilinguals. Although the cognitive effects of an individual's bilingual learning experiences may be mediated by whether or not he attains the hypothesized threshold level of bilingual competence, the attainment of the threshold is itself determined by more fundamental social, attitudinal, educational and cognitive (e.g. language learning aptitude) factors.

What are the characteristics of this threshold level of bilingual competence? In the first place the threshold cannot be defined in absolute terms; rather, it is likely to vary both with the amount of time that is spent through L2 and with the type of cognitive operations that must be expressed through L2. The threshold for a child in a full immersion program is likely to be higher (in absolute terms) than for a child in a bilingual program in which 50% of the time is spent in L1. Because a greater proportion of his cognitive operations in the school setting must be expressed through the medium of his second language, the immersion child is more likely than the child in the bilingual program to suffer cognitively (and academically) if he fails to develop adequate skills in that language. However, by the same token, the immersion experience seems more likely to promote full functional bilingualism than bilingual programs in which a sizeable proportion of the time is spent through L1. Thus, the child in an immersion program may more rapidly gain the threshold level of L2 competence required to reap the cognitive benefits of his bilingual learning experience. This raises the possibility that there may be not one but two thresholds. The attainment of the first threshold would be sufficient to avoid cognitive retardation but the attainment of a second, higher, level of bilingual competence might be necessary to lead to accelerated cognitive growth. This possibility is likely to be investigated in future research on the relationship between bilingualism and cognition. However, for the purposes of exposition in the present paper only one threshold need be posited. In summary, the more time that is spent through the L2, the higher must be the level of second language competence necessary to avoid cognitive deficits.

The threshold is also likely to vary according to the type of cognitive operations appropriate for a child's stage of cognitive development. A grade six child in an immersion program whose L2 competence is below the threshold necessary for the adequate expression of his intelligence may have a much higher level of L2 competence, in absolute terms, than a grade one child whose L2 competence is above the threshold necessary for the adequate expression of *his* intelligence. This is so because between grade one and grade six, or roughly between concrete and formal operations, language is likely to increase in importance as an instrument with which the child can operate on his environment and express his developing intelligence. Possibly one of the reasons why so little cognitive retardation has been observed in the early grades of immersion schooling is that during these grades the child's interaction with the world and, consequently, his cognitive development, is less dependent on the mediation of language than at later grades. This may give the child a 'breather' in which he can overcome the inevitable initial difficulties with language and gain the second language skills necessary to optimally benefit from interaction with an increasingly symbolic environment. Even Piagetian theory, which takes a conservative viewpoint on the relationship between language and thought, admits that as the child approaches the formal operational stage, linguistic symbolism becomes more useful as a means of representing cognitive operations. Thus, linguistic difficulties such as inadequate command of the L2 or interference between L1 and L2 are likely to have a greater effect on the child's expression of his intelligence at the formal operational than at the concrete operational stage. This point will be considered in more detail in a later section.

Much of the evidence (see Macnamara, 1967) linking instruction through a weaker language with cognitive and academic difficulties can be reinterpreted in terms of the threshold hypothesis. These difficulties are due not so much to instruction through a weaker language in itself, as to the failure of pupils to attain the threshold level of L2 competence necessary to benefit from such instruction. Many immersion programs have reported no negative consequences as a result of instruction through a weaker language, the reason being, we would hypothesize, that a relatively high (i.e. threshold) level of L2 skills was attained by pupils in these programs.

What type of linguistic difficulties characterize individuals who fail to attain a threshold level of linguistic competence? This question cannot be answered in any general way due to the fact that the threshold is likely to vary according to the type of bilingual learning situation and the individual's stage of cognitive development. However, Macnamara's (1967) description of the linguistic difficulties experienced by some bilingual children may serve as a guideline for research on the relationship between linguistic competence and cognitive functioning. Macnamara investigated why grade six bilingual children took longer to solve problems in their weaker language and concluded that the reasons lay in an inadequate grasp of the language rather than in ignorance of certain words or syntactic structures. He points out that a bilingual's difficulties with language '... can arise from something other than ignorance of certain words, idioms and syntactic structures; they can arise from a fairly generalized unfamiliarity with and poor control of the standard language, at least in written form, so as to affect a student's problem-solving ability adversely' (1970: 34). In earlier grades, failure to attain the threshold may very well be due to lack of vocabulary or poor command of syntactic structures. However, Macnamara's analysis suggests that in later grades difficulties with language may take quite subtle forms. Elsewhere (1966: 34–48) Macnamara has discussed the roles of interlingual interference, cultural conflict, faulty linguistic models and lack of time in a language as factors which might contribute to a bilingual's difficulties with language.

Few, if any, of the bilingual pupils in the Montreal and Ottawa immersion programs (Lambert & Tucker, 1972; Barik & Swain, 1975) seem to have experienced prolonged difficulties with language. These programs have demonstrated that, under favourable conditions (e.g. the learning of a socially relevant language, a bilingual environment, highly motivated parents, teachers and pupils), the majority of pupils experience little difficulty in attaining relatively high levels of functional bilingualism. Even children with learning difficulties have fared well in the St. Lambert project (Bruck *et al.*, 1974). Thus, in additive bilingual learning situations the proportion of children who fail to attain a threshold level of bilingual competence may be very small. However, in bilingual education programs conducted under less favourable conditions a larger proportion of children may remain very dominant in their L1 and consequently may not optimally benefit from school experiences conducted through L2.

One implication of the threshold hypothesis for evaluations of bilingual education programs is that pupils who have attained the threshold may perform very differently on cognitive and academic tasks from pupils who have failed to attain the threshold. These different levels of cognitive and academic performance may mask each other when the performance of only the total bilingual group is considered. The research reviewed earlier indicated that bilingualism could have both positive and negative cognitive consequences and in the present paper it has been hypothesized that these different consequences may be related to the level of linguistic competence attained by a bilingual. If this hypothesis is valid, then evaluations of bilingual education programs should consider the cognitive and academic consequences not only for the group as a whole, but also separately for those who have attained and those who may have failed to attain high levels of L2 skills.

In summary, as a synthesis of seemingly inconsistent research findings, it has been proposed that there may be a threshold level of bilingual competence which an individual must attain before his access to two languages can begin to positively influence his cognitive functioning. While an individual's competence in L2 and/or L1 remains below this threshold his interaction with the environment through these languages is unlikely to optimally promote his cognitive and academic progress. The threshold hypothesis is doubtless oversimplified and elucidation of the specific characteristics of the threshold in different bilingual learning situations must await future research. Hopefully, however, this hypothesis will have heuristic value since very little research seems to have been carried out in relating a bilingual's level of competence in L1 and L2 to his cognitive and academic progress.

One further problem needs to be considered. In discussing the threshold hypothesis it is clear that certain assumptions have been made regarding the relationships between language and cognitive growth. The final section will state and attempt to justify these assumptions. The problems of how failure to overcome difficulties with language might retard cognitive growth and how the attainment of a threshold level of bilingual competence might positively affect cognitive functioning will be briefly considered in relation to the wider issue of the role of language in cognitive development.

Explaining the Research Findings

The threshold hypothesis makes two theoretical assumptions regarding the relation of bilingualism and cognition. The first assumption is that failure to resolve difficulties in coping with two languages over a prolonged period of time can negatively influence an individual's rate of cognitive development. Secondly, the threshold hypothesis assumes that when a certain level of competence in two languages has been attained, there are aspects either of a bilingual's present access to two languages or of his bilingual learning experiences which can positively influence his cognitive functioning. These assumptions are both supported by the research evidence above but their relationship to the wider theoretical issue of the role of language in cognitive development needs to be made explicit.

Two major contrasting positions on the development inter-relationships of language and thought can be distinguished. The first, which derives from Piaget's (1970) theory of cognitive development, holds that the development of cognitive operations is essentially independent of language. Although language can prepare an operation and extend its range it is neither a sufficient nor necessary condition for the development of operational thought (Furth & Youniss, 1971; Sinclair-de-Zwart, 1967; Piaget, 1970). Vygotsky's (1962) theory, on the other hand, holds that the development of logical thought is dependent on the internalization of speech. Not only logical thought but the totality of an individual's personality is closely integrated with linguistic experience.

Clearly Vygotsky's position creates no problems for the theoretical assumptions of the threshold hypothesis. However, at first sight the Piagetian position appears less compatible with the assumption that a bilingual's linguistic experience can influence his cognitive growth. Macnamara (1970) has drawn out the apparent implications of a Piagetian position for the relationship between bilingualism and cognitive growth. He argues that because the development of cognition owes little to the influence of language and linguistic functioning is to a great extent dependent on many sorts of non-linguistic cognitive functioning '... it seems unlikely that bilingualism should have any effect upon the development of the basic, common, cognitive structures' (1970: 33).

I shall argue, in contrast to Macnamara, that there is no incompatibility between a Piagetian position on the relationship between language and thought and the hypothesis that bilingualism can influence (both positively and negatively under different conditions) the development of cognition.

An appropriate starting point for consideration of the first assumption (i.e. that linguistic difficulties can negatively influence the development of cognition) is Furth's work on the cognitive development of deaf children. The results of an extensive series of studies (Furth, 1966) indicate that deaf children pass through the same operational stages as hearing children even though their performance is somewhat inferior on some tasks. Furth attributes the slight intellectual lag not to the direct influence of language as such but to experiential factors such as the lack of normal social interaction in the deaf which could easily lead to a lower level of intellectual curiosity. Furth and Youniss (1971) sum up their findings as follows:

> In other words, whereas language is never a sufficient or necessary condition of operatory functioning, the evidence from our work with linguistically deficient persons indicates that it may have, at best, an indirect facilitating effect for concrete operations, but can have a direct facilitating effect on certain formal operations precisely because of the close relation between formal operations and symbolic functioning. (1971: 64)

Language, according to Furth and Youniss, is less closely related to concrete than to formal operations because '... for the functioning of concrete operatory structures physical events not verbal propositions are primary objects of thinking' (1971: 63).

From this it can be implied that failure to overcome difficulties with language will have a greater effect on the development of formal operational than on concrete operational thought. By themselves, these difficulties will not prevent an individual from developing formal operational structures but they may retard the process. In addition to the direct relationship between language and some types of formal operational thinking, the scholastic experiences of individuals who have an inadequate grasp of the language of instruction may be less intellectually satisfying and consequently may not promote intellectual curiosity. A lower level of intellectual curiosity could retard the rate of intellectual development even in areas which do not involve the mediation of language. Thus, even though the major negative effects of failure to overcome difficulties in coping with two languages have been identified in areas which require the expression of intelligence through language, more generalized negative effects should not be discounted. In short, because linguistic experience can facilitate the development of cognition, difficulties in coping with two languages are likely to adversely affect a bilingual child's expression of his intelligence through language, and consequently, his interaction with an increasingly symbolic environment.

In order to examine whether or not the second assumption of the threshold hypothesis (i.e. that bilingualism can positively influence cognitive functioning) is compatible with Piagetian theory, it is necessary to summarize the explanations which have been offered by various investigators to account for findings of a positive association between bilingualism and cognition. These explanations can be reduced to three basic hypotheses which I shall term the 'experiential enrichment' hypothesis, the 'switching' hypothesis and the 'objectification' hypothesis. These hypotheses are, for the most part, still in the speculative stage, the objectification hypothesis being the only one supported by empirical evidence.

The experiential enrichment hypothesis holds that the bilingual child may have been exposed to a wider range of experiences due either to attempts by his parents to compensate for the reduced time he will inevitably spend in each language (Liedke & Nelson, 1968), or because his experiences stem from two cultures (Peal & Lambert, 1962). Although this hypothesis seems plausible in general terms there is no empirical evidence for or against it. It has not been demonstrated that bilinguals are exposed to a wider range of social or cultural stimulation than unilinguals or that, even if they were, this would accelerate their rate of cognitive growth.

The switching hypothesis has been proposed by various investigators (Balkan, 1970; Carringer, 1974; Landry, 1974; Peal & Lambert, 1962) to account for their findings that bilingual children exhibited higher levels of cognitive flexibility or divergent thinking. This hypothesis proposes that bilingual children develop a more flexible learning set as a result of switching languages and making use of two different perspectives. The switching hypothesis as expressed by the investigators mentioned above seems to involve two different explanatory factors depending upon whether one emphasizes the different perspectives provided by two *languages* or, alternatively the actual process of *switching* from one language to another. The first interpretation is very similar to the objectification hypothesis and will be considered below. The validity of the second interpretation has been called into question by Cummins and Gulutsan (1975) who found that balanced bilingual and unilingual groups, matched for sex, SES and age, did not differ in ability to extinguish a set as measured by the Uznadze haptic illusion. If bilinguals were, in fact, more adaptable or 'willing to change' (Landry, 1974) as a result of alternating languages, this should have been evident on the haptic set test which requires subjects to change an established set or pattern of response.

In conclusion, it should not be uncritically assumed that the actual process of switching between languages has any consequences for the cognitive functioning of bilinguals. However, it is possible that relevant aspects of problem situations may be brought to the bilingual child's attention by the availability of two different linguistic perspectives. This is the basic tenet of the objectification hypothesis to which we now turn. Since the objectification hypothesis attributes the bilingual's cognitive advantage directly to his access to two linguistic codes, the relationship between this hypothesis and the theories of Piaget and Vygotsky will be considered in some detail.

Cummins and Gulutsan (1975) have suggested that several of the hypotheses put forward to explain bilinguals' higher levels of cognitive performance can parsimoniously be subsumed under what Georgian (USSR) psychologists have termed the 'process of objectification'. The term 'objectification' refers to the process whereby objects become the focus of conscious attention and, according to Uznadze (1966), this process arises in the context of social life and is closely linked to language. The objectification process appears to express the essential component of those explanations which emphasize the interplay between object and word or semantics and phonetics. Lambert and Tucker (1972), for example, note the 'two-way bilingual relay of concepts and linguistic principles' (p. 210) that they have observed among the experimental children in the St. Lambert project from the grade one level on. According to Lambert and Tucker (1972) children in the project 'get caught up in a process of comparing and contrasting two linguistic codes' and 'this children's version of contrastive linguistics helps them immeasurably to build vocabulary and to comprehend complex linguistic functions' (p. 208).

In a similar vein, it has been proposed (e.g. Imedadze, 1960; Leopold, 1949) that the simultaneous acquisition of two languages in early childhood might lead to a faster separation of sound and meaning, thereby directing the bilingual child's attention both to the essential or conceptual attributes of objects (Leopold, 1949) and to the characteristics of his two languages (Imedadze, 1960). Leopold (1949) has argued that

> A bilingual, who constantly hears two words for one thing, is compelled to pay more attention to the meaning expressed than to the word used to express it, whereas the monolingual is often satisfied with a hazy definition of a word and will use it without understanding it fully. (1949: 188)

Imedadze (1960) similarly asserts that when the bilingual child 'first encounters the fact that an object can have two names, a separation of object and name begins. A word, when freed from its referent can easily become the object of special attention' (quoted by Diebold, 1968: 236).

The objectification hypothesis has the advantage that the observations on which it is based have received strong empirical support (Ianco-Worrall, 1972) and the role which it attributes to the bilingual's two linguistic codes in promoting cognitive development is quite compatible with both the Vygotskian and Piagetian positions regarding the role of language in cognitive development.

Ianco-Worrall (1972) supported Leopold's (1949) observations by showing that bilingual children, brought up in a one-person, one-language home environment, were more sensitive than unilingual children to semantic relations between words and were also more advanced in realizing the arbitrary assignment of names to referents. Unilingual children were more likely to interpret similarity between words in terms of an acoustic rather than a semantic dimension and felt that the names of objects could not be interchanged.

The significance of these empirical findings can be appreciated when they are placed in the context of Vygotsky's lucid description of the relationships between words and concepts in the cognitive development of unilingual children. Vygotsky's description of the rigid association between a word and its referent brings into focus the possible advantages of having more than one word available.

> The child must learn to distinguish between semantics and phonetics and understand the nature of the difference. At first he uses verbal forms and meanings without being conscious of them as separate. The word to the child is an integral part of the object it denotes ... We can see how difficult it is for children to separate the name of an object from its attributes ... The fusion of the two planes of speech, semantic and vocal, begins to break down as the child grows older ... (1962: 128–9)

This separation of the semantic and vocal planes of speech, which the research evidence indicates is accelerated by having two words for the same referent, is necessary if the child is to use language effectively as a tool for thinking. Vygotsky (1962: 110) also argued that being able to express the same thought in different languages will enable the child to 'see his language as one particular system among many, to view its phenomena under more general categories, and this leads to awareness of his linguistic operations'.

In an earlier paper directly concerned with multilingualism in children, Vygotsky (1975) argued that, depending on the conditions of acquisition of the second language, bilingualism could have either negative or positive consequences for cognitive development. When child bilingualism develops spontaneously, i.e. outside the influence of training, Vygotsky admitted that it could inhibit the child's mental development through confusion and interference of concepts and associative processes. However, when the application of sound pedagogical principles ensured that each language had an independent sphere of influence, bilingualism could orient the child towards more abstract thought processes 'from the prison of concrete language forms and phenomena' (p. 29). In terms of Vygotsky's theory of cognitive development, it is inconceivable that bilingualism should not affect the child's development (either positively or negatively) since not only intellectual development but also 'character development and emotional development all reflect the direct influence of speech' (p. 24).

In view of the fact that Piaget's (1970) theory is perhaps the most conservative of current theories regarding the role attributed to linguistic experience in promoting cognitive growth, it is somewhat surprising to note that the objectification hypothesis emphasizes precisely the same aspect of language as that emphasized by Genevan investigators. For example, Inhelder et al. (1966) point out that 'language training ... operates to direct the child's interactions with the environment and thus to "focus" on relevant dimensions of task situations' (p. 163). Sinclair-de-Zwart (1967) similarly notes that 'language can direct attention to pertinent factors of a problem, just as it can control perceptual activities ...' (quoted by

Furth, 1969: 130). Although language cannot effect a full transition from one operational stage to another, it can prepare an operation and help children pass to an intermediate stage (Inhelder & Sinclair, 1969). Since operational thinking derives from action not language, linguistic experience, according to Genevan psychologists, is capable of accelerating cognitive growth only to a limited extent.

However, certain differences between the Genevan view of 'language' and the bilingual's linguistic experience should be pointed out. In the context of Genevan research, 'language' usually refers to specific short-term training procedures. The relative ineffectiveness of 'language' in promoting operational growth is due to the fact that operational growth 'does not consist in simply incorporating ready-made and readily available data' (Inhelder & Sinclair, 1969: 21) but in coordinating the feedback derived from the child's own actions on the environment.

The bilingual's access to two linguistic codes represents a very different form of linguistic experience from that provided in short-term verbal training sessions. In the first place the bilingual 'training' experience is likely to be undergone over a period of years. Secondly the 'training' does not consist in the bilingual incorporating ready-made data from outside as in Genevan (and other) verbal training experiments but rather in constantly *generating* data, through his speech actions on the environment, which provide a qualitatively different form of feedback from that provided by a unilingual's speech activity. It is the feedback from these bilingual speech actions which can (according to the objectification hypothesis) accelerate cognitive growth. This assertion is in no way incompatible with Piaget's (1970) statement that 'language does not seem to be the motor of operational evolution, but rather an instrument in the service of intelligence itself' (p. 722). The objectification hypothesis merely asserts that bilingualism represents a more powerful linguistic instrument than unilingualism with which to operate on the environment. Within the theoretical context of Genevan psychology the greater power of the bilingual instrument in facilitating cognitive growth arises from the feedback generated by the bilingual child's own speech actions which help direct his attention both to the conceptual features of the environment and to the characteristics of his linguistic operations.

In summary, I have tried to show how attempts to account for the influence of bilingualism on cognitive functioning might be integrated with theoretical positions on the role of language in cognitive development. More attention has been devoted to the Piagetian position, not because it is necessarily more valid than other theories, but because it takes a conservative position on the developmental relations between language and thought. In addition, an analysis of language and thought, partly based on Piaget's theory, has been used by Macnamara (1970) to argue that there is no theoretical justification for expecting bilingualism to influence cognitive growth. In opposition to this view, I have argued that, provided initial difficulties in coping with two languages are overcome, bilingualism represents an enriched form of experience which is capable of positively influencing cognitive functioning. This hypothesis is not in any way inconsistent with the Piagetian position on the role of language in cognitive growth.

Summary

Recent research findings indicate that access to two languages in early childhood can accelerate the development of both verbal and non-verbal abilities. There is also evidence of a positive association between bilingualism and both cognitive flexibility and divergent thinking. These findings are in contrast to the results of many earlier studies which found that bilingual children performed at a lower level than unilingual children on measures of verbal intelligence and scholastic achievement.

Several differences both in methodology and in setting distinguish these two types of studies. Studies which have reported positive effects associated with bilingualism have tended to involve balanced bilinguals, i.e. bilinguals who have attained a similar level of skills in both languages. In addition, these studies have been carried out in bilingual learning situations where the L2 has been a socially relevant language, the learning of which is unlikely to lead to a replacement of the L1 (usually a prestigious or dominant language). There is evidence that under these conditions a second language can be acquired at no cost to an individual's native language skills. Therefore the balanced bilinguals in recent studies are likely to have had a high level of competence in both their languages.

The bilingual subjects in many earlier studies, however, tended to come from minority language groups for whom the learning of L2 (usually the majority and more prestigious language) is likely to lead to a gradual replacement of the L1. Not surprisingly, the results of these studies produced evidence of a 'balance effect' in language learning, i.e. that a bilingual paid for his increasing L2 competence by a lowering of his competence in L1. Thus, the lower levels of verbal intelligence of the bilingual subjects in these studies may be a reflection of the fact that they are likely to have had less than native-like competence in both their languages.

On the basis of these differences in the linguistic competence of the bilingual subjects in earlier and more recent studies, it is hypothesized that the level of linguistic competence attained by a bilingual child may mediate the effects of his bilingual learning experiences on cognitive growth. In other words, the bilingual's level of competence in L1 and L2 is posited as an intervening variable in the causal chain between cognitive development and more fundamental social, attitudinal, educational and cognitive factors. Specifically, there may be a threshold level of linguistic competence which a bilingual child must attain both in order to avoid cognitive deficits and allow the potentially beneficial aspects of becoming bilingual to affect his cognitive functioning. Bilingualism and unilingualism can both be thought of as instruments which individuals use to operate on their environments. Because of its greater complexity, the bilingual instrument is more difficult to master, but once mastered, has a greater potential than the unilingual instrument for promoting cognitive growth.

One implication of the threshold hypothesis for bilingual education programs is that a program may have a positive influence on the cognitive functioning of children who attain a high level of L2 skills but a negative influence on the development of children who fail to attain adequate L2 skills. In evaluations of such programs the very different cognitive performances of these two groups may mask each other when the performance of only the total group is considered.

In the final section, the theoretical assumptions of the threshold hypothesis that, under different conditions, bilingualism can both positively and negatively influence aspects of cognitive functioning, are examined in relation to the broader issue of the role of language in cognitive development. It is argued that there is no inconsistency between the explanatory hypotheses suggested to account for the influence of bilingualism on cognition and even a conservative theory on the developmental interrelations of language and thought, such as that of Piaget.

Notes

1. I would like to thank Dr John Edwards for reading the original manuscript and making many valuable suggestions.
2. Liedke and Nelson (1968) matched bilingual and unilingual groups on age as well as on IQ, SES and sex. However, in Bain's (1974) study the bilingual children were, on average, five months younger than their unilingual counterparts. Although in this study differences between bilingual and unilingual groups on the rule discovery task, in favour of the bilinguals, only approach significance, the result is interesting both because of the lower chronological age of the bilingual group and the fact that the groups were matched on several cognitive variables, i.e. IQ, school grades and developmental level of operations.
3. The comparison of balanced and non-balanced groups with the unilingual group is only relevant within the context of the second interpretation, i.e. that divergent thinking skills have been influenced by bilingualism. It does *not* constitute support for that interpretation. If the first interpretation is correct, i.e. if divergent thinking skills are a correlate of second language learning ability, no inferences regarding the possible influence of bilingualism on divergent thinking can be made from the Cummins (1975) data. I am indebted to Professor W. Lambert for pointing this out.

References

Bain, B. C. (1974) Bilingualism and cognition: Towards a general theory. In S. Carey (ed.) *Bilingualism, Biculturalism and Education*. Proceedings from the conference at Collège Universitaire Saint-Jean, The University of Alberta.

Balkan, L. (1970) *Les Effets du Bilinguisme Français–Anglais sur les Aptitudes Intellectuelles*. Bruxelles: Aimav.

Barik, H. and Swain, M. (1975) Three-year evaluation of a large scale early grade French immersion program: The Ottawa Study. *Language Learning* 25, 1–30.

Ben-Zeev, S. (1972) The influence of bilingualism on cognitive development and cognitive strategy. Unpublished PhD dissertation, University of Chicago.

Bernstein, B. (1971) *Class Codes and Control.* Vol. 1: *Theoretical Studies towards a Sociology of Language.* London: Routledge and Kegan Paul.

Bruck, M., Lambert, W. E. and Tucker, G. R. (1973) Cognitive and attitudinal consequences of bilingual schooling: The St. Lambert project through grade six. Unpublished research report, McGill University.

Bruck, M., Rabinovitch, M. S. and Oates, M. (1975) The effects of French immersion programs on children with language disabilities – A preliminary report. *Working Papers in Bilingualism* No. 5, January, 47–86.

Carringer, D. C. (1974) Creative thinking abilities of Mexican youth: The relationship of bilingualism. *Journal of Cross-cultural Psychology* 5, 492–504.

Cohen, A. (1975) Successful immersion education in North America. *Working Papers in Bilingualism* No. 5, January, 39–46.

Cummins, J. (1975) Cognitive factors associated with intermediate levels of bilingual skills. Unpublished manuscript, Educational Research Centre, St. Patrick's College, Dublin.

Cummins, J. and Gulutsan, M. (1974a) Some effects of bilingualism on cognitive functioning. In S. Carey (ed.) *Bilingualism, Biculturalism and Education.* Proceedings from the conference at Collège Universitaire Saint-Jean, The University of Alberta.

Cummins, J. and Gulutsan, M. (1974b) Bilingual education and cognition. *Alberta Journal of Educational Research* 5, 259–66.

Cummins, J. and Gulutsan, M. (1975) Set, objectification and second language learning. *International Journal of Psychology* 10, 91–100.

Darcy, N. T. (1953) A review of the literature on the effects of bilingualism upon the measurement of intelligence. *Journal of Genetic Psychology* 82, 21–57.

Davé, R. H. (1963) The identification and measurement of environmental process variables that are related to educational achievement. Unpublished PhD dissertation, University of Chicago.

Diebold, A. R. (1968) The consequences of early bilingualism in cognitive development and personality formation. In E. Norbeck, D. Price Williams and W. M. McCord (eds) *The Study of Personality.* New York: Holt, Rinehart and Winston.

Edwards, J. R. (1975) The speech of disadvantaged Dublin children. Paper presented to the Fourth International Congress of Applied Linguistics, Stuttgart, August.

Engle, P. L. (1975) Language medium in early school years for minority language groups. *Review of Educational Research* 45, 283–325.

Fishman, J. A. (1967) Review of 'Bilingualism and primary education' by John Macnamara. *Irish Journal of Education* 1, 79–83.

Furth, H. G. (1966) *Thinking Without Language: Cognitive Implications of Deafness.* New York: Free Press.

Furth, H. G. (1969) *Piaget and Knowledge.* Englewood Cliffs, NJ: Prentice-Hall.

Furth, H. G. and Youniss, J. (1971) Formal operations and language: A comparison of deaf and hearing adolescents. *International Journal of Psychology* 6, 49–64.

Gowan, J. C. and Torrance, E. P. (1965) An intercultural study of non-verbal ideational fluency. *Gifted Child Quarterly* 9, 13–15.

Hansegard, N. E. (1968) *Tvasprakighet eller halvsprakighet [Bilingualism or Semibilingualism?]* Stockholm: Aldus/Bonniers.

Ianco-Worrall, A. (1972) Bilingualism and cognitive development. *Child Development* 43, 1390–1400.

Imedadze, N. V. (1960) K Psikhologichoskoy prirode rannego dvuyazyehiya [On the psychological nature of early bilingualism]. *Voprosy Psikhologii* 6, 60–8.

Inhelder, B. and Sinclair, H. (1969) Learning cognitive structures. In P. Mussen, J. Langer and M. Covington (eds) *Trends and Issues in Developmental Psychology.* New York: Holt, Rinehart and Winston.

Inhelder, B., Bovet, M., Sinclair, H. and Smock, C. (1966) On cognitive development. *American Psychologist* 21, 160–4.

Jensen, J. V. (1962) Effects of childhood bilingualism, I. *Elementary English* 39, 132–43.

Lambert, W. E. (1975) Culture and language as factors in learning and education. In A. Wolfgang (ed.) *Education of Immigrant Students*. Toronto: Ontario Institute for Studies in Education.

Lambert, W. E. and Anisfeld, E. (1969) A note on the relation of bilingualism and intelligence. *Canadian Journal of Behavioural Science* 1, 123–8.

Lambert, W. E. and Tucker, G. R. (1972) *Bilingual Education of Children: The St. Lambert Experiment*. Rowley: Newbury House.

Landry, R. G. (1974) A comparison of second language learners and monolinguals on divergent thinking tasks at the elementary school level. *Modern Language Journal* 58, 10–15.

Leopold, W. F. (1949) *Speech Development of a Bilingual Child* (Vol. 3). Evanston: Northwestern University Press.

Liedke, W. W. and Nelson, L. D. (1968) Concept formation and bilingualism. *Alberta Journal of Educational Research* 14, 225–32.

Mackey, W. F. (1971) *Bilingual Education in a Binational School*. Rowley: Newbury House.

Macnamara, J. (1966) *Bilingualism and Primary Education*. Edinburgh: Edinburgh University Press.

Macnamara, J. (1967) The effects of instruction in a weaker language. *Journal of Social Issues* 23, 121–35.

Macnamara, J. (1970) Bilingualism and thought. In J. E. Alatis (ed.) *Bilingualism and Language Contact: Anthropological, Linguistic, Psychological and Sociological Aspects*. Report on the Twenty-first Annual Round-Table Meeting. Monograph Series on Languages and Linguistics. Washington, DC: Georgetown University.

Paulston, C. B. (1975) Ethnic relations and bilingual education: Accounting for contradictory data. *Working Papers on Bilingualism* No. 6. Ontario Institute for Studies in Education, May.

Peal, E. and Lambert, W. (1962) The relation of bilingualism to intelligence. *Psychological Monographs* 76, 546.

Piaget, J. (1970) Piaget's theory. In P. Mussen (ed.) *Carmichael's Manual of Child Psychology*. New York: Wiley.

Scott, S. (1973) The relation of divergent thinking to bilingualism: Cause or effect? Unpublished research report, McGill University.

Sinclair-de-Zwart, H. (1967) *Acquisition de langage et développement de la pensée*. Paris: Dunod.

Skutnabb-Kangas, T. (1975) Bilingualism, semilingualism and school achievement. Paper presented to the Fourth International Conference of Applied Linguistics, Stuttgart, August.

Torrance, E. P., Gowan, J. C., Wu, J. M. and Aliotti, N. C. (1970) Creative functioning of monolingual and bilingual children in Singapore. *Journal of Educational Psychology* 61, 72–5.

Tsushima, W. T. and Hogan, T. P. (1975) Verbal ability and school achievement of bilingual and monolingual children of different ages. *Journal of Educational Research* 68, 349–53.

Tucker, G. R., Lambert, W. E. and d'Anglejan, A. (1973) Are French immersion programs suitable for working class children? A pilot investigation. *Language Sciences* 25, 19–26.

United States Commission on Civil Rights (1975) *A Better Chance to Learn: Bilingual–bicultural education*. Clearinghouse Publication 51, May.

Uznadze, D. N. (1966) *The Psychology of Set*. New York: Consultants Bureau.

Vygotsky, L. S. (1962) *Thought and Language*. Cambridge: MIT Press.

Vygotsky, L. S. (1975) Multilingualism in children. Translated by Metro Gulutsan and Irene Arki, Centre for East European and Soviet Studies, The University of Alberta, mimeo, 1975. The essay appears (pp. 53–72) in a collection of essays written by Vygotsky and edited by L. V. Zankov, Zh. I. Shif and D. B. El'konin, *Umstvennoe razvitie detei v protsesse obucheniia, spornik statei* (Mental development of children in the process of education, a collection of essays). Moscow and Leningrad: State Pedagogical Publishing House, 1935.

Wolf, R. (1966) The measurement of environments. In A. Anastasi (ed.) *Testing Problems in Perspective*. Washington, DC: American Council on Education.

Immersion Programs:
The Irish Experience

Recent experimental programs in Canada and the United States (e.g. Cohen, 1974; Lambert & Tucker, 1972; Swain 1974) have demonstrated the viability of a home–school language switch in what Lambert (1975) terms *additive* bilingual learning situations, i.e. in situations where both first (L1) and second (L2) languages are prestigious and L1 is in no danger of replacement by L2. However, for minority language children in 'subtractive' situations where L1 is being replaced by a dominant L2, education through the L1 has been strongly advocated (e.g. Fishman, 1977; Skutnabb-Kangas & Toukomaa, 1976).

The immersion education program in operation in Ireland for over 50 years has several features characteristic of home–school language switch programs in North America. The program is *additive* in that the child's L1 (English) is in no danger of replacement by L2 (Irish); however, the situation differs from North American situations in that Irish is not a prestigious language of wider communication (such as French or Spanish) and the only incentives to learn Irish are ethnic and cultural. The present paper is concerned with the psychological and educational effects of a home–school language switch under these conditions. The findings of Macnamara's (1966) study of bilingualism in Irish primary schools will be critically examined and the results of a survey of teachers in Irish immersion schools will be briefly outlined. First, however, it is necessary to provide some background information on the development of immersion education in Ireland.

History and Recent Developments

The movement to teach infant (kindergarten) and primary school classes through Irish 'as far as possible' began shortly after the founding of the Irish Free State in 1921. The number of immersion or Irish medium primary schools in English-speaking areas reached a peak of almost 300 by the late 1930s; however, concurrent with the growth of Irish medium schools were increasing doubts among teachers and parents about the educational wisdom of teaching children from English-speaking homes through the medium of Irish. A survey of teachers conducted by the Irish National Teachers' Organization in 1941 reported that a majority of teachers who responded felt that pupils received considerably less benefit from instruction through Irish as compared to instruction through English.

Enthusiasm for the revival of Irish was adversely affected by the element of compulsion involved in Government policy. Irish was a compulsory school subject throughout primary and secondary education and in public examinations the awarding of certificates was dependent on the pupil having passed the Irish examination. Teachers were often evaluated by Department of Education inspectors solely on how well they could teach Irish, regardless of their competence in other subject areas.

The recent Committee on Irish Language Attitudes Research (CILAR) report (1975) showed that although a large majority of the population felt that Irish should be taught in schools they were dissatisfied with the way it was taught and opposed Government policies involving compulsion. Almost 80% of the population felt that many children failed their exams because of Irish and 66% felt that most children resented having to learn Irish. 60% considered that children doing subjects through Irish did not do as well in school as those doing them through English.

Widely-held attitudes such as these undoubtedly contributed to the gradual decline in the number of Irish medium schools in English-speaking areas. From a peak of almost 300 in the late 1930s, the number of these schools has fallen to only 18 in the present day.[1] However, about one-third of the present total of Irish medium schools has been founded within the last decade. Thus, among many parents, mainly in the Dublin area, there has been a renewal of interest in having their children educated through Irish. These parents are considerably more committed to the Irish language than many parents of children in earlier Irish immersion schools. As Macnamara (1966) points out

> in rural areas and country towns ... few parents had a choice of schools for their children ... Thus, it is quite unlikely that the parents of children who attended most Irish medium schools in English-speaking areas differed in their attitudes towards Irish or English from the generality of Irish parents.
>
> (1966: 74)

In other words, many of the parents of children in earlier immersion schools would have held neutral or negative attitudes towards Irish and few would have spoken any Irish at home.[2] In contrast many of the recent all-Irish schools were founded through parental pressure and parents are involved both in decision-making and extra-curricular activities. Like immersion programs elsewhere but unlike many earlier Irish immersion programs, emphasis in the early grades is on oral communication rather than grammatical correctness.

A common concern among teachers in present-day Irish medium schools is the desire to follow, and be seen to follow, sound educational principles. This concern with educational soundness was no doubt stimulated by the controversy surrounding John Macnamara's (1966) book *Bilingualism and Primary Education* which claimed to show that teaching through the medium of Irish had detrimental effects on children's academic progress. Macnamara's findings have been widely accepted as supporting what Stern (1973) terms 'a negative theory of bilingualism'. However, a close examination of his study casts doubt on many of his conclusions regarding the educational effects of immersion education in Ireland.

Macnamara's Study

Macnamara (1966) reported that the teaching of arithmetic through Irish to native English-speakers resulted in lower levels of problem but not mechanical arithmetic. He also found that this immersion group performed no better than comparison groups (taught Irish as a school subject) on an Irish achievement test. A third finding was that the English attainment of the *entire sample* of Irish children was very much below that of English children. Macnamara argues from the first result that use of a bilingual's weaker language as a medium of instruction involves retardation in the subject matter taught and from the latter two findings he argues for a 'balance effect' in language learning, i.e. that bilinguals pay for their L2 skills by a decrease in L1 skills.

Cummins (1977a) has argued that Macnamara's finding of lower problem arithmetic scores among the immersion group is uninterpretable since the effects of *testing* through a weaker language are confounded with the effects of *instruction* in a weaker language. The immersion group was administered the problem arithmetic test in Irish (their weaker language) whereas comparison groups were administered an English version of the test. Macnamara attempted to demonstrate the equivalence of Irish and English versions by pretesting the problem arithmetic test in six immersion schools. However, the pretest sample was totally atypical of the immersion sample in Macnamara's main study (see Cummins, 1977a) and consequently it cannot be assumed that the Irish and English versions of the problem arithmetic test were equivalent in difficulty for the immersion pupils, especially since these pupils perform no better than non-immersion pupils in Irish reading. In short, it cannot be argued from Macnamara's data that instruction through a weaker language leads to retardation in subject matter taught since his findings could just as well be due to the effect of testing through a weaker language.

The fact that the Irish reading competence of the immersion pupils was no higher than that of non-immersion pupils suggests that one of the objectives of the immersion schools was not being attained. However, the limitations of using only a test of reading competence as a criterion measure should be pointed out. The CILAR report (1975) found that attendance at an Irish immersion school was a highly significant predictor of later Irish speaking ability and use. Thus, Macnamara's dependent measures may not have been sufficiently sensitive to the objectives of the Irish immersion schools.

Macnamara's finding that the English attainment of Irish children was lower than that of British children may be due to a number of cultural and curricular factors, the most obvious of which is that considerably less time was spent on English instruction. However, within the Irish national sample the immersion group performed at the same level in English as the English-instructed comparison groups. This finding is clearly inconsistent with a balance effect interpretation and is frequently overlooked (e.g. Downing, 1974; Trites, 1976).

In summary, Macnamara's conclusions that there is a balance effect in language learning and that instruction through a weaker language leads to retardation in subject matter taught are by no means clearly supported by his data. In fact, when one considers the unfavourable context (in comparison to North American immersion programs) in which Irish immersion programs operated (e.g. low-prestige, low-utility language, non-supportive parental attitudes) what is surprising is that there is so little evidence of negative academic effects!

As pointed out earlier, present-day Irish immersion schools, unlike many of their predecessors, are quite similar to North American immersion programs and recent studies carried out in these schools show similar positive results. In a study carried out in several Dublin Irish and English medium schools Cummins (1977b) reported that grade 3 Irish medium pupils performed at the same level in English achievement (as in Macnamara's study) but significantly higher in Irish achievement (unlike Macnamara's finding) than a group of English medium pupils matched on IQ, and socio-economic status (SES). A second study (Cummins, 1978) found that at both the grade 3 and grade 6 levels bilingual children in Irish medium schools showed a more analytic orientation to linguistic input and were more aware of certain properties of language than unilingual control groups matched on IQ, sex, SES and age. This finding agrees with the findings of several other studies carried out in very different contexts (Ben-Zeev, 1977a, b; Cummins & Mulcahy, 1978; Ianco-Worrall, 1972).

In considering the effects of a home–school language switch in the Irish context, the experience of teachers in immersion schools is of obvious relevance. Consequently, in order both to supplement and provide a research focus for empirical studies the views of these teachers were investigated in a survey carried out in March and April 1976.

Teachers' Views on the Effects of Irish Immersion

The questionnaire in Irish was designed to gather information regarding Irish immersion schools and also to solicit teachers' opinions on a variety of pedagogic issues related to immersion education. Sixty-three questionnaires were returned from 15 of the 18 Irish medium schools in English-speaking areas. This represents almost two-thirds of the teachers in infant and primary immersion schools. In the section dealing with the effects of immersion, teachers indicated the extent of their agreement or disagreement (on a 5-point scale) with a series of 12 statements. They were also asked whether they felt there were any pupils in all-Irish schools who would be better off in an English medium school, and if so what were the characteristics of these children. The responses to these questions can be briefly summarized.

Teachers strongly agreed (93%) that becoming bilingual confers intellectual advantages on children of above-average intelligence. The majority (72%) also felt that the attempt to make children of below-average intelligence bilingual would not hold back their intellectual development. However, there was considerable disagreement on whether or not education through a second language would increase the linguistic difficulties of children exposed to little linguistic stimulation in the home and also whether or not children of below-average intelligence from homes where no Irish was spoken would be better off attending an English rather than an Irish medium school. On both these items approximately an equal number of teachers agreed and disagreed with the statements. 70% of teachers felt that parental commitment to Irish was essential for children's progress in an all-Irish school while 20% disagreed. Only 9% of teachers felt that it was psychologically healthier to fully develop a child's native language before starting instruction through the medium of a second language.

Teachers' responses were elaborated on the open-ended question regarding the characteristics of children from English-speaking homes who might perform better in an English medium school. 42% felt that Irish immersion schools were suitable for all children. The remainder (58%) who felt that some children might be better off in an English medium school cited four principal traits, one or all of which might characterize such children, viz., below-average intelligence, lack of parental commitment, general lack of academic motivation, shyness or introversion.

Despite the fact that below-average intelligence was frequently cited, several teachers emphasized that *by itself* below-average intelligence was not necessarily a handicap (an opinion which agrees with Genesee's (1976) findings) since many such children develop a good grasp of Irish. It is when low intelligence is combined with one or more of the other factors, i.e. an unsupportive home environment, academic disinterest or reticence that academic difficulties arise.

It is interesting to note that many of the same factors were cited by teachers in English and French medium schools in Montreal in a study conducted by Macnamara, Svarc and Horner (1976). Several teachers in English medium schools felt that an other-language school was not advisable for dull children or those who were shy or lacked confidence. French teachers emphasized that a French school was a bad idea if one parent or the child himself was strongly opposed to French. In the teachers' experience, 'children who were forced did not do well, were inattentive, and tended to become discipline problems' (p. 130).

Future Trends

It has been pointed out that because of strong parental commitment and involvement present-day Irish immersion schools are very different from their predecessors. The available evidence (Cummins, 1977b, 1978) suggests that these schools are providing a favourable environment for academic and cognitive progress. However, despite the success of these schools, the overall decline in the number of all-Irish schools raises questions about the life-expectancy of the Irish language. As the CILAR report (1975) points out

> Those who used Irish at school were also the most likely to continue using it afterwards and to retain it during adult life ... the decline in the number of schools providing instruction through Irish is eroding the base from which language users came in the past. (1975: 230)

Despite their small numbers, however, the present-day Irish immersion schools may provide a basis for generating a more genuine commitment to the Irish language than those in the past. The recent substantial modification of Government policies relating to compulsory Irish increases the probability of such a commitment. However, a necessary condition for an increase in the numbers of immersion schools is a reversal of the belief held by a majority of the population that children doing subjects through the medium of Irish perform less well than children taught through English. The present paper has focused on this issue and has argued that despite the unfavourable climate in which many earlier Irish immersion schools operated, the empirical evidence for negative effects is not convincing. Given the strong parental support among parents in present-day Irish immersion schools (Cummins, 1977b) there is no reason to suspect that these schools are any less successful than their North American counterparts.

Notes

1. According to figures supplied by the Department of Education, Dublin, March 1975.
2. Figures supplied by teachers (April 1975) in present-day Irish immersion schools show that in Dublin schools 11.5% of pupils speak Irish always at home, 23.4% frequently, 25.3% sometimes and 39.8% never. In schools outside Dublin the figures are 6.8% always, 11.2% frequently, 22.5% sometimes, and 59.5% never.

References

Ben-Zeev, S. (1977a) The influence of bilingualism on cognitive development and cognitive strategy. *Child Development* 48, 1009–18.

Ben-Zeev, S. (1977b) The effect of bilingualism in children from Spanish–English low economic neighborhoods on cognitive development and cognitive strategy. *Working Papers in Bilingualism* 14, 83–122.

Cohen, A. D. (1974) The Culver City Spanish immersion programs: The first two years. *The Modern Language Journal* 58, 95–103.

Committee on Irish Language Attitudes Research (CILAR) (1975) *Report*. Dublin: Government Publications.

Cummins, J. (1977a) Immersion education in Ireland: A critical review of Macnamara's findings. *Working Papers in Bilingualism* 13, 121–7.

Cummins, J. (1977b) A comparison of reading achievement in Irish and English medium schools. In V. Greaney (ed.) *Studies in Reading*. Dublin: Educational Co. of Ireland.

Cummins, J. (1978) Bilingualism and the development of metalinguistic awareness. *Journal of Cross-Cultural Psychology* 9, 131–49.

Cummins, J. and Mulcahy, R. (1978) Orientation to language in Ukrainian–English bilinguals. *Child Development* 49, 479–82.

Downing, J. (1974) Bilingualism and learning to read. *The Irish Journal of Education* 8, 77–8.

Fishman, J. A. (1977) Bilingual education: The state of social science inquiry. In *Social Science Perspectives in Bilingual Education*. Arlington, VA: Centre for Applied Linguistics.

Genesee, F. (1976) The suitability of immersion programs for all children. *Canadian Modern Language Review* 32, 494–515.

Ianco-Worrall, A. (1972) Bilingualism and cognitive development. *Child Development* 43, 1390–1400.

Irish National Teachers' Organization (1941) *Report of Committee of Inquiry into the Use of Irish as a Teaching Medium to Children whose Home Language is English*. Dublin: Central Executive Committee.

Lambert, W. E. (1975) Culture and language as factors in learning and education. In A. Wolfgang (ed.) *Education of Immigrant Students*. Toronto: Ontario Institute for Studies in Education.

Lambert, W. E. and Tucker, G. R. (1972) *Bilingual Education of Children: The St. Lambert Experiment*. Rowley, MA: Newbury House.

Macnamara, J. (1966) *Bilingualism and Primary Education*. Edinburgh: Edinburgh University Press.

Macnamara, J., Svarc, J. and Horner, S. (1976) Attending primary school of the other language in Montreal. In A. Simoes, Jr (ed.) *The Bilingual Child: Research and Analysis of Existing Educational Themes*. New York: Academic Press.

Skutnabb-Kangas, T. and Toukomaa, P. (1976) *Teaching Migrant Children's Mother Tongue and Learning the Language of the Host Country in the Context of the Sociocultural Situation of the Migrant Family*. Helsinki: The Finnish National Commission of Unesco.

Stern, H. H. (1973) Psycholinguistics and second language teaching. In J. W. Oller, Jr and J. C. Richards (eds) *Focus on the Learner: Pragmatic Perspectives for the Language Teacher* (pp. 16–28). Rowley, MA: Newbury House.

Swain, M. (1974) French immersion programs across Canada: Research findings. *Canadian Modern Language Review* 31, 117–29.

Trites, R. L. (1976) Children with learning difficulties in primary French immersion. *Canadian Modern Language Review* 33, 193–207.

Linguistic Interdependence and the Educational Development of Bilingual Children

Why does a home–school language switch result in high levels of functional bilingualism and academic achievement in middle-class majority language children (Cohen, 1974; Davis, 1967; Lambert & Tucker, 1972; Swain, 1978a), yet lead to inadequate command of both first (L1) and second (L2) languages and poor academic achievement in many minority language children (US Commission on Civil Rights, 1975; Skutnabb-Kangas & Toukomaa, 1976)? This question has been considered in several recent papers (e.g. Bowen, 1977; Cohen & Swain, 1976; Paulston, 1978; Swain, 1978b; Tucker, 1977) and the marked difference between the outcomes of immersion programs for the majority child and 'submersion' programs for the minority child has usually been attributed to socio-cultural and attitudinal factors such as socioeconomic status (SES), community support for the school program, relative prestige of Ll and L2, teacher expectations, etc. Unlike earlier attempts to explain the poor academic achievement of many minority language children, little importance has generally been attributed to specifically linguistic explanatory factors. Bowen goes so far as to argue that linguistic factors are unimportant and that 'the choice of language of instruction in our schools is linguistically irrelevant' (1977: 116).

In contrast to this position, I shall propose a theoretical framework which assigns a central role to the *interaction* between socio cultural, linguistic and school program factors in explaining the academic and cognitive development of bilingual children. The paucity of meaningful data on the effectiveness or otherwise of bilingual education can be largely attributed to the fact that evaluations have ignored this interaction. Before the interactions between these sets of factors are considered, previous hypotheses regarding the individual role of each will be briefly reviewed.

Linguistic Factors

Early attempts to explain the poor academic achievement of many minority language children tended to attribute a major role to linguistic explanatory factors. A frequent finding was that bilingual children performed poorly on the verbal parts of intelligence tests as well as on academic tasks and several investigators argued that bilingualism itself was a cause of 'mental confusion' and 'language handicaps' (for reviews see Darcy, 1953; Peal & Lambert, 1962). Perhaps the most coherent theoretical statement in this genre was Macnamara's (1966) 'balance effect' hypothesis which proposed that a bilingual child paid for his L2 skills by a decrease in L1 skills.

A somewhat different attempt at explanation is the hypothesis that mismatch between the language of the home and the language of the school leads to academic retardation (Downing, 1974; UNESCO, 1953). This 'linguistic mismatch' hypothesis is exemplified in the well-known UNESCO statement that 'it is axiomatic that the best medium for teaching a child is his mother tongue' (UNESCO, 1953: 11). On the basis of his study of bilingualism in Irish primary schools, Macnamara (1966) also argued that instruction through the medium of a weaker language led to retardation in subject matter taught. Assumptions similar to those of the 'linguistic mismatch' hypothesis underlay much of the impetus for the development of bilingual education in the United States.

However, recent research points clearly to the inadequacy of both the 'linguistic mismatch' hypothesis and the hypothesis that bilingualism itself is a source of academic and cognitive retardation. A large number of recent studies suggest that, rather than being a cause of cognitive confusion, bilingualism can positively influence both cognitive and linguistic development (see Cummins, 1976, 1978c for reviews). In addition, the well-documented success of immersion programs for majority language children is clearly inconsistent with any simplistic notion that linguistic mismatch *per se* causes academic retardation.

In view of the obvious inadequacy of simplistic linguistic explanations of the minority child's academic difficulties, it is not surprising that as educators re-examined the assumptions underlying bilingual education, they have emphasized socio-cultural and school program variables rather than linguistic factors.

Socio-cultural Factors

Two recent reviews (Bowen, 1977; Tucker, 1977) of linguistic perspectives on bilingual education have argued forcefully for the primacy of social factors over specifically linguistic or pedagogical factors in explaining the academic progress of bilingual children. Both Bowen and Tucker reject the generality of the 'vernacular advantage theory' on the basis of the high levels of academic and linguistic skills attained by children in immersion programs. Bowen states that

> what really confirms for me the thesis that the choice of language to be used as medium of instruction is not the determining factor of pedagogical success is the availability of counterevidence, experiments where students studying in a second language matched or excelled over those studying in their mother tongue. This would not be expected to happen if Macnamara's 'balance effect' operates. (1977: 110–1)

Bowen goes on to argue that the choice of medium of instruction 'should be determined by social conditions – not by a preconceived notion that the mother tongue should *per se* be used'.

Tucker's conclusion is similar. He argues that

> social, rather than pedagogical factors will probably condition the optimal sequencing of languages. Thus, in situations where the home language is denigrated by the community at large, where many teachers are not members of the same ethnic group as the pupils and are insensitive to their values and traditions, where there does not exist a pressure within the home to encourage literacy and language maintenance, and where universal primary education is not a reality it would seem desirable to introduce children to schooling in their vernacular language ... Conversely, in settings where the home language is highly valued, where parents do actively encourage literacy and where it is 'known' that the children will succeed, it would seem fully appropriate to begin schooling in the second language. (1977: 39–40)

Bowen and Tucker are undoubtedly correct both in rejecting axiomatic statements regarding the medium of instruction and in assigning a fundamental causal role to social factors. As Paulston (1976) and Fishman (1977) point out, the effects of bilingual education programs can be understood only when these programs are regarded as the result of particular constellations of societal factors rather than as independent variables in their own right.

School Program Factors

Although immersion and submersion programs both involve a home–school language switch, in other respects they are quite dissimilar (Cohen & Swain, 1976; Swain, 1978b). In immersion programs all students start the program with little or no competence in the school language and are praised for any use they make of that language. Children in submersion programs, on the other hand, are mixed together with students whose Ll is that of the school and their lack of proficiency in the school language is often treated as a sign of limited intellectual and academic ability. Children in submersion programs may often become frustrated because of difficulties in communicating with the teacher. These difficulties can arise both because the teacher is unlikely to understand the child's Ll and also because of different culturally-determined expectations of appropriate behavior. In contrast, the immersion teacher is familiar with the child's language and cultural background and can therefore respond appropriately to his needs. The immersion child's Ll is never denigrated by the teacher and its importance is recognized by the fact that it is introduced as a school subject after several grades. The L1 of the minority language child, on the other hand, is often viewed as the cause of his academic difficulties and an impediment to his learning of L2. Consequently, those aspects of the child's identity which are associated with his L1 and home culture are seldom reinforced by the school.

In general, what is communicated to children in immersion programs is their success, whereas in submersion programs children are often made to feel acutely aware of their failure. Thus, as Swain (1978b) points out, despite their superficial similarity, immersion and submersion programs are clearly different programs and it is not surprising that they lead to different results.

The Need for a Theoretical Framework

It is clear that there is no shortage of explanatory variables to account for the different outcomes of immersion and submersion programs. However, what is lacking is a coherent framework within which the relative importance of different variables and the possible interactions between them can be conceptualized. While sociocultural background factors are obviously important, we do not know what are the links in the causal chain through which their effects are translated into academic outcomes. Similarly, we have very little idea of the mechanisms through which many school program variables affect outcomes. To take the obvious example, despite ten years of widespread bilingual education, there is no consensus as to the relative merits of ESL-only, transitional bilingual or maintenance bilingual programs in promoting academic and cognitive skills. There are, in fact, very few interpretable data which are directly related to this central issue.

One of the main reasons for the lack of meaningful research is that evaluators of bilingual education programs have failed to incorporate the possibility of interaction between educational treatment and child input factors into their experimental designs. Not surprisingly, therefore, there has been little consideration of the possibility that inconclusive or ambiguous results may be a function of this interaction. Normally, in order to assess the effects of an experimental program an evaluator will attempt to ensure (either through matching or co-variance analysis) that experimental and control groups are equivalent in terms of background experience and pre-test scores. Where program entrants are heterogeneous with respect to any relevant traits the evaluator will normally take account of possible aptitude by treatment interactions. In evaluations of Canadian immersion programs a variety of possible aptitude by treatment interactions has been investigated in depth, despite the relative homogeneity of program entrants (Bruck, Note 3; Genesee, 1976; Trites, 1976). However, in the United States where there is enormous diversity within different groups of minority language children in terms of motivational, cognitive and linguistic characteristics, evaluations have taken little or no account of possible interactions between these child input factors and educational treatments.

In order for evaluations to incorporate the possibility of interaction between child input and educational treatment variables, it is necessary to specify the relevant child input variables and develop a framework within which school outcomes can be meaningfully related to this interaction. In other words, one must consider the dynamics of the bilingual child's interaction with his educational environment if any answer is to be found to the central question of whether or not the academic progress of children of limited English-speaking ability will be promoted more effectively if initial instruction is in their Ll. It is insufficient to specify merely the regularities between academic outcomes and both societal and program inputs without pursuing the connecting links in the causal chain.

The roles of two main child input factors will be examined in this paper. These are (i) conceptual-linguistic knowledge, (ii) motivation to learn L2 and maintain L1. These factors are conceived as intervening variables which interact with school program factors and mediate the effects of more basic socio-cultural background factors on cognitive and academic outcomes. Before outlining this framework in detail it is necessary to justify the inclusion of a linguistic factor as a critical child input variable and explain what is meant by 'conceptual-linguistic knowledge'.

Linguistic Factors Revisited: Language and Thought in the Bilingual Child

Paulston (1978) points out that there has been little exploration of the relationships between language and cognition in the context of US bilingual education programs. For example, the US Commission on Civil Rights (1975) report contains no reference to empirical work on cognitive development of children in bilingual programs. The argument advanced in this report amounts essentially to a restatement of the linguistic mismatch hypothesis. For example, the report states that

> When language is recognized as the means for representing thought and as the vehicle for complex thinking, the importance of allowing children to use and develop the language they know best becomes obvious.
>
> (US Commission on Civil Rights, 1975: 44)

As pointed out earlier, this argument fails to account for the absence of any negative effects on the linguistic and cognitive development of children in immersion programs.

Paulston (1978) also points out that another current approach to the topic of language and cognition in the bilingual child is to dismiss the issue with vague comments on the invalidity of the instruments and procedures used in early studies. The educational difficulties of the minority child are then attributed to non-linguistic background or school program factors. Related to this approach are reviews which point to the fact that early studies of bilingualism and IQ were poorly controlled and that more recent studies have reported cognitive advantages associated with bilingualism (e.g. Iiams, 1976; Merino, 1975; Ramírez *et al.*, 1977). 'Bilingualism' is then conceived as a positive force in intellectual development which fails to materialize in minority language situations because of socio-economic or educational conditions. However, this approach is usually characterized by uncritical acceptance of the results of recent 'positive' studies and little inquiry into mechanisms through which 'bilingualism' exerts its effects.

The lack of concern for the developmental interrelationships between language and thought in the bilingual child is one of the major reasons why evaluations and research have provided so little data on the dynamics of the bilingual child's interaction with his educational environment. A direct determinant of the quality of this interaction is clearly the level of L1 and L2 competence which the bilingual child develops over the course of his school career. It is impossible to avoid questions like the following if one wishes to explore the assumptions underlying bilingual education: What level of L2 competence must the child possess at various grade levels in order to benefit optimally from instruction in that language? To what extent is a bilingual child who has developed fluent surface skills in L1 and L2 also capable of carrying out complex cognitive operations (e.g. verbal analogies, reading comprehension, mathematical problems) through his two languages? To what extent are L1 and L2 skills interdependent and what are the implications of possible interdependencies for cognitive and academic progress? In other words, do children who maintain and develop their L1 in school develop higher or lower L2 levels of skills than those whose L1 is replaced by their L2? Also to what extent do various patterns of L1–L2 relationship facilitate children's general cognitive and academic progress?

The language–thought issue also has important implications for teaching strategies in bilingual classes. For example, to ask any question regarding the relative merits of concurrent versus separated patterns of L1 and L2 use or whether teachers should encourage or discourage code-switching (Gonzalez, 1977) necessitates considerations of such issues as the developmental relationships between language and thought in the bilingual child.

Two hypotheses have been developed in order to help account for the different outcomes of immersion and submersion programs and also to provide a theoretical framework for research into the developmental interrelations between language and thought in the bilingual child. The 'threshold' hypothesis (Cummins, 1976, 1978a; Toukomaa & Skutnabb-Kangas, 1977) is concerned with the cognitive and academic consequences of different patterns of bilingual skills and the 'developmental interdependence' hypothesis (Cummins, 1978a) addresses the functional interdependence between the development of L1 and L2 skills.

The Threshold Hypothesis

The threshold hypothesis evolved as an attempt to resolve the apparent inconsistencies in the results of early and more recent studies of the relationships between bilingualism and cognition. These studies will be briefly reviewed in order to outline the phenomena which require explanation.

It seems implausible to dismiss the findings of early studies as entirely due to inadequate controls and to argue that specifically linguistic factors do not contribute to the poor academic achievement of many minority language bilinguals. The findings of several recent studies support the early negative findings. Tsushima and Hogan (1975), for example, report lower levels of verbal academic skills among grades 4 and 5 Japanese–English bilinguals compared to a unilingual control group matched on nonverbal IQ. Torrance *et al.* (1970) reported that bilingual children in Singapore performed at a significantly lower level than unilingual children on the fluency and flexibility scales of the Torrance Tests of Creative Thinking. However, the direction of the trend was reversed for the originality and elaboration scales and differences in elaboration in favor of the bilinguals were significant. There is also strong evidence (e.g. Skutnabb-Kangas & Toukomaa, 1976) that some groups of minority language and migrant children are characterized by 'semilingualism', i.e. less than native-like skills in both languages, with its detrimental cognitive and academic consequences.

In contrast to these 'negative' findings, however, there exists a substantial number of recent studies which suggest that bilingualism can positively influence academic and cognitive functioning. Several studies conducted within the context of French immersion programs have reported that the immersion students performed better than controls on measures of English skills despite considerably less instruction through the medium of English (Swain, 1975, 1978a; Tremaine, 1975). Enhancement of linguistic skills as a function of intensity of bilingual learning experiences is also suggested by the evaluation of a trilingual Hebrew, French, English program in Montreal (Genesee, Tucker & Lambert, 1978). It was reported that over time the trilingual students outstripped those in a bilingual Hebrew–English program in Hebrew skills despite essentially the same Hebrew curriculum in experimental and control schools. The findings of Dubé and Hébert (Note 6) suggest that similar processes can operate in minority language contexts when Ll development is promoted by the school. They report enhancement of English (L2) skills by the end of elementary school among children in the St. John's Valley French–English bilingual education project in Maine.

Several recent studies have also reported a more analytic orientation to linguistic and perceptual structures among bilingual children (Balkan, 1970; Ben-Zeev, 1977a,b; Cummins, 1978b; Cummins & Mulcahy, 1978; Feldman & Shen, 1971; Ianco-Worrall, 1972). A possible neuropsychological basis for these findings is suggested by the results of a study by Starck, Genesee, Lambert and Seitz (1977) who demonstrated more reliable ear asymmetry effects on a dichotic listening task among children attending a trilingual Hebrew, French, English program as compared to a control group of children whose instruction was totally in English. The significance of this finding is that right ear advantage on dichotic listening tasks reflects greater development of the more analytic left hemisphere functions in comparison to right hemisphere functions. A plausible explanation for findings of greater analytic orientation to language among bilingual children is Lambert and Tucker's (1972) suggestion that the bilingual child engages in a form of 'contrastive linguistics' by comparing similarities and differences in the vocabulary and syntactic structures of his two languages.

Greater sensitivity to linguistic, perceptual and interpersonal feedback cues has also been reported in association with bilingualism (Bain, 1975, Note 2; Ben-Zeev, 1977a, 1977b; Cummins & Mulcahy, 1978; Genesee, Tucker & Lambert, 1975). Ben-Zeev (1977c) points out that increased attention to feedback cues has adaptive significance for the bilingual child as a way of accommodating to the extra demands of his linguistic environment.

Significant differences have also been reported between bilinguals and unilinguals on measures of both general intellectual development (Bain, 1975, Note 2; Bain & Yu, 1978; Cummins & Gulutsan, 1974; Liedke & Nelson, 1968; Peal & Lambert, 1962) and divergent thinking (Carringer, 1974; Cummins & Gulutsan, 1974; Landry, 1974; Scott, Note 10; Torrance *et al.*, 1970).

Although, in general, these recent studies are better controlled than the earlier studies which reported negative findings, few are without methodological limitations. A problem in many of these studies (Bain, Note 2; Bain & Yu, 1978; Carringer, 1974; Cummins & Gulutsan, 1974; Feldman & Shen, 1971; Landry, 1974; Peal & Lambert, 1962) is the lack of adequate controls for possible background differences between bilingual and unilingual groups. An index of SES based on parental occupation provides inadequate protection against bias. Also, matching only on overall stage of cognitive development (e.g. preoperational, concrete operational, etc.) is insufficient since there can be extremely large individual differences on cognitive variables within stages. Although the remaining studies have matched bilingual and unilingual groups on IQ in addition to SES, the validity of some of the dependent measures used to assess constructs such as 'analytic orientation to language' or 'sensitivity to feedback cues' is open to question. Thus, pending replication and extension, these findings should be evaluated cautiously so that, as Fishman (1977) warns, 'bilingualism will not be spuriously oversold now as it was spuriously undersold (or written off) in the past' (p. 38).

Despite the fact that these recent 'positive' studies are not methodologically flawless, taken together they suggest that under some conditions, access to two languages in early childhood can accelerate aspects of cognitive growth. A distinguishing characteristic of many of these studies is that they involved bilingual subjects whose bilingualism was 'additive' (Lambert, 1975). In other words, since the bilingual's L1 was dominant or at least prestigious it was in no danger of replacement by L2. Consequently the bilingual was adding another language to his repertoire of skills at no cost to his L1 competence. In contrast, many of the 'negative' studies involved bilingual subjects from minority language groups whose L1 was gradually being replaced by a more prestigious L2. Lambert (1975) terms the resulting form of bilingualism 'subtractive' since the bilingual's competence in two languages at any point in time is likely to reflect some stage in the 'subtraction' of L1 and its replacement by L2. Thus, the bilingual child in an additive situation is likely to have relatively high levels of competence in both languages whereas in subtractive situations many bilinguals may be characterized by less than native-like levels in both languages.

This analysis suggests that the level of competence bilingual children achieve in their two languages acts as an intervening variable in mediating the effects of their bilingual learning experiences on cognition. Specifically, there may be threshold levels of linguistic competence which bilingual children must attain both in order to avoid cognitive deficits and to allow the potentially beneficial aspects of becoming bilingual to influence their cognitive growth (Cummins, 1976, 1978a).

The threshold hypothesis assumes that those aspects of bilingualism which might positively influence cognitive growth are unlikely to come into effect until the child has attained a certain minimum or threshold level of competence in a second language. Similarly, if a bilingual child attains only a very low level of competence in the second (or first) language, interaction with the environment through that language, both in terms of input and output, is likely to be impoverished.

The form of the threshold hypothesis which seems to be most consistent with the available data is that there is not one, but two, thresholds (Cummins, 1976; Toukomaa & Skutnabb-Kangas, 1977). The attainment of a lower threshold level of bilingual competence would be sufficient to avoid any negative cognitive effects; but the attainment of a second, higher, level of bilingual competence might be necessary to lead to accelerated cognitive growth. This possibility is expressed in Figure 1.

The Lower Threshold. It can be seen in Figure 1 that negative cognitive and academic effects are hypothesized to result from low levels of competence in both languages or what Scandinavian researchers (e.g. Hansegard, 1975; Skutnabb-Kangas & Toukomaa, 1976) have termed 'semilingualism' or 'double semilingualism' (see Paulston, 1976, for a review of the Scandinavian research). Essentially, the lower threshold level of bilingual competence proposes that bilingual children's competence in a language may be sufficiently weak as to impair the quality of their interaction with their educational environment through that language. The threshold cannot be defined in absolute terms; rather it is likely to vary according to the children's stage of cognitive development and the academic demands of different stages of schooling. Possibly one of the reasons why no cognitive retardation has been observed in the early grades of immersion programs (when instruction is totally through L2) is that during these grades the children's interaction with environment and, consequently, cognitive development, is less dependent on the mediation of language than at later grades. This may give these children a 'breather' in which they can gain the L2 skills necessary to benefit optimally from an increasingly symbolic environment (see Cummins, 1976). Thus, in the early grades the lower threshold may involve only a relatively low level of listening comprehension and expressive skills, but – as the curriculum content becomes more symbolic and requires more abstract formal operational thought processes – the children's 'surface' L2 competence must be translated into deeper levels of 'cognitive competence' in the language. The development of adequate literacy skills is obviously important in this respect. The child whose reading comprehension skills are poorly developed will be handicapped in assimilating most types of subject matter content after the early grades. Olson (1977a) has suggested that the acquisition of literacy skills has more general cognitive significance in that it may be the means by which the child becomes proficient in using the logical or ideational functions of language.

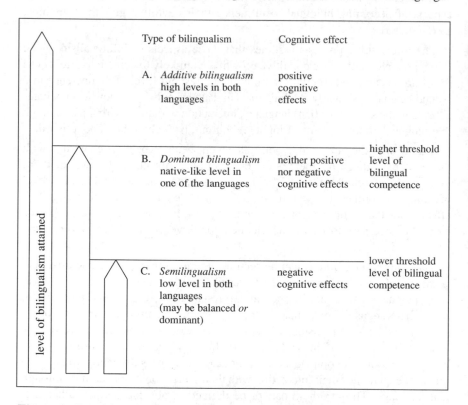

Figure 1 Cognitive effects of different types of bilingualism (adapted from Toukomaa & Skutnabb-Kangas, 1977)

The concept of 'semilingualism' does not in any sense imply that minority children's language is itself deficient. As Skutnabb-Kangas and Toukomaa (1976) point out the term 'cannot be used as a strictly linguistic concept at all' (p. 22). Research which viewed semilingualism as a purely linguistic variable found little support for the concept. However, research which supported the concept of semilingualism 'measured cognitive aspects of the language, understanding of the meanings of abstract concepts, synonyms, etc. as well as vocabulary' (p. 21). Thus, as Skutnabb-Kangas and Toukomaa point out, although parents, teachers and the children themselves considered Finnish migrant children's Swedish to be quite fluent, tests in Swedish which required complex cognitive operations to be carried out, showed that this surface fluency was to a certain extent a 'linguistic facade'.

The Higher Threshold. Because of the widespread academic failure of minority language children and the fact that many of them clearly have less than native-like competence in both languages, the existence of a lower threshold level of bilingual competence is probably less contentious than the existence of a higher threshold. However, direct evidence for the concept of a higher threshold level of bilingual competence is provided in several of the recent studies which suggest that an additive form of bilingualism can positively influence cognitive functioning. If there is a higher threshold level of bilingual competence, then we would expect that as children in immersion programs develop high levels of L2 skills, they would also begin to reap the cognitive benefits of their bilingualism. The findings of Barik and Swain (1976) support this prediction. Using longitudinal data from the Ottawa and Toronto immersion programs, Barik and Swain reported that high French achievers at the grade 3 level performed significantly better than low French achievers on two of the three Otis–Lennon IQ subtests when scores were adjusted for initial IQ and age differences between the two groups. There is no evidence that the low French achievers (i.e. those who remained very dominant in English category B in Figure 1) suffered any cognitive disadvantages since their IQ scores remained unchanged over the three year period. However, the IQ scores of the high French achievers increased over the three year period, suggesting that the attainment of high levels of L2 skills is associated with greater cognitive growth.

Differences between the achievement of children in partial and total immersion programs (Swain, 1978a) can also be interpreted in terms of the threshold hypothesis. Swain reports that children in French–English partial immersion programs who have had approximately 50% of their instruction in English (L1) throughout elementary school take as long as total immersion students to catch up with regular program students in English achievement. In addition, their French skills are considerably lower than those of total immersion students although there is an equivalence of French skills in terms of time spent through French. In other words, the French achievement of grade 2 total immersion students is similar to that of grade 4 or 5 partial immersion students who have spent about the same amount of time learning through French. Swain (1978a) reports that there have been some indications of poorer performance in subject matter taught through French among partial immersion students, but this finding may not be generalizable to immersion programs in general. In addition, by grade 5, total immersion students were performing at a significantly higher level in English as compared to regular program control groups, whereas no such trend was noted for students in partial immersion programs. These findings (together with those of Tremaine, 1975) suggest that because of the more intensive exposure to French in kindergarten and grades 1 and 2 the total immersion students quickly attain a level of functional competence in French which allows them to benefit optimally from interaction with a French school environment and, over the course of elementary school, enhances the development of their English L1 skills. The partial immersion students on the other hand, take considerably longer to attain high levels of French skills. Consequently, they are less likely to experience enhancement of cognitive or academic skills and may have greater difficulty than total immersion pupils in mastering subject matter taught through French. In terms of Figure 1, many of the total immersion students could be classified in category A whereas the majority of partial immersion students would fit the pattern of category B. However, despite the less intensive initial exposure to French, the possibility of cognitive benefits for some partial immersion students who do acquire high levels of French skills should not be ruled out.

It is clear that in minority language situations a prerequisite for attaining a higher threshold level of bilingual competence is maintenance of L1 skills. The findings of several research studies suggest that maintenance of L1 skills can lead to cognitive benefits for minority language children. As mentioned earlier Dubé and Hébert (Note 6) have reported that Franco-American children instructed bilingually performed better in English skills than control children by the end of elementary school. Cummins and Mulcahy (1978) compared two groups of children attending a Ukrainian–English bilingual program with a unilingual control group matched for IQ, SES, sex, age and school at both grades 1 and 3 levels. One group of bilingual children had extensive Ukrainian at home and were judged by their teachers to be relatively fluent in Ukrainian. The second group had little or no Ukrainian at home and were judged by teachers to have little fluency in Ukrainian. Consistent with the threshold hypothesis, it was found that the fluent bilingual group was significantly better able than either the non-fluent bilinguals or unilinguals to analyze ambiguities in sentence structure. In a study of lower SES Spanish–English balanced bilinguals, Ben-Zeev (1977b) has also reported that in comparison to a unilingual control group the response strategies of the bilinguals were characterized by attention to structure and readiness to reorganize cognitive schemata.

In summary, initial research findings support the hypothesis that the level of linguistic competence attained by bilingual children may act as an intervening variable in mediating the effects of bilingualism on their cognitive and academic development. This suggests that the threshold hypothesis can provide a framework with which to predict the academic and cognitive effects of different forms of bilingualism. However, the threshold hypothesis tells us little about how L1 and L2 skills are related to one another or about what types of school programs are likely to promote additive and subtractive forms of bilingualism under different bilingual learning conditions. The 'developmental interdependence' hypothesis addresses itself to these issues.

The Developmental Interdependence Hypothesis

The developmental interdependence hypothesis proposes that the level of L2 competence which a bilingual child attains is partially a function of the type of competence the child has developed in Ll at the time when intensive exposure to L2 begins. When the usage of certain functions of language and the development of Ll vocabulary and concepts are strongly promoted by the child's linguistic environment outside of school, as in the case of most middle-class children in immersion programs, then intensive exposure to L2 is likely to result in high levels of L2 competence at no cost to L1 competence. The initially high level of L1 development makes possible the development of similar levels of competence in L2. However, for children whose L1 skills are less well developed in certain respects, intensive exposure to L2 in the initial grades is likely to impede the continued development of L1. This will, in turn, exert a limiting effect on the development of L2. In short, the hypothesis proposes that there is an interaction between the language of instruction and the type of competence the child has developed in his L1 prior to school.

This basic idea has previously been expressed by Toukomaa and Skutnabb-Kangas (1977). In discussing the threshold hypothesis in minority language situations they argue that

> The basis for the possible attainment of the threshold level of L2 competence seems to be the level attained in the mother tongue. If in an early stage of its development a minority child finds itself in a foreign-language learning environment without contemporaneously receiving the requisite support in its mother tongue, the development of its skill in the mother tongue will slow down or even cease, leaving the child without a basis for learning the second language well enough to attain the threshold level in it. (1977: 28)

I shall first review the research evidence which is related to the developmental interdependence hypothesis and then consider in more detail the mechanisms through which a child's Ll experience may influence the development of L2 skills.

Research Evidence. At a very general level it has frequently been observed that L1 and L2 reading scores are very highly correlated (e.g. Cziko, 1976; Greaney, 1977; Swain, Lapkin & Barik, 1976; Skutnabb-Kangas & Toukomaa, 1976; Tucker, 1975). Also, in middle-class majority language situations, Ll seems to be impervious to 'neglect' by the school. McDougall and Bruck (1976), for example, report that the grade level at which Ll reading is introduced in immersion programs appears to make very little difference to Ll reading achievement. Macnamara, Svarc and Horner (1976) draw a similar conclusion from an investigation of the achievement of children attending primary schools of the 'other' language in Montreal. No differences in English achievement were observed between grade 6 English-speaking children attending French-medium and English-medium schools despite the fact that the children in French schools received no instruction in English until grade 3 or grade 5. Also, there was no evidence that beginning English reading instruction in grade 3 rather than grade 5 made any difference to the grade 6 scores. Macnamara *et al.* conclude that 'school seems to contribute little to reading one's native language apart from some basic mechanical skills' (1976: 123). Another relevant finding is that children in immersion programs achieve levels of L2 reading skills equivalent to native speakers by the end of elementary school (Swain, 1978a).

These data suggest that (i) the prerequisites for acquiring literacy skills are instilled in most middle-class majority language children by their linguistic experience in the home; (ii) the ability to extract meaning from printed text can be transferred easily from one language to another.

The UNESCO report prepared by Skutnabb-Kangas and Toukomaa (1976) provides evidence from a minority language learning situation which is consistent with the developmental interdependence hypothesis. The purpose of the UNESCO investigation

> was to determine the linguistic level and development in both their mother tongue and Swedish or Finnish migrant children attending Swedish comprehensive school. Above all, attention was paid to the interdependence between skills in the mother tongue and Swedish, i.e. the hypothesis was tested that those who have best preserved their mother tongue are also best in Swedish. (p. 48)

This hypothesis was strongly supported by the findings. Although the Finnish migrant children had average levels of nonverbal intellectual ability their skills in both Finnish and Swedish were considerably below Finnish and Swedish norms. The extent to which the mother tongue had been developed prior to contact with Swedish was strongly related to how well Swedish was learned. Children who migrated at age ten maintained a level of Finnish close to Finnish students in Finland and achieved Swedish language skills comparable to those of Swedes. Skutnabb-Kangas and Toukomaa suggest that

> Their skills in the mother tongue have already developed to the abstract level. For this reason they reach a better level in the mastery of Swedish-language concepts in quite a short time than those who moved before or at the start of school, and before long surpass even the migrant children who were born in Sweden. (p. 76)

The situation is very different for children who were 7–8 years of age when they moved to Sweden.

> The verbal development of these children, who moved just as school was beginning, underwent serious disturbance after the move. This also has a detrimental effect on learning Swedish. In this group, and in those who moved before starting school, the risk of becoming semi-lingual is greatest.
> (p. 75)

These findings are consistent with the results of several studies summarized by Engle (1975: 311–2) which reported that children between the ages of 6–8 experience considerable difficulty in language learning. They are also consistent with informal observations (Cardenas, p. 57 in Epstein, 1977; Gonzalez, 1977) that recently-arrived immigrant children from Mexico whose Spanish is firmly established are more successful in acquiring English skills than native-born Mexican–Americans.

However, the UNESCO findings do not agree with data on Canadian immigrant children (Ramsey & Wright, 1974) which suggest that children who arrived at older ages experienced greater educational difficulty than children who arrived prior to school entry or who were born in Canada. Some of the difference between the Swedish and Canadian results can be attributed to motivational factors which will be discussed below. However, another reason for the difference may be that many of the Canadian immigrant children come from rural areas in Southern Europe where educational programs are likely to be less developed than in Canada. Thus, the schooling experiences of the adolescent immigrants may not have been effective in developing the type of linguistic competence necessary to allow them to quickly learn L2 and adapt to a highly abstract school curriculum. In contrast, Finland is a highly industrialized country whose educational system is equivalent to that of Sweden.

Skutnabb-Kangas and Toukomaa also report that mother tongue development is especially important in school subjects which require abstract modes of thought:

> In the upper level Finnish seems to be even more important for achievement in mathematics than Swedish – in spite of the fact that mathematics too is taught in Swedish. This result supports the concept that the abstraction level of the mother tongue is important for mastering the conceptual operations connected with mathematics ... Subjects such as biology, chemistry and physics also require conceptual thinking, and in these subjects migrant children with a good mastery of their mother tongue succeeded significantly better than those who knew their mother tongue poorly. (1976: 69)

The authors go on to suggest that 'the migrant children whose mother tongue stopped developing before the abstract thinking phase was achieved thus easily remain on a lower level of educational capacity than they would originally have been able to achieve' (p. 70).

The UNESCO findings were followed up in a small study conducted with grade 1–2 students on the Hobbema Cree Indian Reserve in Alberta (Leslie, Note 8). Many of the families on the reserve speak both Cree and English at home or a mixture of both and the school is unilingual English. Leslie found high correlations between children's oral Cree competence and English reading skills (r, Gates–McGinitie vocabulary and Cree = 0.76, p <0.001; r, Gates–McGinitie comprehension and Cree = 0.66, p <0.01). This result again suggests the functional significance of the mother tongue in the child's educational development.

An important index of the validity of the developmental interdependence hypothesis is the academic achievement of minority language pupils whose Ll is promoted at school and at home. As mentioned earlier, the issues involved in bilingual education and its evaluation are complex (see Gonzalez, 1977) and there is a scarcity of meaningful data. Here I shall only briefly point to some results which suggest the value of mother tongue maintenance. A comprehensive review of recent studies relevant to this issue can be found in Paulston (1977).

In a study of the academic achievement of minority francophone children in Manitoba, Hébert (1976) found that the percentage of instruction received in French (L1), had no influence on English achievement but was strongly related to French achievement. In other words, promoting children's L1 resulted in higher levels of L1 achievement at no cost to achievement in L2. Ramírez and Politzer (1976) similarly reported that use of Spanish at home resulted in higher levels of Spanish skills at no cost to English achievement while the use of English at home resulted in a deterioration of Spanish skills but no improvement in English. In both these studies a loss in L1 did not result in any gains in L2 despite the increased interaction through L2. In terms of the developmental interdependence hypothesis these findings would be interpreted as indicating that the positive effects on L2 of maintaining L1 compensated for less time spent in L2.

Most of the findings supporting vernacular education are also consistent with the hypothesis. Modiano's (1968) study is usually regarded (e.g. Engle, 1975; Paulston, 1976) as one of the best controlled studies which support the 'vernacular advantage' theory. She reported that Mexican–Indian children who were taught to read in the vernacular and later in Spanish scored significantly higher in Spanish reading after three years than children taught to read only in Spanish.

Findings such as these are sometimes regarded (e.g. Engle, 1975) as contradictory to the findings of immersion programs where initial instruction is in L2. However, when viewed within the framework of the developmental interdependence and threshold hypotheses, it can be seen that identical principles underlie the success of both types of programs. The key to understanding the educational outcomes of a variety of bilingual education programs operating under very different conditions lies in recognizing the functional significance of the child's mother tongue in the developmental process. In immersion programs for majority language children the children's L1 is developed in such a way that it is unaffected by intensive exposure to L2. Consequently, as children develop high levels of L2 skills, their fluent access to two languages can give rise to enhancement both of L1 skills and other aspects of cognitive functioning.

The findings in many minority language situations appear to be just the opposite of those in majority language situations in that initial instruction in L1 has been found to lead to better results than immersion or submersion in L2. The developmental interdependence hypothesis would suggest that the relatively greater success of vernacular education in minority language situations is due, partly at least, to the fact that certain aspects of the minority child's linguistic knowledge may not be fully developed on entry to school. Thus, some children may have only limited access to the cognitive-linguistic operations necessary to assimilate L2 and develop literacy skills in that language.

The 'threshold' and 'developmental interdependence' hypotheses attempt to integrate data which suggest that linguistic factors are important in understanding the dynamics of the bilingual child's interaction with his educational environment. Before considering how these hypotheses fit into an overall model of bilingual education it is necessary to consider in more detail the mechanisms through which children's knowledge of L1 on entry to school might interact with the language of instruction.

L1 Development and Home–School Language Switching

It has been suggested that differences in the way in which children's L1 has been developed by their linguistic experience prior to school contribute to the differential outcomes of a home–school language switch in minority and majority language situations. However, there has been little consideration of which aspects of L1 development interact with medium of instruction. This can be meaningfully discussed only in relation to the types of information which the child is required to process in school. The primary academic task for the child is learning how to extract information efficiently from printed text and subsequent educational progress largely depends upon how well this task is accomplished. Thus, for present purposes, the differential outcomes of a home–school language switch can be discussed in relation to the extent to which the L1 experience of minority and majority language children prior to school has provided them with the prerequisites for acquiring fluent reading skills. This focus is consistent with the research studies reviewed in the previous section, most of which involved interdependence between reading comprehension skills in L1 and L2.

As Smith (1971) points out, fluent reading skills require that the reader's knowledge of language is used to make inferences or predictions about information in the text. A child who has to read word by word will lose much of the information before it can be comprehended. It is possible to distinguish three general aspects of children's knowledge of language which have been hypothesized as important for the acquisition of fluent reading skills. First is what

Becker (1977) has termed the vocabulary-concept knowledge of the child; second is the extent to which the child has acquired certain metalinguistic insights regarding the nature of printed text; and third is the extent to which the child has developed facility in processing language which is decontextualized and possibly in using certain other functions of language. Although these three aspects can be distinguished conceptually, all are determined by the child's linguistic experiences prior to school and are likely to be strongly related to one another empirically.

Vocabulary-concept Knowledge

Becker (1977) uses the term vocabulary-concept knowledge to refer to a child's understanding of the concepts or meanings embodied in words. He argues that the failure of the DISTAR language program to significantly improve reading comprehension skills in contrast to decoding spelling and math skills is due to the fact that reading comprehension is largely dependent on the child's vocabulary-concept knowledge. According to Becker (1977) the learning of vocabulary and concepts usually involves a linear-additive set' in which the learning of one element gives little advantage in learning a new element. This is in contrast to other achievement areas where strategies for problem-solving can be effectively taught.

Several investigators (e.g. Carroll, Note 4; Morris, 1971) have also argued that children's knowledge of vocabulary and the grammatical functions of words play a major role in explaining the progressively poorer performance of minority language children on measures of reading comprehension. This contention is supported by the universally high correlations found between vocabulary and reading comprehension. Morris (1971) has suggested that the purpose of teaching reading at the secondary level is to help students explore, interpret and extend the concepts represented by the written symbols. However, although minority language children can very adequately decode the symbol and produce the word, often the word 'fails to trigger *anything* (original italics) because the concepts it represents to us and to the author simply do not exist for the child, or they exist in a limited vague form' (p. 162). It is clear that efficient prediction of information and fluent reading comprehension are impossible if the reader does not understand the concepts to which the words refer. Morris goes on to suggest that some minority language children may never have had the opportunity to develop the conceptual basis for abstraction in English. The developmental interdependence hypothesis would suggest that this may be due to the fact that their schooling experience has never allowed them to continue to develop the conceptual basis for abstraction in Ll. In other words, the deficient conceptual knowledge which Morris describes at the secondary level results from the interaction between certain forms of educational treatment and a child's input conceptual-linguistic knowledge. If a child on entry to school does not have access to the semantic meanings assumed by beginning reading texts and culturally-different schools the early search for meaning in printed texts is likely to be futile. For many minority language children it appears likely that the semantic prerequisites for literacy skills can be developed more easily through Ll than through L2.

Several investigators have drawn attention to the fact that some bilingual children who have been exposed to both languages in an unsystematic way prior to school, come to school with less than native-like command of the vocabulary and syntactic structures of both Ll and L2 (Gonzalez, 1977; Kaminsky, 1976). Gonzalez (1977) suggests that under these conditions children may switch codes because they do not know the label for a particular concept in the language they are speaking but have it readily available in the other language. Because the languages are not separated, each acts as a crutch for the other with the result that the children may fail to develop full proficiency in either language. Kaminsky (1976) has argued that these bilingual children may fail to develop fluent reading skills since their knowledge of the syntactic rules and vocabulary of each language may be insufficient to make accurate predictions regarding the information in the text.

Metalinguistic Insights

Smith (1977) suggests that children must acquire two insights in order to learn to read. The first is the insight that print is meaningful, and the second that written language is different from speech. Unless children realize that differences on a printed page have a function they will not be motivated to learn to read. Furthermore, if children do not realize that written language is different from spoken language their predictions regarding the meanings in the text are likely to be inaccurate. Smith sums up his discussion of these insights by stating that 'children who can make sense of instruction should learn to read; children confronted by nonsense are bound to fail' (1977: 395).

Decontextualized Language

Related to the differences between spoken and written language is the child's facility in using and assimilating language which is decontextualized, i.e. taken out of the context of the immediate interpersonal situation. As Olson (1977a) points out, a central characteristic of written text is that it is an autonomous representation of meaning and depends on no cues other than linguistic ones. Several investigators (e.g. Elasser & John-Steiner, 1977; Olson, 1976, 1977a; Vygotsky, 1962) have stressed the importance of literacy in promoting the decontextualization and elaboration of thought processes. However, the extent to which children have developed facility in processing linguistic information independent of interpersonal cues prior to school will also clearly influence how easily they acquire literacy skills.

Facility in processing decontextualized language can be regarded as one aspect of an individual's functional linguistic competence. As such it involves what Halliday (1973) has termed the 'representational' function of language which is concerned with the processing and communication of information. The distinction between interpersonal and ideational or logical functions of language (Olson, 1977b) is also relevant. The ideational function of language specifies the semantic and logical relations between subject and predicate of a sentence while the interpersonal function relates the logical component to the requirements of the listener. Olson (1977b) suggests that 'Literate language, especially that of prose text, the language of schooling, is responsible ... for differentiating the logical from the interpersonal functions of language ...' (p. 113).

These aspects of functional linguistic competence appear likely to be most directly related to the development of fluent reading skills. However, individual differences in using other functions of language are clearly important for other aspects of educational adjustment. Halliday (1973), for example, has emphasized the importance of facility in using the personal and heuristic functions of language. The personal function refers to the child's expression of identity and individuality through language while the heuristic function involves the use of language to learn and to explore reality.

The three aspects of linguistic development which have been described are likely to be differentially reinforced by the L1 experience of middle and low SES children. As Olson (1976) suggests, 'Highly literate parents may be expected to communicate the explicit logical structure of printed texts in at least two ways, through their own abstract language and, probably more importantly, through reading printed stories' (p. 201). Smith has also emphasized that the only way children can acquire the insight that written language is different from spoken language is by hearing written language read aloud. Clearly, this is also likely to promote the development of a child's conceptual knowledge. Low SES minority language children are likely to be worse off in this respect than low SES children in a unilingual situation because of unavailability of reading materials in Ll and lack of exposure to Ll on TV and outside the home.

Although these aspects of children's 'input' linguistic knowledge are likely to be highly related to the acquisition of fluent reading skills whether Ll or L2 is used as initial medium of instruction, this does not mean that the language of instruction is 'linguistically irrelevant' as Bowen (1977) argues. The hypothesis advanced in this paper is that there is an interaction between these aspects of Ll development and initial medium of instruction. Medium of instruction may be irrelevant for children whose knowledge of Ll is well advanced. However, for minority language children who have not been exposed to a literate Ll environment prior to school the initial medium of instruction may be vitally important. Such a child's Ll vocabulary-concept knowledge may be limited, there may be difficulty assimilating decontextualized language, and little insight into the fact that print is meaningful and that written language is different from speech. Thus, in Smith's (1977) terms, many of these children may be 'confronted by non-sense' in the task of learning to read and the development of fluent reading skills is likely to be difficult even when instruction is through L1. However, when reading is introduced through L2 the task is likely to be considerably more difficult since there is no way in which the children relate the printed symbols to their knowledge of spoken language. Even where minority language children do have some knowledge of L2 as a result of unsystematic exposure to it prior to school, their knowledge of the language is likely to bear little resemblance to its representation in printed text.

It might be objected that the middle-class immersion child has very little knowledge of the vocabulary and syntax of L2 when L2 reading instruction is begun. However, in contrast to the low SES minority language child, the immersion child is likely both to have developed a certain degree of facility in processing decontextualized information and also to have acquired or be quickly capable of acquiring, the insights that print is meaningful and that written language is different from speech. In addition, through their L1 experience they are likely to have developed an understanding of most of the concepts they will encounter in their early reading of L2. Thus, although initially immersion children may have only a relatively limited knowledge of L2, this is likely to be developed in the process of learning to read L2 since the task is meaningful and children are highly motivated to learn L2. The fact that the children are already familiar with the concepts encountered in learning L2 means that their task is essentially learning a new label for an already existing concept. One might reverse Roger Brown's (1958) dictum and suggest that the presence of the concept is an invitation to acquire the word. This task is clearly very different from that of low SES minority language children who may not have a conceptual basis in either L1 or L2 for the vocabulary encountered in L2. Thus, in order to develop fluent reading skills minority language children may be required to develop or expand their conceptual knowledge by means of a language which they understand poorly. It is not surprising that, under these circumstances, many low SES minority language children become 'semiliterate', i.e. develop less than native-like levels of literacy in both languages. The threshold hypothesis would predict that this would be a progressively deteriorating state and that it would have broader cognitive ramifications in that the children's ability to interact with their educational environment and expand their conceptual knowledge would be reduced.

The fact that, in comparison to middle-class children, low SES minority language children may be more dependent on the school to provide the pre-requisites for the acquisition of literacy skills does not imply that these children's basic cognitive abilities are in any sense deficient nor that their command of the linguistic system of their L1 is necessarily inadequate. It does imply, however, that the school program must be geared to the needs of individual children if they are to attain an additive form of bilingualism involving fluent literacy skills in

L1 and L2. If the process of instruction is to be meaningful it must reflect the child's cultural experiences and build upon his competencies. A low SES minority language child may have less knowledge of some aspects of language and may have developed different functional linguistic skills on entry to school than a middle class child. However, the child's input linguistic knowledge is translated into deficient levels of L1 and L2 competence only when it is reinforced by inappropriate forms of educational treatment. Thus, a child's cognitive, linguistic and academic growth can be conceptualized only in terms of the interaction between child input and educational treatment. This is the basis for the model of bilingual education outlined in the next section.

An Interaction Model of Bilingual Education

As Gonzalez (1977) points out, one of the reasons why bilingual programs for Mexican–American children may have had mixed results is because educators have implicitly assumed that these children constitute a homogeneous group for whom instruction through the medium of a prestige variety of Spanish is uniformly appropriate. He suggests that in order to be optimally effective school programs and teachers must accommodate to the diversity that exists within their student population. To the extent that bilingual programs do not currently do this, it follows that they are differentially effective in promoting academic and cognitive growth for different sub-groups of students.

Given this fact it seems reasonable to suggest that evaluations should aim to discover what are the relevant dimensions of child input and how they interact with different patterns of educational treatment. Instead, much of the controversy surrounding bilingual education has centered around the relative merits of transitional versus maintenance programs versus ESL-only programs, with little attempt to relate the program impact to the diversity of student input. There are very few clearcut data on the academic and cognitive effects of each of these types of programs and virtually none on the mechanisms through which these programs may have exerted their effects. The reason, I would suggest, is that evaluations have ignored the *interaction* between educational treatment variables and student input characteristics. The model outlined in Figure 2 is designed to allow Child Input variables to be systematically related both to Background and Educational Treatment variables.

The influence of both Background and Educational Treatment variables has been considered by several other investigators (e.g. Cohen & Swain, 1976; Fishman, 1977; Paulston, 1976, 1978; Swain, 1978b; Tucker, 1977) and need not be considered in detail here. The two Child Input dimensions of conceptual-linguistic knowledge and motivation to learn L2 and maintain L1 are specified on the basis of data which suggest that individual differences in these dimensions are important determinants of academic outcomes in bilingual programs. The Background variables specified are those which appear most likely to determine

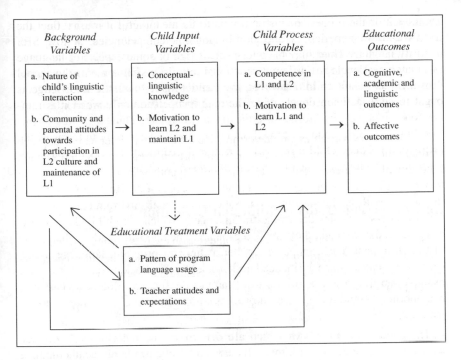

Figure 2 Interaction model of bilingual education

the Child Input variables while the two Educational Treatment dimensions are those most likely to interact with Child Input variables. The pattern of program language usage refers not only to distinctions such as those between maintenance, transitional and ESL-only programs but also to patterns of language usage within the classroom, e.g. concurrent versus separated patterns of L1 and L2 usage. Obviously, all these dimensions are outlined only at a very general level and the purpose of listing them is to indicate the types of variables which evaluations should attempt to assess. At different levels of analysis different sets of variables might assume more relevance than those specified here.

A two-way interaction is posited between Background and Educational Treatment factors. School programs for minority language children are a result of particular constellations of social factors (Paulston, 1976, 1978) but the establishment of a particular program is capable of influencing a community's attitudes and behavior in relation to linguistic issues such as L1 maintenance. The Child Input variables represent those characteristics of students on entry to a particular school program which are likely to interact with patterns of L1 and L2 usage in the school.[1] 'Conceptual-linguistic knowledge' refers to those aspects of L1 development which were specified earlier (viz. vocabulary-concept knowledge, metalinguistic insights, and knowing how to process decontextualized language).

The developmental interdependence hypothesis attempted to specify how the linguistic characteristics of students might interact with the language of instruction. Motivational inputs, whose role is more obvious, will be considered in a later section. The broken arrow between Child Input and Educational Treatment is meant to indicate that the characteristics and needs of students ought to be a factor in determining the appropriate form of educational intervention.

Child Process variables are determined by the initial interaction between Child Input and Educational Treatment and are in constant interaction with Educational Treatment variables. The threshold hypothesis focused on the extent to which the child's process competence in L1 and L2 effectively promotes interaction with an increasingly symbolic educational environment. Although Child Process variables determine the manner in which the child adapts to the educational environment they are also capable of being influenced by changes in that environment (e.g. change of teacher, pattern of program, language usage, etc.). They can also be influenced independently by Background factors; for example, an increase in exposure to L2 and to L2 speakers due to a change of neighborhood could influence both process competence in L2 and motivation to learn L2.

The educational outcomes which are determined by the child's interaction with the educational environment include not only academic and cognitive outcomes but also the broad domain of affective outcomes, e.g. identity, attitudes towards L1 and L2 cultures, etc. Level of absenteeism in particular programs may be a sensitive indicator of some of these affective outcomes.

The relevance of this model for current practice in evaluating bilingual education programs can be seen by considering the recent evaluation of Title VII programs conducted by the American Institutes for Research (AIR) (Note 1). On the basis of pre- and post-tests separated by a five month interval, the AIR reported that bilingual education programs appeared to have little effect on student achievement. However, as pointed out by the Center for Applied Linguistics (Note 5) the AIR findings are uninterpretable since students whose language abilities are extremely varied and who have received a variety of educational treatments are aggregated for purposes of data analysis. Thus, the evaluation reveals no appreciation of the complex interactions which are possible between diverse Child Input and Educational Treatment variables.

Interaction between Linguistic and Motivational Inputs and Educational Treatments

When taken together the developmental interdependence and threshold hypotheses imply that academic and cognitive outcomes are a function of the type of linguistic knowledge which the child brings to the school and the competence in L1 and L2 developed in interaction with educational treatment variables over the course of the school career. These hypotheses imply that for the child whose input conceptual-linguistic knowledge is not conducive to the development of literacy skills, initial instruction should be through the medium of L1. In addition, instruction through L1 should continue after the initial grades in order to develop a cognitively and academically beneficial form of additive bilingualism. However, motivational aspects of Child Input are also likely to interact both with linguistic input variables and Educational Treatments and must be considered before implications can be drawn for program planning.

The motivation of children to learn L2 is closely tied to their attitudes towards L2 speakers (e.g. Lambert, 1967; Wong Fillmore, Note 11). Where there is a strong desire to identify with members of the L2 group, the children will be highly motivated to learn L2. Conversely, motivation to learn L2 is likely to be low when the learning of L2 is regarded as a threat to the children's identity. As Lambert (1967) points out, there are four possible ways in which minority language children can work out their identity in relation to their participation in two cultures: (1) harmonious identification with both L1 and L2 cultures; (2) identification with L2 culture, rejection of L1 culture; (3) identification with L1 culture, rejection of L2 culture; (4) failure to identify with either culture. These patterns of identification are intimately tied up with the learning of L1 and L2. For example, a child who identified closely with both cultures is more likely to achieve high levels of competence in both languages than a child who identified with neither. Similarly, a child who identifies only with the L2 group is likely to actively promote the replacement of L1 by L2 while a child who rejects the L2 culture will be resistant to the learning of L2.

Wong Fillmore (Note 11) has illustrated the potency of motivational variables in a one year longitudinal study of five Spanish-speaking children learning English. There were enormous differences between the five children in the progress they made during the year and these differences were strongly related to differences in the extent to which the children sought out the company of English speakers and desired to identify with them. After three months of exposure to English the most social and outgoing child, Nora, had learned more English than two of the others would learn by the end of the year. Wong Fillmore (Note 12) suggests that for the child who does not spontaneously seek out L2 input and actively analyze that input an ESL component in bilingual education may be beneficial.

Harmonious identification with both cultures is a stated goal in most recent educational programs for minority language children. The central question is which patterns of L1 and L2 usage in the school will be most effective in promoting this type of identification for which children. Again, it is essential to take into account the interactions between motivational Child Inputs and Educational Treatment variables. For example, for a child such as Nora in Wong Fillmore's study, an L2 total immersion program in kindergarten and grade 1 with L1 introduced as a medium of instruction for part of the school day in subsequent grades (see Epstein, 1977) may be effective in producing an additive form of bilingualism and harmonious identification with both cultures. However, for a child whose attitudes towards L2 speakers are more ambivalent, gradual introduction of L2 as a medium of instruction would seem more appropriate.

At this stage it is possible only to speculate on the ways in which motivational and linguistic Child Input factors interact and on their relative importance in different situations. For example, in an earlier section it was suggested that the relatively superior academic performance of Finnish children who migrated to Sweden at the age of 10 in comparison to those who migrated earlier or were born in Sweden (Skutnabb-Kangas & Toukomaa, 1976) might be due to the fact that their L1 was well-developed when intensive exposure to Swedish began. However, the findings are equally susceptible to a motivational explanation. It could be argued that children who were born in Sweden had internalized their parents' negative perceptions of Swedish speakers and that these negative perceptions had been reinforced by a Swedish-only school system, many of whose teachers may have had negative expectations of Finnish children. The 'semilingualism' of these children is likely to reflect, partially at least, an inability to feel comfortable with either their Finnish or Swedish identities.

As suggested earlier, motivational factors may help explain the fact that data on Canadian immigrant children in the Toronto School System (Ramsey & Wright, 1974; Rogers & Wright, Note 9) do not appear to be consistent either with the Finnish findings or what has been informally observed in relation to Mexican–American children (Cardenas, in Epstein, 1977). In the Canadian situation, minority language children may not have been subject to negative attribution to the same extent as Finnish or Mexican–American children and consequently may have had greater motivation to learn L2.

High levels of motivation are also likely to contribute to the reasonably good performance of Italian background children in French–English immersion programs (Edwards & Casserly, Note 7; Genesee, 1976). These data are somewhat difficult to interpret due to the fact that specific characteristics of the Italian background children are not known; however, as Genesee points out 'there is nothing in these data to suggest that French immersion would not be suitable for third language children' (1976: 510). It is possible that in this type of situation the use of French rather than English as the primary medium of instruction might reduce the tendency to replace the child's home language with English.

The implications of the interactions between Child Inputs and Educational Treatments can be stated quite simply. If the same treatment is differentially effective for children with different input characteristics, then program planners must adopt what Gonzalez (1977) has termed a differentiated approach to bilingual education which would attempt to match different student inputs with the most appropriate treatments. The only way to discover how educational treatments interact with student inputs is by means of 'planned variation' research (Epstein, 1977) which would compare the value of different approaches for different children.

In designing this type of research it is necessary to develop hypotheses regarding the ways in which Child Inputs might interact with Educational Treatments. The possible interactions between two patterns of Child Input variables and four patterns of Educational Treatment variables are outlined in Table 1.

Only the extreme cases of 'high' and 'low' levels of both motivation to learn L2 and conceptual-linguistic knowledge are considered. At this stage there is little point in speculating on the effects of having low levels of one factor but high levels of the other. Submersion programs refer to the regular L2 programs which make no concessions either to the culture or language of the minority language child. The L2 immersion/L1 maintenance program refers to the type of program outlined by Epstein (1977) where L2 is used as an instructional medium in kindergarten and grade 1 but L1 is introduced as an instructional medium for part of the school day at grade 2. Transitional bilingual programs refer to the use of L1 as an instructional medium in the early grades but phasing out to exclusive use of L2 as soon as the child has developed sufficient L2 skills to follow instruction in that language. Finally, maintenance programs would use both languages as media of instruction throughout the child's school career with the aim of developing and maintaining proficiency in both.

Table 1 Hypothesized interactions between Child Input and Educational Treatment variables

| | Child Inputs | |
Educational Treatments	High Language/ High Motivation	Low Language/ Low Motivation
1. Submersion	−	−
2. L2 Immersion/L1 Maintenance	++	−
3. Transitional Bilingual	+	+
4. Maintenance Bilingual	++	++

−: academic and cognitive performance below comparable unilingual children
+: academic and cognitive performance similar to comparable unilingual children
++: academic and cognitive performance superior to comparable unilingual children

The present analysis would suggest that minority language children who are highly motivated to learn L2 and whose L1 experience has promoted the pre-requisites for the acquisition of literacy skills may very well develop a cogni-tively enriching form of additive bilingualism under treatments 2 and 4. Their L2 skills will develop adequately in a transitional bilingual program but because of the likely regression of L1 skills they will probably fail to experience any cognitive advantages in comparison to unilingual children. In a submersion program they are likely to perform below their potential for a variety of reasons considered earlier.

Children whose motivation to learn L2 is low and whose conceptual-linguistic knowledge is not conducive to the acquisition of literacy skills are likely to fail in both submersion and L2 immersion programs. Neither program seems likely to provide an educational context in which the child's initial school learning experiences would be successful and non-traumatic. This may be provided to a greater extent by a transitional program. However, only a program which attempts to promote the child's academic and cognitive development through both L1 and L2 is likely to result in a cognitively and academically beneficial form of additive bilingualism.

Summary and Conclusion

In the course of this paper evidence relating to several seemingly paradoxical and contradictory findings has been reviewed. First is the question of why a home–school language switch leads to such different outcomes in majority and minority language learning situations. Second is the fact that early studies reported a negative association between bilingualism and intelligence whereas more recent studies have consistently reported a positive association. Finally, there is the lack of any simple relationship between instructional time spent through the medium of a language and achievement in that language. In bilingual programs for minority language children, time spent through the medium of L1 appears to have no detrimental effects on the development of L2 skills while in immersion programs for majority language children the grade level at which L1 reading instruction is introduced makes very little difference to L1 reading achievement.

The model of bilingual education which has been elaborated is designed to provide a framework within which these apparently paradoxical findings can be resolved. The core of the model is its explicit assumption that the outcomes of bilingual education can be understood only in the context of the interaction between Educational Treatments and Child Input and Process variables. If this is the case then it carries important implications for both program planning and evaluation. For program planning it implies that educators take account of the diversity of input characteristics of their students and adopt a differentiated approach to bilingual education. Evaluations must follow a 'planned variation' approach in order to find the optimum blends of Input and Treatment characteristics under different socio-cultural conditions. Failure to take account of possible Input x Treatment interactions is likely to result in uninterpretable data.

Obviously, a central question for both program planning and evaluation is the extent to which different Child Input and Process variables interact with Educational Treatments to determine outcomes. Future research must determine which

Input and Process variables are most relevant. It was suggested that motivational and linguistic variables might be important to consider in interaction with Educational Treatments and several hypotheses regarding these interactions were proposed as possible ways of integrating apparently inconsistent research findings. The major educational implication of these hypotheses is that if *optimal* development of a minority language child's cognitive and academic potential is a goal, then the school program must aim to promote an additive form of bilingualism involving literacy in both L1 and L2.

Note

1. Although cognitive abilities and styles (see, for example, Ramírez *et al.*, 1977) clearly interact with various educational treatment variables, they are not specified in the present model because they do not appear to carry specific implications with regard to the initial pattern of L1 and L2 usage in particular school programs. For example, individual differences in degree of field-sensitivity or field-independence do not appear likely to interact with patterns of L1 and L2 usage in the school. Clearly, however, a more inclusive model which was not confined to bilingual program evaluation would include input variables related to children's strategies for learning.

Reference Notes

1. American Institutes for Research (1977) Evaluation of the impact of ESEA Title VII Spanish/English bilingual education programs. Report submitted to US Office of Education.
2. Bain, B. C. (1976) The consequence of unilingualism, disruptive bilingualism and creative bilingualism for the development of the body schema: A cross-cultural study in Canada, Italy and West Germany. Paper presented at the First International Christian University Symposium on Pedolinguistics, Mitaka, Tokyo, Japan.
3. Bruck, M. (1978) The suitability of early French immersion programs for the language disabled child. Manuscript.
4. Carroll, J. B. (1971) *Learning from Verbal Discourse in Educational Media: A Review of the Literature.* Princeton, NJ: Educational Testing Service.
5. Center for Applied Linguistics (1978) Challenge to USOE final evaluation of the impact of ESEA Title VII Spanish/English bilingual education programs. Manuscript.
6. Dubé, N. C. and Hébert, G. (1975) St John Valley Bilingual Education Project: Five-year evaluation report 1970–1975. Prepared for US Department of Health, Education and Welfare (mimeo).
7. Edwards, H. P. and Casserly, M. C. (1973) Evaluation of second language programs in the English schools. Annual report, Ottawa Roman Catholic Separate School Board.
8. Leslie, D. (1977) Bilingual education and Native Canadians. Unpublished research report, The University of Alberta.
9. Rogers, R. S. and Wright, E. N. (1969) The school achievement of kindergarten pupils for whom English is a second language. A longitudinal study using data from the study of achievement. Research report, Board of Education for the City of Toronto.
10. Scott, S. (1973) The relation of divergent thinking to bilingualism: Cause or effect? Unpublished research report, McGill University.
11. Wong Fillmore, L. (1976) Individual differences in second language acquisition. Paper presented to Asilomar Conference on Individual Differences in Language Ability and Language Behavior. Monterey, CA.
12. Wong Fillmore, L. (1978) ESL: A role in bilingual education. Paper presented at Ninth Annual California TESOL Conference.

References

Balkan, L. (1970) *Les Effets du Bilinguisme Français–Anglais sur les Aptitudes Intellectuelles*. Bruxelles: AIMAV.

Bain, B. C. (1975) Toward an integration of Piaget and Vygotsky: Bilingual considerations. *Linguistics* 160, 5–20.

Bain, B. C. and Yu, A. (1978) Toward an integration of Piaget and Vygotsky: A cross-cultural replication (France, Germany, Canada) concerning cognitive consequences of bilinguality. In M. Paradis (ed.) *Aspects of Bilingualism*. Columbia, SC: Hornbeam Press.

Barik, H. C. and Swain, M. A. (1976) A longitudinal study of bilingual and cognitive development. *International Journal of Psychology* 11, 251–63.

Becker, W. C. (1977) Teaching reading and language to the disadvantaged: What we have learned from field research. *Harvard Educational Review* 47, 518–44.

Ben-Zeev, S. (1977a) The influence of bilingualism on cognitive development and cognitive strategy. *Child Development* 48, 1009–18.

Ben-Zeev, S. (1977b) The effect of Spanish–English bilingualism in children from less privileged neighborhoods on cognitive development and cognitive strategy. *Working Papers on Bilingualism* No. 14, 83–122.

Ben-Zeev, S. (1977c) Mechanisms by which childhood bilingualism affects understanding of language and cognitive structures. In P. Hornby (ed.) *Bilingualism: Psychological, Social and Educational Implications*. New York: Academic Press.

Bowen, J. D. (1977) Linguistic perspectives on bilingual education. In B. Spolsky and R. Cooper (eds) *Frontiers of Bilingual Education*. Rowley, MA: Newbury House.

Brown, R. (1958) *Words and Things*. Glencoe, IL: Free Press.

Carringer, D. C. (1974) Creative thinking abilities of Mexican youth: The relationship of bilingualism. *Journal of Cross-cultural Psychology* 5, 492–504.

Cohen, A. D. (1974) The Culver City Spanish immersion program: The first two years. *The Modern Language Journal* 58, 95–103.

Cohen, A. D. and Swain, M. (1976) Bilingual education: The immersion model in the North American context. *TESOL Quarterly* 10, 45–53.

Cummins, J. (1976) The influence of bilingualism on cognitive growth: A synthesis of research findings and explanatory hypotheses. *Working Papers on Bilingualism* 9, 1–43.

Cummins, J. (1978a) Educational implications of mother tongue maintenance in minority-language children. In S. T. Carey (ed.) *The Canadian Modern Language Review* 34, 395–416.

Cummins, J. (1978b) Bilingualism and the development of metalinguistic awareness. *Journal of Cross-cultural Psychology* 9, 131–49.

Cummins, J. (1978c) The cognitive development of children in immersion programs. *The Canadian Modern Language Review* 34, 855–983.

Cummins, J. and Gulutsan, M. (1974) Some effects of bilingualism on cognitive functioning. In S. Carey (ed.) *Bilingualism, Biculturalism and Education*. Edmonton: The University of Alberta Press.

Cummins, J. and Mulcahy, R. (1978) Orientation to language in Ukrainian–English bilingual children. *Child Development* 49, 1239–42.

Cziko, G. (1976) The effects of language sequencing on the development of bilingual reading skills. *The Canadian Modern Language Review* 32, 534–9.

Darcy, N. T. (1953) A review of the literature on the effects of bilingualism upon the measurement of intelligence. *Journal of Genetic Psychology* 82, 21–57.

Davis, F. B. (1967) *Philippine Language-teaching Experiments*. Quezon City: Alemar-Phoenix.

Downing, J. (1974) Bilingualism and learning to read. *The Irish Journal of Education* 8, 77–88.

Elasser, N. and John-Steiner, V. P. (1977) An interactionist approach to advancing literacy. *Harvard Educational Review* 47, 355–69.

Engle, P. L. (1975) Language medium in early school years for minority language groups. *Review of Educational Research* 45, 283–325.

Epstein, N. (1977) *Language, Ethnicity and the Schools.* Washington, DC: Institute for Educational Leadership.

Feldman, C. and Shen, M. (1971) Some language-related cognitive advantages of bilingual five-year olds. *Journal of Genetic Psychology* 118, 235–44.

Fishman, J. A. (1977) The social science perspective. In *Bilingual Education: Current Perspectives.* Vol. 1: *Social Science.* Arlington, VA: Center for Applied Linguistics.

Genesee, F. (1976) The suitability of immersion programs for all children. *Canadian Modern Language Review* 32, 494–515.

Genesee, F., Tucker, G. R. and Lambert, W. E. (1975) Communication skills of bilingual children. *Child Development* 46, 1013–8.

Genesee, F., Tucker, G. R. and Lambert, W. E. (1978) An experiment in trilingual education: Report 3. In S. T. Carey (ed.) *The Canadian Modern Language Review* 34, 621–43.

Gonzalez, G. (1977) Teaching bilingual children. In *Bilingual Education: Current Perspectives.* Vol. 2: *Linguistics.* Arlington, VA: Center for Applied Linguistics.

Greaney, V. (1977) Review of reading research in the Republic of Ireland. In V. Greaney (ed.) *Studies in Reading.* Dublin: Educational Co. of Ireland.

Halliday, M. A. K. (1973) *Explorations in the Functions of Language.* London: Edward Arnold.

Hansegard, N. E. (1975) *Tvasprakighet eller Halvsprakighet? [Bilingualism or Semilingualism?].* Stockholm: Aldus/Bonniers.

Hébert, R. (1976) *Rendement académique et langue d'enseignement chez les élèves franco-manitobains.* Saint-Boniface, Manitoba: Centre de Recherches du College Universitaire de Saint-Boniface.

Ianco-Worrall, A. (1972) Bilingualism and cognitive development. *Child Development* 43, 1390–400.

Iiams, T. M. (1976) Assessing the scholastic achievement and cognitive development of bilingual and monolingual children. In A. Simoes (ed.) *The Bilingual Child.* New York: Academic Press.

Kaminsky, S. (1976) Bilingualism and learning to read. In A. Simoes (ed.) *The Bilingual Child.* New York: Academic Press.

Lambert, W. E. (1967) A social psychology of bilingualism. *Journal of Social Issues* 23, 91–109.

Lambert, W. E. (1975) Culture and language as factors in learning and education. In A. Wolfgang (ed.) *Education of Immigrant Students.* Toronto: Ontario Institute for Studies in Education.

Lambert, W. E. (1978) Cognitive and socio-cultural consequences of bilingualism. In S. T. Carey (ed.) *The Canadian Modern Language Review* 34, 537–47.

Lambert, W. E. and Tucker, G. R. (1972) *Bilingual Education of Children: The St. Lambert Experiment.* Rowley: Newbury House.

Landry, R. G. (1974) A comparison of second language learners and monolinguals on divergent thinking tasks at the elementary school level. *The Modern Language Journal* 58, 10–15.

Liedke, W. W. and Nelson, L. D. (1968) Concept formation and bilingualism. *Alberta Journal of Educational Research* 14, 225–32.

Macnamara, J. (1966) *Bilingualism and Primary Education.* Edinburgh: Edinburgh University Press.

Macnamara, J., Svarc, J. and Horner, S. (1976) Attending a primary school of the other language in Montreal. In A. Simoes Jr (ed.) *The Bilingual Child.* New York: Academic Press.

McDougall, A. and Bruck, M. (1976) English reading within the French immersion program: A comparison of the effects of the introduction of reading at different grade levels. *Language Learning* 26, 37–43.

Merino, B. (1975) Early bilingualism and cognition: A survey of the literature. In T. Gonzales and S. Gonzales (eds) *Perspectives on Chicano Education.* Stanford: Chicano Fellows.

Modiano, N. (1968) National or mother tongue language in beginning reading: A comparative study. *Research in the Teaching of English* 2, 32–43.

Morris, J. (1971) Barriers to successful reading for second-language students at the secondary level. In B. Spolsky (ed.) *The Language Education of Minority Children.* Rowley: Newbury House.

Olson, D. R. (1976) Culture, technology, and intellect. In L. B. Resnick (ed.) *The Nature of Intelligence.* Hillsdale, NJ: Lawrence Erlbaum Associates.

Olson, D. R. (1977a) From utterance to text: The bias of language in speech and writing. *Harvard Educational Review* 47, 257–81.

Olson, D. R. (1977b) The formalization of linguistic rules. In J. Macnamara (ed.) *Language Learning and Thought.* New York: Academic Press.

Paulston, C. B. (1976) Ethnic relations and bilingual education: Accounting for contradictory data. In J. Alatis and K. Twaddell (eds) *English as a Second Language in Bilingual Education.* Washington, DC: TESOL.

Paulston, C. B. (1977) Research viewpoint. In *Bilingual Education: Current Perspectives.* Vol. 2: *Linguistics.* Arlington, VA: Center for Applied Linguistics.

Paulston, C. B. (1978 in press) Bilingual–bicultural education. *Review of Research in Education.*

Peal, E. and Lambert, W. E. (1962) The relation of bilingualism to intelligence. *Psychological Monographs* 76, 546.

Ramírez, A. G. and Politzer, R. L. (1976) The acquisition of English and maintenance of Spanish in a bilingual education program. In J. E. Alatis and K. Twaddell (eds) *English as a Second Language in Bilingual Education.* Washington, DC: TESOL.

Ramírez, M., Macaulay, R. K. S., Gonzalez, A., Cox, B. and Perez, M. (1977) *Spanish–English Bilingual Education in the US: Current Issues, Resources and Research Priorities.* Arlington, VA: Center for Applied Linguistics.

Ramsey, C. A. and Wright, E. N. (1974) Age and second language learning. *The Journal of Social Psychology* 94, 115–21.

Skutnabb-Kangas, T. and Toukomaa, P. (1976) *Teaching Migrant Children's Mother Tongue and Learning the Language of the Host Country in the Context of the Sociocultural Situation of the Migrant Family.* Helsinki: The Finnish National Commission for UNESCO.

Smith, F. (1971) *Understanding Reading.* New York: Holt, Rinehart and Winston.

Smith, F. (1977) Making sense of reading and of reading instruction. *Harvard Educational Review* 47, 386–95.

Starck, R., Genesee, F., Lambert, W. E. and Seitz, M. (1977) Multiple language experience and the development of cerebral dominance. In S. J. Segalowitz and F. A. Gruber (eds) *Language Development and Neurological Theory.* New York: Academic Press.

Swain, M. (1975) Writing skills of grade 3 French immersion pupils. *Working Papers on Bilingualism* 7, 1–38.

Swain, M. (1978a) French immersion: Early, late or partial? In S. T. Carey (ed.) *The Canadian Modern Language Review* May, 34, 557–85.

Swain, M. (1978b) Home–school language switching. In J. C. Richards (ed.) *Understanding Second Language Learning: Issues and Approaches.* Rowley, MA: Newbury Press.

Swain, M., Lapkin, S. and Barik, H. C. (1976) The cloze test as a measure of second language proficiency for young children. *Working Papers in Bilingualism* 11, 32–43.

Torrance, E. P., Gowan, J. C., Wu, J. M. and Aliotti, N. C. (1970) Creative functioning of monolingual and bilingual children in Singapore. *Journal of Educational Psychology* 61, 72–5.

Toukomaa, P. and Skutnabb-Kangas, T. (1977) *The Intensive Teaching of the Mother Tongue to Migrant Children of Pre-school Age and Children in the Lower Level of Comprehensive School.* Helsinki: The Finnish National Commission for UNESCO.

Tremaine, R. V. (1975) *Syntax and Piagetian Operational Thought.* Washington, DC: Georgetown University Press.

Trites, R. L. (1976) Children with learning difficulties in primary French immersion. *Canadian Modern Language Review* 33, 193–207.

Tsushima, W. T. and Hogan, T. P. (1975) Verbal ability and school achievement of bilingual and monolingual children of different ages. *Journal of Educational Research* 68, 394–53.

Tucker, G. R. (1975) The development of reading skills within a bilingual program. In S. S. Smiley and J. C. Towner (eds) *Language and Reading.* Bellingham, WA: Western Washington State College.

Tucker, G. R. (1977) The linguistic perspective. In *Bilingual Education: Current Perspectives.* Vol. 2: *Linguistics.* Arlington, VA: Center for Applied Linguistics.

UNESCO (1953) *The Use of Vernacular Languages in Education.* Monographs on fundamental education.

United States Commission on Civil Rights (1975) *A Better Chance to Learn: Bilingual–bicultural Education.* Clearinghouse Publication 51, May.

Vygotsky, L. S. (1962) *Thought and Language.* Cambridge, MA: MIT Press.

Research Findings from French Immersion Programs Across Canada: A Parent's Guide

Immersion education refers to the use of a language other than the child's home language as a medium of instruction. Fifteen years ago this type of educational program was almost nonexistent in Canada. Today immersion programs are in operation in every province and every major city from St. John's, Newfoundland to Victoria, BC. The vast majority of these programs use French and English as media of instruction. However, bilingual programs involving a variety of other languages also exist. For example, in Edmonton, Alberta, Ukrainian, German, Hebrew and Cree programs are offered at the elementary level.

The first reaction of many parents to the idea of learning through the medium of a second language is one of incredulity. It is assumed that even if children in an immersion program do become reasonably fluent in French (or whatever the second language is) they will lose out somewhere along the line. Surely, children's achievement in English and other school subjects must suffer when a large proportion of school time is spent through French; some parents also fear that mental confusion will result from the necessity to think through two languages; or, even if logical thinking is unaffected, maybe immersion in a second language environment will stunt the child's spontaneity and power of creative thinking. Other parents wonder what the effects on the child's emotional adjustment will be.

Even parents who are familiar with the general trend of the research results often wonder whether such a program is suitable for *their* child. Are immersion programs suitable only for extremely bright children or can average or below average children benefit just as much? Should children who have speech or language disorders consider enrolling in an immersion program? How about the child who speaks a third (i.e. non-English, non-French) language at home?

Another issue which is sometimes raised is whether or not French immersion programs are equally successful in totally anglophone areas as they are in areas where there is more opportunity to use French outside of school (e.g. Montreal,

Ottawa). Underlying any discussion of the effects of immersion is the question of how the different program options compare with one another. First, then, it is appropriate to describe the major varieties of French immersion programs which are offered in Canada.

Varieties of French Immersion Programs

Three basic types of French immersion programs which aim to develop a high level of bilingualism can be distinguished:

(i) *Early total immersion.* The usual pattern of early total immersion is one where kindergarten and grade 1 are totally through French, one period of English language arts is introduced in grade 2 or 3, leading to approximately 50% of the time through English by grades 5 or 6. Reading is introduced in French.

(ii) *Early partial immersion.* Kindergarten is usually through French, grades 1–6 are 50% English, 50% French. Reading is introduced in English.

(iii) *Intermediate and late immersion.* Into this category can be grouped a variety of immersion programs which begin after the initial grades of elementary school (i.e. anywhere from grade 3 to grade 12). Late immersion programs (grade 7 up) are favoured by many school boards because they are easier to administer than early immersion programs. Children may or may not have taken regular French-as-a-second language courses ('core' FSL) before entry.

What are the 'pros' and 'cons' of each of these basic types of program? Specifically, how do they compare in relation to children's achievement in (a) French, (b) English, (c) other subjects, (d) intellectual development, (e) emotional and attitudinal development. To what extent are each of the programs suitable for all children?

French Achievement

Evaluations have shown that each of the three basic program types can be an effective route to bilingualism and, in terms of French achievement, it is not clear whether one program type is superior to the others.

It has been consistently found that by the end of elementary school early total immersion students approach native-like levels in French listening comprehension and reading skills, although they are still clearly distinguishable from native francophones in speaking and writing skills. This is not surprising since their only source of French language input is the teacher. Sustained interaction with native francophone children appears to be necessary to develop native-like speaking abilities. This can be seen in the fact that English-speaking children in francophone schools in Montreal are judged by their teachers to be almost indistinguishable from their francophone classmates in terms of French fluency, pronunciation and accent.

Comparisons of the French achievement of early total and partial immersion students show, as one would expect, differences in favour of the total immersion students. For example, within the Ottawa Roman Catholic Separate School Board (ORCSSB) the French achievement of grade 5 partial immersion students was intermediate between that of students in total immersion and extended French. However, all of these program options appear to meet their objectives rather well and the ORCSSB partial immersion model (half-day K French, grades 1–6 half-day French, half-day English taught by different teachers) has been successfully implemented for more than 90% of students in the system.

Middle immersion programs starting in grades 4 or 5 have recently been implemented in several cities across Canada and initial evaluation results are encouraging in that students make rapid progress in French at no apparent cost to English or subject matter content.

Comparisons of the acquisition of French in early and late immersion programs show that late immersion students make rapid gains in French proficiency, sometimes performing as well as equivalent grade students who have gone through an early immersion program. For example, it has been found in Montreal that students who have had six years of core French in elementary school and who enter an intensive grade 7 immersion program (80% French in grade 7 and 8) perform as well in listening, speaking, reading and writing French in grades 5 and 9 as students who have gone through an early immersion program. This result has been attributed to the fact that the early immersion students had only 40% French from grades 5–9 and recent findings from the Ottawa–Carleton evaluation suggest that this indeed may be an important factor. In this system early immersion students showed a consistent superiority in French proficiency over late immersion students. The apparent discrepancy in results is probably due to the fact that considerably more time is spent through French in grades 3–8 in the Ottawa–Carleton early immersion program than in the Montreal program. However, it is clear that other immersion programs are certainly a viable option in that, like other program varieties, they tend to meet their objectives very well. From a theoretical point of view, the success of late immersion shows that the use of the second language to convey meaningful content (Penfield's 'mother's method') is considerably more significant in language learning than the age of the learner (at least up to the early teens). With the possible exception of accent, there is little evidence for an optimal age for second language acquisition, contrary to what Penfield had suggested. However, students who begin early have the obvious potential advantage of greater exposure to the second language and it has been suggested that there are cognitive advantages associated with a relatively early bilingualism.

In summary, early, middle and late immersion programs all appear to meet their second language teaching objectives very well in that students in all three program types develop a high degree of fluency and literacy skills in French.

English Achievement

In early total immersion programs there are temporary lags in some aspects of English skills until formal English instruction is introduced. When English language arts is introduced, immersion students catch up to children in regular programs very rapidly, suggesting that considerable transfer of language skills takes place from French to English. It usually takes longer for children to catch up in the technical aspects of English skills, e.g. capitalization, spelling, etc., where the lag may persist until grade 3 or 4. However, it has been found in some evaluations that, despite the early lags, children in early immersion programs tend to perform better than children in regular programs on several aspects of English achievement by the end of elementary school.

In most early partial immersion programs little or no delay has been noted in the development of English language skills. Studies conducted within the context of partial immersion programs have also found differences in English language skills in favour of immersion students. However, the extent of beneficial effects on English may be a function of the amount of French students have learned. This is suggested by a study conducted in the Edmonton Public School System partial immersion program which compared grade 3 high French achievers, low French achievers, and regular program students on a series of English language processing tasks. The three groups had similar academic potential at the kindergarten level, but by grade 3 those children who had developed high levels of French proficiency also performed significantly better than the other two groups on several measures of English language processing.

In late immersion programs no differences have appeared between immersion and regular program students in English academic skills. However, less research has been conducted on this in late immersion than in early immersion programs and the possibility of subtle benefits should not be ruled out.

These results have two interesting implications. First, at least among middle-class anglophone children, the influence of schools on the development of English language skills appears to be less than was hitherto assumed. This is most convincingly illustrated in the study of anglophone children attending francophone schools in Montreal mentioned earlier. Despite the fact that for many children English language arts was not introduced until grade 5, children performed as well on measures of English achievement as comparable children in regular English schools. It appears that skills learnt through a second language can be easily transferred to the child's native language. Also, the main ingredient in the development of fluent reading comprehension is the vocabulary knowledge of the child which is much more dependent on the child's environment outside the school (e.g. literacy level of the home) than it is on school factors.

The relevance of these results lies in the fact that in the past, some parents have opted for a partial immersion program rather than total immersion program because of fears regarding their child's English development. These fears appear to have little basis. The greater exposure to French in early total immersion has no detrimental effects on children's achievement in English.

The second implication is that it may be possible to devise teaching methods and programs which would exploit the child's knowledge of two languages. The research results showing a tendency for the immersion students to perform better on aspects of English skills are consistent with the results of a considerable number of studies which suggest that there may be some cognitive advantages associated with attaining high levels of competence in two languages. For example, it has been reported in several studies that bilingual children are better able to analyze aspects of language in comparison to unilingual children. It would not be at all surprising if this were the case in view of the enormous amount of analyzing and processing of language that must be involved in becoming bilingual. One possible explanation which has been suggested to account for the superior performance of bilingual children on some language tasks is that, as they acquire more proficiency in their second language, they begin to compare and contrast the ways in which their two languages organize reality, e.g. word orders, grammatical structures, vocabulary, pronunciation, etc. In other words knowledge of a second language may help bring into focus aspects of children's first language of which they might otherwise be unaware. However, not all children in immersion programs are likely to engage in this form of contrastive analysis to the same extent. Some may do it consciously and explicitly, others not at all. Thus, there may be considerable potential for parents and teachers to devise means of encouraging children to become aware of similarities and differences in the ways in which they use French and English to express their thoughts. This type of approach might increase children's understanding of how language itself works. The ability and motivation to engage in this form of contrastive analysis is likely to be partially a function of the level of French competence which a child has attained.

Achievement in Other Subjects

Students in early total immersion programs have tended to perform as well as comparison groups in all school subjects other than English or French. In addition, they are able to transfer their knowledge from one language to the other. For example, when mathematics is taught through French, early immersion students perform equally well whether tested in English or French.

In one early partial immersion program in Ontario there were several instances of poorer performance in subject matter taught through French, especially in the later grades of elementary school. For example, the grade 6 students did not perform as well as their English-educated peers in either science or mathematics possibly, as Merrill Swain suggests, because 'their level of French was not adequate to deal with the more sophisticated level of mathematical and scientific concepts being presented to them in French'.

By contrast, in the Ottawa partial immersion program, students have performed as well as comparison groups in all academic subjects. This is probably related to the fact that students' French proficiency in the Ottawa partial immersion program was considerably better developed than in the other Ontario programs.

In late immersion programs some temporary lags in subject matter taught through French have been experienced but in no case has the difficulty been long-term. Usually, by the end of the second year of the program, students have caught up with their regular program peers in all subjects taught through French. There is some evidence that a relatively high degree of motivation may be necessary among late immersion students in order to 'keep up' in subjects taught through French. This may be due to the greater abstractness of curriculum content. At this stage the 'language barrier' is very evident whereas younger early immersion students 'have overcome the language barrier before they even knew it existed' (H. H. Stern). Thus, although late immersion programs have been highly successful among students who are willing to work exceptionally hard, early immersion programs may be a more viable proposition for a larger number of students.

Intellectual Development

There has been no evidence that immersion programs have any negative effects on children's intellectual or creative development. Any differences that have been found have tended to favour children in immersion programs.

Emotional and Attitudinal Development

Studies have shown no evidence of any problems in emotional or social adjustment among students in any of the different types of immersion program. Children's introduction to early immersion programs is 'gentle' in that they continue to express themselves in English in kindergarten – only the teacher speaks French. This experience builds up sufficient listening comprehension in French that when academic content is introduced in grade 1, children have little difficulty in following what is going on.

Studies of children's attitudes towards francophones have shown that children in immersion programs continue to maintain strong feelings of identity with the anglophone group but they perceive less 'psychological distance' separating themselves and francophone children than do children in regular programs.

How Successful is Immersion in Totally Anglophone Areas?

Intuitively one might expect immersion to be more successful in bilingual cities such as Montreal or Ottawa–Hull than in totally unilingual areas. However, this does not appear to be the case. Evaluations have shown quite clearly that immersion programs can be highly successful anywhere in Canada. The reason why a bilingual location does not appear to confer any advantage is that, for the most part, children in immersion programs use little or no French outside of school. The only television programs they are likely to watch on the French channel are hockey games (when there are none on the English channel) or Saturday morning cartoons. In both these cases the visual image is to a large extent independent of the verbal accompaniment. However, studies have shown that although children in immersion programs tend not to actively seek out opportunities to use French outside of school, they feel relatively comfortable in situations where they are required to use French. In contrast, children in core FSL programs tend to feel threatened by such situations.

In summary, a major reason why immersion works just as well in a unilingual as compared to a bilingual environment is that students in immersion programs tend to make relatively little use of opportunities for using French outside the classroom. It is possible that highly motivated students in high school (who have been in either an early or late immersion program) may make more effort to use French outside of school if they perceive knowledge of French as playing a useful or desirable role in their life plans.

Are Immersion Programs Suitable for All Children?

There is no more reason to expect immersion programs to be the best possible educational program for all children than there is to expect regular English programs to be. However, despite a considerable number of studies addressed to the issue, research to date has failed to identify any category of student for whom immersion programs are not suitable.

Intelligence

Immersion programs are certainly not just for the very bright. Studies have consistently shown that although IQ is strongly related to the development of reading and writing skills in both early and late French immersion programs (as in regular programs), it is much less related to the development of French speaking skills. In other words, children of relatively low IQ develop as much fluency in French as high IQ children. Although this finding may appear surprising at first sight, it makes a lot of sense when one realizes that the immersion experience is designed to mimic the process through which children learned their first language. Except in the case of some severely retarded or autistic children, virtually all children learn to communicate in their first language, irrespective of level of intelligence. Thus, there is no reason to expect that the acquisition of second language speaking skills in a French immersion program should be determined by a child's level of intelligence.

Home Background

It has also been found that children from working-class backgrounds and those who speak a third language at home appear to do well in immersion. In fact there is some evidence that children from certain linguistic backgrounds (e.g. Italian) may have an advantage in learning French because of the similarity between languages.

Motivation

As mentioned previously, a high level of motivation to learn French is probably a prerequisite for success in late immersion programs. This does not mean that a high level of motivation is not necessary in early immersion programs. It is; however, one can assume high motivation more easily at the kindergarten and grade 1 levels than one can in junior high and high school. The relatively concrete nature of the curriculum at the younger age level provides children with a 'breather' in which to acquire sufficient French skills to master academic content; however, at the older age level students must be motivated to work extremely hard to overcome the language barrier and master the complex curriculum content being presented through French. Thus, late immersion programs may be suitable only for children who are motivated to work extra hard to succeed.

Learning Disabilities

It has been suggested by Dr Ronald Trites of the Neuropsychological Laboratory at the Royal Ottawa Hospital that some children are more predisposed to develop learning disabilities in early immersion programs than they would be in a regular English program. Other researchers have not found Dr Trites' evidence convincing. Dr Maggie Bruck of the Montreal McGill Children's Hospital has conducted an extensive longitudinal study of children with language disabilities in early French immersion. She has found that these children do as well in immersion as comparable children in regular programs. In addition, they acquire fluent French skills. It is interesting to note that language disabled children experience considerable difficulty in core FSL courses. Some of the reasons which have been suggested to explain why these children perform relatively well in early total French immersion are (a) reading skills may be easier to acquire in French since sound–symbol relationships are more systematic in French than in English; (b) the language disabled child's self-esteem may be boosted by the fact that s/he is acquiring relatively fluent French skills, something that other siblings or peers may not have.

In summary, it is still an open question as to whether or not early French immersion programs are suitable for all children. However, research to date has provided no evidence that they are not. Late immersion programs may be less suited for all children because of the high level of motivation necessary to overcome the language barrier.

Should Children Who Experience Learning Problems in Early French Immersion Transfer out or Remain in?

Here again Dr Trites and Dr Bruck take opposing views. Dr Trites argues that children who experience difficulties should be switched to an English program whereas Dr Bruck suggests that the disadvantages associated with such a switch will usually far outweigh any benefits. Dr Trites' case is weakened by the detailed statistical analyses in his report (Trites & Price, 1977) to the Ontario Ministry of Education. These analyses indicate that a large majority of children who switched to an English program repeated or dropped back a grade level, and, although they made good progress in reading and other subjects *in relation to the grade level which they repeated,* they fell further behind equivalent children who remained in French immersion in terms of the level of performance that would be expected on the basis of their age.

However, in statistical analyses it is easy to lose sight of the individual child and it is important to emphasize that when children encounter difficulties in French immersion, each case must be judged on its individual merits. What researchers can do is suggest some of the potentially important factors which should be considered by those who are responsible for deciding whether or not to transfer a child to an English program.

(1) Parents and teachers should not assume that the French immersion program is to blame for a child's learning problems. There is no greater incidence of learning disability in French immersion than in regular programs and Dr Bruck's evidence would suggest that children with problems in immersion would likely have experienced the same problems in a regular English program.

(2) If a child has been unhappy for a prolonged period of time in an immersion program and wants to switch, then it is probably right to do so. However, one should consider the reasons for the child's unhappiness. If the child's relationship with a particular teacher is the source of the problems and the school year is almost finished, then transfer may not be necessary.

(3) Transfer to an English program may damage a child's self-image and the stigma of failure may compound the learning problems.

(4) When a child transfers to an English program in the early grades of elementary school, s/he will probably be even further behind than in the immersion program because of not having had any formal English instruction. Teachers in the regular program may resent the extra work which transferred children represent and thus harmonious learning relationships may be difficult to establish.

(5) Despite problems in academic subjects, the child experiencing learning difficulties in immersion will usually be developing relatively fluent French speaking skills. Not only is this likely to boost his or her self-esteem since

siblings or parents may not have acquired French, but it also represents an asset which will enhance future chances of personal satisfaction and economic success in present-day Canada. Immersion may be the only means through which such a child can acquire facility in French since s/he is likely to have the same difficulty in a core FSL program as s/he does in other academic subjects.

Thus, there are a number of factors to consider, and teachers and parents should not assume that a child who experiences difficulties in French immersion would necessarily be better off in a regular program. A sizeable proportion of children experience academic difficulties in any type of school program. Teachers must accept the fact that children in immersion programs also experience their share of difficulties, and they should individualize their program accordingly rather than automatically taking the easy way out by transferring children to the regular program.

Further information

1. *So You Want Your Child to Learn French!* (1979). A handbook for parents produced by Canadian Parents for French. Available from Canadian Parents for French, 309 Cooper St, Suite 400 B, Ottawa, Ontario K2P 0G5.
2. Seven special issues of *The Canadian Modern Language Review* have been published with financial assistance from the Secretary of State. These special issues deal with current Canadian research on immersion education and second language learning. The volumes still in print can be obtained free of charge from The Canadian Modern Language Review, 4 Oakmount Road, Welland, Ontario L3C 4X8.
   (i)   Bilingualism in Education (out of print).
   (ii)   Attitude and Motivation in Language Learning.
   (iii) Immersion Education for the Majority Child.
   (iv) Alternative Programs for Teaching French as a second Language in the Schools of the Carleton and Ottawa School Boards (out of print).
   (v)   Needs Oriented Language Teaching.
   (vi) Language Acquisition and Bilingualism in Education.
   (vii) Proceedings of the First ACPI/CAIT Conference.
3. Merrill Swain and Sharon Lapkin (1982) *Evaluating Bilingual Education: A Canadian Case Study*. Clevedon: Multilingual Matters.

Section Two: The 1980s

Section 2 begins with a classic paper. Published in the *NABE Journal* in 1980, 'The entry and exit fallacy in bilingual education' was originally a lecture given at San Diego State University and then at the 9th Annual NABE Conference in California in April 1980. The paper continues a theme that has lasted throughout Jim Cummins' career: the small impact of research on bilingual education is due not to a small volume of research but rather to absent or weak theoretical assumptions underlying such research. To provide a stronger theoretical base for bilingual education, he proposed the now famous BICS and CALP distinction. Everyday conversational language (Basic Interpersonal Communication Skills, or BICS) is different from the academic language of the classroom (Cognitive Academic Language Proficiency, or CALP).

By distinguishing between two different forms of language proficiency, a radical critique of bilingual education practices in the United States and elsewhere became possible. Such a distinction also helped conceptualize a solution. Children from minority language backgrounds with everyday conversational skills in English were not ready to enter mainstream English language classrooms. Exiting children from a bilingual program to an English-only program (to promote more thoroughly their English language development) results in much educational failure. Such early-exited students do not have the cognitive and academic language to cope in a mainstream classroom.

This article introduces other ideas that have become globally influential: the iceberg representation of language proficiency, the Separate Underlying Proficiency (SUP) model of bilingualism and the Common Underlying Proficiency (CUP) model of bilingualism. While these concepts attracted criticism, they have also influenced policy and practice in a truly international manner.

This influential paper criticizes United States transitional bilingual education. Yet 20 years later, the preference in the US for an early exit of language minority students to mainstream classrooms, and a preference for replacing a child's home linguistic skills with English, are still as evident and in need of refutation as they were when Cummins wrote this paper and delivered the 1980 NABE lecture.

The second paper was published by the National Clearinghouse for Bilingual Education in 1982. Jim Cummins, particularly in his graduate university days, had gained much expertise on tests and testing. While this paper demonstrates his expertise in relating psychometric tests to bilingual issues, it also provides his initial thinking on two dimensions of communication: cognitively demanding/ undemanding; context reduced/embedded. These two dimensions provided a theoretical proposition about the relationship between language proficiency and academic achievement. Such dimensions are immediately related to forms of bilingual education in which immigrant children are placed. One implication Cummins outlines is that it takes about two years for a child to achieve context-embedded communicative proficiency but five to seven years to achieve context-reduced academic communicative proficiency. This implies that an immigrant student in the US needs five to seven years of English language learning before they can cope in a mainstream classroom.

The third paper in this section is an extract from Jim Cummins' (1984) book entitled *Bilingualism and Special Education: Issues in Assessment and Pedagogy*. Chapter 7 of that book asks whether bilingual education is suitable for all children, including those who have learning difficulties. In a thorough review of available research, Cummins concludes that an enrichment form of bilingual education is suitable for all students, majority and minority, for those with learning difficulties and those who are less academically able.

The next paper appeared in the prestigious *Harvard Educational Review* in 1986. It is another of Jim Cummins' papers that has reached a large international audience. It shows a development in his thinking, with a deepening appreciation of the political nature of bilingual education, of power and status relationships in blocking enrichment forms of bilingual education, and of the need to empower minority language students against whom there is much prejudice.

Rather than starting from psychological research, educational program evaluations or educational theory, the paper is immediately contextualized within policies that institutionalize minority language student failure. He proposes a theoretical framework for the empowerment of minority language students that accounts for dominant/dominated power relationships, culture, community, pedagogy and assessment. The framework is valuable not only for predicting the effects of Submersion and Transitional Bilingual Education, but also how the empowerment of students can be achieved when collaboration and advocacy are part of a political solution to an educational issue.

The fifth paper returns to the psychological assessment of minority language students, but with a political perspective. The paper is particularly important in redefining the role of psychological assessment of bilingual students. It suggests that psychological assessment too often has a legitimizing function whereas an advocacy approach is needed for minority language groups. The psychologist must not legitimize the minority child's under-performance by blaming the child or the parents. Rather the societal and educational context surrounding the language minority child must be considered. This means, for example, the psychologist should examine relationships between dominant and subordinate groups, and how power relationships in politics and the community create impoverished education contexts. Such sociopolitical contexts must be understood so that remedies are achieved at system levels rather than simply blaming the child and parents.

The sixth paper is remarkable for its early understanding of the importance and influence of new technologies. Published in 1988 in the early days of computers in a classroom, it is prophetic and powerful. The final sentence of the first paragraph could have been written today: 'The challenge for our educational system is not only to provide children from all social and ethnic groups with sufficient and equal access to computers and other technological advances but also to provide them with the opportunities to develop the critical thinking skills and creativity to control the technology rather than being controlled by it.'

Jim Cummins argued in 1988 that the computer has the potential to make the global village a reality for school students by involving them in interacting with other students around the world. Cultural interchange, collaborative discovery learning and problem solving, meaningful language use, intrinsic motivation and critical and creative thinking all become possible with a microcomputer (and today, by use of the World Wide Web).

The seventh paper is a chapter in a book entitled *Minority Education: From Shame to Struggle* edited by Tove Skutnabb-Kangas and Jim Cummins (1988). Jim Cummins' chapter in that book analyses bilingualism and bilingual education in Ontario from a multicultural and anti-racist education perspective. Encapsulating perspectives from education, sociocultural studies, politics and community relations, the chapter discusses the changes needed in politics, provision, policy and practice to ensure that a strong form of multiculturalism, prejudice reduction and anti-racism permeates all levels of the educational system, from teachers to politicians. Jim Cummins argues that challenging societal power structures and relationships between the dominant and dominated has to be attempted to challenge the institutionalized racism that is all too frequent.

The final paper in this section, published in 1988, is a position paper on the role and use of educational theory in formulating language policy. The context of the paper is the United States bilingual education policy debate. The paper provides a succinct cross-disciplinary overview of US bilingual education issues, with two strong conclusions. First, that sociopolitical factors dominate the interpretation of United States research on bilingual education. Second, coherent theories that predict outcomes under varying conditions are important if a more rational and effective approach to bilingual education in the United States is to be achieved.

The Entry and Exit Fallacy in Bilingual Education[1]

It is frequently claimed (e.g. Perez, 1980; Troike, 1978) that bilingual education in the United States is in critical need of research in order to document the validity (or otherwise) of its basic psycho-educational assumptions. Troike (1978) for example, points out that bilingual education was undertaken largely as an act of faith based on the UNESCO declaration of 1953 that 'it is axiomatic that the best medium for teaching a child is his mother tongue', as well as on positive reports from a few scattered projects in the United States and elsewhere (Engle, 1975; Modiano, 1968). However, after 10 years of bilingual education in the United States he could find only 13 evaluations that were reasonably well-controlled. The fact that these evaluations do appear to support bilingual education is counter-balanced by the fact that there is as yet no clear evidence that bilingual education is reducing inequality of educational opportunity on the large scale that was originally envisaged (e.g. Danoff, 1978).

The urgent need for large-scale research documentation for the psycho-educational assumptions of bilingual education is highlighted by the growing sociopolitical backlash against bilingual education, illustrated by frequent warnings in the popular press that bilingual education will lead to social fragmentation and Quebec-style separatist movements. This fear of bilingual education is often rationalized in psychoeducational terms, namely, that if minority children are deficient in English then they need instruction in English, not their first language (L1). The alternative argument, for bilingual education, rests on the counter-intuitive assumption that instruction in L1 will promote English skills more effectively than instruction in English. It is not surprising that this 'Less Equals More' rationale would be difficult both for proponents to articulate and for opponents to swallow. Consequently, there appears to be widespread confusion about the goals and methods of bilingual education at all levels of the educational hierarchy, from teachers to policy makers.

Much of the recent debate, both political and pedagogical, has centered around the question of entry and exit criteria in transitional bilingual education. There is considerable disagreement about *who* should enter bilingual education programs, *why* they should be there, and *how* to identify them. Similarly, there is disagreement about *who* should exit from bilingual programs, *why* they should exit, and *how* to identify students who should exit.

The confusion regarding these issues exists just as much among those who favour bilingual education as among those who are opposed. Although research documentation is lacking on some of the issues, there is abundant research available on others. Thus, the roots of the confusion lie not so much in the conflict between sociopolitical and psychoeducational concerns, nor in the absence of adequate research documentation, but in the *real* confusion which underlies the rationale for transitional programs. This confusion is evident in the attempt both to identify educationally meaningful entry and exit criteria and to operationalize these criteria by means of tests of language dominance and proficiency.

I shall argue in the present paper that the questionable validity of many of the assumptions underlying transitional bilingual education stems from a failure to adequately conceptualize the construct of language proficiency and its cross-lingual dimensions. In other words, there has been relatively little inquiry into what forms of language proficiency are related to the development of literacy skills in school contexts, and how the development of literate proficiency in Ll relates to the development of literate proficiency in L2. When these questions are considered, the educational rationale for trying to establish entry and exit criteria vanishes. Furthermore, consideration of the nature of language proficiency and its crosslingual dimensions suggests that many widely used tests of language dominance and proficiency may be of doubtful validity for educational placement purposes. In other words, 1 shall try to show that analysis of the development of language proficiency in bilingual children is of central importance in constructing an adequate rationale for bilingual education and in answering the *who, why* and *how* questions outlined earlier.

Cognitive/Academic Language Proficiency

Oller (see Oller, 1978, 1979; Oller & Perkins, 1978) has argued on the basis of a large number of studies that 'there exists a global language proficiency factor which accounts for the bulk of the reliable variance in a wide variety of language proficiency measures' (1978: 413). This factor is strongly related to IQ and to other aspects of academic achievement. Most of the data reported by Oller and Perkins involved performance on discrete-point measures of literacy-related skills (e.g. vocabulary and reading comprehension tests) or on integrative tests such as oral and written cloze and dictation. Farhady (1979) has shown that there is no difference between discrete-point and integrative tests in terms of their loadings on a global proficiency factor.

Oller's general position is supported by a large body of research showing high correlations between literacy skills and general intellectual skills. Verbal intellectual skills are more strongly related to reading than are nonverbal skills. For example, Strang (1945) reported correlations of 0.41–0.46 between nonverbal abilities and reading, and of 0.80–0.84 between verbal abilities and reading. Consistent with these empirical findings, several theorists have emphasized the importance of *reasoning* in the reading process (Downing, 1979; Singer, 1977;

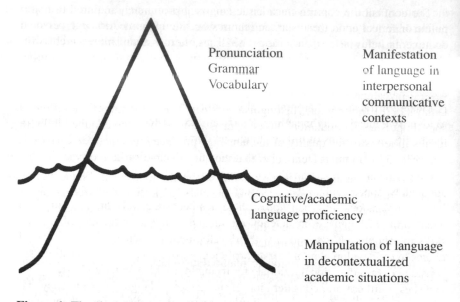

Figure 1 The 'iceberg' representation of language proficiency

Vernon, 1971) while others (e.g. Goodman, Goodman & Flores, 1979; Smith, 1971) have pointed out that fluent reading skills require that readers make use of their total knowledge of language and of the world to make predictions about information in the text.

However, it is clear that not all aspects of language proficiency are related to cognitive and literacy skills. For example, with the exception of severely retarded and autistic children, everybody acquires basic interpersonal communicative skills (BICS) in a first language, regardless of IQ or academic aptitude. As Chomsky (1965) has pointed out, the phonological, syntactical and lexical skills necessary to function in everyday interpersonal contexts are universal across native speakers. There are individual differences in the ways in which native speakers manifest these linguistic skills in interpersonal communicative contexts, e.g. oral fluency, but for the most part these differences are not strongly related to cognitive or academic performance. Thus, I prefer to use the term 'cognitive/academic language proficiency' (CALP) in place of Oller's 'global language proficiency' to refer to the dimension of language proficiency that is related to literacy skills. BICS refers to cognitively undemanding manifestations of language proficiency in interpersonal situations.

It is possible to diagrammatically present the distinction between CALP and BICS by adapting Roger Shuy's (1976) 'iceberg' metaphor.[2] In Figure 1, the 'visible' language proficiencies of pronunciation, vocabulary, grammar, which are manifested in everyday interpersonal communicative situations, are above the surface, but the cognitive/academic language proficiency required to manipulate or reflect upon these surface features outside of immediate interpersonal contexts is below the surface, and I shall argue, has usually been ignored in policy decisions regarding language of instruction.

Distinctions similar to that between CALP and BICS have been made by several investigators. Hernandez-Chavez, Burt and Dulay (1978) and Burt and Dulay (1978) for example, distinguish between 'natural communication' tasks and 'linguistic manipulation' tasks which, they report, 'give quite different results in terms of the quality of the language produced' (Hernandez-Chavez *et al.*, 1978: 52). Burt and Dulay (1978) define this distinction as follows:

> A natural communication task is one where the focus of the student is on communicating something to someone else – an idea, some information, or an opinion in a natural manner … On the other hand, a linguistic manipulation task is one where the focus of the student is on performing the conscious linguistic manipulation required by the task. (p. 184)

Burt and Dulay regard linguistic manipulation tasks as primarily assessing metalinguistic awareness, although the decontextualized non-communicative tasks such as oral and written cloze, sentence repetition, dictation, etc. that they include in this category would not usually be regarded as measures of metalinguistic awareness. In terms of the present framework, metalinguistic awareness is regarded as one specialized aspect of CALP. Several studies have reported that development of metalinguistic skills is significantly related to overall cognitive development (see Ryan & Ledger, 1979, for a review).

A similar distinction to that proposed by Burt and Dulay (1978) has been noted by Krashen (1978) in discussing the 'Words in Sentences' subtest of the *Modern Language Aptitude Test* (Carroll & Sapon, 1959). Krashen notes that this subtest involves 'a conscious awareness of language and grammar, quite different from the tacit knowledge or "competence" Chomsky (1965) claims all native speakers have of their language' (1978: 9). Further evidence for the distinction comes from the finding that the oral language production skills of preschoolers are only weakly related to the later acquisition of reading skills in school (Wells, 1979). The CALP–BICS distinction is also parallel to the distinction which Olson (1977) makes between the social and ideational functions of language and Halliday's (1975) distinction between pragmatic and mathetic functions of speech.

The CALP–BICS distinction can be further illustrated by considering their developmental trends as outlined in Figure 2.

The main difference between these idealized curves is that CALP follows the curve of overall cognitive development which begins to flatten out around mid-adolescence, whereas BICS tends to reach a plateau soon after the age of about five or six (see, e.g. Chomsky, 1965). However, at any given age level there are substantial individual differences between individuals (within cultural groups) in

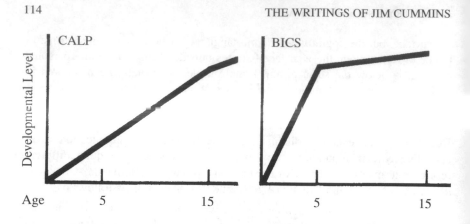

Figure 2 Developmental trends of CALP and BICS

the extent to which CALP has been developed. There are also large differences between individuals in some aspects of BICS (e.g. oral fluency, sensitivity to paralinguistic cues, etc.). A major difference, however, is that individual differences in CALP are strongly related to academic progress whereas individual differences in BICS are largely unrelated to academic progress. The relationships between CALP, overall language proficiency, cognitive skills, and academic progress are presented in Figure 3.

It should be noted that the development of CALP is not independent of interpersonal communication. On the contrary, as suggested by Wells' (1979) longitudinal study, the quality of communication between adults and children, both in the home and school, is a primary determinant of CALP development. The point is that in L1, certain aspects of BICS reach a developmental plateau considerably sooner than CALP, and thus proficiency in L1 BICS carries no implications in regard to level of development of L1 CALP, despite the fact that the development of both is dependent on interpersonal communication.

In other words, it is important to stress the 'B' in BICS. Only cognitively undemanding or 'everyday' aspects of communicative skills are included in the construct. It is certainly possible to construct an interpersonal communicative task which is cognitively demanding and requires the use of decontextualized information. In terms of the present framework, such a task would be regarded more as an index of CALP than BICS. Clearly, in an L2 context, where proficiency is as yet inadequately developed, a wider range of interpersonal communicative tasks are cognitively demanding than in an L1 context.

CALP and BICS in L2 Contexts

In L2 contexts there is not always the clear distinction between CALP and BICS that is evident in L1 contexts. For example, Oller (1980) has reported that

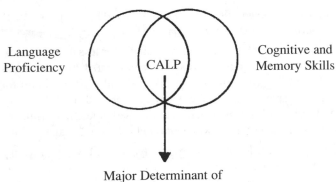

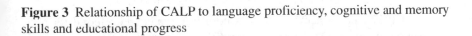

Major Determinant of
Educational Progress

Figure 3 Relationship of CALP to language proficiency, cognitive and memory skills and educational progress

measures of L2 communicative proficiency loaded on the same global proficiency factor as measures of L2 CALP in a sample of adult migrant workers in the Southwestern United States. However, in contrast to these findings there is abundant evidence that, under some conditions, proficiency in L2 BICS is independent of proficiency in both L1 and L2 CALP. For example, many studies have reported that grammatical competence is not a reliable predicator of communicative competence (see Canale & Swain, 1980, Overall, 1978; Rosansky, 1980 for reviews). Studies conducted in two very different contexts – immigrant language learning situations and French immersion programs – illustrate the fact that acquisition of L2 BICS becomes differentiated from development of L2 CALP in a similar manner to the differentiation of L1 BICS and CALP.

Studies in immigrant language learning situations

Skutnabb-Kangas and Toukomaa (1976) reported that although parents, teachers and the children themselves considered Finnish immigrant children's Swedish to be quite fluent, tests in Swedish which required cognitive operations to be carried out showed that this surface fluency was not reflected in the cognitive/academic aspects of Swedish proficiency.

Similar findings are reported by Cummins (1980b) in a study of more than 400 minority language children referred for psychological assessment. Throughout the teachers' referral forms and psychologists' assessment reports there are references to the fact that children's English communicative skills are considerably better developed than their academic language skills. The following examples illustrate the point:

PS (094): referred for reading and arithmetic difficulties in grade 2; teacher commented that 'since PS attended grade 1 in Italy I think his main problem is language, although he understands and speaks English quite well'. Verbal (V) IQ, 75, Performance (P) IQ 84.

GG (184): Although he had been in Canada for less than a year, in November of the grade 1 year, the teacher commented that 'he speaks Italian fluently and English as well . However, she also referred him for psychological assessment because 'he is having a great deal of difficulty with the grade 1 program' and she wondered if he had 'specific learning disabilities or if he is just a very long way behind children in his age group'.

DM (105): Arrived from Portugal at age 10 and was placed in a grade 2 class; three years later, in grade 5, her teacher commented that 'her oral answering and comprehension is so much better than her written work that we feel a severe learning problem is involved, not just her non-English background'. Her P IQ (grade 5) was 101 but V IQ was below 70.

BM (017): this grade 1 child was born in Canada and referred for poor school progress. On the referral form the teacher asked 'How can BM, 7 years old, speak such good English when mother can speak only Italian, little English, and father can speak only Czechoslovakian, little English?' V IQ 79, P IQ 74.

These examples illustrate the influence of the environment in developing L2 BICS. Television and peer interaction are likely to be the major factors. Although it is obviously not possible to generalize from the children in this study, it is clear that among these children acquisition of fluent English speaking and listening skills does not necessarily imply commensurate development of English conceptual abilities.

Another example comes from Wong Fillmore's (1979) one-year longitudinal study of five Spanish-speaking kindergarten children learning English. There was considerable variation in the extent to which the children sought out the company of English speakers and desired to identify with them. After three months of exposure to English the most social and outgoing child, Nora, had learned more English than two of the others would learn by the end of the year. Wong Fillmore (1979) argues that 'the secret of Nora's spectacular success as a language learner can be found in the special combination of interests, inclinations, skills, temperament, needs, and motivations that comprised her personality' (p. 221). She suggests that the differences between the five children in rate of English communicative skills acquisition 'presumably had nothing to do with intellectual or cognitive capacity' (p. 227). Thus, we would not necessarily expect Nora to excel the other children to the same extent in development of English literacy skills, since overall cognitive abilities appear to underlie these to a greater extent than personality variables.

Another study, Cummins (1980c) has shown that it took immigrant children, who arrived in Canada after the age of six, between five and seven years, on the average, to approach grade norms in English CALP. However, the study of minority children referred for psychological assessment (Cummins, 1980b), as well as common observance, shows clearly that immigrant children acquire a high level of English communicative proficiency in interpersonal situations in a considerably shorter period of time than five years. In summary, a high level of L2 BICS does not imply a commensurate level of L2 CALP.

Studies in French immersion programs

Genesee (1976) tested anglophone students in grades 4, 7, and 11 in French immersion and 'core' French programs in Montreal on a battery of French language tests. He reported that although IQ was strongly related to the development of academic French language skills (reading, grammar, vocabulary, etc.), it was, with one exception, unrelated to ratings of French oral productive skills at any grade level. The exception was pronunciation at the grade 4 level which was significantly related to IQ. Listening comprehension (measured by a standardized test) was significantly related to IQ only at the grade 7 level.

A similar pattern of relative independence between L2 BICS and both L1 and L2 CALP is reported by Bruck (1978) in a longitudinal study of children diagnosed as learning disabled in Montreal French immersion programs. Although the learning disabled children experienced considerable difficulty in both English and French reading, their acquisition of French interpersonal communicative skills was largely unaffected. The parallels with findings in immigrant language acquisition contexts are clear.

It should be noted that the argument is *not* that acquisition of L2 BICS will necessarily be unrelated to L1 and L2 CALP, but that, under certain conditions, L2 BICS and L2 CALP will become differentiated in a similar way to the differentiation observed between L1 BICS and L1 CALP. Two necessary conditions for L2 CALP and L2 BICS differentiation appear to be, first, extensive opportunities for interpersonal contact in L2, and second, motivation to take advantage of these opportunities. Briefly, L2 BICS will be acquired only through exposure to 'acquisition on-rich' (in Krashen's, 1978, sense) environments. However, this is not a necessary condition for development of L2 CALP. For example, high levels of L2 reading proficiency could be developed through home study without interpersonal contact.

In summary, although measures of L2 BICS and L2 CALP may be strongly related in the early stages of acquisition, or in situations where acquisition of both L2 BICS and L2 CALP has reached a plateau considerably below native speaker levels, they will tend to become differentiated from one another as the acquisition process continues. The main implication for bilingual education is that just as in a unilingual situation, L1 BICS (e.g. fluency) tells us virtually nothing about L1 CALP; native-like L2 BICS in a bilingual situation tells us very little about a child's ability to survive educationally in an L2-only classroom. This is because, as illustrated previously, native-like L2 BICS may hide large gaps in L2 CALP. Thus, performance on 'natural communication' tests such as

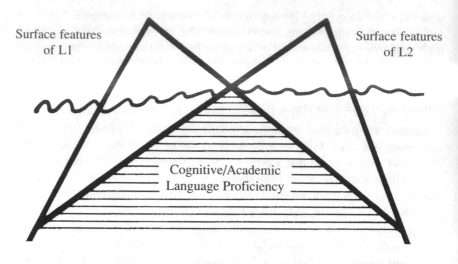

Figure 4 The 'dual-iceberg' representation of bilingual proficiency

the *Bilingual Syntax Measure* or *Basic Inventory of Natural Language*, that attempt to assess L1 and L2 BICS, may have very little predictive validity for educational performance. This is because academic progress is largely dependent on CALP. The analysis in the next section suggests that measures of L1 CALP may be sensitive indicators of future academic potential in L2-only contexts.

Interdependence of CALP Across Languages

Oller does not consider in detail the question of whether his global language proficiency factor underlies an individual's performance in different languages. In fact, the entire question of how the development of L1 proficiency relates to the development of L2 proficiency has received little attention until recently in the context of bilingual education. However, it has been hypothesized that the cognitive/academic aspects of Ll and L2 are interdependent and that the development of proficiency in L2 is partially a function of the level of Ll proficiency at the time when intensive exposure to L2 begins (Cummins, 1979a; Skutnabb-Kangas & Toukomaa, 1976). In other words, previous learning of literacy-related functions of language (in L1) will predict future learning of these functions (in L2). This interdependence hypothesis is illustrated in Figure 4.

Figure 4 expresses the point that despite the obvious differences between L1 and L2 in terms of the surface features of phonology, syntax and lexicon, there is a common underlying proficiency that determines an individual's performance on cognitive/academic tasks (e.g. reading) in both Ll and L2. The dual-iceberg diagram also allows for the possibility that there may be non-surface aspects of proficiency in each language that are not interdependent and that may not be related to CALP. In this respect it is useful to distinguish, as Genesee (1979) does, between language-specific skills and more general aspects of language proficiency. Genesee suggests that

> One might expect the language-specific skills (those which are not easily transferable from language to language) to include the more technical aspects of language, such as spelling patterns or syntactic rules, whereas the transferable skills may be more in the nature of cognitive processes, such as the use of one's knowledge of the syntactic transitional probabilities of a language in reading. (1979: 74–5)

Genesee's (1979) discussion is related only to transfer of reading skills but some sociolinguistic rules may also be language-specific.

It is important to note that although language-specific skills may not be easily transferable across languages, there may be high correlations between language-specific skills (e.g. L1 spelling and L2 spelling) if CALP underlies an individual's acquisition of these skills in each language. In general, also, one would expect proficiency in languages that are similar to be more highly correlated than proficiency in languages that are dissimilar.

Also, the hypothesized interdependence between L1 and L2 does not exist in an affective or experiential vacuum and there are several factors which might reduce the relationships between L1 and L2 measures of CALP in comparison to those between intralanguage (L1–L1, L2–L2) measures. For example, when motivation to learn L2 (or maintain L1) is low, CALP will not be applied to the task of learning L2 (or maintaining L1). The interdependent hypothesis also presupposes adequate exposure to both languages.

Empirical support for the interdependence hypothesis comes from correlational studies, studies on the 'optimal age' question in L2 acquisition, and evaluations of bilingual education programs for both minority and majority language students.

Correlational studies

If L1 and L2 CALP are manifestations of a common underlying proficiency, it would be predicated that L2 CALP will be significantly related to measures of L1 CALP and each will show a similar pattern of correlations with other variables such as verbal and nonverbal ability. Evidence supporting this prediction from nine recent studies is presented in Cummins (1979b). In these studies the correlations between L1 and L2 CALP ranged from 0.77 to 0.42 with the majority in the range of 0.6 to 0.7. In addition, L1 and L2 showed a very similar pattern of correlations with language aptitude and IQ variables. For example, the relationships between both L1 and L2 and verbal IQ or language aptitude measures were, for the most part, in the 0.6 to 0.7 range while those between L1 and L2 and nonverbal IQ tended to be in the 0.4 to 0.5 range.

Age and L2 acquisition

The interdependence hypothesis would predict that older L2 learners whose Ll CALP is better developed, will acquire cognitive/academic L2 skills more rapidly than younger learners. Recent reviews of research on the age issue confirm this prediction (Cummins, 1980c, 1980d; Ekstrand, 1978; Genesee, 1978; Krashen, Long & Scarcella, 1979). In no study did younger learners acquire L2 CALP more rapidly than older learners. No advantage for older learners in acquiring L2 BICS would be predicted on the basis of the interdependence hypothesis. The research shows no clear trend in aspects of L2 proficiency directly related to communicative skills, such as oral fluency, phonology, and listening comprehension. In some studies older learners display an advantage whereas in others younger learners perform better. A variety of factors might affect rate of acquisition of L2 communicative skills (see Cummins, 1980c; Genesee, 1978; Krashen *et al.*, 1979). However, the consistency of the findings in relation to L2 CALP acquisition, strongly suggest that level of Ll CALP is a major determinant.

Bilingual program evaluations

The success of French immersion programs for majority language anglophone children in Canada and elsewhere is well documented (see, e.g. Cummins, 1979a; Swain, 1978) and need not be considered in detail. Briefly, evaluations have consistently shown that children instructed mainly through French (L2) in the early grades suffer no adverse academic or cognitive consequences and catch up with regular program comparison groups in English language skills shortly after formal English language arts is introduced (usually about grade 2 or 3). Many investigators have remarked on the rapid transfer of reading skills from French to English (e.g. Genesee, 1979; Lambert & Tucker, 1972).

Immersion programs in other contexts show very similar results (see, e.g. Cohen & Swain, 1976; Cummins, 1977b). For example, Macnamara's (1966) study of bilingualism in Irish primary education shows that using Irish as a major medium of instruction for children whose Ll is English results in higher achievement in Irish at no cost to achievement in English (see Macnamara, 1966, Table 11.1, p. 101). Macnamara's findings have been frequently misinterpreted as support for the linguistic mismatch hypothesis (e.g. Downing, 1978; see Cummins, 1977a, 1978 for discussion of Macnamara's results).

The findings from immersion programs are sometimes regarded as inconsistent with findings that, for many groups of minority language children, instruction through L1 is more effective in promoting literacy skills in both L1 and L2 than instruction through L2 (see Cummins, 1979a). However, the inconsistency disappears when the data are viewed within the context of the interdependence hypothesis, rather than in terms of home–school language switching, or linguistic mismatch.

Many evaluations of Ll-medium or bilingual education programs for minority language children demonstrate a very similar transfer of language skills across languages to that observed in immersion programs. For example, several studies involving minority francophone students in Canada show that instruction through French (L1) is just as effective in promoting English proficiency as instruction through English. Carey and Cummins (1979) reported that grade 5 children from French-speaking home backgrounds in the Edmonton Catholic School System bilingual program (80% French, 20% English, from K-12) performed at an equivalent level in *English* skills to anglophone children of the same IQ in either the bilingual or regular English programs. A similar finding is reported in a large-scale study carried out by Hébert *et al.* (1976) among grades 3, 6, and 9 francophone students in Manitoba. At all grade levels there was a significant positive relationship between percentage of instruction in French and French achievement but no relationship between percentage of instruction in French and English achievement. In other words, francophone students receiving 80% instruction in French and 20% instruction in English did just as well in English as students receiving 80% instruction in English and 20% in French.

The findings of a longitudinal evaluation of the bilingual program for Navajo students at Rock Point (Rosier & Farella, 1976) in which all initial literacy skills were taught in Navajo, showed that by grades 5 and 6, students were performing at the National US norm in English reading. Prior to the institution of the bilingual program, students at Rock Point were two years below the norm in English reading despite intensive ESL instruction in the school. Troike (1978) has reviewed findings from other bilingual programs in the United States which showed that minority students performed as well or better in English skills as compared to students in English-only programs, and examples continue to multiply (e.g. Legaretta, 1979).

The evaluation of a recent 'language shelter' program for Finnish immigrant children in Sodertalje in Sweden reports findings very similar to those of the Rock Point Navajo evaluation. The extremely poor academic performance of Finnish L1 children in Swedish-only schools has been documented by Skutnabb-Kangas and Toukomaa (1976). The Sodertalje program, however, used Finnish as the exclusive language of instruction in the first two years of school and Swedish was gradually introduced in the third year. In subsequent years Swedish became the main language of instruction but teaching of Finnish was continued throughout the school. By grade 6, children's performance in this program in both Finnish and Swedish was almost at the same level as that of equivalent Swedish-speaking children in Finland, which was a considerable improvement in both languages compared to their performance in Swedish-only programs (Hanson, 1979).

In these programs for minority language children as well as in immersion programs for majority children, instruction through the *minority* language has been effective in promoting proficiency in *both* languages. These findings support the following formulation of the interdependence hypothesis:

To the extent that instruction in L_x is effective in promoting cognitive/ academic proficiency in L_x, transfer of this proficiency to L_y will occur provided there is adequate exposure to L_y (either in school or environment) and adequate motivation to learn L_y.

In summary, two main points have been made:

(1) CALP is a reliable dimension of individual differences in decontextualized literacy-related functions of language which appears to be distinct from interpersonal communicative skills in L1 and L2;

(2) L1 and L2 CALP are interdependent, i.e. manifestations of a common under-lying proficiency. The immediate psychoeducational implication of these hypotheses for bilingual education is that instruction through a minority language for either minority or majority language students will be just as, or more effective in promoting literacy skills in the majority language as instruction through the majority language.

Application of Theoretical Analysis of Bilingual Proficiency to Transitional Bilingual Education

The theoretical analysis of language proficiency and its crosslingual dimen-sions carries several implications for the currently controversial issues of who should enter bilingual programs, when they should exit from these programs, and how to validly operationalize entry and exit criteria. The CALP–BICS distinc-tion and the interdependence hypothesis are most directly relevant to the third issue and this will be considered first. Then the theoretical assumptions under-lying entry criteria will be critically analysed. Finally, I shall argue that current procedures for existing students from bilingual programs are logically incon-sistent, contrary to empirical data, and display a simplistic conception of what it means to be proficient in a language.

Operationalizing entry and exit through language proficiency assessment

A cursory examination of the many tests of language proficiency and domi-nance currently available for assessing bilingual students (see, e.g. DeAvila & Duncan, 1978; Dieterich *et al.,* 1979) reveals enormous variation in what they purport to measure. Of the 46 tests examined by DeAvila and Duncan (1978), only four included a measure of phoneme production, 43 claimed to measure various levels of lexical ability, 34 included items assessing oral syntax compre-hension and nine attempted to assess pragmatic aspects of language. This varia-tion is not surprising given the fact that the complexity of language necessitates making a choice as to what aspects to include in a test that can be administered in a reasonable amount of time. For example, Hernandez-Chavez *et al.* (1978) have outlined a model of language proficiency comprising 64 separate profici-encies, each of which, hypothetically at least, is independently measurable.

What criteria should guide the choice of which aspects of language to assess and how to do so? These *what* and *how* questions can only be answered when we consider the *why* of language proficiency testing for bilingual students. The impetus to devise measures of language proficiency and dominance arose as a result of the assumption that linguistic mismatch between home and school was a major cause of school failure among minority language children. Consequently, it was assumed that children who were not proficient in English ought to be educated through both their Ll and English in the initial grades until they had acquired sufficient proficiency to benefit fully from English-only instruction. Implementation of the transitional bilingual programs which are the logical outcome of this assumption necessitated operational procedures for entry into and exit from bilingual programs. Thus, a central purpose in assessing minority children's language dominance patterns is to assign children to classes taught through the language in which it is assumed they are most capable of learning and in which they will most readily acquire literacy skills.

This analysis suggests that, when used for placement purposes, measures of language proficiency and dominance should assess CALP, i.e. literacy-related aspects of language. The empirical data reviewed above suggest that 'linguistic manipulation' tasks are likely to be more appropriate than 'natural communication' tasks for this purpose. The most critical feature of the validity of such a placement test is its predictive validity, i.e. the extent to which placement decisions based on test performance assign students to instructional programs that facilitate the acquisition of literacy to a greater extent than would be the case in alternative programs.

However, the assumptions advocated by most sociolinguists and which underlie many of the tests currently in existence are directly contrary to those outlined above. First, it is argued (e.g. Burt & Dulay, 1978; Dieterich *et al.*, 1979; Shuy, 1976) that language proficiency ideally ought to be assessed in a naturally occurring communicative context. The internal (mainly content) validity of the test is regarded as critical whereas the predictive validity of the test for placement purposes is rarely discussed. Natural communication tasks are regarded as very much preferable to linguistic manipulation tasks, especially if the latter are discrete-point. For example, Burt and Dulay (1978) argue that 'it is not at all clear how the results of a linguistic manipulation task relate to a student's overall communicative proficiency, leaving the validity of linguistic manipulation tasks in some doubt if their results are to be used as an indicator of general level of communicative ability or proficiency' (p. 186). Dieterich *et al.* (1979) make a similar point in relation to a sentence repetition or mimicry task arguing that 'it mirrors no real speech situation and is thus of questionable validity in assessing proficiency' (p. 541). They also argue that the diagnostic uses of tests are more important for the classroom teacher than their uses in placement: 'If there is any payoff for teachers from testing, it is when the test yields diagnostic information about a student's language abilities, something more than whether the child will benefit from instruction in English or from a program of bilingual instruction' (p. 547).

Similar assumptions appear to underlie many of the tests currently in use. Despite the fact that these tests are ostensibly being used for placement purposes, they appear to be designed specifically *not* to relate language proficiency to educational performance because it is felt that the construct of language proficiency should be independent of cognitive and academic development. For example, it is reported (see Oakland, 1977: 199) that on the *Basic Language Competence Battery* there is little or no increase in scores across the elementary grades among native speakers. This is interpreted as evidence for the construct validity of the battery in that the battery is indeed measuring 'language knowledge' rather than intellectual abilities or educational achievement.

The emphasis on assessing language proficiency in naturally-occurring communicative contexts rather than in decontextualized situations, on eliminating cognitive demands in the test, and on content validity rather than on predictive validity, are all appropriate if the aim of the assessment is to diagnose weaknesses or gaps in students' basic interpersonal communicative skills. However, the relevance of tests based on these assumptions to the placement of children in linguistically-appropriate classrooms is questionable in view of the evidence, reviewed above, that L2 BICS may quickly become differentiated from and independent of L2 cognitive/academic performance. Thus, classification as 'English-proficient' on a natural communication task in no way implies that a student has 'sufficient' English proficiency to benefit fully from English-only instruction, since the acquisition of grade-appropriate English CALP may take considerably longer than the acquisition of English BICS. Empirical support for this scepticism regarding commonly used measures of language proficiency and dominance comes from Perez' (1980) report that in a large-scale Texas study five measures of English language proficiency showed low correlations among themselves and with standardized tests.

What assessment procedures ought to be used in the context of transitional bilingual programs? It will be argued below that there is no educational logic to the mainstreaming endeavor in bilingual education. However, if School Districts are required to mainstream, then the most logical criterion of ability to benefit from English instruction is performance on a standardized measure of English academic (CALP) skills, since these are universally used in the United States to assess educational performance. In other words, because standardized tests of English CALP are the criterion measures, the predicator measures should also assess English CALP.

This procedure may not be palatable to advocates of a 'quick-exit' policy in transitional programs, since data from several bilingual programs show that it is not until the later grades of elementary school that minority students (in the more successful programs) reach US norms on English literacy skills (see, e.g. Troike, 1978). However, the data reviewed above supporting the interdependence hypothesis suggest that measures of Ll CALP are reliable predictors of L2 CALP. Thus, if it were thought necessary for political reasons to mainstream students as quickly as possible (e.g. before they had attained an adequate level of English CALP), then the criterion least likely to damage students educationally would be a high level of L1 CALP. In other words, if we take two students, one of whom scores at the 60th percentile on L1 CALP and at the 20th percentile on L2 (English) CALP, and the other at the 40th percentile on L1 CALP and the 30th percentile on L2 CALP, it is the former (other things being equal) who is most likely to survive in an English-only program, despite the fact that his/her English proficiency is currently less well developed.

In summary, it has been argued that measures of language proficiency and dominance have proliferated with little regard for the purpose they were supposed to serve in the context of bilingual education. This purpose is to provide a rational basis for assigning children to classes taught through the language in which they are most capable of learning. Thus, in the context of bilingual education the construct of 'language proficiency' should include the notion of 'ability to benefit from instruction through that language'. Yet this is seldom, if ever, addressed in the validity statements of those tests whose manuals consider the question of validity at all. Based on the interdependence hypothesis and the CALP–BICS distinction, it was suggested that measures of Ll CALP would provide a more adequate basis for exiting from a bilingual program (if this were considered imperative) than measures of English BICS.

The entry fallacy

Although early statements of the rationale of bilingual education (e.g. Gaarder, 1977) emphasized both cultural and linguistic mismatch as important contributors to academic failure among bilingual children, linguistic factors have become the predominant focus of attempts to develop criteria for entry to bilingual programs. Thus, minority students classified as limited or non-English proficient (LEP or NEP) currently qualify in most States. However, it was initially implicitly assumed that students who were limited English proficient would be proficient in their mother tongue. However, Burt and Dulay (1980) have pointed out that this is not necessarily the case. They identified three groups of LEP students and discussed what types of instructional programs were appropriate for each. The first group was termed 'Primary Language Superior' and it was recommended that these children be placed in bilingual programs in which content subjects would be taught in the primary language while English was being learned. The second group of 'English Superior' students should be instructed in English, while the third group of 'Limited Balanced' (i.e. equally limited in L1 and L2) should be taught through whichever language is spoken at home.

Burt and Dulay's recommendations have proven controversial in California, because, if implemented, they would considerably reduce the numbers of LEP students receiving bilingual education. However, it is difficult for those who advocate bilingual education for all LEP students to argue against the Burt and Dulay proposals without appearing to undermine the entire theoretical foundation of bilingual education, which has come to rest on the linguistic mismatch hypothesis. Thus, it is appropriate to examine the validity of this hypothesis.

The linguistic mismatch hypothesis

Although several writers have pointed out that the success of immersion programs for majority language children casts doubt on the linguistic mismatch hypothesis or 'vernacular advantage theory' (Bowen, 1977; Epstein, 1977; Tucker, 1977), it is still widely assumed that introducing children to reading in L2 will lead to academic disadvantages. The most coherent recent statement of the linguistic mismatch hypothesis comes from Downing (1978) who tries to incorporate the findings from immersion programs within the theory. He claims that

> ... serious retardation in the development of literacy occurs when the initial instruction is delivered in L2. Even with strong positive motivation towards learning L2, literacy instruction in L2 still causes cognitive confusion. (p. 328)

Downing (1978) argues that the cognitive difficulties that derive from L2-medium instruction are often compounded by negative emotional reactions towards the L2. This is often the case when the majority L2 is imposed as an instructional medium on minority groups. As evidence for the combined adverse effects of cognitive confusion and negative affect Downing cites Garcia de Lorenzo's analysis of the low reading achievement of Fronterizo-dialect speaking children on the border of Uruguay and Brazil, and Macnamara's (1966) analysis of bilingualism in Irish primary schools. He also argues that initial cognitive confusion results even when there are positive attitudes towards the L2, as in Canadian French immersion programs, although here he admits that the longer term effect seems more favorable for the development of literacy skills.

Downing's attribution of cognitive confusion as a result of initial reading instruction in L2 is questionable in all three of the situations he analyses. In the Fronterizo situation, as in most other situations where minority students manifest low L2 reading scores (see Cummins, 1980a), the linguistic mismatch is confounded by the ambivalence of children towards their own dialect and towards the L2. Thus, the precise role of linguistic mismatch, by itself is unclear.

The problems in Macnamara's interpretation of his study of bilingualism in Ireland have been considered previously (Cummins, 1977a, 1978). For present purposes, however, it is sufficient to note that grade 5 Irish children introduced to reading in L2 (Irish) and instructed largely through L2, performed at the same level in *English* reading as Irish children introduced to reading in L1 (English) and instructed largely through L1 (see Macnamara, 1966, Table 11.1, p. 101).

This finding is clearly inconsistent with the linguistic mismatch hypothesis but consistent with findings of immersion programs elsewhere.

The fact that children in French immersion programs experience a lag in the development of English (L1) reading skills until about grade 2 or 3 is interpreted by Downing as support for the linguistic mismatch hypothesis. However, he points out that they perform as well as French-speaking controls in French reading in the early grades. The lag in English reading observed in virtually all early French immersion programs (Swain, 1978) is hardly surprising in view of the fact that formal teaching of English language arts is generally not introduced until about grade 2 or 3. In evaluations conducted in Ontario (Swain, 1978), a consistent trend had emerged for the immersion students to perform *better* in English language skills in comparison to regular program controls by about grade 4 or 5. Again, these data provide no evidence of retardation in reading skills as a result of linguistic mismatch.

The inability of the linguistic mismatch hypothesis to account for the research findings derives from two factors. First, it focuses on the obvious differences between L1 and L2 in surface manifestations of language (grammar, vocabulary, phonology) and ignores the cognitive/academic language proficiency which underlies successful literacy development whether initial instruction is in L1 or L2. Secondly, the sociocultural determinants of minority children's poor academic performance are ignored.

Sociocultural determinants

The importance of these sociocultural factors is clear from the differences between minority groups in academic performance under identical home–school languages with conditions. Consider, for example, the performance of minority group children (born in Canada) as revealed in the Toronto Board of Education Every Student Survey conducted in the late 1960s (see Cummins, 1980a for a review of these data). It was found that most groups of minority language students born in Canada tended to perform *better* academically than native unilingual English students. The major exception to this trend was the Franco-Ontarian group whose academic performance (in English-only programs) was considerably inferior to that of unilingual English students.

It is clear that it is not possible to account for the academic failure of minority children in terms of home–school switching or lack of school system sensitivity *per se* because different groups exposed to similar educational conditions react in very different ways. Thus, there must be an interaction between the affective or cognitive characteristics which children bring to the school and the educational conditions.

An examination of the sociocultural characteristics of minority groups that tend to perform poorly in L2-only school situations suggests that the attitudes of these groups towards the majority group and towards their own identity may be an important factor in interaction with educational treatment. Specifically, groups such as Finns in Sweden, North American Indians, Spanish-speakers in the US, and Franco-Ontarians in Canada all tend to have ambivalent or negative feelings towards the majority culture and often also towards their own culture. This pattern has been clearly documented for Finnish immigrants in Sweden by Skutnabb-Kangas and Toukomaa (1976). For example, they quote Heyman's (1973) conclusion:

> Many Finns in Sweden feel an aversion, and sometimes even hostility, towards the Swedish language and refuse to learn it under protest. There is repeated evidence of this, as there is, on the other hand, of Finnish people – children and adults – who are ashamed of their Finnish language and do not allow it to live and develop.

The same pattern of ambivalence of hostility towards the majority cultural group and insecurity about one's own language and culture is found, to a greater or lesser extent, in other minority groups that have tended to perform poorly in school. For example, many Franco-Ontarians tend to regard their own dialect of French as inferior and to show low aspirations for social and economic mobility in the majority anglophone culture. In contrast, minority groups that do well in school tend to be highly motivated to learn the majority language and often (though not always) have a strong sense of pride in their own cultural background.

How does the pattern of parental ambivalence towards home and majority cultures get translated into school failure among minority language children? First, obviously, these same attitudes get transmitted (probably unconsciously) to the children so that they may not be strongly motivated either to maintain L1 or succeed in school. Teachers may contribute to this pattern either through low expectations of the child's ability to learn L1 or through insensitivity towards the child's cultural background.

However, a second way in which the home environment affects the child's school performance is through the linguistic stimulation (or lack of it) that children receive in L1. Because parents are ashamed of their cultural background or feel they speak an inferior dialect of L1, they may not strongly encourage children to develop L1 skills in the home. For example, they may communicate with the child only when necessary or use a mixture of L1 and L2 in the home. Thus, children's L1 abilities (i.e. the development of concepts and thinking skills in L1) may be poorly developed on entry to school. This leaves children without a conceptual basis for learning L2 in an L2-only school situation and consequently they may achieve only low levels of proficiency (e.g. reading skills) in both languages.

According to this interpretation, the success of bilingual programs derives from the fact that children and parents are encouraged to take pride in their own language and culture as well as from the fact that schools try to build on the cognitive and linguistic abilities which children bring to the school.

In summary, the 'entry fallacy' consists of the assumption that a consideration of purely linguistic factors is adequate to determine whether or not a particular student, or sub-group of students, 'needs' bilingual education. As suggested by the Interaction Model of Bilingual Education (Cummins, 1979a) the input characteristics of students will interact in as yet undetermined ways with educational treatments. The initial rationale for bilingual education was based on assumptions regarding input-by-treatment interactions, namely, that mismatch between the culture and language that the child brought to school and those reflected in the school curriculum would lead to academic retardation. As a general principle the 'linguistic mismatch hypothesis' clearly has little validity, since many groups of minority and majority language students perform extremely well under conditions of a home–school language switch. Yet it is this narrow linguistic factor that has come to be almost the sole criterion of entry into a bilingual education program.

I have suggested that among minority language students, levels of input CALP are likely to be more important to consider in interaction with educational treatment than the surface manifestations of language considered in the linguistic mismatch hypothesis (Cummins, 1979a). The sociocultural characteristics of the community will also interact with educational treatment. Specifically, minority language groups that tend to perform poorly under conditions of a home–school language switch appear to be characterized by ambivalence towards both their own culture and the majority culture. However, considerably more research is required to explicate the interactions between educational treatments, students' input CALP, and the sociocultural characteristics of the community.

What are the implications of this analysis for Burt and Dulay's (1980) suggestion that 'English superior' LEP students should not enter bilingual education programs? First, it is clearly an unproven assumption with no empirical support; second, insofar as it is based on the linguistic mismatch hypothesis, its theoretical assumptions are invalid; third, the focus only on surface manifestations of language ignores the sociocultural determinants of minority children's school failure. The evidence for these sociocultural determinants is considerably stronger than for linguistic factors *per se,* although the specific ways in which they translate into educational failure are as yet inadequately understood. However, perhaps the most pertinent point is that there is no evidence that 'English-superior' LEP students have fared any better in English-only programs, in the era prior to bilingual education, than have other groups of Hispanic and Native minority children. Thus, Burt and Dulay's recommendation amounts to backing a horse with a dismal track record without any logical or valid reason for doing so.

The exit fallacy

The 'exit fallacy' consists in the assumption that mainstreaming minority children out of a bilingual program into an English-only program will promote the development of English literacy skills more effectively than if children were maintained in a bilingual program. This fallacious assumption is deeply ingrained in the thinking of policy makers. For example, Mazzone (1980) noted that legislators in Massachusetts were concerned that the reason Spanish and Portuguese background children were found, in a recent survey, to be between 9 and 14 percentage points below native English-speakers on reading and mathematics tests, was because they may have been kept too long in transitional bilingual programs. However, data showed that this was not the case since a large majority had been in bilingual programs for three years or less. In fact, it was more likely that children were transferred too early, since it was found that children made more rapid academic progress in the bilingual program than out of it.

The assumption that children must be mainstreamed 'in order to learn English' is essentially a rejection of the counter-intuitive 'Less Equals More' rationale of bilingual education, i.e. less English instruction leads to greater achievement in English. Those who argue for English-only programs and for quick-exit from bilingual programs implicitly assume the validity of a *Separate Underlying Proficiency* (SUP) model of bilingual proficiency. The SUP model illustrated in Figure 5 involves the misconception that a bilingual's two 'balloons' or sets of linguistic abilities are separate. Therefore, stimulation of one implies that the other is not being stimulated and will consequently decline in relation to the language ability of unilingual speakers of that language. In other words, a direct link is assumed between amount of exposure to English in school (and home) and achievement in English literacy. It follows that instruction in L1 will result in lower levels of English proficiency than instruction in English.

An example will illustrate how the 'common-sense' assumptions of the SUP model get expressed at a policy level. The example is taken from Bethell's (1979) article, 'Against Bilingual Education: Why Johnny Can't Speak English' where he approvingly quotes congressman John Ashbrook's opposition to bilingual education:

> The program is actually preventing children from learning English. Someday, somebody is going to have to teach those young people to speak English or else they are going to become public charges. Our educational system is finding it increasingly difficult today to teach English-speaking children to read their own language. When children come out of the Spanish-language schools or Choctaw-language schools which call themselves bilingual, how is our educational system going to make them literate in what will still be a completely alien tongue …? (1979: 32–3)

These 'common-sense' assumptions of the SUP model are widely believed at all levels of the educational hierarchy, despite the fact that they are patently false. Among the hundreds of evaluations of bilingual programs for both minority and majority language children carried out all over the world during the past 20 years, I know of *none* which provides any support for such a model. As pointed

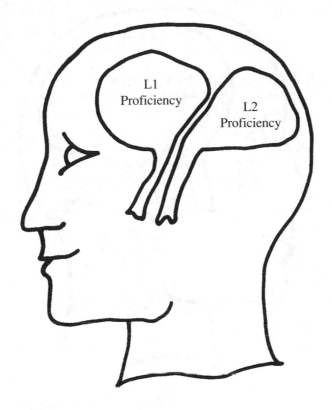

Figure 5 The *Separate Underlying Proficiency* (SUP) model of bilingualism

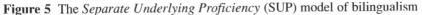

out earlier, the pattern of results revealed in a large majority of these evaluations is one where there is a significant relationship between amount of instructional time through the minority language and achievement in the minority language, but no relationship between amount of instructional time through the majority language and achievement in that language.

It is thus necessary to reject the SUP model for a *Common Underlying Proficiency* (CUP) model of bilingualism in which the cognitive/academic proficiencies underlying literacy skills in L1 and L2 are assumed to be interdependent. This model is illustrated in Figure 6.

The essential characteristics of the CUP model have been outlined earlier in considering the interdependence hypothesis.[3] Briefly, in the CUP model experience with either language can, theoretically, promote the development of the proficiency underlying both languages, given adequate motivation and exposure to both, either in school or wider environment.

The problems in the psychoeducational rationale underlying the quick-exit policy in transitional programs can be illustrated with reference to the SUP and

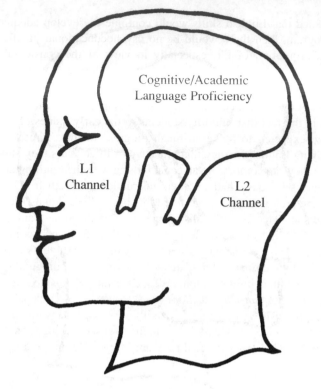

Figure 6 The *Common Underlying Proficiency* (CUP) model of bilingualism

CUP models. These problems derive from both logical inconsistency and contrary empirical evidence.

Internal logic of the transitional rationale

On the one hand, transitional programs assume that bilingual instruction in the
early grades will be *more* effective in raising the level of *English* proficiency of
LEP and NEP students than instruction only through the medium of English. In
other words, *less* time through the medium of English will result in *greater*
development of the English language skills underlying literacy. In terms of Figure
5, the assumption is that inflating the L1 balloon will simultaneously succeed in
inflating the L2 balloon *to a greater extent* than if attempts were made to inflate
only the L2 balloon. In other words, in the initial grades the SUP model is
rejected in favor of the CUP model. However, despite the implicit endorsement
of a CUP model in the early grades, transitional programs revert to a SUP model
by assuming (without any evidence) that children's English skills will not
develop adequately unless they are mainstreamed to an English-only program. If

it were assumed that English skills would continue to develop adequately in a bilingual program, then there would be no psychoeducational justification for aborting the promotion of L1, especially in view of the considerable funds currently being expended in the United States on foreign language teaching (President's Commission, 1979).

The extent of the logical contradiction involved in the mainstreaming process can be seen in the fact that minority students in the early grades of transitional programs are expected to make so much progress in the cognitive/academic skills underlying English literacy that after two or three years they should be at a level where they can compete on an equal footing with their unilingual English-speaking peers who have had all their instruction in English. The findings reviewed in the present paper suggest that this basic 'Less Equals More' expectation is realistic; what is not realistic, however, is the time frame. The data suggest that 'equality' of academic potential and performance is not attained until the later grades of elementary school. Many minority students will be fluent in English prior to that time and may qualify to exit from a bilingual program on the basis of a 'natural communication' task such as the *Bilingual Syntax Measure* or the *Basic Inventory of Natural Language*. However, as emphasized earlier, fluency in English BICS does not necessarily imply commensurate proficiency in English CALP. The evidence reviewed in the next section suggests that rate of growth in English CALP in bilingual programs accelerates in the later grades of elementary school.

Cumulative benefits

A considerable body of recent evidence, again from both minority and majority situations, suggests that in its effort to avoid the taint of cultural pluralism, transitional bilingual education may also deny minority children the opportunity to reap the educational benefits of their bilingualism. As outlined above, there is no logical psychoeducational reason to assume that bilingual instruction will be any less effective in promoting the cognitive/academic proficiency underlying English literacy in the later grades of elementary school than it is assumed by transitional programs to be in the early grades. In fact, as Troike (1979) points out, several longitudinal evaluations (Gonzalez, 1977; Leyba, 1978; Rosier & Farella, 1976) suggest that the full benefit of bilingual instruction may not become apparent until the fifth or sixth year of instruction. In these evaluations, students in the bilingual program reached national grade-level norms in English reading only in the fifth grade. As outlined earlier, the Sodertalje program for Finnish immigrant children in Sweden (Hanson, 1979) showed a similar pattern of cumulative growth in L2 proficiency.

Several 'enrichment' bilingual programs for majority language children also show a trend for achievement gains in majority language literacy skills to become apparent in the later grades of elementary school. For example, students in French immersion programs in Ontario have consistently performed significantly better than comparison groups in aspects of English language skills in grades 5 and 6 (see Swain, 1978). Recent findings from the longitudinal evaluation of a Ukrainian–English bilingual program in Edmonton, Alberta, also show that the bilingual students in grade 5 perform significantly better than the comparison group in English reading comprehension skills despite 50% less instructional time through the medium of English. In previous grades no significant group differences were observed in English language skills (Edmonton Public School Board, 1979).

These findings of cumulative advantages as a result of bilingual education are consistent with the 'threshold' hypothesis (Cummins, 1979a) that there may be threshold levels of bilingual proficiency which bilingual children must attain both in order to avoid cognitive/academic deficits and to allow the potentially beneficial aspects of becoming bilingual to influence their cognitive/academic growth. The research findings reviewed by Cummins (1979a) and by Duncan and DeAvila (1979) suggest that cognitive/academic benefits accrue to students who reach a 'higher threshold' level of bilingual proficiency, i.e. high levels of proficiency in both languages. The fact that students in bilingual programs begin to pull ahead of comparison groups in the later grades of elementary school, when literacy skills in both languages have become well-established, is clearly consistent with the threshold hypothesis.

Conclusion

1 have argued that the empirical data support two theoretical positions:

(1) CALP becomes differentiated and can be empirically distinguished from BICS in both L1 and L2.

(2) L1 and L2 CALP are interdependent – i.e. manifestations of the same under-lying dimension.

These theoretical positions have the following implications for bilingual education in the United States:

(1) *Placement* of bilingual children in different types of instructional programs should *not* be based only on 'natural communication' (BICS) tasks. Develop-mental level of L1 and L2 CALP should also be taken into account.

(2) The linguistic mismatch hypothesis provides an inadequate theoretical basis for determining *entry criteria* for bilingual programs because (a) it focuses only on obvious surface differences between L1 and L2 and ignores CALP; (b) it ignores the sociocultural determinants of minority children's poor aca-demic performance.

(3) The *'quick exit' policy* in transitional bilingual programs (a) is logically inconsistent with the initial assumption of such programs that LEP or NEP children will make more rapid academic progress in English skills in a bilingual rather than an English-only program; (b) is contrary to empirical

research showing that minority children in bilingual programs tend to reach grade norms in English reading only in the later grades of elementary school. This pattern of cumulative benefits of bilingual instruction is what would be predicted on the basis of the threshold hypothesis (Cummins, 1979a).

A prediction that follows from the present theory is that children mainstreamed to English-only programs on the basis of adequate attainment on measures of either Ll or L2 CALP will fare better academically than children mainstreamed only on the basis of adequate attainment on measures of L2 BICS. To establish precisely what constitutes 'adequate' or 'threshold' levels of Ll or L2 CALP in criterion-referenced terms for different grade levels is an important task for future research.

Notes

1. This paper was originally given as a keynote address at the Workshop on 'Comparative Review of Identified District Continua' sponsored by the National Origin Desegregation LAU Center, San Diego State University in coordination with the Bilingual Education Service Center, San Diego State University at the 9th Annual Bilingual Bicultural Education Conference (NABE), Anaheim, California, April, 1980.
2. Shuy's use of the iceberg metaphor is principally to illustrate the fact that the visible features of language which are assessed by most tests are not necessarily those that are most critical. He suggests that the less visible dimensions of semantic and functional meaning are critical for language functioning but are seldom assessed. The emphasis in the present paper is clearly different from Shuy's, but the two approaches are compatible if CALP is viewed as one aspect of semantic and functional meaning.
3. The CUP model illustrated in Figure 6 embodies the same assumptions as the 'dual-iceberg' model in Figure 4. The two illustrations, however, permit different aspects to be highlighted. Specifically, the dual-iceberg model illustrates the distinction between surface and underlying dimensions of language proficiency, whereas the CUP model allows the instructional component to be illustrated by means of the 'balloon-inflation' metaphor.

References

Bethell, T. (1979) Against bilingual education. *Harper's,* February.

Bowen, J. D. (1977) Linguistic perspectives on bilingual education. In B. Spolsky and R. Cooper (eds) *Frontiers of Bilingual Education.* Rowley, MA: Newbury House.

Bruck, M. (1978) The suitability of early French immersion programs for the language-disabled child. *Canadian Journal of Education* 3, 51–72.

Burt, M. and Dulay, H. (1978) Some guidelines for the assessment of oral language proficiency and dominance. *TESOL Quarterly* 12, 177–92.

Burt, M. and Dulay, H. (1980) Relative proficiency of limited English-proficient students. In J. E. Alatis (ed.) *31st Annual Georgetown University Round Table on Languages and Linguistics.* Washington, DC: Georgetown University Press.

Canale, M. and Swain, M. (1980) Theoretical bases of communicative approaches to second language teaching and testing. *Applied Linguistics* 1, 1–47.

Carey, S. T. and Cummins, J. (1979) English and French achievement of grade 5 children from English, French and mixed French–English home backgrounds attending the Edmonton Separate School System English–French immersion program. Report submitted to the Edmonton Separate School System, April.

Carroll, J. B. and Sapon, S. M. (1959) *Modern Language Aptitude Test*. New York: Psychological Corporation.

Chomsky, N. (1965) *Aspects of the Theory of Syntax*. Cambridge, MA: MIT Press.

Cohen, A. D. and Swain, M. (1976) Bilingual education: The immersion model in the North American context. *TESOL Quarterly* 10, 45–53.

Cummins, J. (1977a) Immersion education in Ireland: A critical review of Macnamara's findings. *Working Papers in Bilingualism* No. 13.

Cummins, J. (1977b) A comparison of reading achievement in Irish and English medium schools. In V. Greaney (ed.) *Studies in Reading*. Dublin: Educational Co. of Ireland.

Cummins, J. (1978) Immersion programs: The Irish experience. *International Review of Education* 24, 273–82.

Cummins, J. (1979a) Linguistic interdependence and the educational development of bilingual children. *Review of Educational Research* 49, 222–51.

Cummins, J. (1979b) Cognitive/academic language proficiency, linguistic interdependence, the optimal age question and some other matters. *Working Papers in Bilingualism* No. 19.

Cummins, J. (1980a) The language and culture issue in the education of minority language children. *Interchange* 10, 72–88.

Cummins, J. (1980b) Psychological assessment of immigrant children: Logic or intuition? *Journal of Multilingual and Multicultural Development* 1, 97–111.

Cummins, J. (1980c) Age on arrival and immigrant second language learning: A reanalysis of the Ramsey and Wright data. Unpublished manuscript, Ontario Institute for Studies in Education.

Cummins, J. (1980d) The cross-lingual dimensions of language proficiency: Implications for bilingual education and the optimal age question. *TESOL Quarterly* 14, 175–87.

Danoff, M. N. (1978) Evaluation of the impact of ESEA Title VII Spanish/English bilingual education program: Overview of study and findings. Palo Alto: American Institutes for Research.

DeAvila, E. A. and Duncan, S. E. (1978) A few thoughts about language assessment: The LAU decision reconsidered. *Bilingual Education Paper Series*, National Dissemination and Assessment Center, Vol. 1, No. 8.

Dieterich, T. G., Freeman, C. and Crandall, J. A. (1979) A linguistic analysis of some English proficiency tests. *TESOL Quarterly* 13, 535–50.

Downing, J. (1978) Strategies of bilingual teaching. *International Review of Education* 329–46.

Downing J. (1979) Cognitive clarity and linguistic awareness. Paper presented at the International Seminar on Linguistic Awareness and Learning to Read, Victoria, Canada.

Duncan, S. E. and DeAvila, E. A. (1979) Bilingualism and cognition: Some recent findings. *NABE Journal* 4, 15–50.

Edmonton Public School Board (1979) Evaluation of the Bilingual (English–Ukrainian) Program, Fifth Year. Research Report.

Ekstrand, L. H. (1978) Bilingual and bicultural adaptation. Doctoral dissertation, University of Stockholm.

Engle, P. L. (1975) Language medium in early school years for minority language groups. *Review of Educational Research* 65, 283–325.

Epstein, N. (1977) *Language, Ethnicity and the Schools*. Washington, DC: Institute for Educational Leadership.

Farhady, H. (1979) The disjunctive fallacy between discrete-point and integrative tests. *TESOL Quarterly* 13, 347–58.

Gaarder, A. B. (1977) *Bilingual Schooling and the Survival of Spanish in the United States*. Rowley, MA: Newbury House.

Garcia de Lorenzo, M. E. (1975) Frontier dialect: A challenge to education. *Reading Teacher* 28, 563–658.

Genesee, F. (1976) The role of intelligence in second language learning. *Language Learning* 26, 267–80.

Genesee, F. (1978) Is there an optimal age for starting second language instruction? *McGill Journal of Education* 13, 145–54.

Genesee, F. (1979) Acquisition of reading skills in immersion programs. *Foreign Language Annals,* February.

Gonzalez, G. A. (1977) Brownsville Independent School District Bilingual Education Program Title VII – Final Report for 1976–77. Brownsville, TX.

Goodman, K., Goodman, Y. and Flores, B. (1979) *Reading in the Bilingual Classroom: Literacy and Biliteracy.* Rosslyn, VA: National Clearinghouse for Bilingual Education.

Halliday, M. A .K. (1975) *Learning How to Mean.* London: Edward Arnold.

Hanson, G. (1979) The position of the second generation of Finnish immigrants in Sweden: The importance of education in the home language to the welfare of second generation immigrants. Paper presented at symposium on the position of the second generation of Yugoslav immigrants in Sweden, Split, October.

Hébert, R. *et al.* (1976) *Rendement Académique et Langue d'Enseignement chez les Élèves Franco-manitobains.* Saint-Boniface, Manitoba: Centre de recherches du College Universitaire de Saint-Boniface.

Hernandez-Chavez, E., Burt, M. and Dulay, H. (1978) Language dominance and proficiency testing: Some general considerations. *NABE Journal* 3, 41–54.

Heyman, A. (1973) *Invandrarbarn: Slutrapport.* Stockholm: Stockholms Invandrarnamd.

Krashen, S. D. 1978. The monitor model for second-language acquisition. In R. C. Gingras (ed.) *Second-Language Acquisition and Foreign Language Teaching.* Arlington: CAL.

Krashen, S. D., Long, M. A. and Scarcella, R. C. (1979) Age, rate and eventual attainment in second language acquisition. *TESOL Quarterly* 13, 573–82.

Lambert, W. E. and Tucker, G. R. (1972) *Bilingual Education of Children: The St. Lambert Experiment.* Rowley, MA: Newbury House.

Legaretta, D. (1979) The effects of program models on language acquisition by Spanish speaking children. *TESOL Quarterly* 13, 521–34.

Leyba, C. F. (1978) Longitudinal study title VII bilingual program Santa Fe Public Schools, Santa Fe, New Mexico. National Dissemination and Assessment Center, California State University, Los Angeles.

Macnamara, J. (1966) *Bilingualism and Primary Education.* Edinburgh: Edinburgh University Press.

Mazzone, E. (1980) Current trends in the assessment of language minority students in Massachusetts. In J. E. Alatis (ed.) *31st Annual Georgetown University Round Table on Languages and Linguistics.* Washington, DC: Georgetown University Press.

Modiano, N. (1968) National or mother tongue language in beginning reading: A comparative study. *Research in the Teaching of English* 2, 32–43.

Oakland, T. (1977) *Psychological and Educational Assessment of Minority Children.* New York: Brunner/Mazel.

Oller, J. W. (1978) The language factor in the evaluation of bilingual education. In J. E. Alatis (ed.) *Georgetown University Round Table on Languages and Linguistics.* Washington, DC: Georgetown University Press.

Oller, J. W. (1979) *Language Tests at School: A Pragmatic Approach.* New York: Longman.

Oller, J. W. Jr (1980) A language factor deeper than speech: More data and theory for bilingual assessment. In J. E. Alatis (ed.) *Current Issues in Bilingual Education* (Georgetown University Round Table on Languages and Linguistics, 1980) (pp. 14–30). Washington, DC: Georgetown University Press.

Oller, J. W. and Perkins, K. (1978) *Language in Education: Testing the Tests.* Rowley, MA: Newbury House.

Olson, D. R. (1977) The formalization of linguistic rules. In J. Macnamara (ed.) *Language Learning and Thought.* New York: Academic Press.

Overall, P. T. 1978. An assessment of the communicative competence in English of Spanish-speaking children in the fourth and sixth grades. Doctoral dissertation, Stanford University.

Perez, E. (1980) Current trends in the assessment of language minority students in Texas. In J. E. Alatis (ed.) *31st Annual Georgetown University Round Table on Languages and Linguistics*. Washington, DC. Georgetown University Press.

Rosansky, E. (1980) Research efforts in the development of multiple indicators of communicative competence and effects of bilingual education. In J. E. Alatis (ed.) *31st Annual Georgetown University Round Table on Languages and Linguistics*. Washington, DC: Georgetown University Press.

Rosier, P. and Farella, M. (1976) Bilingual education at Rock Point – some early results. *TESOL Quarterly* 10, 379–88.

Ryan, E. G. and Ledger, G. W. (1979) Children's awareness of sentence grammaticality. Paper presented to the Annual Meeting of the Psychonomic Society in Phoenix, Arizona.

Shuy, R. W. (1976) Problems in assessing language ability in bilingual education programs (mimeo).

Singer, H. (1977) IQ is and is not related to reading. In S. F. Wanat (ed.) *Issues in Evaluating Reading*. Arlington, VA: Center for Applied Linguistics.

Skutnabb-Kangas, T. and Toukomaa, P. (1976) *Teaching Migrant Children's Mother Tongue and Learning the Language of the Host Country in the Context of the Socio-cultural Situation of the Migrant Family*. Helsinki: The Finnish National Commission for UNESCO.

Smith, F. (1971) *Understanding Reading*. New York: Holt, Rinehart and Winston.

Strang, R. (1945) Variability in reading scores on a given level of intelligence test scores. *Journal of Educational Research* 38, 440–6.

Swain, M. (1978) French immersion: Early, late or partial. *The Canadian Modern Language Review* 34, 577–86.

Swain, M. (1979) Bilingual education: Research and its implications. In C. A. Yorio, K. Perkins and J. Schachter (eds) *On TESOL '79: The Learner in Focus*. Washington, DC: TESOL.

Troike, R. (1978) Research evidence for the effectiveness of bilingual education. *NABE Journal* 3, 13–24.

Troike, R. (1979) Research findings demonstrate the effectiveness of bilingual education. *Institute for Cultural Pluralism Newsletter* 1, 67.

Tucker, G. R. (1977) The linguistic perspective. In *Bilingual Education: Current Perspectives*. Vol. 2: *Linguistics*. Arlington, VA: Center for Applied Linguistics.

UNESCO (1953) *The Use of Vernacular Languages in Education*. Monographs on fundamental education.

Vernon, M. D. (1971) *Reading and its Difficulties*. London: Cambridge University Press.

Wells, G. (1979) Describing children's linguistic development at home and at school. *British Educational Research Journal* 5, 75-89.

Wong Fillmore, L. (1979) Individual differences in second language acquisition. In C. J. Fillmore, D. Kempler and W. S.-Y. Wang (eds) *Individual Differences in Language Ability and Language Behavior*. New York: Academic Press.

Tests, Achievement, and Bilingual Students

> ... The number of aliens deported because of feeble-mindedness ... increased approximately 350 per cent in 1913 and 570 per cent in 1914 ... This was due to the untiring efforts of the physicians who were inspired by the belief that mental tests could be used for the detection of feeble-minded aliens ... (Goddard, 1917)

Most educators would consider that the assumptions underlying the widespread use of ability and achievement tests in our schools are very far removed from the naive assumptions of early practitioners of IQ testing. In contrast to the early assumption that IQ tests measured 'innate potential', most educators today would agree that IQ tests measure 'academic potential', as evidenced by the high correlations between IQ and academic achievement tests, and that performance is determined by both hereditary and environmental factors. They would also readily agree that IQ tests have certain limitations. For example, extreme caution is necessary in assessing the intelligence of students from backgrounds other than the dominant cultural group because of the possibility of cultural or linguistic bias. Labelling such children as 'low IQ' can adversely affect their academic progress because of the way labels tend to shape teachers' expectations.

All of this is 'known' by most teachers, psychologists, and administrators in our school systems because they have learned it in university courses in educational or clinical psychology. However, there is abundant evidence that this 'knowledge' about the dangers of testing culturally and linguistically different students does not readily translate into educational practice and that a disproportionate number of bilingual students are still being 'deported' into special education and vocational classes as a combined result of the indiscriminate use of mental tests and the cultural and linguistic orientation of school programs.

However, during the past decade, US educators have been forced to begin to address the issue of bias in educational programs and tests as a result of court decisions and legislative mandates. Bilingual education is intended to reduce the language barriers to students' achievement while court rulings in California (e.g. *Diana* v. *California State Board of Education*, 1970) have made it mandatory to assess bilingual students in their dominant language, where feasible.

Such changes, although clearly necessary and worthwhile, are as yet only scratching the surface of the problem. Most minority language students are still taught predominantly in English by non-bilingual teachers and most are still assessed by monolingual psychologists with assessment tools and procedures that were designed only for children from the majority Anglo group. Myths about the 'causes' of bilingual students' low achievement still persist (e.g. 'bilingualism gives rise to language handicaps', 'inadequate home experiences lead to low verbal abilities', etc.) and these myths appear to be reinforced by the results of biased educational and psychological assessment procedures. Because of this it is not uncommon to find bilingual teachers who suspect that some of their students may have learning disabilities that might benefit from appropriate diagnosis and remediation but who refuse to send the students for psychological assessment. The teachers know that the students will return with a permanent label and a one-way ticket to a monolingual English special education class.

Court decisions and legislative mandates may eventually force 'compliance', but the only compliance that will have any lasting impact is one that is rooted in sympathy with the intended aims and understanding of the conceptual issues. Although presumably most educators would claim to support the goal of equal educational opportunity, relatively few know enough about the process of second language acquisition and bilingual academic development to translate this support into effective educational practice.

The reason for this is quite simply that research evidence has, until recently, been lacking. In the absence of research, however, educators have naturally tended to revert to 'common sense' as a basis for decision-making. Often the common-sense assumptions that guide (or misguide) educational policy and practice are regarded as self-evident. An example is the assumption of educators, until recently, that schools had to eradicate the first language (L1) of minority students (often by means of physical punishment) in order to help them learn English (L2) and identify with the dominant cultural group. Research carried out in the context of bilingual programs (Cummins, 1981) shows clearly that this assumption is entirely false and served only to create and sustain academic deficits in minority students, thereby 'reproducing the caste of assembly-line workers' (Skutnabb-Kangas, 1978).

A more subtle but equally prevalent misconception concerns the specific issue of how long it takes minority language students to become 'proficient' in English, an issue that is part of the more general question of what it means to 'know' a language. Teachers and psychologists tend to assume that minority language students have 'learned English' or become 'English proficient' when they have acquired peer-appropriate fluency in everyday face-to-face communication (usually within 18 months to two years of exposure to English). Once students have become 'proficient' in English, there appears to be no linguistic reason why they should not be administered an English psychological test or transferred from a bilingual to an English-only program.

The dangers of these implicit assumptions can be illustrated by some concrete examples from a recent study in which the psychological assessments of over 400 minority language students were analyzed (Cummins, 1980).

Three Psychological Assessments

Student LT (225): LT was referred by his second-grade teacher, who noted that he 'appears to be of average intelligence but is only at a primer instructional level'. No mention was made of an English as a second language (ESL) background. On the Wechsler Intelligence Scale for Children – Revised (WISC-R), LT's verbal IQ was 70 and his performance IQ was 102. The verbal subtest scores were: Information 3, Similarities 3, Arithmetic 10, Vocabulary 4, Comprehension 6, Digit Span 13. In other words, the child performed at an average (i.e. score of 10) or above-average level on the two least verbally loaded subtests. The psychologist's report read:

> Psychometric rating as determined by the WISC-R places LT in the low average range of intellectual development. An extreme discrepancy between verbal and performance abilities is indicated. The low verbal ability IQ may be collectively attributed to limited general information fund or long term learning; poor ability to form generalizations or make abstractions; poor verbal expressive abilities and limited meaningful vocabulary in comparison with peers of similar age range; and poor judgement with respect to practical solutions to everyday problems or common sense ...

> With regard to general test behaviour, LT made no attempt to volunteer information or initiate conversation, and tended to require some prodding to make responses ...

Ten days later the following entry appeared in the child's file:

> Telephoned the mother and gave a brief summary of the testing results. [The mother] indicated that Portuguese is normally spoken at home and this would certainly at least partially account for LT's low verbal abilities development.

This example shows how easy it is for psychologists to interpret test scores automatically when they are not sensitized to manifestations of cultural/linguistic differences. After speaking to the child's mother, the psychologist qualifies the previous interpretation of test results. Interestingly, the psychologist persists in using 'deficit semantics' by attributing the child's 'low verbal abilities development' rather than 'present level of cognitive/academic functioning in English' to the use of Portuguese at home.

In this example, the psychologist (and possibly also the teacher) was unaware that the child came from a non-English background (despite some clues in the child's test behavior) and had no hesitation in administering a psychological assessment and interpreting it as though the child were from a monolingual English background. The following example shows that awareness of the child's non-English background does not guarantee any change in test interpretation. A major reason for this is the child's apparent fluency in English.

Student PR (283): PR was referred for psychological assessment because he was experiencing difficulty in the regular first-grade work despite the fact that he was repeating the grade. The principal noted that 'although PR was in Portugal for part (six months) of the year there is a suspicion of real learning disability. WISC testing would be a great help in determining this'. PR's scores on the WISC-R were: verbal IQ, 64; performance IQ, 101; full scale IQ, 80. After noting that 'English is his second language but the teacher feels that the problem is more than one of language', the psychologist continued:

> Psychometric rating, as determined by the WISC-R, places PR in the dull normal range of intellectual development. Assessment reveals performance abilities to be normal while verbal abilities fall in the mentally deficient range. It is recommended that PR be referred for resource room placement for next year and if no progress is evident by Christmas, a Learning Centre placement should be considered.

This assessment illustrates well the abuses to which psychological tests can be put. It does not seem at all unreasonable that a child from a non-English background who has spent six months of the previous year in Portugal should perform very poorly on an English verbal IQ test. Yet, rather than admitting that no conclusions regarding the child's academic potential can be drawn, the psychologist validates the teacher's 'suspicion' of learning disability by means of a 'scientific' assessment and the use of inappropriate terminology ('dull normal', 'mentally deficient'). An interesting aspect of this assessment is the fact that neither the teacher nor the psychologist makes any reference to difficulties in English as a second language and both considered that the child's English proficiency was adequate to perform the test. This again implies no obvious deficiencies in English communicative skills despite a severe lag in English academic proficiency.

These examples (and many more from the same study), as well as both research evidence (e.g. Snow & Hoefnagel-Höhle, 1978) and common observation, show that within about 18 months to two years of starting to acquire a second language, most minority language students are able to function fluently in it for everyday face-to-face situations. As a result of children's fluency, teachers and psychologists tend to assume that language difficulties due to learning English as a second language have been overcome. In other words, the child has learned English and can be classified as 'English proficient'. According to this apparent logic there is thus no reason why such minority language students should not be given a psychological assessment in English or transferred from a bilingual to a regular all-English classroom. If the child then experiences academic difficulties or shows low 'verbal abilities' on an IQ test, this must be due to intrinsic cognitive or motivational deficiencies within the child (e.g. 'learning disabled', 'educable mentally retarded', 'lazy'). These, in turn, can be attributed to the child's deficient background experiences (e.g. 'cultural deprivation', 'bilingualism', etc.). Before examining the fallacies in this logic, it is worth considering another example that illustrates the destructive potential of making children's home language or bilingual proficiency the scapegoat for their 'low academic abilities'.

Student MF (237): MF was referred for psychological assessment by her first-grade teacher, who noted that she had difficulty in all aspects of learning. She was given both speech and hearing and psychological assessments. The former assessment found that all structures and functions pertaining to speech were within normal limits and hearing was also normal. The findings were summarized as follows: 'MF comes from an Italian home where Italian is spoken mainly. However, language skills appeared to be within normal limits for English.'

The psychologist's conclusions, however, were very different. On the Wechsler Preschool and Primary Scale of Intelligence (WPPSI), MF obtained a verbal IQ of 89, a performance IQ of 99, and a full scale IQ of 93. The report to MF's teacher read:

> MF tended to be very slow to respond to questions, particularly if she were unsure of the answers. Her spoken English was a little hard to understand, which is probably due to poor English models at home (speech is within normal limits). Italian is spoken almost exclusively at home, and this will be further complicated by the coming arrival of an aunt and grandmother from Italy.

> There is little doubt that MF is a child of low average ability whose school progress is impeded by lack of practice in English. Encourage MF's oral participation as much as possible, and try to involve MF in extracurricular activities where she will be with her English-speaking peers.

Despite the fact that the speech assessment revealed no deficiencies in MF's spoken English, the psychologist has no hesitation ('there is little doubt ...') in attributing MF's academic problems to the use of Italian in the home. The implicit message to the teacher is clear: MF's communication in L1 with parents and relatives detracts from her school performance, and the aim of the school program should be to expose MF to as much L2 as possible in order to compensate for these deficient linguistic and cultural background experiences. It is likely that in reporting the results of this psychological assessment to MF's parents, the psychologist or teacher would encourage them (and presumably the soon-to-arrive aunt and grandmother) to use more English with MF, in which case the child would, in all likelihood, be exposed to poor English models in the home as well as to a considerably impoverished linguistic environment.

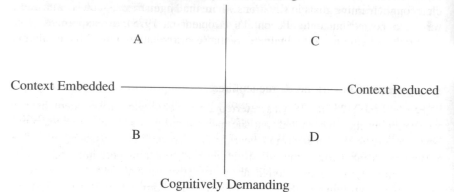

Figure 1 Range of contextual support and degree of cognitive involvement in communicative activities

Research Evidence: Language Proficiency and Academic Achievement

The major misconceptions about the nature of language proficiency illustrated in the psychological assessments considered above are very much in evidence in the education of minority language students in the United States. These misconceptions reflect a failure to recognize the crucial differences between the 'language proficiency' involved in face-to-face communication and that involved in most academic tasks, and the considerably greater time required to attain age-appropriate levels of academic skills in a second language as compared with face-to-face communicative skills. The research evidence relating to these misconceptions has been considered in detail elsewhere (Cummins, 1980, 1981) and will be reviewed here only briefly.

There is clear evidence that not all aspects of language proficiency are related to academic achievement, whether in a monolingual or bilingual context. For example, most children classified as learning disabled have no ostensible abnormalities in face-to-face communicative skills. Also, it has been found that L1 cognitive/academic proficiency is more strongly related to the acquisition of L2 academic skills than are personality factors, whereas the opposite is true for the acquisition of L2 face-to-face communicative skills (Cummins, Swain *et al.*, 1981).

The relationship between language proficiency and academic achievement has been described in terms of two continua as illustrated in Figure 1. The distinction between context-embedded and context-reduced language proficiency relates to the range of contextual support for expressing or receiving meaning.

Context-embedded language proficiency refers to students' ability to achieve their communicative goals in situations where the linguistic message is embedded within 'a flow of meaningful context' (Donaldson, 1978), i.e. supported by a wide range of situational and paralinguistic (e.g. intonation, gestures, etc.) cues. Context-reduced proficiency, on the other hand, refers to students' ability to handle the communicative demands of situations where the range of extralinguistic supports is very much reduced (e.g. reading a difficult text, writing an essay). Clearly, context-embedded communication is more typical of the everyday world outside the classroom, whereas many of the linguistic demands of the classroom reflect communication that is closer to the context-reduced end of the continuum. For example, sharing a communication partner (i.e. the teacher) with 30 other students is more context reduced than a one-to-one, face-to-face situation. The crucial implication is that acquisition of meaning in context-reduced classroom situations requires more knowledge of the language itself than is typically required in context-embedded face-to-face situations.

The vertical continuum relates to the degree of active cognitive involvement in the task or activity; in other words, to the amount of information that must be processed simultaneously or in close succession by the individual in order to carry out the communicative activity. As language skills are progressively mastered or automatized they become less cognitively demanding. It is clear that some language subskills are mastered more rapidly than others (e.g. pronunciation and syntax in L1). In fact, for many L1 context-reduced (e.g. reading, writing) and context-embedded (e.g. oratory) skills it is not appropriate to speak of mastery, but rather degrees of proficiency, since considerable differences among individuals persist throughout adulthood.

What are the implications of this framework for bilingual education and psychological assessment? Many minority language students acquire certain context-embedded English skills and become almost indistinguishable from native speakers in face-to-face situations within a relatively short period. In other words, they quickly acquire quadrant A communicative skills. However, this does not imply that such students have sufficient proficiency in context-reduced (quadrant D) aspects of English to survive academically in an all-English class on an equal footing with native speakers of English. In fact, data from studies of immigrant students' learning of English (Cummins, 1980, 1981) and from successful bilingual programs show that it takes approximately from five to seven years, on the average, for minority language students to approach grade norms in academic (context-reduced) aspects of English proficiency. As shown in Figure 2, a major reason for this is that native English-speaking students are not standing still waiting for minority language students to catch up with them (compare, for example, the vocabulary and conceptual knowledge of monolingual 14-year-old and six-year-old children). By contrast, differences between 14-year-old and six-year-old children are less salient in face-to-face situations.

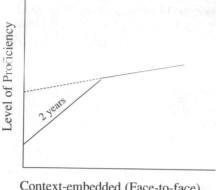
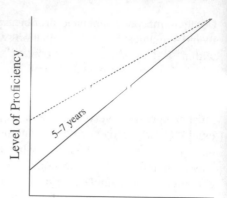

Context-embedded (Face-to-face)   Context-reduced (Academic)
Communicative Proficiency   Communicative Proficiency

------------------ Native English speakers
                                       (From *NABE Journal* 5, No. 3: 35, used by
——————————— ESL learners   permission)

Figure 2 Length of time required to achieve age-appropriate levels of context-embedded and context-reduced communicative proficiency

In summary, educators risk creating academic deficits in minority language students by extrapolating from the considerable English proficiency that these students display in context-embedded face-to-face communication to their ability to handle the context-reduced communicative demands of an all-English classroom or an English psychological test. The implicit identification of adequate surface structure control with 'English proficiency' leads teachers to eliminate 'lack of English proficiency' as an explanatory variable. As a result, low academic performance or test scores among minority language students are attributed to deficiencies in the student or in his or her background experiences. In this way the process of 'blaming the victim', which has characterized the 'education' of minority language children in North America throughout this century, is perpetuated.

References

Cummins, J. (1980) Psychological assessment of immigrant children: Logic or intuition? *Journal of Multilingual and Multicultural Development* 1, 97–111.
Cummins, J. (1981) The role of primary language development in promoting educational success for language minority students. In *Schooling and Language Minority Students: A Theoretical Framework.* Compiled by the California State Department of Education, Los Angeles, National Dissemination and Assessment Center.
Cummins, J., Swain, M., Nakajima, K., Handscombe, J., Green, D. and Tran, C. (1981) Linguistic interdependence in Japanese and Vietnamese immigrant students. Research report submitted to InterAmerica Research Associates, Inc., Rosslyn, VA. October.

Donaldson, M. (1978) *Children's Minds*. Glasgow: Collins.

Goddard, H. H. (1917) Mental tests and the immigrant. *Journal of Delinquency* 2, 271.

Skutnabb-Kangas, T. (1978) Semilingualism and the education of migrant children as a means of reproducing the caste of assembly line workers. In N. Dittmar, H. Haberland, T. Skutnabb-Kangas and U. Teleman (eds) *Papers from the First Scandinavian–German Symposium on the Language of Immigrant Workers and their Children*. Roskilde, Denmark: Roligpapir.

Snow, C. E. and Hoefnagel-Höhle, M. (1978) The critical period of language acquisition: Evidence from second language learning. *Child Development* 49, 1114–28.

Learning Difficulties in 'Immersion' Programmes

In the previous chapter* it was pointed out that it was necessary to posit a 'common underlying proficiency' to account for the transfer of academic skills across languages which is invariably observed in bilingual programmes for both minority and majority students. The most common form of bilingual education for majority students has been termed 'immersion' in that students are immersed in a second language classroom, initially with little or no instruction through their first language. These programmes may begin at any grade level, the most frequent being kindergarten, grades 4 or 5 and grade 7 or 8 (respectively termed early, intermediate and late immersion). As briefly described in previous chapters*, the large number of French immersion programmes implemented across Canada have been highly successful; students achieve high levels of proficiency in French at no long-term cost to English or other academic skills (see Swain & Lapkin, 1982; California State Department of Education, 1984 for comprehensive reviews).

However, despite the consistency and apparently straightforward nature of the evaluation results, immersion programmes have given rise to considerable controversy in both the United States and Canada. In the United States the issue concerns the implications of immersion programmes for minority students; specifically, it has been suggested (Baker & de Kanter, 1981; Epstein, 1977) that the success of initial instruction through L2 refutes the usual rationale for bilingual education, namely, that home–school linguistic mismatch causes academic retardation. On the basis of the Canadian data, many US politicians and educational administrators have endorsed 'English immersion' (i.e. a monolingual English programme) as the appropriate response to minority students' underachievement.

In Canada, the spread of French immersion has aroused hostility among some teachers and sectors of the community who feel threatened for a variety of reasons (e.g. teacher job security, availability and quality of monolingual English programmes in neighbourhood schools). The predominantly middle-class composition of the student population in immersion has also given rise to accusations of élitism (see e.g. Burns & Olson, 1981). However, the most relevant issue in the present context concerns the suitability of immersion programmes for all students; in other words, are there any unique individual factors at work in determining success and failure in French immersion such that some students experience learning difficulties in immersion who would not have done so in a regular English programme?

Although the contexts are very different, the issues in the United States and Canada are similar insofar as both concern the conditions under which immersion in a second language is associated with academic success or failure. The obvious difference, of course, is that in the Canadian context the students are predominantly of English language background and the major language of instruction (French) is the minority language of the society; in the United States, on the other hand, the issue under debate is the appropriacy of immersing students from minority language backgrounds in programmes conducted exclusively through English, the majority language. It should be noted that there are also L2 immersion programmes (in Spanish, French and German) for English-background students in the United States, although on a much more limited scale than in Canada.

The controversy in the United States about the relative effectiveness of 'immersion' versus 'bilingual education' programmes for underachieving minority students derives from two main sources: (1) faulty assumptions on both sides of the debate about the causes of minority student underachievement; (2) misunderstanding about what exactly an immersion programme entails.

As discussed in previous chapters*, policy in the United States in relation to minority language students has tended to ignore the societal context and focus on the issue of linguistic mismatch or home–school language switching as the major cause of students' academic difficulties. The adequacy of this assumption is refuted by a considerable amount of data, among which is the success of L2 immersion programmes for majority students. However, advocates of immersion programmes also typically ignore the societal context and base their case on an equally untenable 'maximum exposure' or 'separate underlying proficiency' assumption. Also, their conception of immersion usually bears very little resemblance to the successful Canadian model.[1]

In order to clarify some of the issues concerning the appropriacy of 'immersion' programmes under different societal conditions, the distinction between 'immersion' and 'submersion' will first be considered; then three central components of the Canadian early immersion model will be outlined, and finally, the extent to which a variety of programmes labelled 'immersion' in the US context incorporate these components will be examined. The second part of the chapter will examine some of the individual variables that might determine the extent to which immersion programmes are suitable for all students.

'Immersion' for Minority Students Academically at Risk

Immersion and submersion

In considering the implications of Canadian immersion programmes for the education of minority students, Cohen and Swain (1976) contrasted the immersion methodology with what they termed 'submersion'. Submersion refers to the 'sink or swim' approach where no adjustments are made in the school pro- gramme to take account of the minority child's cultural and linguistic difference; in other words, the instructional approach that has characterized the education of minority students throughout most of this century.

Cohen & Swain point out that in immersion programmes all students start the programme with little or no competence in the school language and are praised for any use they make of that language. Children in submersion programmes, on the other hand, are mixed together with students whose L1 is that of the school and their lack of proficiency in the school language is often treated as a sign of limited intellectual and academic ability. Children in submersion programmes may often become frustrated because of difficulties in communicating with the teacher. These difficulties can arise both because the teacher is unlikely to under- stand the child's L1 and also because of different culturally-determined expecta- tions of appropriate behaviour. In contrast, the immersion teacher is familiar with children's language and cultural background and can therefore respond appro- priately to their needs. The immersion child's L1 is never denigrated by the teacher and its importance is recognized by the fact that it is introduced as a school subject after several grades. The L1 of minority language children, on the other hand, is often viewed as the cause of academic difficulties and an impedi- ment to the learning of L2. Consequently, those aspects of children's identity which are associated with the L1 and home culture are seldom reinforced by the school.

In general, what is communicated to children in immersion programmes is their success, whereas in submersion programmes children are often made to feel acutely aware of their failure. Thus, as Swain (1979) points out, despite their superficial similarity, immersion and submersion programmes are clearly differ- ent programmes and it is not surprising that they lead to different results.

Defining characteristics of an immersion programme

What many policy-makers and media commentators appear to understand by the term 'immersion' is some form of 'high-intensity' monolingual English pro- gramme which would simultaneously 'Americanize' minority students while teaching them English; in other words, a programme not very far removed from submersion but with the possible addition of an ESL component. Other com- mentators and educators are more sophisticated in realizing that 'immersion' involves special pedagogical adjustments designed to provide students with what Krashen (1982) has termed 'comprehensible input' in the L2; however, the pro- gramme is still conceived as a monolingual English programme and often proposed as an alternative to bilingual education (e.g. Baker & de Kanter, 1981).

Advocates of both these forms of 'immersion' invoke the Canadian pro- gramme evaluations as evidence of the appropriacy of immersion for minority students. However, in so doing they reveal a very superficial understanding of what the Canadian programmes involve. Three major components of the Canadian early immersion model can be distinguished:

(1) Bilingual teachers who are proficient in both the child's L1 and the language of instruction.

(2) Meaning communicated initially by means of extensive use of paralinguistic cues (e.g. intonation, gestures, etc.), concrete context and linguistic redundancy and repetition. This 'fine-tuning' of L2 instruction to make it comprehensible is facilitated by homogeneous grouping, although this is not necessarily essential.

(3) In order to ensure an additive form of bilingualism and biliteracy, L1 instruction is increasingly emphasized in early immersion over the course of elementary school such that about half the instruction is through L1 by grade 5 or 6.

It is clear that, transposed into a minority context, this form of 'genuine immersion' programme would entail considerably more emphasis on developing L1 literacy skills than do typical transitional bilingual programmes in the United States which attempt to 'exit' the child from the bilingual programme as rapidly as possible. In light of the analysis of minority student underachievement presented in previous chapters*, there appears to be little reason why such a 'genuine immersion' programme might not be successful. However, the relevance of sociocultural variables associated with student ambivalence *vis-à-vis* L1 and L2 suggests that there should be an L1 component from the beginning of the programme. This is not necessary in the majority context because the child's identity is not under threat.

It is possible to distinguish four distinct programmes designed for minority students that have been labelled as 'immersion' and whose advocates draw on the Canadian data for empirical support. These are examined in the next section in terms of the three defining characteristics of immersion programmes as implemented in Canada.

Four types of 'immersion' programme for minority students

The four major types of 'immersion' programme that have been implemented for minority students in the United States represent a continuum in terms of adjustment made to the child's non-English cultural and linguistic background. At one end of the continuum *submersion* programmes, representing virtually no concessions to the child's language or culture, have well-documented negative results for many minority students. None of the defining characteristics of genuine immersion programmes form a part of submersion programmes.

Next come '*monolingual immersion*' programmes which take account of the need to provide minority students with modified L2 input (characteristic no. 2) but which dispense with bilingual teachers and L1 literacy promotion. Little systematic observation has been made of the effects of monolingual immersion.

However, such a programme might be appropriate under certain conditions; for example, in classes with a large number of languages represented, it might not be feasible to actively promote L1 literacy because of the lack of teachers or instructional aides fluent in children's languages. Also, for minority children who do not appear to be academically at risk, a monolingual immersion programme might be effective in developing English fluency.

It is worth noting, however, that even for minority students who are not academically at risk, there is evidence that bilingual programmes produce somewhat better academic results than do monolingual English programmes. This is illustrated by the Southwest Educational Development Laboratory study of 112 grades 4–6 Chinese-background students in Seattle, Washington (Hoover, 1983; Cummins, 1983a). It was found that students whose initial schooling was in the United States tended to perform somewhat above-average (roughly 50–60th percentile) in English reading and considerably above-average (80th percentile) in mathematics, regardless of whether they experienced bilingual or monolingual English schooling. Thus, lack of or minimal bilingual education did not result in academic deficits. However, regression analyses revealed that the amount of Chinese–English bilingual instruction students received was significantly related to how well they performed in English reading. The trends in the data can be seen in students' scored on the Interactive Reading Assessment Scales (IRAS) (Calfee & Calfee, 1981); students who received only 0–2 semesters of Chinese–English bilingual instruction scored 6.2 on the IRAS whereas those who received 8 semesters scored 7.5 (these figures are roughly similar to grade equivalent scores). In short, the fact that some groups of minority students survive academically in monolingual immersion or submersion programmes does not mean that these are necessarily the most appropriate programmes for these students.

For minority students who are academically at risk, a monolingual immersion programme is unlikely to significantly reverse the pattern of underachievement because it responds only partially to the causes of that underachievement. Although, as outlined in the previous chapter*, it is not possible to specify precisely the interactions between different factors in determining minority student underachievement, there is considerable evidence that academic progress is facilitated by means of programmes that strongly reinforce students' cultural identity and promote L1 language and literacy development. The Carpinteria evaluation, for example, suggested the importance of a strong L1 component both in providing children with a cognitive/academic foundation to make L2 academic input comprehensible and in facilitating parental involvement in their children's development.

In monolingual immersion programmes a subtractive form of bilingualism is likely to develop because of the lower status of students' L1 and the lack of exposure to L1 literacy experiences. In other words, the conditions for linguistic interdependence or transfer across languages are met to a much lesser extent in monolingual immersion than in programmes where the *minority* language is used for instruction.

In summary, although undoubtedly less inappropriate than submersion programmes for underachieving minority students, monolingual immersion programmes respond only to narrowly linguistic impediments to student success. For the many minority students whose academic failure is much more deeply rooted, monolingual immersion programmes appear to have only limited potential.

The third form of immersion programme conforms much more closely to the Canadian model in that it incorporates the three defining characteristics outlined above: teachers are bilingual, the instruction is modified, and first language literacy is promoted. One such programme has been implemented in McAllen, Texas, with encouraging results at the kindergarten level (Baker & de Kanter, 1981). Mexican–American students in this immersion variant of bilingual education who received about one hour a day of Spanish literacy-related instruction performed significantly better in both English and Spanish than equivalent students in a transitional bilingual programme. Because students are 'immersed' in the societal majority language (English), this type of programme can be labelled '*Majority Language Bilingual Immersion*'.

The fourth programme type that has been labelled 'immersion' is the '*Minority Language Bilingual Immersion*' programme discussed in the previous chapter* with reference to the San Diego results. This type of 'immersion' in L1 represents a considerably stronger commitment to promoting minority students' first language than Majority Language Bilingual Immersion programmes, although in both programme types the support for literacy in the minority language is more genuine and sustained than in most transitional bilingual programmes.

Researchers involved with the evaluations of Canadian immersion programmes have consistently advocated Minority Language Bilingual Immersion programmes for minority students although this term has not been used (e.g. Cummins, 1979a; Genesee, 1984; Lambert, 1975; Swain, 1983; Tucker, 1980). They emphasize that the appropriate implication from the Canadian immersion data is that the language whose development is most likely to be neglected (i.e. the minority or subordinate language) should be strongly promoted in the school programme in order to produce an additive form of bilingualism.

Table 1 shows clearly why the two types of bilingual immersion programmes appear to have more potential for success than the other three options. In the bilingual immersion programmes students are likely to be exposed to considerably more comprehensible academic input than in other programmes and they are also likely to experience any positive cognitive and academic benefits that may result from attaining proficiency in two languages.

Similarly, only the bilingual immersion programmes appear to respond adequately to the causes of minority students' underachievement. The implicit

Table 1 'Immersion' programmes and minority students: conformity with the principles underlying the success of the Canadian model

Program	COMPREHENSIBLE INPUT		
	1. Bilingual Teacher	2. L2 Modified Input	3. L1 Literacy Promotion
A. *Monolingual*			
1. Submersion	–	–	–
2. Monolingual Immersion	–	+	–
B. *Bilingual*			
3. Majority Language Bilingual Immersion	+	+	+
4. Minority Language Bilingual Immersion	+	+	+
5. Quick-Exit Transitional Bilingual	+	?	–[a]

+: principle incorporated in programme
–: principle not incorporated in programme
?: extent of incorporation will vary across programmes

[a] In transitional programmes which are not of the quick-exit variety (e.g. some L1 instruction from kindergarten through until the later elementary grades), L1 literacy skills are likely to be promoted.

assumptions of the five programme types in Table 1 with respect to remedies for minority students' underachievement are as follows: submersion assumes that students require only maximum exposure to L2; the assumption underlying monolingual immersion is that students need modified input in L2 to facilitate comprehension; both majority and minority language bilingual immersion assume that minority students who are academically at risk require comprehensible linguistic *and academic* input as well as reinforcement of L1 and cultural identity, the difference between them being in the strength of L1 and cultural identity reinforcement assumed to be necessary. The only consistency in transitional bilingual programmes is in their acceptance of linguistic mismatch as the causal factor underlying minority students' underachievement; after the initial mismatch has been resolved most programmes opt for maximum L2 exposure although some continue to reinforce students' L1 and cultural identity. It is clear that the assumptions of the two bilingual immersion programmes conform much more closely to the analysis of the causes of minority student underachievement presented in Chapter 5* than do the other three programme options.

Other programmes that lie between Majority Language Bilingual Immersion and Minority Language Bilingual Immersion have also been labelled as 'immersion' programmes. For example, Baker and de Kanter (1981) suggest that the 50% Spanish, 50% English kindergarten programme reported by Legaretta (1979) to be highly successful is in fact an 'alternate immersion' programme. The same reasoning could be used to label alternate day bilingual programmes (e.g. one day English-medium instruction, next day Spanish-medium instruction) as 'immersion'. Clearly, the term 'immersion' is not neutral in its sociopolitical overtones and the semantic jungle which the term has generated serves to obscure both the principles underlying the success of immersion programmes for majority students and the implications of these principles for minority programmes.

In summary, there are no data to support the implementation of English-only immersion (or, obviously, submersion) programmes for underachieving minority students. The Canadian immersion programmes, however, do have implications for the education of minority students who are academically at risk. Specifically, they reinforce the notion of a common underlying proficiency and suggest that minority students' L1 proficiency can be strongly promoted at no long term cost to the development of English proficiency. That there be *genuine* sustained reinforcement of minority students' L1 (as opposed to its transitional use in most US bilingual programmes) is probably ultimately more important than the specific amount of L1 instructional time (e.g. 80% in San Diego early grades, 20% in McAllen) or the language in which reading is introduced. The relative efficacy of majority language and minority language bilingual programmes is an empirical question at this point. On theoretical grounds the latter programme model appears to have the edge because of the greater probability of additive bilingualism and the integration of minority and majority students, with each group providing comprehensible L2 input for the other. Either of these two bilingual models, however, is likely to be superior to the quick-exit variety of transitional bilingual programme.

Immersion Programmes and Learning Difficulties in the Majority Context

The research that has addressed this issue has been conducted in the context of French immersion programmes for majority children. Despite the overall success of French immersion in imparting high levels of L2 skills at no long-term cost to the development of L1, educators and parents have wondered whether some children might be predisposed to experience learning difficulties in immersion which they might not experience in a regular English programme. Related to this is the question of whether to maintain children who are experiencing difficulty in immersion or, alternatively, transfer them to the English programme without delay. Thus, the issues are superficially similar to those in US bilingual education insofar as they concern entry into and exit out of the programme.

These issues will be considered in three sections. First, the question of whether academic ability (IQ), SES, or ethnic language background *differentially* predict success in French immersion programmes in comparison to English programmes is examined. Then, we consider the specific issue of whether some children are predisposed to experience learning difficulties in early French immersion (i.e. Kindergarten entry) as a result of a maturational lag in the temporal lobe regions of the brain, as argued by Trites (in press). Finally, research is reviewed relating to the issue of whether students who do experience learning difficulties in immersion should be transferred to the English programme.

In examining this research our concern is not just with its immediate practical relevance for French immersion programmes. The focus is rather on understanding the implications of the findings for the underlying theoretical issues. For example, what do the research findings imply with regard to the nature of L2 acquisition, the relationships between conversational and academic L2 skills, as well as those between L1 and L2 proficiency. Clearly, the question of whether academic difficulties manifest themselves in both languages is of obvious relevance to the notion of a common underlying proficiency.

Differential prediction of learning difficulty

Clearly, factors such as IQ and SES are likely to predict academic success within both French immersion and regular English programmes. The issue here, however, concerns *differential* success and failure, i.e. whether students with, for example, low academic ability, will do worse in immersion than they would have done in an all-English programme.

(i) Academic ability

Studies by Genesee (1976a) using IQ measures and by Bruck (1982) using L1 cognitive/academic measures show that although these indices of academic ability are strongly related to students' academic performance in both regular and immersion programmes, and within immersion, to both French and English academic skills, there is no differential effect across programmes. The same lack of differential effects for academic ability has been reported in the context of the Ukrainian–English programme in Edmonton (Edmonton Public Schools, 1979) and, as noted in the previous chapter*, in Malherbe's (1946) Afrikaans–English study in South Africa. In other words, immersion or bilingual programmes are just as appropriate for students with low academic ability as they are for students with higher ability.

Related to this issue is the fact that although IQ scores significantly predict academic performance in French (and English), they tend to show an inconsistent and much weaker pattern of relationships with French conversational skills (Bruck, 1984; Genesee, 1976a; Swain & Lapkin, 1982). These results are consistent with the different developmental trends shown by immigrant students acquiring L2 conversational and academic skills (see Chapter 6*) as well as with the fact that, in L1, cognitive abilities appear relatively independent of basic conversational fluency.

(ii) SES

Genesee (1976b) has reviewed several studies carried out in the Montreal area which investigated the suitability of French immersion programmes for students from working-class backgrounds. The results of all these studies were similar to those obtained in evaluations of programmes involving middle-class students. Students are reported to gain impressive French skills at no long-term cost to English or subject-matter learning.

(iii) Language background

Studies of the achievement of minority or 'third' (i.e. non-English, non-French) language groups conducted within the context of French immersion programmes have generally failed to control for SES and other confounding variables (e.g. Edwards & Casserly, 1973). The results of such comparisons have, however, been generally encouraging. Genesee (1976b) concludes his review of these studies as follows:

> The findings that the third language children scored as well as they did on some of the English tests is remarkable considering their lack of formal instruction in English. At the same time, their French language skills were comparable to the English based groups, despite differences in social class background ... there is nothing in these data to suggest that French immersion would not be suitable for third language children. (1976b: 510)

In summary, the available data provide no evidence that French immersion programmes are inappropriate for children from minority language backgrounds. However, studies of this question have tended to be small-scale and few in number and the issues are by no means resolved. For example, we know virtually nothing about the possible differential appropriacy of early versus late or intermediate. immersion, or early total versus early partial (i.e. approximately 50% French K-6) immersion for students from different minority language backgrounds.

Perhaps the most convincing evidence that immersion programmes are not just for an élite group of bright, middle-class majority-background students comes from the experience of the multi-language schools in Milwaukee. This programme illustrates very clearly some general principles about how both language and academic skills are acquired as well as pointing to some of the ways in which the implicit assumptions of some Canadian immersion educators have inadvertently helped create an élitist programme.

The Milwaukee magnet multi-language schools

In the mid-70s a series of magnet alternative schools were instituted in Milwaukee in response to federal racial desegregation requirements as an

Table 2   Distribution of 1981 grade 3 Reading and Mathematics scores for Milwaukee German and French immersion programmes[a]

	Reading %			Mathematics %		
	low	average	high	low	average	high
Eighty-Second Street School	2	80	18	5	64	31
City-wide	23	60	17	15	61	24
National	23	54	23	23	54	23

[a] From Milwaukee Public Schools Task Force Report on Foreign Language Programmes, 1982.

alternative to 'forced busing'. These were 'magnet' schools in the sense that students from outside the immediate school area were attracted to the school by the special programme offered there. Among these special programmes are French, German and Spanish immersion programmes modelled on Canadian French immersion programmes. Formal English reading instruction is introduced in grade 3 and each language is used for about the same proportion of time by grade 5. A major difference from the Canadian programmes, however, is that about half the students are from minority groups (mainly Black) and students show a normal distribution of IQ scores and come from varied socio-economic backgrounds. The racial balance is by design in view of the fact that the magnet schools were set up to overcome the segregation of inner-city Black students.

Although no formal evaluation of the multi-language schools has been published, achievement test results suggest a programme which is working extremely well. Table 2 presents the grade 3 Metropolitan Achievement Test results for Reading and Mathematics for the Eighty-Second Street School (composed of German and French immersion) in comparison to City-wide and National norms. These test data are from 1981 and represent grade 3 German programme students who started immersion in kindergarten while the grade 3 French programme students tested in that year started immersion in grade 1.

These results are consistent with those found in previous years for the programme and are remarkable in view of the fact that English reading has been formally taught for only one school year and many of the students in the programme are relatively low SES Black students who have traditionally tended not to excel in regular English programmes.

How do we explain the fact that these students appear to be performing better in a 'challenging' immersion programme than in programmes which are specifically designed to remediate their presumed 'deficits'? Teacher expectations are clearly likely to be an important factor, but, in addition, students' academic self-esteem appears to be increased by virtue of the fact that they are acquiring fluency in a second language. Newspaper reports strongly emphasize the positive attitudes of students in the immersion programmes (e.g. *The Milwaukee Journal*, 1980, May 7; 1981, February 9), as the following extract illustrates:

> Ironically, one of the few people in the school who speaks only English is the principal, Frank H. Henke, and the students don't let him forget it. Henke tells of a first grader who proudly pointed him out to a visitor, and said, 'I know more words than he does'.
>
> (*The Milwaukee Journal*, 1981, February 9:
> Magnet Grade Schools: Vive la Différence!)

It is interesting to place these findings in the context of Canadian French immersion programmes where, despite the research findings, many administrators and teachers see the immersion experience as too 'challenging' for less bright or low SES students. Such students are often discouraged from entering the programme and are often recommended for transfer to the regular English programme if they experience learning difficulties (Burns & Olson, 1981). The reluctance of some teachers to deal with the full range of learning abilities within the immersion programme has been reinforced by the research of Ronald Trites, a neuropsychologist at the Royal Ottawa Hospital, who argues that immersion programmes give rise to learning disabilities in some children and that procedures should be implemented to screen out those children who are more predisposed to develop learning disabilities in early immersion than they would be in a regular programme. Trites also argues that children who develop learning disabilities in early immersion should be switched to an English programme without delay. This issue is considered in the next section.

Learning 'disabilities' and French immersion

The question of whether French immersion programmes are suitable for all children is currently extremely problematic for Canadian policy-makers, educators and parents because the two major research efforts concerned with this issue, involving almost a decade of research, have reached diametrically opposed conclusions. On the one hand, Trites' (in press) studies in Ottawa suggest that some children are predisposed to experience difficulty in early immersion and, consequently, screening procedures should be instituted to identify such children before they enter the programme. Margaret Bruck (1984) in Montreal, on the other hand, reports that learning disabled or 'language-impaired' children in immersion acquire basic academic skills at a comparable rate to similar children in English programmes. In addition, they develop fluent interpersonal communicative skills in French, although at a slower rate than non-language-impaired children. Bruck (1984) also reports significant correlations between French and English literacy skills, suggesting that level of literacy is not language-specific but a function of some underlying general abilities. The fact that, in her studies, children's academic difficulties tended to persist after they were transferred from immersion to English programmes supports this conclusion. Bruck strongly recommends that learning disabled children remain in the immersion programme and receive appropriate remedial assistance.

The research carried out by Trites and by Bruck will be considered in turn. The basic argument will be that Bruck's position is considerably more convincing than that of Trites: (a) because her empirical studies are methodologically well-conceived whereas there are serious design problems with Trites' studies; (b) because the findings that emerge from Bruck's studies are consistent with a large body of theory and research relating to bilingualism and second language acquisition whereas Trites' findings are not.

A. Trites' studies

Trites' position derives from three basic studies. The first study (Trites & Price, 1976) compared the test profile of 32 children referred to the Neuropsychology Laboratory of the Royal Ottawa Hospital because of difficulties in early French immersion, with the profiles obtained from seven other problem groups selected from the files of the Laboratory. Each child had received a six- to eight-hour neuropsychological examination consisting of a variety of cognitive, linguistic, motor and perceptual tests. The aim of the study was to see if the French immersion difficulty group was characterized by a unique profile.

The second study (Trites & Price, 1977) was carried out in response to criticism (Stern et al., 1976) that the 'clinical' group of French immersion difficulty students in the original study may not have been representative of children in general who experience difficulty in French immersion. In this study a group of 16 drop-outs from French immersion was compared to 16 children who were successful in immersion on a similar battery of tests to that used in the original study.

The third study was an attempt to predict success and failure in French immersion on the basis of students' entry characteristics as revealed by the neuropsychological test battery. Four-year-old kindergarten children were initially tested and followed through to grade 4. The aim was to develop a screening battery which would predict the likelihood of dropping out of French immersion. The progress in the English programme of children who dropped out of immersion has also been followed by Trites and reported in the context of the latter two studies.

Trites' first two studies have been criticized in some detail on conceptual, methodological and statistical grounds (Cummins, 1979b, 1983b; Stern et al., 1976) and the major points will be reviewed here. The same criticisms are equally applicable to the more recent longitudinal study. Problems in the logic of Trites' theoretical argument will be considered first; then it will be argued that the basic research designs are incapable of providing answers to the research questions, and finally, it will be pointed out that contrary to Trites' claims, his own data show that students who transferred out of immersion actually made *poorer* progress in English reading than students who remained in immersion despite difficulties.

Maturational lags in French immersion: logic or speculation?

Trites' specific claim is that 'some children, of above average potential and normal abilities for school progress in their native language, experience difficulty or fail in a primary immersion programme in a second language as a result of a mild specific maturational lag' (1976: 200–1). The suggestion that children who experience difficulties in French immersion are characterized by a specific maturational lag in the temporal lobe regions of the brain is based on the assertion that in all three studies children who experienced difficulty in immersion performed more poorly than comparison groups on the Tactual Performance Test (TPT) a complex psychomotor problem-solving task (Halstead, 1947). On the TPT the subject is required to place blocks of various shapes in a formboard while blindfolded, first with the dominant hand, then with the non-dominant hand and finally with both hands together.

Trites claims that 'performance on this test has specific implications with regard to adequacy of functioning of the temporal lobes. In turn, it is well established in the neuropsychological literature that the temporal lobes are important brain structures for subserving language, memory and auditory perceptual functions' (1976: 198). He goes on to argue that the relatively poor performance of the French immersion difficulty group on the TPT in the initial study 'is compatible with the interpretation of a maturational lag in the temporal lobe regions' (1976: 200). Trites (in press) suggests that this interpretation is supported by the poorer TPT performance of the French immersion drop-outs in the subsequent 'cross-validation' study and in the longitudinal study. The reason a maturational lag in the temporal lobes could cause difficulties for children in French immersion is that 'since the primary auditory cortex is situated in the temporal lobes, children who have a mild maturational deficit affecting these areas would have difficulty in a complex language learning situation' (Trites & Price, 1976: 135).

The apparent logic in this argument falls apart when one takes account of the fact that the left and right temporal lobes are specialized for different types of information processing. The left temporal lobe is specialized for the processing of verbal material, particularly in the auditory modality. The right temporal lobe, on the other hand, is less involved with the speech system (see e.g. Luria, 1973), being primarily involved in perception of space, both visual and nonvisual (see e.g. Gazzaniga, 1972; Milner, 1954).

Trites and Price (1976, 1977) consistently maintain that the TPT is related to 'temporal lobe functioning', but they cite no evidence to back up this claim nor do they say whether left or right temporal lobe functioning is involved, although they do admit that right and left temporal lobes subserve different psychological functions (1977: 18; Trites, in press). The logic of their argument, however, implies that the TPT involves the left temporal lobe since this is the primary localization of speech and language functions. If the TPT is dependent upon the right or nondominant temporal lobe, its relationship to the difficulties some children experience in a complex language task is less evident.[2]

An examination of the neuropsychological literature relating to the TPT (e.g. Klove, 1963; Knights, 1966; Lezak, 1976) provides no evidence that it is in any way associated with left temporal lobe functioning. It would be curious indeed if any such connection were to emerge since the TPT involves spatial integration in the tactual modality and has no linguistic or auditory component. The available neuropsychological evidence (e.g. Milner, 1954: 58), as well as the fact that in Trites and Price's (1977) own studies the TPT related significantly to non-verbal ability measures, suggests that the TPT may reflect right rather than left hemispheric functions. However, what in fact it is measuring is sufficiently unclear as to make any interpretation speculative. Similar scepticism about the construct validity of Trites' measures is expressed by Albert and Obler (1979: 33) who regard the claim that these measures assess temporal lobe maturational lag as 'extreme'.

In summary, there is no logical or theoretical basis for expecting a relationship between TPT performance and difficulty in early immersion. The empirical evidence for such a relationship is equally unconvincing.

Both the second 'cross-validation' study and the longitudinal study involved a comparison between drop-outs from French immersion and successful students. As would be expected in a comparison of drop-outs and successful students in *any* academic programme on *any* battery of cognitive tests, significant group differences were found in both studies on intellectual, psycholinguistic and reading abilities as well as on parent and teacher rating scales. In the cross-validation study one of the few variables where differences between drop-out and success groups did *not* attain significance was the TPT (see Trites & Price, 1977: 43 Table 10).[3]

In the longitudinal study, there were no significant differences between students who had dropped out of immersion by the end of grade 1 and high achievers in immersion on the TPT administered at age four as part of the Early Identification Assessment Battery. When the same groups were compared on the TPT administered at age five in kindergarten, differences were statistically significant. However, the level of significance was not large (F = 5.57, $p < 0.05$), as can be seen from the fact that of 13 significant group differences the TPT was placed only tenth in order of magnitude. In the discriminant function analyses designed to identify the variables that distinguished the drop-outs from successful immersion students, the TPT played a relatively minor role, placing twelfth in order of importance on the battery of tests administered to the four-year olds and tenth in importance on the battery administered to the five-year olds. The amount of variance in grade 1 French or English academic achievement uniquely accounted for in the regression analyses by any of the TPT variables was minuscule (no more than 1%). English cognitive/academic proficiency, on the other hand, was strongly related to grade 1 French academic skills.

Even if anybody really knew what the TPT was measuring, its inconsistent and weak effect in predicting academic achievement and in distinguishing drop-outs from successful students hardly justifies the central role Trites attributes to 'maturational lags in the temporal lobe regions of the brain' in explaining difficulty in French immersion. In fact, no inferences whatsoever can be drawn from Trites' studies about any unique pattern of deficits characterizing students who have difficulty in immersion because of a fundamental flaw in the design of both the cross-validation and longitudinal studies.

Research design and the issue of differential programme effects

The assumption underlying the development of a screening battery for French immersion is that such a battery would identify students who are likely to experience difficulty in immersion but who would not experience similar difficulty in a regular English programme. In other words, the question is whether there is a *differential* programme impact on students with similar entering characteristics. In order to answer this question it is not sufficient to compare only the performance of drop-outs and successful students within immersion because the test profile of the drop-out group might be very similar to the test profile of students who have academic difficulty in a regular programme. In other words, we would not know whether the test profile is unique to difficulties within French immersion and we could say *nothing* about differential programme effects. By the same logic, Trites' studies tell us nothing about differential programme effects; we do not know, for example, whether poor TPT performance characterizes low achievers in regular programmes as he suggests it does in immersion.

Bruck's (1984) studies are considerably more convincing from a design standpoint because they compare the performance over time of 'difficulty' and 'success' groups in both immersion and regular programmes. The fact that Bruck finds no evidence of differential programme effects suggests that Trites' entire screening endeavour is without empirical foundation.

However, if we examine the scores of Trites' subjects in the original study and in the early identification longitudinal study, there appears to be some evidence that the immersion drop-outs are different in certain respects from regular programme students who experience academic difficulty. Most obviously, the immersion drop-outs are characterized by relatively high IQ scores. In the longitudinal study, for example, the drop-outs had Full Scale and Verbal IQ's of 115 compared to 121 for the immersion students who were not experiencing difficulty. Performance IQ's for both groups were about four points lower. Trites (in press) reports that after transferring, their academic progress in the regular programme was satisfactory, as would be expected from students with such high academic ability. As Trites (in press) points out, this drop-out group appears very different from the 'language-impaired' or French immersion problem children studied by Bruck (1984) whose Verbal IQ's were below 100 and about 13 points lower than their Performance IQ's. Bruck's sample of both English and French programme difficulty students appears much more typical of students generally characterized as 'learning disabled'.

One interpretation which this suggests is that many of Trites' drop-out students in the longitudinal study may not have been 'drop-outs' so much as 'push-outs'. In other words, because they were below the extremely high average of their class-mates they may have had difficulty in meeting teachers' expectations and may consequently have been viewed as academically-weak and unable to meet the 'challenge' of immersion. In other words, their 'failure' in immersion may not be due to any 'intrinsic neurological impairments' but rather to negative perceptions on the part of the teacher of their relative academic ability, and the teacher's consequent assumption that the student would be better off in the regular programme. The teacher's assumption that the child has some form of 'learning disability' and its reinforcement by neurological speculation that sounds impressive but is, in reality, vacuous, follows the pattern of 'blaming the victim' discussed in previous chapters*. The 'disabling' of the child and the institution of screening procedures in effect 'screens' the pedagogy from critical scrutiny.

In the next section we consider what actually does happen to students who transfer from immersion to the regular programme.

The effects of transfer out of immersion

A detailed technical analysis of Trites' claim that students who transfer out of immersion into the English programme make better progress than students who remain in immersion despite difficulty is presented in Cummins (1979b). A variety of statistical problems characterize the data analysis presented in Trites and Price (1977). However, the most clearcut refutation of their claim comes from their own data. Although not acknowledged in their report, Trites and Price's data show clearly that a large majority of children who switched to an English programme repeated or dropped back a grade level, and, although they made good progress in reading and other subjects *in relation to the grade level which they repeated,* they fell further behind equivalent children who remained in French immersion in terms of the level of performance that would be expected on the basis of their age. Specifically, whereas children who remained in immersion despite difficulty maintained their expected rate of progress in reading skills, those who dropped out fell back by about a quarter of a grade level in terms of what would be expected based on their age (see Cummins, 1979; Trites, 1979).

In summary, Trites' studies are characterized by a variety of conceptual and methodological problems which cast serious doubts on his assertion that school systems ought to institute screening programmes for children entering French immersion.[4] These doubts are reinforced by the fact that Bruck's (in press) studies show a very different pattern of findings.

B. Bruck's studies

Among the conceptual and methodological problems discussed in relation to Trites' studies are: (i) the fact that the nature of immersion drop-out children's learning difficulties is unclear; they may not be 'disabled' or 'delayed' in any intrinsic sense but rather 'pushed-out' of the programme as a result of school, teacher and parent expectations; (ii) the fact that although the studies were intended to provide evidence of differential programme effects, the research designs are incapable of providing any information on this issue. Both of these problems are largely overcome in Bruck's studies.

In Bruck's major study, students entering both French immersion and English kindergarten (five-year olds) were screened for language problems over a period of six years. The following screening procedure was employed: first, in October kindergarten teachers were asked to list any children from English-speaking backgrounds whom they felt had problems with language; next, the referred children were interviewed individually and given a diagnostic screening test by a specialist in child language development. This test consisted of object manipulation, story retelling, sentence imitation and echolalia subtests and was designed so that children with normal language development would have little difficulty. Many of the items were similar to those used in other diagnostic tests of language skills such as the Boehm Test of Basic Concepts or the Detroit Tests of Learning Aptitude. Children included in the French immersion and English programme 'problem' groups scored lower than 35 (out of a possible 59) on the diagnostic screening test, their IQ scores were in the normal range (i.e. Verbal or Performance IQ's above 85) and were judged by the interviewer to have a language problem which was not due to shyness, dialect difference, etc. After the problem children were identified, each was matched with a control child not experiencing language problems, on the basis of sex, age, classroom teacher and father's occupation. The total sample consisted of 147 children at kindergarten, a figure that declined to 101 at grade 2 due to attrition.

Trites (in press) has criticized Bruck's (1978, 1984) study on the grounds that there was high attrition from the French immersion problem group and thus those who remained in the immersion programme through grade 2 or 3 may represent a select, more able, group compared to the problem group in the English programme. However, Bruck (1984) points out that the majority of students who left the programme did so because the family moved to a district which did not offer immersion, and furthermore, the kindergarten and grade 1 test data of those who left the project were similar to those who remained in immersion, suggesting that those who remained were not a select group.

The kindergarten students were administered four sets of measures:

(1) Wechsler Preschool and Primary Scale of Intelligence (WPPSI)

(2) Peabody Picture Vocabulary Test (PPVT)

(3) Receptive and Expressive subtests of the Northwestern Syntax Screening Test (NSST)

(4) Seven subtests of the Illinois Test of Psycholinguistic Abilities (ITPA).

These measures were re-administered in grades 1 and 2 together with measures of French, English and math skills as well as other measures of cognitive/academic abilities.

The following issues were addressed in Bruck's (1984) study: (1) Are French immersion programmes equally suitable for language-impaired students as English programmes; in other words, is there a differential programme effect for these students? (2) What is the relationship between L1 cognitive/academic skills on entry to immersion programmes and subsequent acquisition of communicative and academic French skills? In other studies Bruck (1978/79, 1980) has compared the progress of children who dropped out of immersion with that of children who remained in immersion despite academic difficulties. These findings will also be reviewed.

Bruck (in press) reports no differential effects of the immersion and English programmes on children with language impairments. Although the children with language problems in immersion had lower L1 literacy skills in grade 1 and 2 than children with language problems in the English programme, the level of difference was similar to that between French and English programme control children and consistent with what is usually observed in the early grades of immersion. Both groups of problem children were closer to the controls in language and cognitive skills at grade 2 than either grade 1 or kindergarten, suggesting, according to Bruck, that the problem children were maturationally slower in language skills when assessed in kindergarten but that with time they began to approach normal levels of development. Bruck (in press) concludes that after three years (K–grade 2) of education in a second language environment, the language impaired children's linguistic and cognitive skills were equivalent to those of similar children who had been totally schooled in their first language (except for 40 minute daily periods of French-as-a-second-language instruction).

In terms of the acquisition of French skills, Bruck (1984) reports that the immersion problem children made good progress in listening comprehension, being rated as at least average by their teachers, but progress was slower in terms of French oral production ($^1/_3$ were considered below average). Bruck points out that the immersion problem children's ability to acquire fluency in French, albeit more slowly than normal, would appear surprising to many people in view of their problems in L1 oral language and the fact that similar children have been reported to experience extreme difficulty in learning a second language when taught by traditional methods (e.g. Bruck, 1981; Rudel, 1981). For example, the

English problem group made little or no progress in French despite three years of 40 minutes of instruction daily. In a different follow-up study of adults who had as children been diagnosed as 'learning disabled', Bruck (1981) found that 52% of the learning disabled group did not know enough French to cope in most daily situations compared to only 22% of a control group of non-disabled subjects. However, the relatively well-developed French communicative skills of the French immersion problem group can presumably be attributed to the fact that in the early grades of immersion, communication between teacher and students is embedded in a meaningful concrete context and supported by a wide range of paralinguistic cues. This 'comprehensible input' allows students to infer the intended meaning and simultaneously acquire the second language, despite their problems in L1.[5]

Neither the immersion nor English programme problem children performed as well as their controls in L1 or L2 academic and cognitive skills. The fact that L1 cognitive/academic ability is predictive of L2 academic skills (as reported by both Bruck and Trites) is clearly consistent with the notion of a common underlying proficiency.

The fact that children with language and learning problems make equivalent academic progress in immersion to similar children in English programmes suggests that there is little justification for assuming (as many educators and parents do) that such children should be switched to an English programme. In fact, Bruck's (1978/79, 1980) studies suggest that switching may damage a child's self-esteem and the stigma of failure may compound the learning problems. Also, when children transfer in the early grades of an immersion programme, they will probably be even further behind in English academic skills because of not having had any formal English instruction. Switching can also contribute to tension within the school because regular programme teachers may resent the extra work which transferred children represent.

Bruck (1980) also carried out detailed case studies of 17 grade 6 students who had experienced difficulty in immersion. Twelve of these switched to the English programme while five remained in immersion despite difficulties. Those who switched did so as a result of a combination of factors: all were doing poorly academically; many (seven out of 12) were considered by teachers as disruptive and difficult to manage in the classroom; some of the children were not receiving adequate remedial help for their problems within the immersion programme; and parents tended to be less committed to French than those of children who remained in the programme.

Most of the children who switched out of immersion experienced feelings of frustration and unhappiness during the year after the switch. For some, self-esteem was low either because they had to repeat a grade or because they felt that the English stream class was of lower status than the immersion class. Others experienced frustration because of the academic demands of the English stream and the fact that their new class-mates had received more years of English language arts instruction. Only three of the twelve who switched made good initial academic and emotional adjustments. Bruck (1980) points out that if a child is to be switched there must be careful educational and social planning in order to promote personal and academic adjustment.

Despite the fact that the Verbal and Performance IQs of the children who remained in immersion and of those who switched out were similar (in both cases Verbal scores were below 100 and at least 12 points below Performance scores), the switch-out group performed more poorly than the immersion group in English academic skills. Bruck attributes this to the fact that the problems of the immersion 'stay-in' group tended to be identified earlier (in grade 1 or 2) and they received intensive individualized help; although children who switched-out received similar amounts of remediation to those who stayed-in over the course of elementary school, they tended to receive less early assistance. Thus, Bruck emphasizes the importance of early and appropriate intervention in helping children with learning difficulties to progress within the immersion (or English) programme.

Several of the findings of this study are relevant to the theoretical constructs proposed in the previous chapter. First, French and English reading comprehension skills were highly correlated ($r = 0.73$, $p < 0.01$) suggesting that literacy skills in each language are a function of some underlying general abilities. Second, literacy skills in French and English were unrelated to French oral communication skills, as measured by a cognitively undemanding task (picture descriptions). Third, the severity of the learning problem (as indicated by amount of remediation) was related to French reading skills but not to French oral communication skills.

These findings are parallel to those obtained in studies of immigrant students (see Chapter 6*) in that there appears to be a certain degree of independence between L2 conversational and L2 academic skills. Also, in both contexts the development of L2 academic skills is a function both of exposure to the L2 *and* L1 cognitive/academic proficiency. Wyszewianski's (1977) study of Puerto Rican minority Spanish–English bilingual students similarly demonstrated the cross-lingual nature of language disorders in that academic and language difficulties were equally evident in L1 (Spanish) as in English.

Bruck's (1980, 1982) findings have clear practical implications for the teaching of second languages to children with language or learning problems. Specifically, they show that such children can acquire high levels of L2 fluency in an immersion or bilingual learning context where there is considerable exposure to comprehensible input in the L2. One of the unfortunate aspects of traditional second language programmes for children with learning difficulties is that the teaching methods in these programmes typically involve language drills which stress repetition of phrases and structures in nonmeaningful contexts. The auditory sequential processing and rote memory skills required for success in learning under these conditions are often those which are particularly problematic for children with academic difficulties (Das & Cummins, 1982).

It should be stressed, however, that when children encounter difficulties in an immersion programme, each case must be judged on its individual merits. Although in general the drawbacks of switching appear to outweigh any potential advantages, under some conditions it might be appropriate to transfer the child to an English programme. For example, if a child has been unhappy for a prolonged period of time in an immersion programme and wants to switch, then it is probably right to do so. Also, if the programme or teacher expectations are tuned to very academically-able students such that average students are seen as less bright or as having learning difficulties then such students might be better off in a programme which does not inappropriately label them in this way. In these cases, however, the problem clearly lies with the particular implementation of the immersion methodology rather than with either the student or the concept of immersion itself.[6]

The research data reviewed in this and the previous chapter* (e.g. Bruck, 1982; Genesee, 1976a; Malherbe, 1946; Milwaukee Public Schools, 1982) clearly show that bilingual and L2 immersion programmes are appropriate for children with a wide range of learning abilities and language skills. As Bruck (1984) suggests, the issue of concern should change from 'Are French immersion programmes suitable for the language impaired, learning disabled, or low-IQ child?' to 'How can French immersion programmes be made more suitable for these children?' Three ways are immediately apparent: (1) provision of appropriate remedial services (in French) for students who encounter difficulties in immersion; (2) dissemination of information to educators and parents about the research data showing that neither immersion itself nor bilingualism contributes to children's academic problems; (3) ensuring that literacy and other academic instruction in immersion is such that students of both high and low ability are motivated to become intrinsically involved in learning (see Chapter 9*).

In short, it is extremely important for educators to address the 'push-out' phenomenon in immersion programmes because of its serious negative consequences for both the individual student (e.g. loss of self-esteem and French skills) and for the society as a whole (reserves second language enrichment for an élite group of students).

Conclusion

In response to the frequently asked question of whether 'immersion' programmes are suitable for all children, the answer that emerges from research in both minority and majority contexts is that immersion programmes, properly understood and implemented, appear to represent an appropriate form of enrichment bilingual education for all students, majority and minority, learning 'disabled' and non-disabled. Such programmes result in additive bilingualism at no apparent cost to children's personal or academic development.

However, despite the relative clarity of the research findings, confusion about immersion programmes is extremely common among educators and policy-makers. In the United States, for example, most educators do not realize that the Canadian immersion programmes are, in fact, enrichment bilingual programmes designed to promote additive bilingualism in a particular sociopolitical context (i.e. a dominant group whose L1 is prestigious and strongly reinforced outside the school). They then use the Canadian results to argue for monolingual English-only programmes (submersion plus ESL, or monolingual immersion) which would be implemented in a very different sociopolitical context (i.e. a sub-ordinate group whose L1 is neither prestigious nor reinforced in the society). There are clearly two logical flaws in this argument: first, in arguing for mono-lingual programmes on the basis of the success of bilingual programmes, and second, in extrapolating from a particular sociopolitical context to one that is very different.

Essentially, the very superficial reasoning evident in the policy-debate on this issue is indicative of the failure to understand the role of *theory* in research interpretation and policy formulation. As discussed in Chapter 5*, the extent to which a particular theory is valid is precisely the extent to which it can account for a variety of findings from different contexts. Thus, the theoretical principles underlying the success of immersion programmes for majority students must be consistent with those which have been used to account for the patterns of aca-demic achievement of minority groups under various instructional conditions.

In this regard, the research findings from both contexts show many points of convergence. The interdependence hypothesis, for example, is strongly supported by the general patterns of evaluation results in minority and majority contexts as well as by more specific research studies involving children with learning difficulties (Bruck, 1980, 1984). The distinction between face-to-face conver-sational skills and cognitive/academic proficiency is also consistent with the findings of several studies involving very different groups of students acquiring second language skills.

Another theme that has emerged is the total absence of empirical support for the concerns of many educators that bilingual instruction is inappropriate (e.g. too 'challenging', confusing) for students who are at risk academically or who may be experiencing learning difficulties. This finding is of particular relevance to special educators who often assume that children with learning problems (whether minority or majority) would be better-off in an English-only pro-gramme.

These points of convergence are at the level of psychological processes involved in language and learning. However, the data also show clearly that psychological factors at the level of the individual student are inadequate by themselves to account for all the research data. Differences in the achievement of majority and minority students are fundamentally determined by sociopolitical factors associated with language prestige and cultural identity. The underachievement of minority students is much more complex in nature than a mere lack of English fluency and consequently is unlikely to be reversed by monolingual immersion programmes. Sociopolitical factors must be invoked to explain why many majority students are likely to perform adequately in, for example, a French monolingual immersion or even submersion programme in Montreal (see e.g. Macnamara *et al.*, 1976) whereas many minority students tend to fail academically under these conditions.

Notes

* Reference to another part of the volume where this chapter was originally published *(Bilingualism and Special Education: Issues in Assessment and Pedagogy).*
1. The very different approaches to bilingual education in the two countries can be seen in the fact that exit from the Canadian enrichment programme to the regular classroom is an indication of academic difficulty whereas exit from the US remedial bilingual programme is, in theory at least, indicative that academic difficulties associated with L2 acquisition have been overcome.
2. Recent research provides some evidence for a link between right hemisphere functioning and both learning disabilities (Witelson, 1977) and bilingualism (Vaid & Genesee, 1980), and it is conceivable that Trites could try to make a speculative case for right hemisphere involvement in some immersion students' academic difficulties based on these relations. However, considerably more research with measures whose validity is less uncertain than the TPT would be required before one could even begin to suggest policy implications.
3. In subsequent analyses the samples were divided into those above and below nine years of age, and significant differences emerged in the younger but not the older age group. However, these differences appear to be largely a function of non-verbal IQ differences between the groups, since there are strong correlations between TPT and non-verbal IQ, and significant non-verbal IQ differences between the groups. In the analysis of group differences on all other dependent variables *except* TPT, the influence of non-verbal IQ was statistically removed through analysis of covariance.
4. Trites has recently (July and August, 1983) instituted his own early identification programme for prospective French immersion students which consists of five hours of testing for four- and five-year old children as well as interviews with parents and teachers. The cost of the programme is $350 per child. This type of procedure is certainly consistent with Trites' interpretation of his data. However, it appears unfortunate to subject four-year old children to five hours of testing in light of the conceptual and empirical problems in the research upon which this early identification procedure is based.
5. A further point emphasized by Bruck (1980, 1984) is that the acquisition of a second language can benefit the self-concept of children with learning problems. Because they are successfully acquiring a skill that siblings or parents may not have, they tend to feel better about themselves and about school than equivalent children in a regular programme. An example from the recently completed Significant Instructional Features in Bilingual Education study (Tikunoff, 1983; Guthrie, 1981) illustrates this potential. The performance of Calvin, a grade 5 Black student who had been classified as learning disabled, is described. The student was in a Chinese–English bilingual classroom where non-native speakers of Chinese received about an hour a day of Chinese-as-a-second-language (CSL) instruction. English was used as the major medium of instruction for the rest of the day. According to the teacher:

Calvin had a lot of difficulty with all his classes except Chinese. She felt the Chinese class had done wonders for his self-image. From the beginning he had done as well as any of the other CSL students. The teacher thought that because they all started off at the same level, they all started off knowing nothing, he was able to keep up. In all his other subjects he was so far behind, catching up seemed impossible. Now he had gained some self-confidence, however, his performance in other areas had begun to improve as well. (Guthrie, 1981b: 54)

In short, the acquisition of a second language is not necessarily too difficult for students with learning problems in their first language. Their success will depend on the extent to which the instruction is meaningful and motivates them to become intrinsically involved in the learning process.

6. There are indications that some immersion programmes tend to place excessive reliance on seat work and ditto sheet exercises to the exclusion of more pedagogically appropriate ways of promoting literacy and other academic skills (see Cummins *et al.*, 1984). As discussed in Chapter 9, it is not sufficient only to have the medium comprehensible, the academic message must also be meaningful and motivating for students. Failure to embed the academic content into meaningful activities (e.g. expressive writing) is likely both to contribute to the difficulties of some children in immersion and to increase the number of these children who are 'pushed-out'. An 'activity-based' approach to late immersion methodology which is consistent with the pedagogical principles discussed in Chapter 9 has recently been proposed by Stevens (1983).

References

Albert, M. L. and Obler, L. K. (1979) *The Bilingual Brain*. New York: Academic Press.

Baker, K. A. and de Kanter, A. A. (1981) *Effectiveness of Bilingual Education: A Review of the Literature*. Washington, DC: Office of Planning and Budget, US Department of Education.

Bruck, M. (1978) The suitability of early French immersion programs for the language-disabled child. *Canadian Journal of Education* 3, 51–72.

Bruck, M. (1978/79) Switching out of French immersion. *Interchange* 9, 86–94.

Bruck, M. (1980) The consequences of switching out of French immersion: A pilot study. Research report submitted to the Quebec Ministry of Education.

Bruck, M. (1981) The adult functioning of children with specific learning disabilities. Final Report to Health and Welfare Canada.

Bruck, M. (1982) Language impaired children's performance in an additive bilingual education program. *Applied Psycholinguistics* 3, 46–60.

Bruck, M. (1984) The feasibility of an additive bilingual program for language-impaired children. In Y. Lebrun and M. Paradis (eds) *Early Bilingualism and Child Development*. Amsterdam: Swets and Zeitlinger.

Burns, G. E. and Olson, P. (1981) *Implementation and Politics in French Immersion*. Toronto: Ontario Institute for Studies in Education.

Calfee, R. C. and Calfee, K. H. (1981) Interactive Reading Assessment System. Unpublished manuscript. Stanford University.

California State Department of Education (1984) *Basic Principles for the Education of Language-Minority Students: An Overview*. Sacramento: California State Department of Education.

Cohen, A. D. and Swain, M. (1976) Bilingual education: The immersion model in the North American context. In J. E. Alatis and K. Twaddell (eds) *English as a Second Language in Bilingual Education*. Washington, DC: TESOL.

Cummins, J. (1979a) Linguistic interdependence and the educational development of bilingual children. *Review of Educational Research* 49, 222–51.

Cummins, J. (1979b) Should the child who is experiencing difficulties in early immersion be switched to the regular English program? A reinterpretation of Trites' data. *The Canadian Modern Language Review* 36, 139–43.

Cummins, J. (1983a) *Policy Report: Language and Literacy Learning in Bilingual Instruction*. Austin, TX: Southwest Educational Development Laboratory.

Cummins, J. (1983b) Language proficiency, biliteracy and French immersion. *Canadian Journal of Education* 8, 117–38.

Cummins, J., Abrey, R., Burrows, A., Falter, P., O'Donoghue, B., Robichaud, D. and Stern, M. (1984). French immersion: Second generation issues. Unpublished manuscript, The Ontario Institute for Studies in Education.

Das, J. P. and Cummins, J. (1982) Language processing and reading disability. In K. D. Gadow and I. Bialer (eds) *Advances in Learning and Behavioral Disabilities: A Research Annual*. Greenwich, CT: JAI Press.

Edmonton Public Schools (1979) *Evaluation of the Bilingual Program (English–Ukrainian), Fifth Year*. Edmonton: Edmonton Public School Board.

Edwards, H. P. and Casserly, M. C. (1973) *Evaluation of Second Language Programs in the English Schools*. Ottawa: Ottawa Roman Catholic School Board.

Epstein, N. (1977) *Language, Ethnicity and the Schools*. Washington, DC: Institute for Educational Leadership.

Gazzaniga, M. (1972) One brain – two minds? *American Scientist* 60, 311–17.

Genesee, F. (1976a) The role of intelligence in second language learning. *Language Learning* 26, 267–80.

Genesee, F. (1976b) The suitability of immersion programs for all children. *Canadian Modern Language Review* 32, 494–515.

Genesee, F. (1984) Historical and theoretical foundations of immersion education. In California State Department of Education, *Studies on Immersion Education: A Collection for U.S. Educators*. Sacramento: State Department of Education.

Guthrie, L. F. (1981) *An Ecological Case Study of Bilingual Instruction (English/Cantonese), Grade 5, Site 5*. Appendix B6, Significant Bilingual Instructional Features Study. San Francisco: Far West Laboratory for Educational Research and Development.

Halstead, W. C. (1947) *Brain and Intelligence: A Quantitative Study of the Frontal Lobes*. Chicago: University of Chicago Press.

Hoover, W. (1983) *Language Learning in Bilingual Instruction: Cantonese Site Analytic Study*. Austin, TX: Southwest Educational Development Laboratory.

Klove, H. (1963) Clinical neuropsychology. *The Medical Clinics of North America* 47, 1647–58.

Knights, R. M. (1966) *Normative Data on Tests for Evaluating Brain Damage in Children from 5 to 14 Years of Age*. Research Bulletin No. 20, Department of Psychology. London, Ontario: The University of Western Ontario.

Krashen, S. D. (1982) *Principles and Practice in Second Language Acquisition*. Oxford: Pergamon Press.

Lambert, W. E. (1975) Culture and language as factors in learning and education. In A. Wolfgang (ed.) *Education of Immigrant Students*. Toronto: The Ontario Institute for Studies in Education.

Legaretta, D. (1979) The effects of program models on language acquisition by Spanish-speaking children. *TESOL Quarterly* 13, 521–34.

Lezak, M. D. (1976) *Neuropsychological Assessment*. New York: Oxford University Press.

Luria, A. R. (1973) *The Working Brain*. New York: Basic Books.

Macnamara, J., Svarc, J. and Horner, S. (1976) Attending a primary school of the other language in Montreal. In A. Simoes (ed.) *The Bilingual Child*. New York: Academic Press.

Malherbe, E. G. (1946) *The Bilingual School.* Johannesburg: Bilingual School Association.

Milner, B. (1954) Intellectual function of the temporal lobes. *Psychological Bulletin* 51, 42–61.

Milwaukee Public Schools (1982) *Report of the Foreign Language Task Force.* Milwaukee: Milwaukee Public Schools.

Rudel, R. G. (1981) Residual effects of childhood reading disabilities. *Bulletin of the Orton Society* 31, 89–102.

Stern, H. H., Swain, M., McLean, L. D., Friedman, R. J., Harley, B. and Lapkin, S. (1976) *Three Approaches to Teaching French.* Toronto: Ministry of Education, Ontario.

Stevens, F. (1983) Activities to promote learning and communication in the second language classroom. *TESOL Quarterly* 17, 259–72.

Swain, M. (1979) Bilingual education: Research and its implications. In C. A. Yorio, K. Perkins and J. Schachter (eds) *On TESOL '79: The Learner in Focus.* Washington, DC: TESOL.

Swain, M. (1983) Bilingualism without tears. In M. A. Clarke and J. Handscombe (eds) *On TESOL '82: Pacific Perspectives on Language Learning and Teaching.* Washington DC: TESOL.

Swain, M. and Lapkin, S. (1982) *Evaluating Bilingual Education: A Canadian Case Study.* Clevedon: Multilingual Matters.

Tikunoff, W. J. (1983) Five significant bilingual instructional features: A summary of findings from Part 1 of the SBIF descriptive study. In C. Fisher *et al., The Significant Bilingual Instructional Features Study.* Final report submitted to The National Institute of Education.

Trites, R. L. (1976) Children with learning difficulties in primary French immersion. *Canadian Modern Language Review* 33, 193–216.

Trites, R. L. (1979) A reply to Cummins. *Canadian Modern Language Review* 36, 143–46.

Trites, R. L. (in press) Early immersion in French at school for anglophone children: Learning disabilities and prediction of success. In Y. Lebrun and M. Paradis (eds) *Early Bilingualism and Child Development.* Amsterdam: Swets and Zeitlinger.

Trites, R. L. and Price, M. A. (1976) *Learning Disabilities Found in Association with French Immersion Programming.* Toronto: Ministry of Education, Ontario.

Trites, R. L. and Price, M. A. (1977) *Learning Disabilities Found in Association with French Immersion Programming: A Cross-validation Study.* Toronto: Ministry of Education, Ontario.

Tucker, G. R. (1980) Implications for US bilingual education: Evidence from Canadian research. *Focus,* No. 2.

Vaid, J. and Genesee, F. (1980) Neuropsychological approaches to bilingualism: A critical review. *Canadian Journal of Psychology* 34, 417–45.

Witelson, S. F. (1977) Development dyslexia: Two right hemispheres and none left. *Science* 195, 309–11.

Wyszewianski, H. L. (1977) *Determining a Language Disorder in a Bilingual Spanish–English Population.* Ann Arbor, MI: University Microfilms International.

Empowering Minority Students: A Framework for Intervention

During the past 20 years educators in the United States have implemented a series of costly reforms aimed at reversing the pattern of school failure among minority students. These have included compensatory programs at the preschool level, myriad forms of bilingual education programs, the hiring of additional aides and remedial personnel, and the institution of safeguards against discriminatory assessment procedures. Yet the dropout rate among Mexican–American and mainland Puerto Rican students remains between 40 and 50% compared to 14% for whites and 25% for blacks (Jusenius & Duarte, 1982). Similarly, almost a decade after the passage of the nondiscriminatory assessment provision of PL94–142,[1] we find Hispanic students in Texas over-represented by a factor of 300% in the 'learning disabilities' category (Ortiz & Yates, 1983).

I have suggested that a major reason previous attempts at educational reform have been unsuccessful is that the relationships between teachers and students and between schools and communities have remained essentially unchanged. The required changes involve *personal redefinitions* of the way classroom teachers interact with the children and communities they serve. In other words, legislative and policy reforms may be necessary conditions for effective change, but they are not sufficient. Implementation of change is dependent upon the extent to which educators, both collectively and individually, redefine their roles with respect to minority students and communities.

The purpose of this paper is to propose a theoretical framework for examining the types of personal and institutional redefinitions that are required to reverse the pattern of minority student failure. The framework is based on a series of hypotheses regarding the nature of minority students' educational difficulties. These hypotheses, in turn, lead to predictions regarding the probable effectiveness, or ineffectiveness, of various interventions directed at reversing minority students' school failure.

The framework assigns a central role to three inclusive sets of interactions or power relations: (1) the classroom interactions between teachers and students,

175

(2) relationships between schools and minority communities, and (3) the intergroup power relations within the society as a whole. It assumes that the social organization and bureaucratic constraints within the school reflect not only broader policy and societal factors but also the extent to which *individual educators* accept or challenge the social organization of the school in relation to minority students and communities. Thus, this analysis sketches directions for change for policymakers at all levels of the educational hierarchy and, in particular, for those working directly with minority students and communities.

The Policy Context

Research data from the United States, Canada, and Europe vary on the extent to which minority students experience academic failure (for reviews, see Cummins, 1984; Ogbu, 1978). For example, in the United States, Hispanic (with the exception of some groups of Cuban students), Native American, and black students do poorly in school compared to most groups of Asian-American (and white) students. In Canada, Franco-Ontarian students in English language programs have tended to perform considerably less well academically than immigrant minority groups (Cummins, 1984), while the same pattern characterizes Finnish students in Sweden (Skutnabb-Kangas, 1984).

The major task of theory and policy is to explain the pattern of school success and failure among minority students. This task applies both to students whose home language and culture differ from those of the school and wider society (language minority students) and to students whose home language is a version of English but whose cultural background is significantly different from that of the school and wider society, such as many black and Hispanic students from English language backgrounds. With respect to language-minority students, recent policy changes in the United States have been based on the assumption that a major cause of students' educational difficulty is the switch between the language of the home and the language of the school. Thus, the apparently plausible assumption that students cannot learn in a language they do not understand gave rise in the late 60s and early 70s to bilingual education programs in which students' home language was used in addition to English as an initial medium of school instruction (Schneider, 1976).

Bilingual programs, however, have met with both strong support and vehement opposition. The debate regarding policy has revolved around two intuitively appealing assumptions. Those who favor bilingual education argue that children cannot learn in a language they do not understand, and, therefore, L1 (first language) instruction is necessary to counteract the negative effects of a home/ school linguistic mismatch. The opposition contends that bilingual education is illogical in its implication that less English instruction will lead to more English achievement. It makes more sense, the opponents argue, to provide language-minority students with maximum exposure to English.

Despite the apparent plausibility of each assumption, these two conventional wisdoms (the 'linguistic mismatch' and 'insufficient exposure' hypotheses) are each patently inadequate. The argument that language minority students fail primarily as a result of a home/school language switch is refuted by the success of many minority students whose instruction has been totally through a second language. Similarly, research in Canada has documented the effectiveness of 'French immersion programs' in which English background (majority language) students are instructed largely through French in the early grades as a means of developing fluent bilingualism. In spite of the home/school language switch, students' first language (English) skills develop as well as those of students whose instruction has been totally through English. The fact that the first language has high status and is strongly reinforced in the wider society is usually seen as an important factor in the success of these immersion programs.[2]

The opposing 'insufficient exposure' hypothesis, however, fares no better with respect to the research evidence. In fact, the results of virtually every bilingual program that has been evaluated during the past 50 years show either no relationship or a negative relationship between amount of school exposure to the majority language and academic achievement in that language (Baker & de Kanter, 1981; Cummins, 1983a, 1984; Skutnabb-Kangas, 1984). Evaluations of immersion programs for majority students show that students perform as well in English academic skills as comparison groups despite considerably less exposure to English in school. Exactly the same result is obtained for minority students. Promotion of the minority language entails no loss in the development of English academic skills. In other words, language minority students instructed through the minority language (for example, Spanish) for all or part of the school day perform as well in English academic skills as comparable students instructed totally through English.

These results have been interpreted in terms of the 'interdependence hypothesis', which proposes that to the extent that instruction through a minority language is effective in developing academic proficiency in the minority language, transfer of this proficiency to the majority language will occur given adequate exposure and motivation to learn the majority language (Cummins, 1979, 1983a, 1984). The interdependence hypothesis is supported by a large body of research from bilingual program evaluations, studies of language use in the home, immigrant student language learning, correlational studies of L1–L2 (second language) relationships, and experimental studies of bilingual information processing (for reviews, see Cummins, 1984; McLaughlin, 1985).

It is not surprising that the two conventional wisdoms inadequately account for the research data, since each involves only a one-dimensional linguistic explanation. The variability of minority students' academic performance under different social and educational conditions indicates that many complex, interrelated factors are at work (Ogbu, 1978; Wong Fillmore, 1983). In particular, sociological and anthropological research suggests that status and power relations between groups are an important part of any comprehensive account of minority students' school failure (Fishman, 1976; Ogbu, 1978; Paulston, 1980). In addition, a variety of factors related to educational quality and cultural mismatch also appear to be important in mediating minority students' academic progress (Wong Fillmore, 1983). These factors have been integrated into the design of a theoretical framework that suggests the changes required to reverse minority student failure.

A Theoretical Framework

The central tenet of the framework is that students from 'dominated' societal groups are 'empowered' or 'disabled' as a direct result of their interactions with educators in the schools. These interactions are mediated by the implicit or explicit role definitions that educators assume in relation to four institutional characteristics of schools. These characteristics reflect the extent to which (1) minority students' language and culture are incorporated into the school program; (2) minority community participation is encouraged as an integral component of children's education; (3) the pedagogy promotes intrinsic motivation on the part of students to use language actively in order to generate their own knowledge; and (4) professionals involved in assessment become advocates for minority students rather than legitimizing the location of the 'problem' in the students. For each of these dimensions of school organization the role definitions of educators can be described in terms of a continuum, with one end promoting the empowerment of students and the other contributing to the disabling of students.

The three sets of relationships analyzed in the present framework – majority/minority societal group relations, school/minority community relations, educator/minority student relations – are chosen on the basis of hypotheses regarding the relative ineffectiveness of previous educational reforms and the directions required to reverse minority group school failure. Each of these relationships will be discussed in detail.

Intergroup Power Relations

When the patterns of minority student school failure are examined from an international perspective, it becomes evident that power and status relations between minority and majority groups exert a major influence on school performance. An example frequently given is the academic failure of Finnish students in Sweden, where they are a low-status group, compared to their success in Australia, where they are regarded as a high-status group (Troike, 1978). Similarly, Ogbu (1978) reports that the outcast Burakumin perform poorly in Japan but as well as other Japanese students in the United States.

Theorists have explained these findings using several constructs. Cummins (1984), for example, discusses the 'bicultural ambivalence' (or lack of cultural identification) of students in relation to both the home and school cultures. Ogbu (1978) discusses the 'caste' status of minorities that fail academically and ascribes their failure to economic and social discrimination combined with the internalization of the inferior status attributed to them by the dominant group. Feuerstein (1979) attributes academic failure to the disruption of inter-generational transmission processes caused by the alienation of a group from its own culture. In all three conceptions, widespread school failure does not occur in minority groups that are positively oriented towards both their own and the dominant culture, that do not perceive themselves as inferior to the dominant group, and that are not alienated from their own cultural values.

Within the present framework, the *dominant* group controls the institutions and reward systems within society; the *dominated* group (Mullard, 1985) is regarded as inherently inferior by the dominant group and denied access to high-status positions within the institutional structure of the society. As described by Ogbu (1978), the dominated status of a minority group exposes them to condi-tions that predispose children to school failure even before they come to school. These conditions include limited parental access to economic and educational resources, ambivalence toward cultural transmission and primary language use in the home, and interactional styles that may not prepare students for typical teacher/student interaction patterns in school (Heath, 1983; Wong Fillmore, 1983). Bicultural ambivalence and less effective cultural transmission among dominated groups are frequently associated with a historical pattern of coloni-zation and subordination by the dominant group. This pattern, for example, char-acterizes Franco-Ontarian students in Canada, Finns in Sweden, and Hispanic, Native, and black groups in the United States.

Different patterns among other societal groups can clearly be distinguished (Ogbu & Matute-Bianchi, in press). Detailed analysis of patterns of intergroup relations go beyond the scope of this paper. However, it is important to note that the minority groups characterized by widespread school failure tend overwhelm-ingly to be in a dominated relationship to the majority group.[3]

Empowerment of students

Students who are empowered by their school experiences develop the ability, confidence, and motivation to succeed academically. They participate compe-tently in instruction as a result of having developed a confident cultural identity as well as appropriate school-based knowledge and interactional structures (Cummins, 1983b; Tikunoff, 1983). Students who are disempowered or 'disabled' by their school experiences do not develop this type of cognitive/academic and social/emotional foundation. Thus, student empowerment is regarded as both a mediating construct influencing academic performance and as an outcome variable itself.[4]

Although conceptually the cognitive/academic and social/emotional (identity-related) factors are distinct, the data suggest that they are extremely difficult to separate in the case of minority students who are 'at risk' academically. For example, data from both Sweden and the United States suggest that minority students who immigrate relatively late (about ten years of age) often appear to have better academic prospects than students of similar socioeconomic status born in the host country (Cummins, 1984; Skutnabb-Kangas, 1984). Is this because their L1 cognitive/academic skills on arrival provide a better foundation for L2 cognitive/academic skills acquisition, or alternatively, because they have not experienced devaluation of their identity in the societal institutions, namely schools of the host country, as has been the case of students born in that setting?

Similarly, the most successful bilingual programs appear to be those that emphasize and use the students' L1 (for reviews, see Cummins, 1983a, 1984). Is this success due to better promotion of L1 cognitive/academic skills or to the reinforcement of cultural identity provided by an intensive L1 program? By the same token, is the failure of many minority students in English-only immersion programs a function of cognitive/academic difficulties or of students' ambivalence about the value of their cultural identity (Cohen & Swain, 1976)?

These questions are clearly difficult to answer; the point to be made, however, is that for minority students who have traditionally experienced school failure, there is sufficient overlap in the impact of cognitive/academic and identity factors to justify incorporating these two dimensions within the notion of 'student empowerment,' while recognizing that under some conditions each dimension may be affected in different ways.

Schools and power

Minority students are disabled or disempowered by schools in very much the same way that their communities are disempowered by interactions with societal institutions. Since equality of opportunity is believed to be a given, it is assumed that individuals are responsible for their own failure and are, therefore, made to feel that they have failed because of their own inferiority, despite the best efforts of dominant-group institutions and individuals to help them (Skutnabb-Kangas, 1984). This analysis implies that minority students will succeed educationally to the extent that the patterns of interaction in school reverse those that prevail in the society at large.

Four structural elements in the organization of schooling contribute to the extent to which minority students are empowered or disabled. As outlined in Figure 1, these elements include the incorporation of minority students' culture and language, inclusion of minority communities in the education of their children, pedagogical assumptions and practices operating in the classroom, and the assessment of minority students.

SOCIETAL CONTEXT

Dominant Group

Dominated
Group

SCHOOL CONTEXT

Educator Role Definitions

Cultural/Linguistic Incorporation	Additive	–	Subtractive
Community Participation	Collaborative	–	Exclusionary
Pedagogy	Reciprocal Interaction-Oriented	–	Transmission-Oriented
Assessment	Advocacy-Oriented	–	Legitimization-Oriented

EMPOWERED
STUDENTS

DISABLED
STUDENTS

Figure 1 Empowerment of minority students: a theoretical framework

Cultural/linguistic incorporation. Considerable research data suggest that, for dominated minorities, the extent to which students' language and culture are incorporated into the school program constitutes a significant predictor of academic success (Campos & Keatinge, 1984; Cummins, 1983a; Rosier & Holm, 1980). As outlined earlier, students' school success appears to reflect both the more solid cognitive/academic foundation developed through intensive L1 instruction and the reinforcement of their cultural identity.

Included under incorporation of minority group cultural features is the adjustment of instructional patterns to take account of culturally conditioned learning styles. The Kamehameha Early Education Program in Hawaii provides strong evidence of the importance of this type of cultural incorporation. When reading instruction was changed to permit students to collaborate in discussing and interpreting texts, dramatic improvements were found in both reading and verbal intellectual abilities (Au & Jordan, 1981).

An important issue to consider at this point is why superficially plausible but patently inadequate assumptions, such as the 'insufficient exposure' hypothesis, continue to dominate the policy debate when virtually all the evidence suggests that incorporation of minority students' language and culture into the school program will at least not impede academic progress. In other words, what social function do such arguments serve? Within the context of the present framework, it is suggested that a major reason for the vehement resistance to bilingual programs is that the incorporation of minority languages and cultures into the school program confers status and power (jobs, for example) on the minority group. Consequently, such programs contravene the established pattern of dominant/dominated group relations. Within democratic societies, however, contradictions between the rhetoric of equality and the reality of domination must be obscured. Thus, conventional wisdoms such as the insufficient exposure hypothesis become immune from critical scrutiny, and incompatible evidence is either ignored or dismissed.

Educators' role definitions in relation to the incorporation of minority students' language and culture can be characterized along an 'additive–subtractive' dimension.[5] Educators who see their role as adding a second language and cultural affiliation to their students' repertoire are likely to empower students more than those who see their role as replacing or subtracting students' primary language and culture. In addition to the personal and future employment advantages of proficiency in two languages, there is considerable, though not conclusive, evidence that subtle educational advantages result from continued development of both languages among bilingual students. Enhanced metalinguistic development, for example, is frequently found in association with additive bilingualism (Hakuta & Diaz, 1985; McLaughlin, 1984).

It should be noted that an additive orientation does not require the actual teaching of the minority language. In many cases a minority language class may not be possible for reasons such as low concentration of particular groups of minority students. Educators, however, communicate to students and parents in a variety of ways the extent to which the minority language and culture are valued within the context of the school. Even within a monolingual school context, powerful messages can be communicated to students regarding the validity and advantages of language development.

Community participation. Students from dominated communities will be empowered in the school context to the extent that the communities themselves are empowered through their interactions with the school. When educators involve minority parents as partners in their children's education, parents appear to develop a sense of efficacy that communicates itself to children, with positive academic consequences.

Although lip service is paid to community involvement through Parent Advisory Committees (PAC)[6] in many education programs, these committees are frequently manipulated through misinformation and intimidation (Curtis, 1984). The result is that parents from dominated groups retain their powerless status, and their internalized inferiority is reinforced. Children's school failure can then be attributed to the combined effects of parental illiteracy and lack of interest in their children's education. In reality, most parents of minority students have high aspirations for their children and want to be involved in promoting their academic progress (Wong Fillmore, 1983). However, they often do not know how to help their children academically, and they are excluded from participation by the school. In fact, even their interaction through L1 with their children in the home is frequently regarded by educators as contributing to academic difficulties (Cummins, 1984).

Dramatic changes in children's academic progress can be realized when educators take the initiative to change this exclusionary pattern to one of collaboration. The Haringey project in Britain illustrates just how powerful the effects of simple interventions can be (Tizard et al., 1982). In order to assess the effects of parental involvement in the teaching of reading, the researchers established a project in the London borough of Haringey whereby all children in two primary level experimental classes in two different schools read to their parents at home on a regular basis. The reading progress of these children was compared with that of children in two classes in two different schools who were given extra reading instruction in small groups by an experienced and qualified teacher who worked four half-days at each school every week for the two years of the intervention. Both groups were also compared with a control group that received no treatment.

All the schools were in multi-ethnic areas, and there were many parents who did not read English or use it at home. It was found, nevertheless, to be both feasible and practicable to involve nearly all the parents in educational activities such as listening to their children read, even when the parents were non-literate and largely non-English-speaking. It was also found that, almost without exception, parents welcomed the project, agreed to hear their children read, and completed a record card showing what had been read.

The researchers report that parental involvement had a pronounced effect on the students' success in school. Children who read to their parents made significantly greater progress in reading than those who did not engage in this type of literacy sharing. Small-group instruction in reading, given by a highly competent specialist, did not produce improvements comparable to those obtained from the collaboration with parents. In contrast to the home collaboration program, the benefits of extra reading instruction were least apparent for initially low-achieving children.

In addition, the collaboration between teachers and parents was effective for children of all initial levels of performance, including those who, at the beginning of the study, were failing in learning to read. Teachers reported that the children showed an increased interest in school learning and were better behaved. Those teachers involved in the home collaboration found the work with parents worthwhile, and they continued to involve parents with subsequent classes after the experiment was concluded. It is interesting to note that teachers of the control classes also adopted the home collaboration program after the two-year experimental period.

The Haringey project is one example of school/community relations; there are others. The essential point, however, is that the teacher's role in such relations can be characterized along a *collaborative–exclusionary* dimension. Teachers operating at the collaborative end of the continuum actively encourage minority parents to participate in promoting their children's academic progress both in the home and through involvement in classroom activities. A collaborative orientation may require a willingness on the part of the teacher to work closely with mother-tongue teachers or aides in order to communicate effectively, in a non-condescending way, with minority parents. Teachers with an exclusionary orientation, on the other hand, tend to regard teaching as *their* job and are likely to view collaboration with minority parents as either irrelevant or detrimental to children's progress.

Pedagogy. Several investigators have suggested that many 'learning disabilities' are pedagogically induced in that children designated 'at risk' frequently receive intensive instruction which confines them to a passive role and induces a form of 'learned helplessness' (Beers & Beers, 1980; Coles, 1978; Cummins, 1984). This process is illustrated in a micro-ethnographic study of 14 reading lessons given to West Indian Creole-speakers of English in Toronto, Canada (Ramphal, 1983). It was found that teachers' constant correction of students' miscues prevented students from focusing on the meaning of what they were reading. Moreover, the constant corrections fostered dependent behavior because students knew that whenever they paused at a word the teacher would automatically pronounce it for them. One student was interrupted so often in one of the lessons that he was able to read only one sentence, consisting of three words, uninterrupted. In contrast to a pattern of classroom interaction which promotes instructional dependence, teaching that empowers will aim to liberate students from instruction by encouraging them to become active generators of their knowledge. As Graves (1983) has demonstrated, this type of active knowledge generation can occur when, for example, children create and publish their own books within the classroom.

Two major pedagogical orientations can be distinguished. These differ in the extent to which the teacher retains exclusive control over classroom interaction as opposed to sharing some of this control with students. The dominant instructional model in North American schools has been termed a transmission model (Barnes, 1976; Wells, 1982). This model incorporates essentially the same assumptions about teaching and learning that Freire (1970, 1973) has termed a 'banking' model of education. This transmission model will be contrasted with a 'reciprocal interaction' model of pedagogy.

The basic premise of the transmission model is that the teacher's task is to impart knowledge or skills that she or he possesses to students who do not yet have these skills. This implies that the teacher initiates and controls the interaction, constantly orienting it towards the achievement of instructional objectives. For example, in first- and second-language programs that stress pattern repetition, the teacher presents the materials, models the language patterns, asks questions, and provides feedback to students about the correctness of their response. The curriculum in these types of programs focuses on the internal structure of the language or subject matter. Consequently, it frequently focuses predominantly on surface features of language or literacy such as handwriting, spelling, and decoding, and emphasizes correct recall of content taught by means of highly structured drills and workbook exercises. It has been argued that a transmission model of teaching contravenes central principles of language and literacy acquisition and that a model allowing for reciprocal interaction among students and teachers represents a more appropriate alternative (Cummins, 1984; Wells, 1982).[7]

A central tenet of the reciprocal interaction model is that 'talking and writing are means to learning' (Bullock Report, 1975: 50). The use of this model in teaching requires a genuine dialogue between student and teacher in both oral and written modalities, guidance and facilitation rather than control of student learning by the teacher, and the encouragement of student/student talk in a collaborative learning context. This model emphasizes the development of higher level cognitive skills rather than just factual recall, and meaningful language use by students rather than the correction of surface forms. Language use and development are consciously integrated with all curricular content rather than taught as isolated subjects, and tasks are presented to students in ways that generate intrinsic rather than extrinsic motivation. In short, pedagogical approaches that empower students encourage them to assume greater control over setting their own learning goals and to collaborate actively with each other in achieving these goals.

The development of a sense of efficacy and inner direction in the classroom is especially important for students from dominated groups whose experiences so often orient them in the opposite direction. Wong Fillmore (1983) has reported that Hispanic students learned considerably more English in classrooms that provided opportunities for reciprocal interaction with teachers and peers. Ample opportunities for expressive writing appear to be particularly significant in promoting a sense of academic efficacy among minority students (Cummins *et al.*, 1986). As expressed by Daiute (1985):

> Children who learn early that writing is not simply an exercise gain a sense
> of power that gives them confidence to write – and write a lot ... Beginning

writers who are confident that they have something to say or that they can find out what they need to know can even overcome some limits of training or development. Writers who don't feel that what they say matters have an additional burden that no skills training can help them overcome. (pp. 5–6)

The implications for students from dominated groups are obvious. Too often the instruction they receive convinces them that what they have to say is irrelevant or wrong. The failure of this method of instruction is then taken as an indication that the minority student is of low ability, a verdict frequently confirmed by subsequent assessment procedures.

Assessment. Historically, assessment has played the role of legitimizing the disabling of minority students. In some cases assessment itself may play the primary role, but more often it has been used to locate the 'problem' within the minority student, thereby screening from critical scrutiny the subtractive nature of the school program, the exclusionary orientation of teachers towards minority communities, and transmission models of teaching that inhibit students from active participation in learning.

This process is virtually inevitable when the conceptual base for assessment is purely psycho-educational. If the psychologist's task is to discover the causes of a minority student's academic difficulties and the only tools at his or her disposal are psychological tests (in either L1 or L2), then it is hardly surprising that the child's difficulties will be attributed to psychological dysfunctions. The myth of bilingual handicaps that still influences educational policy was generated in exactly this way during the 1920s and 1930s.

Recent studies suggest that despite the appearance of change brought about by PL 94–142, the underlying structure of assessment processes has remained essentially intact. Mehan *et al.* (1986), for example, report that psychologists continued to test children until they 'found' the disability that could be invoked to 'explain' the student's apparent academic difficulties. Diagnosis and placement were influenced frequently by factors related to bureaucratic procedures and funding requirements rather than to students' academic performance in the classroom. Rueda and Mercer (1985) have also shown that designation of minority students as 'learning disabled' as compared to 'language impaired' was strongly influenced by whether a psychologist or a speech pathologist was on the placement committee. In other words, with respect to students' actual behavior, the label was essentially arbitrary. An analysis of more than four hundred psychological assessments of minority students revealed that although no diagnostic conclusions were logically possible in the majority of assessments, psychologists were most reluctant to admit this fact to teachers and parents (Cummins, 1984). In short, the data suggest that the structure within which psychological assessment takes place orients the psychologist to locate the cause of the academic problem within the minority student.

An alternative role definition for psychologists or special educators can be termed an 'advocacy' or 'delegitimization' role.[8] In this case, their task must be to delegitimize the traditional function of psychological assessment in the educational disabling of minority students by becoming advocates for the child in scrutinizing critically the societal and educational context within which the child has developed (Cazden, 1985). This involves locating the pathology within the societal power relations between dominant and dominated groups, in the reflection of these power relations between school and communities, and in the mental and cultural disabling of minority students that takes place in classrooms. These conditions are a more probable cause of the 300% over-representation of Texas Hispanic students in the learning disabled category than any intrinsic processing deficit unique to Hispanic children. The training of psychologists and special educators does not prepare them for this advocacy or delegitimization role. From the present perspective, however, it must be emphasized that discriminatory assessment is carried out by well-intentioned individuals who, rather than challenging a socio-educational system that tends to disable minority students, have accepted a role definition and an educational structure that makes discriminatory assessment virtually inevitable.[9]

Empowering Minority Students: The Carpinteria Example

The Spanish-only preschool program of the Carpinteria School District, near Santa Barbara, California, is one of the few programs in the United States that explicitly incorporates the major elements hypothesized in previous sections to empower minority students. Spanish is the exclusive language of instruction, there is a strong community involvement component, and the program is characterized by a coherent philosophy of promoting conceptual development through meaningful linguistic interaction.

The proposal to implement an intensive Spanish-only preschool program in this region was derived from district findings showing that a large majority of the Spanish-speaking students entering kindergarten each year lacked adequate skills to succeed in the kindergarten program. On the School Readiness Inventory, a district-wide screening measure administered to all incoming kindergarten students, Spanish-speaking students tended to average about eight points lower than English-speaking students (approximately 14.5 compared to 23.0, averaged over four years from 1979 to 1982) despite the fact that the test was administered in students' dominant language. A score of 20 or better was viewed by the district as predicting a successful kindergarten year for the child. Prior to the implementation of the experimental program, the Spanish-background children attended a bilingual preschool program – operated either by Head Start or the Community Day Care Center – in which both English and Spanish were used concurrently but with strong emphasis on the development of English skills. According to the district kindergarten teachers, children who had attended these programs often mixed English and Spanish into a 'Spanglish'.

The major goal of the experimental Spanish-only preschool program was to bring Spanish-dominant children entering kindergarten up to a level of readiness for school similar to that attained by English-speaking children in the community. The project also sought to make parents of the program participants aware of their role as the child's first teacher and to encourage them to provide specific types of experiences for their children in the home.

The preschool program itself involved the integration of language with a large variety of concrete and literacy-related experiences. As summarized in the evaluation report: 'The development of language skills in Spanish was foremost in the planning and attention given to every facet of the pre-school day. Language was used constantly for conversing, learning new ideas, concepts and vocabulary, thinking creatively, and problem-solving to give the children the opportunity to develop their language skills in Spanish to as high a degree as possible within the structure of the pre-school day' (Campos & Keatinge, 1984: 17).

Participation in the program was on a voluntary basis and students were screened only for age and Spanish-language dominance. Family characteristics of students in the experimental program were typical of other Spanish-speaking families in the community; more than 90% were of low socioeconomic status, and the majority worked in agriculture and had an average educational level of about sixth grade.

The program proved to be highly successful in developing students' readiness skills, as evidenced by the average score of 21.6 obtained by the 1982–83 incoming kindergarten students who had been in the program, compared to the score of 23.2 obtained by English-speaking students. A score of 14.6 was obtained by Spanish-speaking students who experienced the regular bilingual preschool program. In 1983–84 the scores of these three groups were 23.3, 23.4, and 16.0, respectively. In other words, the gap between English-background and Spanish-background children in the Spanish-only preschool had disappeared; however, a considerable gap remained for Spanish-background students for whom English was the focus of preschool instruction.

Of special interest is the performance of the experimental program students on the English and Spanish versions of the Bilingual Syntax Measure (BSM), a test of oral syntactic development (Hernandez-Chavez *et al.*, 1976). Despite the fact that they experienced an exclusively Spanish preschool program, these students performed better than the other Spanish-speaking students in English (and Spanish) on entry to kindergarten in 1982 and at a similar level in 1983. On entrance to grade one in 1983, the gap had widened considerably, with almost five times as many of the experimental-program students performing at level 5 (fluent English) compared to the other Spanish-background students (47% *vs.* 10%) (Campos & Keatinge, 1984).

The evaluation report suggests that:

although project participants were exposed to less *total* English, they, because of their enhanced first language skill and concept knowledge were better able to comprehend the English they were exposed to. This seems to be borne out by comments made by kindergarten teachers in the District about project participants. They are making comments like, 'Project participants appear more aware of what is happening around them in the classroom,' 'They are able to focus on the task at hand better' and 'They demonstrate greater self-confidence in learning situations.' All of these traits would tend to enhance the language acquisition process.

(Campos & Keatinge, 1984: 41)

Campos and Keatinge (1984) also emphasize the consequences of the pre-school program for parental participation in their children's education. They note that, according to the school officials, 'the parents of project participants are much more aware of and involved in their child's school experience than non-participant parents of Spanish speakers. This is seen as having a positive impact on the future success of the project participants – the greater the involvement of parents, the greater the chances of success of the child' (p. 41).

The major relevance of these findings for educators and policymakers derives from their demonstration that educational programs *can* succeed in preventing the academic failure experienced by many minority students. The corollary is that failure to provide this type of program constitutes the disabling of minority students by the school system. For example, among the students who did not experience the experimental preschool program, the typical pattern of low levels of academic readiness and limited proficiency in both languages was observed. These are the students who are likely to be referred for psychological assessment early in their school careers. This assessment will typically legitimize the inadequate educational provision by attributing students' difficulties to some vacuous category, such as learning disability. By contrast, students who experienced a preschool program in which (a) their cultural identity was reinforced, (b) there was active collaboration with parents, and (c) meaningful use of language was integrated into every aspect of daily activities were developing high levels of conceptual and linguistic skills in *both* languages.

Conclusion

In this article I have proposed a theoretical framework for examining minority students' academic failure and for predicting the effects of educational interventions. Within this framework the educational failure of minority students is analyzed as a function of the extent to which schools reflect or counteract the power relations that exist within the broader society. Specifically, language-minority students' educational progress is strongly influenced by the extent to which individual educators become advocates for the promotion of students' linguistic talents, actively encourage community participation in developing students' academic and cultural resources, and implement pedagogical approaches that succeed in liberating students from instructional dependence.

The educator/student interactions characteristic of the disabling end of the proposed continua reflect the typical patterns of interaction that dominated societal groups have experienced in relation to dominant groups. The intrinsic value of the group is usually denied, and 'objective' evidence is accumulated to demonstrate the group's 'inferiority'. This inferior status is then used as a justification for excluding the group from activities and occupations that entail societal rewards.

In a similar way, the disabling of students is frequently rationalized on the basis of students' 'needs'. For example, minority students need maximum exposure to English in both the school and home; thus, parents must be told not to interact with children in their mother tongue. Similarly, minority children need a highly structured drill-oriented program in order to maximize time spent on tasks to compensate for their deficient preschool experiences. Minority students also need a comprehensive diagnostic/prescriptive assessment in order to identify the nature of their 'problem' and possible remedial interventions.

This analysis suggests a major reason for the relative lack of success of the various educational bandwagons that have characterized the North American crusade against underachievement during the past 20 years. The individual role definitions of educators and the institutional role definitions of schools have remained largely unchanged despite 'new and improved' programs and policies. These programs and policies, despite their cost, have simply added a new veneer to the outward facade of the structure that disables minority students. The lip service paid to initial L1 instruction, community involvement, and nondiscriminatory assessment, together with the emphasis on improved teaching techniques, have succeeded primarily in deflecting attention from the attitudes and orientation of educators who interact on a daily basis with minority students. It is in these interactions that students are disabled. In the absence of individual and collective educator role redefinitions, schools will continue to reproduce, in these interactions, the power relations that characterize the wider society and make minority students' academic failure inevitable.

To educators genuinely concerned about alleviating the educational difficulties of minority students and responding to their needs, this conclusion may appear overly bleak. I believe, however, that it is realistic and optimistic, as directions for change are clearly indicated rather than obscured by the overlay of costly reforms that leave the underlying disabling structure essentially intact. Given the societal commitment to maintaining the dominant/dominated power relationships, we can predict that educational changes threatening this structure will be fiercely resisted. This is in fact the case for each of the four structural dimensions discussed earlier.[10]

In order to reverse the pattern of widespread minority group educational failure, educators and policymakers are faced with both a personal and a political challenge. Personally, they must redefine their roles within the class-room, the community, and the broader society so that these role definitions result in interactions that empower rather than disable students. Politically, they must attempt to persuade colleagues and decision-makers – such as school boards and the public that elects them – of the importance of redefining institutional goals so that the schools transform society by empowering minority students rather than reflect society by disabling them.

Acknowledgements

Discussions at the Symposium on 'Minority Languages in Academic Research and Educational Policy' held in Sandbjerg Slot, Denmark, April 1985, contri-buted to the ideas in the paper. I would like to express my appreciation to the participants at the Symposium and to Safder Alladina, Jan Curtis, David Dolson, Norm Gold, Monica Heller, Dennis Parker, Verity Saifullah Khan, and Tove Skutnabb-Kangas for comments on earlier drafts. I would also like to acknow-ledge the financial support of the Social Sciences and Humanities Research Council (Grant No. 431-79-0003) which made possible participation in the Sandbjerg Slot symposium.

Notes

1. The Education of All Handicapped Children Act of 1975 (Public Law 94–142) guarantees to all handicapped children in the United States the right to a free public education, to an individualized education program (IEP), to due process, to education in the least segregated environment, and to assessment procedures that are multidimensional and non-culturally discriminatory.
2. For a discussion of the implications of Canadian French immersion programs for the education of minority students, see California State Department of Education (1984).
3. Ogbu (1978), for example, has distinguished between 'caste,' 'immigrant,' and 'auto-nomous' minority groups. Caste groups are similar to what has been termed 'domi-nated' groups in the present framework and are the only category of minority groups that tends to fail academically. Immigrant groups have usually come voluntarily to the host society for economic reasons and, unlike caste minorities, have not internalized negative attributions of the dominant group. Ogbu gives Chinese and Japanese groups as examples of 'immigrant' minorities. The cultural resources that permit some minority groups to resist discrimination and internalization of negative attributions are still a matter of debate and speculation (for a recent treatment, see Ogbu & Matute-Bianchi, in press). The final category distinguished by Ogbu is that of 'autonomous' groups who hold a distinct cultural identity but who are not subordinated economically or politi-cally to the dominant group (for example, Jews and Mormons in the United States).
   Failure to take account of these differences among minority groups both in patterns of academic performance and socio-historical relationships to the dominant group has contributed to the confused state of policymaking with respect to language minority students. The bilingual education policy, for example, has been based on the implicit assumption that the linguistic mismatch hypothesis was valid for all language minor-ity students, and, consequently, the same types of intervention were necessary and appropriate for all students. Clearly, this assumption is open to question.
4. There is no contradiction in postulating student empowerment as both a mediating and an outcome variable. For example, cognitive abilities clearly have the same status

in that they contribute to students' school success and can also be regarded as an outcome of schooling.

5. The terms 'additive' and 'subtractive' bilingualism were coined by Lambert (1975) to refer to the proficient bilingualism associated with positive cognitive outcomes on the one hand, and the limited bilingualism often associated with negative outcomes on the other.

6. PACs were established in some states to provide an institutional structure for minority parent involvement in educational decision making with respect to bilingual programs. In California, for example, a majority of PAC members for any state-funded program was required to be from the program target group. The school plan for use of program funds required signed PAC approval.

7. This 'reciprocal interaction' model incorporates proposals about the relation between language and learning made by a variety of investigators, most notably in the Bullock Report (1975), and by Barnes (1976), Lindfors (1980), and Wells (1982). Its application with respect to the promotion of literacy conforms closely to psycholinguistic approaches to reading (Goodman & Goodman, 1977; Holdaway, 1979; Smith, 1978) and to the recent emphasis on encouraging expressive writing from the earliest grades (Chomsky, 1981; Giacobbe, 1982; Graves, 1983; Temple, Nathan & Burris, 1982). Students' microcomputing networks such as the *Computer Chronicles Newswire* (Mehan *et al.*, 1984) represent a particularly promising application of reciprocal interaction model of pedagogy.

8. See Mullard (1985) for a detailed discussion of delegitimization strategies in anti-racist education.

9. Clearly, the presence of processing difficulties that are rooted in neurological causes is not being denied for either monolingual or bilingual children. However, in the case of children from dominated minorities, the proportion of disabilities that are neurological in origin is likely to represent only a small fraction of those that derive from educational and social conditions.

10. Although for pedagogy the resistance to sharing control with students goes beyond majority/minority group relations, the same elements are present. If the curriculum is not predetermined and presequenced, and the students are generating their own knowledge in a critical and creative way, then the reproduction of the societal structure cannot be guaranteed – hence the reluctance to liberate students from instructional dependence.

References

Au, K. H. and Jordan, C. (1981) Teaching reading to Hawaiian children: Finding a culturally appropriate solution. In H. Trueba, G. P. Guthrie and K. H. Au (eds) *Culture and the Bilingual Classroom. Studies in Classroom Ethnography* (pp. 139–52). Rowley, MA: Newbury House.

Baker, K. A. and de Kanter, A. A. (1981) *Effectiveness of Bilingual Education: A Review of the Literature.* Washington, DC: US Department of Education, Office of Planning and Budget.

Barnes, D. (1976) *From Communication to Curriculum.* New York: Penguin.

Beers, C. S. and Beers, J. W. (1980) Early identification of learning disabilities: Facts and fallacies. *Elementary School Journal* 81, 67–76.

Bethell, T. (1979) Against bilingual education. *Harper's*, February, 30–3.

Bullock Report (1975) *A Language for Life* (Report of the Committee of Inquiry Appointed by the Secretary of State for Education and Science under the Chairmanship of Sir Alan Bullock). London: HMSO.

California State Department of Education (1984) *Studies on Immersion Education: A Collection for United States Educators.* Sacramento: Author.

Campos, J. and Keatinge, B. (1984) *The Carpinteria Preschool Program: Title VII Second Year Evaluation Report*. Washington, DC: Department of Education.

Cazden, C. B. (1985) The ESL teacher as advocate. Plenary presentation to the TESOL Conference, April, New York.

Chomsky, C. (1981) Write now, read later. In C. Cazden (ed.) *Language in Early Childhood Education* (2nd edn, pp. 141–49). Washington, DC: National Association for the Education of Young Children.

Cohen, A. D. and Swain, M. (1976) Bilingual education: The immersion model in the North American context. In J. E. Alatis and K. Twaddell (eds) *English as a Second Language in Bilingual Education* (pp. 55–64). Washington, DC: TESOL.

Coles, G. S. (1978) The learning disabilities test battery: Empirical and social issues. *Harvard Educational Review* 48, 313–40.

Cummins, J. (1979) Linguistic interdependence and the educational development of bilingual children. *Review of Educational Research* 49, 222–51.

Cummins, J. (1983a) *Heritage Language Education: A Literature Review*. Toronto: Ministry of Education.

Cummins, J. (1983b) Functional language proficiency in context: Classroom participation as an interactive process. In W. J. Tikunoff (ed.) *Compatibility of the SBIS Features with Other Research on Instruction for LEP Students* (pp. 109–31). San Francisco: Far West Laboratory.

Cummins, J. (1984) *Bilingualism and Special Education: Issues in Assessment and Pedagogy*. Clevedon: Multilingual Matters.

Cummins, J., Aguiar, M., Bascunan, L., Fiorucci, S., Sanaoui, R. and Basman, S. (1986) *Literacy Development in Heritage Language Programs*. Toronto: National Heritage Language Resource Unit (unpublished report).

Curtis, J. (1984) Bilingual education in Calistoga: Not a happy ending. Report submitted to the Instituto de Lengua y Cultura, Elmira, NY.

Daiute, C. (1985) *Writing and Computers*. Reading, MA: Addison-Wesley.

Feuerstein, R. (1979) *The Dynamic Assessment of Retarded Performers: The Learning Potential Assessment Device, Theory, Instruments, and Techniques*. Baltimore: University Park Press.

Fishman, J. (1976) *Bilingual Education: An International Sociological Perspective*. Rowley, MA: Newbury House.

Freire, P. (1970) *Pedagogy of the Oppressed*. New York: Seabury.

Freire, P. (1973) *Education for Critical Consciousness*. New York: Seabury.

Giacobbe, M. E. (1982) Who says children can't write the first week? In R. D. Walshe (ed.) *Donald Graves in Australia. 'Children Want to Write'* (pp. 99–103). Exeter, NH: Heinemann Educational Books.

Goodman, K. S. and Goodman, Y. M. (1977) Learning about psycholinguistic processes by analyzing oral reading. *Harvard Educational Review* 47, 317–33.

Graves, D. H. (1983) *Writing: Teachers and Children at Work*. Exeter, NH: Heinemann Educational Books.

Hakuta, K. and Diaz, R. M. (1985) The relationship between degree of bilingualism and cognitive ability: A critical discussion and some new longitudinal data. In K. E. Nelson (ed.) *Children's Language* (Vol. 5, pp. 319–45). Hillsdale, NJ: Erlbaum.

Heath, S. B. (1983) *Ways with Words*. Cambridge: Cambridge University Press.

Hernandez-Chavez, E., Burt, M. and Dulay, H. (1976) *The Bilingual Syntax Measure*. New York: The Psychological Corporation.

Holdaway, D. (1979) *The Foundations of Literacy*. Sydney, Australia: Ashton Scholastic.

Jusenius, C. and Duarte, V. L. (1982) *Hispanics and Jobs: Barriers to Progress*. Washington, DC: National Commission for Employment Policy.

Lambert, W. E. (1975) Culture and language as factors in learning and education. In A. Wolfgang (ed.) *Education of Immigrant Students* (pp. 55–83). Toronto: OISE.

Lindfors, J. W. (1980) *Children's Language and Learning.* Englewood Cliffs, NJ: Prentice-Hall.

McLaughlin, B. (1984) Early bilingualism: Methodological and theoretical issues. In M. Paradis and Y. Lebrun (eds) *Early Bilingualism and Child Development* (pp. 19–46). Lisse: Swets & Zeitlinger.

McLaughlin, B. (1985) *Second Language Acquisition in Childhood.* Vol. 2. *School-age Children.* Hillsdale, NJ: Erlbaum.

Mehan, H., Hertweck, A. and Meihls, J. L. (1986) *Handicapping the Handicapped: Decision Making in Students' Educational Careers.* Palo Alto: Stanford University.

Mehan, H., Miller-Souviney, B. and Riel, M. M. (1984) Research currents: Knowledge of text editing and control of literacy skills. *Language Arts* 65, 154–9.

Mullard, C. (1985) The social dynamic of migrant groups: From progressive to transformative policy in education. Paper presented at the OECD Conference on Educational Policies and the Minority Social Groups, January, Paris.

Ogbu, J. U. (1978) *Minority Education and Caste.* New York: Academic Press.

Ogbu, J. U. and Matute-Bianchi, M. E. (in press) Understanding sociocultural factors: Knowledge, identity and school adjustment. In California State Department of Education (ed.) *Sociocultural Factors and Minority Student Achievement.* Sacramento: Author.

Ortiz, A. A. and Yates, J. R. (1983) Incidence of exceptionality among Hispanics: Implications for manpower planning. *NABE Journal* 7, 41–54.

Paulston, C. B. (1980) *Bilingual Education: Theories and Issues.* Rowley, MA: Newbury House.

Ramphal, D. K. (1983) An analysis of reading instruction of West Indian Creole-speaking students. Unpublished doctoral dissertation, Ontario Institute for Studies in Education.

Rosier, P. and Holm, W. (1980) *The Rock Point Experience: A Longitudinal Study of a Navajo School.* Washington, DC: Center for Applied Linguistics.

Rueda, R. and Mercer, J. R. (1985) Predictive analysis of decision making with language-minority handicapped children. Paper presented at the BUENO Center 3rd Annual Symposium on Bilingual Education, June, Denver.

Schneider, S. G. (1976) *Revolution, Reaction or Reform: The 1974 Bilingual Education Act.* New York: Las Americas.

Skutnabb-Kangas, T. (1984) *Bilingualism or Not: The Education of Minorities.* Clevedon: Multilingual Matters.

Smith, F. (1978) *Understanding Reading* (2nd edn). New York: Holt, Rinehart & Winston.

Temple, C. A., Nathan, R. G. and Burris, N. A. (1982) *The Beginnings of Writing.* Boston: Allyn & Bacon.

Tikunoff, W. J. (1983) Five significant bilingual instructional features. In W. J. Tikunoff (ed.) *Compatibility of the SBIS Features with Other Research on Instruction for LEP Students* (pp. 5–18). San Francisco: Far West Laboratory.

Tizard, J., Schofield, W. N. and Hewison, J. (1982) Collaboration between teachers and parents in assisting children's reading. *British Journal of Educational Psychology* 52, 1–15.

Troike, R. (1978) Research evidence for the effectiveness of bilingual education. *NABE Journal* 3, 13–24.

Wells, G. (1982) Language, learning and the curriculum. In G. Wells (ed.) *Language, Learning and Education* (pp. 205–26). Bristol: Centre for the Study of Language and Communication, University of Bristol.

Wong Fillmore, L. (1983) The language learner as an individual: Implications of research on individual differences for the ESL teacher. In M. A. Clarke and J. Handscombe (eds) *On TESOL '82: Pacific Perspectives on Language Learning and Teaching* (pp. 157–71). Washington, DC: TESOL.

Psychological Assessment of Minority Students: Out of Context, Out of Focus, Out of Control?

For more than 50 years educators have pointed to the abuses of psychological tests when applied to students from cultural or linguistic minority groups (e.g. Mercer, 1973; Sanchez, 1934). These concerns finally found legal expression in 1975 with the passage of Public Law (PL) 94–142 which entailed what appeared to be strong provisions against discriminatory assessment.

Recent studies, however, suggest that the implementation of PL 94–142 does not eliminate discrimination (Mehan *et al.*, in press; Ortiz & Yates, 1983). Ortiz and Yates, for example, reported that Hispanic students in Texas were over-represented by a factor of 300% in the 'learning disabilities' category. The ethnographic study conducted by Mehan *et al.* found no empirical basis for teachers' referrals of students for psychological assessment. Yet, the referral exercised a major influence on the actual psychological assessment in that psychologists continued to test until they 'found' the disability that could be invoked to 'explain' the student's apparent academic difficulties.

A similar conclusion emerged from the analysis of more than 400 psychological assessments of minority students conducted by Cummins (1984). Although no diagnostic conclusions were logically possible in the majority of assessments, psychologists were most reluctant to risk their professional credibility by admitting this fact to teachers and parents.

The argument in the present paper is that discriminatory assessment of minority students is virtually inevitable when the process focuses exclusively on the student and ignores the societal context within which minority students develop and schools attempt to educate. Legislation such as PL 94–142 is largely ineffective in altering discriminatory assessment procedures because it leaves essentially unchanged the *role relationships* between teachers, psychologists and students, on the one hand, and between schools and the minority communities they serve, on the other. Within this system of role relationships, the psychological assessment has operated to screen from critical scrutiny both the societal roots of

195

minority students' academic difficulties and the educational treatment experienced by the child. This screening is achieved through the adoption of a medical model of assessment that necessitates that the 'problem' be located within the child.

The Context of Minority Student Assessment

Typically, assessment procedures take little account of the context within which minority students have developed. The standardization procedures for tests such as the verbal scale of the WISC–R make it inevitable that items that might be uniquely fair to any particular minority group will be screened out in the item analysis phase since these items are unlikely to be 'fair' to the majority group which, by definition, will constitute the bulk of any representative sample. Ribeiro (1980), for example, gives many examples of how WISC–R items discriminate against Azorean children. On item 12 of the Comprehension subtest ('Why is it usually better to give money to a well-known charity than to a street beggar?'), Ribeiro suggests that for a child raised within an Azorean cultural milieu, the 'intelligent' response is that it is better to give money to a street beggar, since within the Azorean context giving to a beggar amounts to giving to God, whereas well-organized charities are almost non-existent.

Thus, typical psychological assessment procedures not only fail to sample the culturally-specific skills and knowledge of the minority child, they frequently penalize children for demonstrating this knowledge.

In addition, current psychological assessment practices ignore the historical context within which the 'myth of bilingual handicaps' was created. Many educators still attribute minority students' academic difficulties to their bilingualism or use of a minority language at home. Parents are frequently advised to switch to English in the home on the grounds that they jeopardize their children's academic prospects by exposing them to a language other than the school language. Although many studies carried out during the past decade totally discredit these assumptions (see Cummins, 1984, for a detailed review), they persist because they provide a convenient 'explanation' for the low verbal scores often observed in assessments of minority students.

The myth that bilingualism causes academic difficulties gained credibility largely as a result of the administration of IQ tests to low socioeconomic status (SES) minority children in their weaker language (English). Comparisons were usually made with non-bilingual students from middle-class backgrounds. The minority students frequently were experiencing active eradication of their language and cultural identity at school (often through physical punishment). Psychological assessment of minority students as intellectually inferior legitimizes the educational treatment of attributing students' failure to characteristics of the students themselves.

Despite the outward appearance of change, this structure still persists. Psychological assessment is still oriented towards discovery of the *student's* problem. The societal context and the classroom context are taken for granted, thereby limiting possible explanations of academic difficulties to intrinsic characteristics or cultural background of the student. Lack of exposure to the school language is still a favored explanation for minority students' school failure. The consequent advice to parents ('Speak English') appears logical despite the likelihood that this advice will expose children to poor models of English and reduce the emotional and conceptual quality of parent–child communication. Research pointing to power relations between dominant and subordinate groups as a major contributor to minority students' academic difficulties (Cummins, 1984; Ogbu, 1978) is ignored as is research suggesting that bilingualism enhances academic functioning when a minority students' home language is encouraged to develop (Cummins, 1984).

In short, the current role relations between psychologists and minority students mirror those that helped create the myth of bilingual handicaps more than 50 years ago. Attempts to render the assessment tools used by psychologists less discriminatory will be effective only to the extent that the new tools require a change in the role relationships between assessor and assessed.[1]

The Focus of Minority Student Assessment

Location of the 'problem' within the child is virtually inevitable when the conceptual base for the psychological assessment process is purely psychoeducational. If the psychologist's task is to discover the causes of a minority student's academic difficulties and the only tools at her disposal are psychological tests (in either L1 or L2), then it is hardly surprising that the child's difficulties will be attributed to psychological dysfunctions.

Currently, the favored diagnostic category for minority students appears to be that of 'learning disability' (e.g. Ortiz & Yates, 1983; Tucker, 1980). The assumption underlying the designation of diagnostic categories (such as 'learning disability') is that they can be coherently defined, reliably identified and measured, and that specific implications for remediation exist. None of these conditions are met in the case of 'learning disabilities'. Definitions of the construct are regarded as highly problematic by many investigators and practitioners (e.g. McIntyre *et al.*, 1980), no valid measures of the construct exist (e.g. Coles, 1978), incidence estimates in the school population vary between 2% and 20% (Wallace & McLoughlin, 1975), and, it has been argued, remedial pedagogy frequently violates central principles of language learning. As pointed out by Farnham-Diggory (1978), within the scope of the field called 'learning disabilities' there are:

> ... notions of brain damage, hyperactivity, mild forms of retardation, social–emotional adjustment, language difficulties, subtle forms of deafness,

perceptual problems, motor clumsiness, and, above all, reading disorders –
almost the entire field of special education. (1978: 2)

It is hardly surprising that the learning disability category has become a
dumping ground for minority students who are failing academically. The label is
regarded as an explanation. No further inquiry is necessary or desirable. The
focus is on the child and the problem has been identified.

Psychologists who operate within this pattern of role definition ignore the
possibility that the 'learning disabilities' they have identified are pedagogically-
induced. They also ignore the social pathology reflected in some patterns of
dominant–subordinate group relations that gives rise to academic and identity
problems for minority students. There is considerable evidence that when educators redefine the pattern of role relationships established between teachers and
minority students within the classroom and between schools and minority communities, the incidence of learning difficulties is greatly reduced (Campos &
Keatinge, 1984; Tizard et al., 1982). Psychologists who operate within the traditional narrow-focus model of assessment unwittingly legitimize the educational
disabling of many minority students.

Redefining the Role of Psychological Assessment

The alternative role definition that is required to reverse the traditional 'legitimizing' function of assessment can be termed an 'advocacy' or 'delegitimization' role (see Mullard, 1985, for discussion of delegitimization strategies
in anti-racist education). The psychologist's or special educator's task must be
to 'delegitimize' the traditional function of psychological assessment in the
educational disabling of minority students; in other words, they must be prepared
to become the advocate for the child (Cazden, 1985) in critically scrutinizing the
societal and educational context within which the child has developed. This
involves locating the pathology within the societal power relations between
dominant and subordinate groups, in the reflection of these power relations
between school and communities, and in the mental and cultural disabling of
minority students that has taken and still does take place in classrooms. These
conditions are the cause of the 300% over-representation of Texas Hispanic
students in the 'learning disabled' category rather than any intrinsic processing
deficit unique to Hispanic children.

Sensitivity to intrinsic processing deficits among minority children is also a
legitimate function but only within the context of an 'advocacy' role definition
where social and educational pathologies are equally subject to critical scrutiny
as contributors to minority students' academic difficulties.

Realistically, large-scale change from a 'legitimization' to an 'advocacy' role on
the part of psychologists is unlikely. To the extent that the legitimization process
functions as an integral part of a social system, it cannot change independently

of that system. However, the analytic focus with respect to change presented in the present paper has been on *individual* role definitions. Thus, to the extent that individual psychologists question the assumptions underlying their role, they also challenge the social and educational structures that disable students.

An implication that follows from the present analysis is that those who train psychologists and other educators to use certain tools and fulfill particular roles within social systems have an ethical responsibility to simultaneously train them to question those role definitions and challenge a social system that disables minority students. Discriminatory assessment is carried out by individual people who have accepted a role definition and a socio-educational system that makes discriminatory assessment virtually inevitable.

Note

1. Feuerstein's (1979) Learning Potential Assessment Device does achieve a positive change in role relationships and is arguably the least discriminatory of current assessment procedures.

References

Campos, J, and Keatinge, B. (1984) *The Carpinteria Pre-school Program: Title VII Second Year Evaluation Report*. Report submitted to the Department of Health, Education, and Welfare, Office of Education, Washington, DC.

Cazden, C. B. (1985) The ESL teacher as advocate. Plenary presentation to the TESOL Conference, New York. April.

Coles, G. S. (1978) The learning disabilities test battery: Empirical and social issues. *Harvard Educational Review* 48, 313–40.

Cummins, J. (1984) *Bilingualism and Special Education: Issues in Assessment and Pedagogy*. San Diego, CA: College-Hill Press.

Farnham-Diggory, S. (1978) *Learning Disabilities*. Cambridge, MA: Harvard University Press.

Feuerstein, R. (1979) *The Dynamic Assessment of Retarded Performers: The Learning Potential Assessment Device, Theory, Instruments and Techniques*. Baltimore, MD: University Park Press.

McIntyre, R. B., Keeton, A. and Agard, R. (1980) *Identification of Learning Disabilities in Ontario: A Validity Study*. Toronto: Ministry of Education, Ontario.

Mehan, J., Hertweck, A. and Meihls, J. L. (in press). *Handicapping the Handicapped: Decision-making in Students' Educational Careers*. Palo Alto, CA: Stanford University Press.

Mercer, J. R. (1973) *Labelling the Mentally Retarded*. Los Angeles, CA: University of California Press.

Mullard, C. (1985) The social dynamic of migrant groups: From progressive to transformative policy in education. Paper presented at the OECD Conference on Educational Policies and the Minority Social Groups, Paris, January.

Ogbu, J. U. (1978) *Minority Education and Caste*. New York: Academic Press.

Ortiz, A. A. and Yates, J. R. (1983) Incidence of exceptionality among Hispanics: Implications for manpower planning. *NABE Journal* 7, 41–54.

Ribeiro, J. L. (1980) Testing Portuguese immigrant children: Cultural patterns and group differences in responses to the WISC–R. In D. P. Macedo (ed.) *Issues in Portuguese Bilingual Education*. Cambridge, MA: National Assessment and Dissemination Center for Bilingual Education.

Sanchez, G. I. (1934) Bilingualism and mental measures: A word of caution. *Journal of Applied Psychology* 18, 765–72.
Tizard, J., Schofield, W. N. and Hewison, J. (1982) Collaboration between teachers and parents in assisting children's reading. *British Journal of Educational Psychology* 52, 1–15.
Tucker, J. (1980) Ethnic proportions in classes for the learning disabled: Issues in non-biased assessment. *Journal of Special Education* 14, 93–105.
Wallace, G. and McLoughlin, J. (1975) *Learning Disabilities: Concepts and Characteristics*. Columbus, OH: Charles E. Merrill.

From the Inner City to the Global Village: The Microcomputer as a Catalyst for Collaborative Learning and Cultural Interchange[1]

> With the computer as the instrument, writing is more like talking. Writers interact with the computer instrument, while the pen and the typewriter are static tools. The computer enhances the communication functions of writing not only because it interacts with the writers but also because it offers a channel for writers to communicate with one another and because it can carry out a variety of production activities. Writing on the computer means using the machine as a pencil, eraser, typewriter, printer, scissors, paste, copier, filing cabinet, memo pad, and post office. Thus, the computer is a communication channel as well as a writing tool.
>
> (Collette Daiute, *Writing and Computers*, 1985: xiv)

Introduction

Much has been written about the technological revolution that is sweeping most aspects of modern life, including education. It is clear that the generation of students currently in school will require knowledge and skills related to the uses of technology far beyond anything achieved by their parents. However, they will also be faced increasingly with critical social issues related to the appropriate uses of the new technology. The challenge for our educational system is not only to provide children from all social and ethnic groups with sufficient and equal access to computers and other technological advances but also to provide them with opportunities to develop the critical thinking skills and creativity to control the technology rather than being controlled by it.

Research conducted during the past five years in the United States and Canada (see e.g. Canale *et al.*, 1984; US Congress Office of Technology Assessment, 1987, for reviews) on the ways that computers are being used educationally does not engender confidence that schools are meeting this challenge. Certainly an increasing number of computers are being placed in schools; however, these computers are predominantly used for drill and practice activities requiring only relatively low level cognitive skills of rote memory and application (Becker, 1982; Center for Social Organization of Schools, 1983); in addition, female students and those from low income and ethnic minorities tend not to have the same access to computers as do their male, middle-income, non-minority counterparts; and when minority groups or students with special learning difficulties do get access they are more likely to be assigned to drill and practice rather than to problem-solving activities (Mehan *et al.*, 1986).

We tend to view the computer as the culprit for the narrow educational uses to which it is frequently applied. However, the computer is simply a machine which has been programmed by people who are operating with certain implicit or explicit assumptions about teaching and learning. It is a tool whose educational uses are still being explored.

The two major points that I want to make are first, that the question about how computers should be used in schools and whether their impact is likely to be positive or negative is not, in reality, a question about computers; it is a question about educational philosophy and about the psychology of learning and teaching. All educational software incorporates assumptions about how children learn best and about appropriate ways of teaching children. Critical examination of the underlying pedagogical model is a prerequisite for the evaluation of software and appropriate use of microcomputer hardware.

The second point is that when microcomputers are applied with an appropriate pedagogical framework, they have the potential to radically improve the quality of education children receive. Specifically, the computer has the potential to make the 'global village' a reality for students by allowing them to interact directly with other students around the world. In other words, when used appropriately, the computer has enormous potential for cultural interchange and reinforcement; by interacting through writing with their peers in different parts of the world, students simultaneously explore the values and history of other cultures and, in the process, discover what is unique about their own. Enhancement of basic language and literacy skills are important by-products of this interaction.

Transmission versus Interactive/Experiential Models of Pedagogy

The predominant use of computers for reinforcing skills and knowledge reflects an underlying educational philosophy which has been termed a 'transmission' model of teaching (Barnes, 1976). The basic premise of this model is that the teacher's task is to impart knowledge or skills that s/he possesses to students who do not yet have these skills. This implies that the teacher initiates and controls the interaction, constantly orienting it towards the achievement of instructional objectives. For example, in first and second language programs that stress pattern repetition, the teacher presents the materials, models the language patterns, asks questions, and provides feedback to students about the correctness of their response. Both in the case of regular curriculum development and educational software development, the transmission model emphasizes analysis of academic task demands, establishment of sequential learning objectives based on this task analysis, and 'direct instruction' of individual task components, proceeding from 'simpler' lower level subskills to more complex integrations of these subskills.

While transmission of information is clearly appropriate within our educational systems, it is by no means the only or the most important goal of education. As recently suggested by David Suzuki in an article highly critical of teaching 'computer literacy' in isolation from specific pedagogical goals (*Globe and Mail,* February 14, 1987), schools should be concerned not just with the transmission of information but with developing students' abilities to access information when needed and to critically evaluate the information obtained and apply it in appropriate ways. These critical thinking skills require discussion and interaction among teachers and students (through active use of language) for their development rather than solitary work at a computer.

In short, reliance on a transmission model of education is increasingly inappropriate in view of both the information explosion and the critical social issues that our children's generation will be required to resolve (e.g. issues related to genetic engineering, pollution, nuclear waste disposal, etc.). Information is increasing at such a rate that nobody (student or adult) is capable of absorbing and remembering more than a fraction of potentially relevant knowledge; furthermore, the information presented in textbooks or computer courseware is likely to be out of date before it ever gets into students' heads. Schools should not be trying to drill isolated facts and skills into reluctant skulls; they should rather provide students with ample opportunities to access information that is relevant to issues they are analyzing or problems they are trying to resolve. Our global future is likely to be dependent upon our children's ability to critically analyze situations and collaborate with others (both locally and in distant locations) in creatively solving problems.

If a transmission approach to pedagogy is not appropriate for the future needs of society, to what extent might the classroom computer act as a catalyst for a fundamentally different approach to education, one where the emphasis in on interpretation and use of information for collaborative problem-solving? Rather than being used to 'program' the student more effectively, might the computer be used as a tool to dramatically increase social interaction and amplify rather than constrict students' experiences?

Such uses of the computer would fall within what has been termed an interactive/experiential approach to pedagogy (see Barnes, 1976; Cummins, 1984;

Wells, 1982 for discussion of similar notions). The basic theoretical premise underlying interactive/experiential approaches to pedagogy (and computer use) is that learning is an active process of constructing cognitive schemata through the integration of previous and new experiences; this process is strongly enhanced through social interaction.

In this broader view of education, genuine understanding is seen as involving active discovery on the part of the child rather than just consumption of pre-determined knowledge. Similarly, the development of higher levels of cognitive and literacy skills requires considerably more active and intrinsically-motivated involvement on the part of the student than is implied by the transmission model.

A central tenet of an interactive/experiential approach to pedagogy is that 'talking and writing are means to learning' (Bullock Report, HMSO, 1975: 50). Its major characteristics in comparison to a transmission model are as follows:

- genuine dialogue between student and teacher in both oral and written modalities;
- guidance and facilitation rather than control of student learning by the teacher;
- encouragement of student–student talk in a collaborative learning context;
- encouragement of meaningful language use by students rather than a focus only on correctness of surface forms;
- conscious integration of language use and development with all curricular content rather than teaching language and other content as isolated subjects;
- a focus on developing higher level cognitive skills rather than factual recall;
- task presentation that generates intrinsic rather than extrinsic motivation.

In this interactionist view of children are seen as explorers of meaning, as critical and creative thinkers who have contributions to make both in the classroom and in the world beyond. Rather than regarding children only as consumers of predetermined knowledge, the emphasis in language and literacy teaching is on enriching the child through literature and on helping the child become a creator of literature. This interactionist view of children's learning is consistent with Piaget's theory which stresses action on the environment as crucial for the development of cognitive operations and with Vygotsky's theory which emphasizes social interaction as the matrix within which higher level thought processes develop.[2]

Clearly, very different applications of microcomputers are likely to result from each of these two pedagogical models. The transmission model is likely to give rise to more efficient procedures of task presentation and sequencing that can be individualized according to children's current level of knowledge of the subject matter. There is evidence, in fact, that the computer is more efficient at transmission of facts and lower-level skills than instruction that is not computer-mediated (US Congress Office of Technology Assessment, 1987). However, there is virtually no data on the issue of cost-effectiveness; in other words, to put it crudely, is the increased efficiency of transmission sufficient to offset the difference between 25 cents for a ditto sheet and approximately $2,000 for a computer?

In contrast to the transmission model emphasis on the computer as a tutor (Taylor, 1980), the interactive/experiential model emphasizes the computer as a tool that can enhance a variety of active learning activities, but particularly written communication.

In order to understand the potential role of the microcomputer in promoting creative writing and cultural interchange, it is necessary to consider recent developments in our understanding of how writing is acquired and how it can best be encouraged in the classroom.

Recent Developments in the Teaching of Writing

The extent to which writing activities had declined in North American schools was forcefully brought home to educators with the publication of Donald Graves' (1978) study entitled 'Balance the Basics. Let Them Write'. Graves documented the fact that writing received minimal attention in comparison to reading and most of the writing that students did carry out was copying. Feedback that students received on their writing tended to focus on the correctness of surface forms (e.g. grammar and spelling). This preoccupation with correctness of surface forms persisted despite considerable evidence that correction of students' writing errors and explicit teaching of grammar were not particularly effective. For example, Elley (1981) summarizes the findings of his extensive longitudinal study on the teaching of grammar as follows:

> Pupils who had no formal grammar lessons for three years were writing just as clearly, fluently and correctly as those who had studied much grammar, the only apparent difference being that the pupils who hadn't studied grammar enjoyed English more … The research evidence overwhelmingly shows that increasing the amount of analytic study of language has no positive effect on pupils' ability to read or write. (1981: 12)

Many teachers operating from within a transmission model have difficulty in accepting that 'errors' in grammar or spelling should not necessarily be immediately corrected, despite the evidence from both first and second language acquisition that explicit error correction is ineffective. The analogy with spoken language acquisition helps to explain the function of developmental 'errors' in the acquisition of written competence. In drawing this analogy, Temple *et al.* (1982), for example, point out that the two processes are similar in that children normally take a great deal of initiative in learning both to talk and to write and for both processes to occur, children must be surrounded by language used in meaningful ways. They go on to note that

> Children learn to talk by formulating tentative rules about the way language works, trying them out, and gradually revising them. At first, they

make many mistakes in speech, but they gradually correct them. In writing we see errors of letter formation, spelling, and composition occurring as children make hypotheses about the rules that govern the writing system; errors give way to other errors before they arrive at correct forms. (1982: 9)

In other words, if children are exposed to a wide variety of written language and if they are allowed to continue to express themselves in writing, then errors will gradually approximate adult usage without explicit correction.

Correction, in fact, can have negative consequences for writing development in much the same way as for spoken language acquisition. As expressed by Smith (1983):

Children do not learn from being corrected but from wanting to do things the right way. Most of the immense labor teachers put into correcting their students' work is wasted; it is ignored. If it is not ignored, then it may have a negative effect, with children avoiding the words they fear they cannot spell or pronounce correctly. They do not become better spellers or speakers by writing or talking less. Correction is useful, and it is only paid serious attention to, when the student wants it and would indeed be offended if it were not given. (1983: 138)

In conclusion, children acquire writing skills by engaging in writing activities that are creative and intrinsically interesting. Formal skills are gradually acquired in the context both of continued reading (Smith, 1982) and of projects to which children are actively committed. As Smith points out, children do not want 'spelling mistakes in the poster they put on the wall, the story they are circulating, or the letter they will mail' (1983: 138). Rather than attempting to control this process, the teacher's roles include being a guide, facilitator, and most important, communication partner. Essentially, teachers organize the classroom in such a way that children's active involvement is maximized in projects to which the children themselves are committed.

Graves' (1983) work has begun to bring about a major change in the way writing is taught in North American schools. The change is essentially one from a transmission approach to one that focuses on encouraging children to express and share their experiences in the classroom through both talking and writing. The 'process' writing approach that Graves has advocated emphasizes writing as a meaningful communicative activity in which there is a real purpose (e.g. publication of a book within the classroom), a genuine audience (e.g. peers, teachers, parents), and support systems to assist children work through the editing of successive drafts.

This section has outlined an approach to the teaching of writing that derives from principles of an interactive/experiential model of pedagogy. The microcomputer is clearly not an essential part of this approach. However, the computer has tremendous potential to enhance this process by increasing the audience for students' writing and by facilitating the editing and production process. The research evidence also indicates that, in addition to providing possibilities for international communication, microcomputers can increase the immediate social interaction within the classroom.

The Microcomputer as a Tool for Social Interaction and Cultural Exchange

A number of investigators have stressed that the computer encourages a positive form of social interaction and collaboration among students. Canale *et al.* (1984), for example, conclude

> What stands out in all these cases is the social nature of computer use. Perhaps it is one of the virtues of necessity, but the scarcity of hardware brings with it what all teachers we have observed generally agree is a positive benefit – authentic interaction among the students as they negotiate both for access to the machines and while using them. (1984: 7)

Mehan *et al.* (1984) have similarly stressed that 'while the microcomputer itself cannot transform unskilled writers into skilled ones, it does present a medium that makes a new social organization for reading and writing possible' (p. 516). They attribute the positive effects they observed on students' writing to this social organization:

> The presence of this 'other' during the writing process helps students generate ideas and gives immediate responses to the written text. Students frequently challenge one another's sentences as 'not making any sense' or correct the spelling of a word as it was typed. Less frequently, but more important for the writing process, students discuss whether two sentences should be conjoined, how run-on sentences should be divided, or how to substitute for overused words. (1984: 517–8)

It appears clear from these studies that the microcomputer has the potential to reorient instruction from transmission towards interactional classroom structures. From the perspective of language learning theory, the presence of both immediate and distant audiences is especially significant in students' use of computers for writing. Swain and Wong Fillmore (1984) recently proposed a synthesis of the views of leading second language acquisition researchers whom they interviewed in the form of an 'interactionist theory' whose major proposition is that 'interaction between learner and target language users is the major causal variable in second language acquisition' (p.18).

The potential of microcomputers to provide immediate and direct access to an international audience clearly has significant implications for language and literacy development as well as for cultural exchange and reinforcement. The technology exists to send written documents around the world in a matter of seconds and even to have written 'conversations' with individuals in distant countries.

A significant innovation in recent years has been the institution of computer writing networks through which classes of students create newsletters, books, and other forms of information exchange that can be shared with other classes tied into the same network. Some of these experiences are briefly described in the next section.

Computer Networking: Examples and Scenarios

During the past two years, several networking projects have been implemented in school systems in the United States, Britain, and Canada. For example, in the United States, schools in San Diego have been linked with schools in Mexico, Hawaii, Alaska and Japan (Mehan *et al.*, 1986) using English as the major language of communication. A related project with Spanish–English bilingual students entitled 'De Orilla a Orilla' (From Shore to Shore) links students in Puerto Rico, Connecticut, San Diego and Tijuana (Mexico) on a daily basis. In addition to exchange of newsletters and stories created on the computer, students in some classes have exchanged videotapes which they have made of their communities (Sayers, 1986). In Britain, seven schools in the southwest of the country have carried out joint science projects with schools in Tasmania, with whom they have had daily contact through a computer network. The RAPPI system in Canada, supported by the Department of Communications, has linked 45 schools across Canada with about 35 schools in France, Britain and Italy. The system has operated through the mainframe computer at the University of British Columbia. In addition, during the past six months, the National Heritage Language Resource Unit (NHLRU) of the Ontario Institute for Studies in Education (OISE) has been involved in a cooperative project with IBM Canada exploring options and applications of computer networking for schools. Students from Portuguese backgrounds in Toronto have sent through the BITNET computer network newsletters (written in students' first language and English) to Spanish–English bilingual students in Tucson, Arizona. Observations of teachers and researchers suggested that the exchange appeared to stimulate students' interest in and awareness of language as they explored the similarities between Portuguese and Spanish (personal communication, Luis Moll).[3]

The initial experiences of these projects have been encouraging in that they demonstrate that computer networking among schools is feasible both from a financial and operational point of view. It is also clear that considerable enthusiasm is generated among both students and teachers for the cross-cultural exchange, and teachers report that students are motivated to write much more than previously. Some future directions for expanding the potential of computer networking are outlined in the hypothetical illustrative scenarios depicted below.

1. 'The basics': Reading and writing

A consortium of grade 3 classes from 5 school districts in different provinces choose an 'author of the month'. During the month all children, working in groups, read this author's books and discuss them in light of their own experiences and feelings. They also react critically to the stories (e.g. what other ways might the author have ended the story? Why does she or he make character X so nasty? etc.) and write stories themselves based on some of the ideas (or on the style) of the author. Peer conferencing would be used in the editing of these stories. Within classes, each group enters the fruits of its discussion and writing into the computer, prints it out and shares it with other groups. Several times a week the class may participate in a computer conference with the other classes who are reading the same material. Thus, they will see how other children in different parts of Canada (or outside Canada) are reacting to the same stories they have read. In addition, the author himself or herself, participates in this network (possibly twice a week), reads what the children are discussing in relation to his/her books, what questions they have generated, and responds to comments that they have made.

The result is that the children are in direct communication not only with children of their own age in distant locations but also with the author whose books they are reading. It is clear that this can help them gain tremendous insight into the process through which stories are created and they can begin to apply this insight to their own writing. Students essentially will have become apprentices in literacy.

Publishers might also get involved in this type of project through subsidizing purchase of books by schools or parents or by formally publishing the best stories that students in the network created during the course of the year.

2. Science

A network of several grade 7 classes undertakes a series of joint science projects that relate directly to issues that are of current concern globally and in all of the specific sites (e.g. environmental pollution, global politics, nuclear contamination, etc.). For example, they might research pollution of maritime or lakewater life in the different settings. This would involve first, library/database research on types, causes, and effects of such pollution, with particular attention to data from the local area (e.g. articles from local newspapers and magazines [possibly using the *Globe and Mail*'s InfoGlobe on-line database searching service, or the Groeller Encyclopedia now available on Compact Disk ROM], input from local university biology departments, etc.); the results of this research could be shared between the different groups. The second phase would involve collaboratively (across groups and teachers) designing a project to collect data from the local area (e.g. sampling and analysing water samples, fish caught locally, etc.). The final phase would involve publishing a report (e.g. for a local or school newspaper) which describes the procedures and results of the projects in the different locations.

As in the previous scenario, students are using language actively for clarifying and generating meaning. The project clearly incorporates the principle of 'language across the curriculum' in that oral and written language development are integrated with both science and social studies.

Several variations of this type of project can be implemented. For example, as in the previous scenario, an expert facilitator might join the computer conferences in order to provide additional guidance and react to students' work. Also, all classes in the network might subscribe to magazines such as *National Geographic* or the Greenpeace monthly magazine which contain considerable information regarding the social consequences of scientific advances. Discussion of this material both within and across classes will clearly promote reading and writing skills, as well as science knowledge and critical awareness of current social studies issues. Once again, the interaction in the context of a shared activity is the fuel which promotes cognitive and academic progress.

3. Second language/culture learning

As mentioned above, theorists (e.g Swain & Wong Fillmore, 1984) are agreed that interaction is fundamental to second language acquisition. Computer networks linking students in different countries (e.g. Canada and France) or within countries (Ontario and Quebec) can stimulate direct interaction in the target language through exchange of creative writing (e.g. newsletters, books of stories, science projects, etc.). Thus, Ontario students in French immersion programs might exchange such material (in English and/or French) with francophone students in Quebec who are learning English, or Portuguese-background students in Toronto and Winnipeg might communicate with Portuguese-background students in the New England area or in the Azores.

The type of activity that has taken place in the Orillas project (Sayers, 1986) illustrates the potential of networking for second (and first) language and literacy development. Students go through the process of collaborating with each other and with their teachers in developing newsletters that report/comment on events that are of interest to the students and that also publish students' creative writing. These newsletters are then exchanged among classes in the network. At this point, students undertake the task of publishing for a wider audience (e.g. the entire school) an international newsletter with what they consider the best/most interesting writing in the newsletters produced by students in the different countries. This involves students working in small groups, with each group assigned to edit the different sections of the international newsletter. For example, the group editing the articles in the fiction section will read and discuss the various articles that have appeared in the individual newsletters, decide which ones are most interesting, and what editing changes may be required prior to publication in the international newsletter. A similar process will go on for the sports section, current events, etc. In this process, the students are finding out what makes a good piece of writing, why one story is more interesting than another, and how it might be improved. They are also likely to be dramatically improving their second language skills as well as overall literacy skills.

Major Objectives of Computer Networking

The major objectives of computer networking are summarized below:

- *Language Learning/Maintenance.* As outlined above, the computer network is capable of supplying the one essential ingredient that is often lacking in second language classrooms, namely sufficient communicative interaction with speakers of (or text in) the target language. It is also capable of encouraging minority students to continue to develop literacy skills in their mother tongues.

- *Literacy Development.* The effectiveness of 'process' approaches to writing, popularized by Graves, in which students actively generate their own creative writing and publish it for real audiences is seldom questioned. However, it requires a change of orientation among teachers from a transmission to an interactive/experiential mode of teaching. In other words, teachers must be prepared to acknowledge that active student use of language (both talking and writing) are important means to learning. Many teachers (in both regular and second language classrooms) find it difficult to reorient their teaching from an emphasis on transmission of knowledge and skills to one where the generation and exploration of ideas through dialogue and interaction are encouraged. The incentive provided by international communication is likely to encourage a greater number of teachers to redefine their teaching roles and allow students more opportunities to develop their literacy skills through writing. Clearly, the reading and editing for publication of other students' writing from around the world will also contribute to literacy skills development.

- *Cultural Exchange and Reinforcement.* In an era where our images of other cultures and nations are considerably influenced by television-reinforced stereotypes, the educational relevance of establishing a system for genuine communication and real cultural exchange is obvious. Within Canada, for example, few would dispute the desirability of greater possibilities for interchange between French-speaking students in Quebec and English-speaking (or French-speaking) students in other parts of Canada. A significant increase in cross-cultural understanding and sensitivity is likely to result from a writing exchange made possible by the computer network.

- *Artistic Expression.* Newer generations of computer programs permit easy integration of text and graphics. It is thus possible for students to illustrate their stories on the computer and transmit the illustrations as well as the text.

- *Computer Literacy.* As children use the computer and see its possibilities they are likely to want to explore other applications of computers to their lives. Among older students, programming applications should be encouraged and, once again, international exchange of programs is likely to provide considerable incentive.

- *International Educational Cooperation.* The computer connections established between classes of students will also allow their teachers to communicate with each other and will encourage cross-national contact and cooperation in a variety of other educational areas. For example, student exchanges where students spend periods of time in other countries are likely to be encouraged by the writing connection. The impact of such exchanges is likely to increase if followed or preceded by a computer writing exchange.

Conclusion

We are at a cross-roads with respect to the ways computers will be used in schools. Many lie unused or are used for trivial purposes not because teachers do not understand the technical aspects but because the underlying pedagogical issues have not been resolved. If a teacher has only one computer in her class and is using a transmission approach to teaching, then the computer cannot achieve very much since only one student can be 'programmed' at a time. However, if that computer is used within an interactive approach to pedagogy, it can dramatically enhance the learning experiences of all the children in the classroom by acting as a catalyst for cooperative learning, process writing, critical literacy and discovery approaches to science. In short, rather than dehumanizing education, as some critics fear, the microcomputer has the potential to greatly enhance the educational experience of both teachers and students by putting the inner-city classroom in touch with the global village.

Notes

1. Paper presented at conference on 'The Challenge of Microcomputers in K-12 Education', Winnipeg, May 1987, InfoTech Resource Centre, Manitoba Ministry of Education.
2. It is interesting to note that these assumptions characterize the education of 'gifted' children in most North American schools. 'Gifted' students are seen as active, inquiring, involved, individuals who thrive on self-directed problem-solving and learning which is not provided in regular classrooms. The implicit assumptions underlying such programs are that 'non-gifted' students are much less capable of

active inquiry and would not benefit from the opportunity to become actively involved in adopting and pursuing their own learning goals; therefore, regular curricula should not (and hence, do not) foster active involvement by students in independent learning. These implicit assumptions are closely associated with transmission approaches to teaching and are likely to become self-fulfilling.

3. A variety of options for computer networking currently exist; for example, commercial networking and database-access systems (e.g. Compuserve, The Source, iNet [in Canada]) provide efficient but potentially expensive communication possibilities; subsidized networks such as the TTNS system in Britain and RAPPI in Canada overcome the problem of expense but may lack stability due to the need for external subsidy; highly promising are private Bulletin Board Systems (BBS) combined with E-mail programs. The Orillas project in the US utilizes such a system for Apple II computers while the OPUS BBS combined with the SEAdog E-mail program is beginning to be used for educational purposes with MS-DOS machines in Canada. Since these systems avoid communication through mainframe computers, it is possible to use relatively powerful specialized software between compatible micros that preserves particular formats, graphics, and diacritics (accents).

References

Barnes, D. (1976) *From Communication to Curriculum*. Harmondsworth: Penguin.

Becker, H. J. (1982) *Microcomputers in the Classroom: Dreams and Realities*. CSOS, The Johns Hopkins University, Report No. 319.

Canale, M., Barker, G., Belanger, M., MacRuary, K., McLean, R. S. and Ragsdale, R. G. (1984) *Microcomputer Software for Language Arts in Ontario: Survey and Analysis*. Final report of OISE project, 82-3916.

Center for Social Organization of Schools (1983) *School Uses of Microcomputers: Reports from a National Survey*. Baltimore, MD: The Johns Hopkins University, Center for the Organization of Schools.

Cummins, J. (1984) *Bilingualism and Special Education: Issues in Assessment and Pedagogy*. Clevedon: Multilingual Matters. Co-published in the United States by College-Hill Press, San Diego.

Daiute, C. (1985) *Writing and Computers*. Reading, MA: Addison-Wesley.

Elley, W. B. (1981) Why teach a centipede to walk? *Education* (New Zealand) 3, 11–13.

Graves, D. (1983) *Writing: Children and Teachers at Work*. Exeter, NH: Heinemann.

HMSO (1975) *A Language for Life*. Report of the Committee of Inquiry appointed by the Secretary of State for Education and Science under the chairmanship of Sir Alan Bullock. London: HMSO.

Mehan, H., Miller-Souviney, B. and Riel, M. M. (1984) Knowledge of text editing and the development of literacy skills. *Language Arts* 65, 154–9.

Mehan, H. *et al.* (1986) *The Write Help: Resources and Activities for Word Processing*. Glenview, IL: Scott Foresman.

Office of Technology Assessment, US Congress (1987) *Trends and Status of Computers in Schools: Use in Chapter 1 Programs and Use with Limited English Proficient Students*. Staff Paper, Washington, DC.

Sayers, D. (1986) Sending messages: Across the classroom and around the world. *TESOL Newsletter* 20, 7–8.

Smith, F. (1978) *Understanding Reading* (2nd edn). New York: Holt, Rinehart & Winston.

Smith, F. (1982) *Writing and the Writer*. New York: Holt, Rinehart & Winston.

Smith, F. (1983) Afterthoughts. In F. Smith *Essays into Literacy*. Exeter, NH: Heinemann Educational Books.

Suzuki, D. (1987) Student 'computer literacy': An outmoded teaching idea. *Globe and Mail*, Saturday, February 14.

Swain, M. and Wong Fillmore, L. (1984) Child second language development: Views from the field on theory and research. Paper presented at the 18th Annual TESOL Conference, Houston, TX. March.

Taylor, R. (1980) *The Computer In the School: Tutor, Tool, Tutee.* New York: Teachers' College Press.

Temple, C. A., Nathan, R. G. and Burris, N. A. (1982) *The Beginnings of Writing.* Boston: Allyn & Bacon.

Wells, G. (1982) Language, learning and the curriculum. In G. Wells (ed.) *Language, Learning and Education.* Bristol: Centre for the Study of Language and Communication, University of Bristol.

From Multicultural to Anti-racist Education: An Analysis of Programmes and Policies in Ontario

Overview

Since the declaration of an official policy of multiculturalism in Canada by Prime Minister Trudeau in 1971, and the subsequent endorsement of this policy by provincial governments, Canadian educators have attempted to develop and implement 'multicultural education' policies in classrooms across the country. Many of the larger urban boards of education set up workgroups in the mid-1970s to develop such policies and since that time teacher in-service activities have regularly focused on 'multicultural education'. However, to many observers it appears that by the time 'multicultural education' policies filter down to the classroom, they amount to little more than recognition of holidays/festivals from a few cultures in addition to those observed by Anglo-Celtic Canadians, and the presence of some 'visible minority' referents in textbooks and other curriculum materials. The advent of 'multicultural education' has not given rise to dramatic changes in the interactions between educators and students. In most classrooms, the hidden curriculum still conforms largely to the ideology of 'Anglo-conformity' (Troper, 1979).

In this chapter, I examine some of the reasons why the rhetoric of 'multicultural education' has failed to translate into reality and I illustrate the disjunction between rhetoric and reality with reference to policies and programmes in Ontario during the past decade. The argument presented is that the overt goals of multicultural education can be realized only when policy-makers, educators and communities acknowledge the subtle (and sometimes not so subtle) forms of institutionalized racism that permeate the structure of schools and mediate the interactions between educators and students. In other words, unless it becomes 'anti-racist education', 'multicultural education' may serve only to provide a veneer of change that in reality perpetuates discriminatory educational structures.

Clearly, a theoretical framework is required to document the ways in which institutionalized racism manifests itself in the educational system and the change processes required to combat this racism, i.e. to shift from an Anglo-conformity to an anti-racist orientation. A framework is presented that analyses the ways in

215

which educators define their roles with respect to four overlapping dimensions of schooling: (1) incorporation of minority students' language and culture; (2) minority community participation; (3) orientation to pedagogy; and (4) assessment of minority students. These dimensions reflect the power relations in the society at large and thus the framework provides a means of analysing the extent to which educators challenge or accept the societal racism that is reflected in schools. The focus is on ways in which the structural power relations in society are realized within schools and manifested psychologically within individual educators. A central assumption is that implementation of anti-racist educational changes requires *personal redefinitions* of the way in which classroom teachers and other educators interact with the children and communities they serve. In other words, legislative and policy reforms may be necessary conditions for effective change, but they are not sufficient. Implementation of change is dependent on the extent to which educators, both collectively and individually, redefine their roles with respect to minority students and communities.

In the first section, a brief outline of the historical and social context of 'multicultural education' in Canada is presented and this is followed by a discussion of the meaning of the term 'institutionalized racism' and the ways it manifests itself in the interactions between educators and minority students. The theoretical framework outlined above for conceptualizing strategies for countering institutionalized racism in schools and empowering minority students is then discussed. The dynamics of the change processes required are illustrated with concrete examples from recent educational conflicts in Ontario. Finally, the broader context of planning and implementing change is considered with respect to the roles of ministries of education, universities, school board officials (i.e. administrators, principals, etc.) and ethnocultural communities.

Historical and Social Context of Multicultural Education

Harold Troper (1979) has argued cogently that multiculturalism has come to play a role in filling an 'identity vacuum' among English Canadians brought about by the gradual weakening of the bonds with Britain, partly as a result of large-scale immigration during the past 40 years. The prevailing attitude towards ethnic diversity in English Canada during the first part of the 20th century was that ethnic groups should give up their own languages and cultures and become assimilated to the dominant British group. This Anglo-conformity orientation is well expressed by a speaker to the 1913 Presbyterian Pre-Assembly Congress in Toronto:

> The problem is simply this: take all the different nationalities, German, French, Italian, Russian and all the others that are sending their surplus into Canada: mix them with the Anglo-Saxon stock and produce a uniform race wherein the Anglo-Saxon peculiarities shall prevail.
>
> (Quoted by Harney & Troper, 1975: 110)

The current endorsement of multiculturalism as national and provincial policy tends to obscure the strong assimilationist orientation of Canadian educators in the past and the racist character of much of our past public policy (e.g. immigration regulations). Despite recent reminders of the exclusion of Jews before and during World War II (Abella & Troper, 1983), the continuing saga of compensation for racism against Japanese-Canadians during the war, and the failure to alleviate the deplorable conditions of many Native Canadians, Canadians still tend to view themselves as having always been a tolerant and open society. As expressed by Troper (1979):

> Perhaps every country needs its myths and national clichés. For English speaking Canada one current and often repeated cliché is that Canada owes its distinctive character to a long fostered tolerance of cultural diversity – we are a mosaic while the Americans are a melting pot ... If anything the opposite is closer to the truth. The survival of active and distinct ethnic communities in Canada ... occurred in spite of public policy and sentiment not because of them ... Ethnicity, if tolerated at all, was seen as a temporary stage through which one passed on the road to full assimilation. Prolonged ethnic identification ... was seen as a pathological condition to be overcome, not as a source of national enrichment and pride. (1979: 9)

Given the recency of an official multiculturalism policy and the strong Anglo-conformity tradition that preceded it, it is hardly surprising that the orientations of many individuals within Canadian society (including educators) continue to reflect assimilationist assumptions. Nevertheless, serious attempts have been and continue to be made to change the assimilationist orientation in many schools. A recent statement by the Ontario Ministry of Education in a memorandum to Chairpersons of boards of education (announcing a province-wide conference on race relations and multiculturalism) can be taken as indicative of the desired reality towards which change is directed:

> The philosophy of multiculturalism ... should permeate the school's curriculum, policies, teaching methods and materials, courses of study, and assessment and testing procedures, as well as the attitudes and expectations of its staff and all of its community. (December 1985: 1)

Certain aspects of this statement are worth highlighting: first, the *role definitions* of educators are included as an important component of a multicultural orientation in schools. The statement implies that the attitudes and expectations of school staff should reflect a positive orientation towards the cultural and linguistic diversity of both students and communities. In addition, significant dimensions of programme delivery are highlighted; specifically, curriculum, which can be taken to include materials and courses of study, teaching methods and assessment/testing procedures.

Clearly, all of these are admirable objectives. However, up to this point the implementation of multicultural education policies appears to have lacked coherence and dynamism in many parts of Canada. With some noteworthy exceptions (e.g. the multicultural assessment system in the North York Board of Education) there has been little structural change either in the ways schools relate to minority communities or in the interactions students experience in schools. Following Appel (this volume)* several reasons can be suggested for this: first, 'multicultural education' focuses only on the educational system rather than on the power relations in the broader society. As societal institutions, schools tend to reflect the values and priorities of the dominant group and to reproduce the status and power differences between class and ethnic groups that are so evident in the wider society. No programme of 'multicultural education' can be successful unless it takes account of the logic of its own rhetoric: namely, rather than reflecting the values and priorities of the dominant group in the wider society and reproducing the inequalities between class and ethnic groups, the rhetoric of multicultural education requires that schools actively challenge the societal power structure by empowering minority students. It is hardly surprising that few 'multicultural education' initiatives have succeeded in even addressing this goal. Those that appear to challenge, even to a minor extent, the societal power structure and the priorities of the dominant group (e.g. heritage language initiatives,[1] bilingual assessment, etc.) tend to generate fierce opposition, a reaction which is entirely predictable (see below).

A second reason why 'multicultural education' has often appeared to lack coherence is that there tends to be no clear position articulated with respect to minority languages and the extent to which schools (and taxpayers) have a role to play in encouraging their retention. For example, although official federal and provincial policies generally assert the close link between language and culture, many advocates of 'multicultural education' are highly ambivalent about heritage language programmes which they see as being divisive and as erecting intercultural barriers rather than breaking them down. The ambivalence with respect to heritage language development reflects the lack of a coherent theoretical framework for analysing the multiple dimensions and goals of 'multicultural education'.

Related to this last point is the fact that multicultural education does not address, either theoretically or programmatically, the causes of minority students' academic difficulties nor explain the wide variation in achievement of different groups (see e.g. Cummins, 1984a; Ogbu, 1978; Wright & Tsuji, 1984).

In short, while the rhetoric of 'multicultural education' articulates a variety of positive goals, it is necessary to examine critically the extent to which this rhetoric is symbolic, simply reflecting the 'myth of multiculturalism' (Troper, 1979), or whether it reflects a real commitment to fully eradicating the racism that has characterized much of Canadian education in the past. As we shall see, the record in Ontario is mixed in that major changes have occurred in some areas while in other areas the institutionalized structure has made virtually no accommodation to students' cultural diversity.

Institutionalized Racism and Anti-racist Education

Institutionalized racism can be defined as ideologies and structures which are systematically used to legitimize unequal division of power and resources (both material and non-material) between groups which are defined on the basis of race (see Mullard, this volume*, Phillipson, this volume*, and Skutnabb-Kangas, this volume* (Chapter 1) for discussion of parallels between 'racism', 'linguicism', 'ethnicism' and other 'isms'). The term 'racism' is being used here in a broad sense to include discrimination against both ethnic and racial minorities. The discrimination is brought about both by the ways particular institutions (e.g. schools) are organized or structured and by the (usually) implicit assumptions that legitimize that organization. For example, the over-representation of certain groups of minority students in vocational programmes at the secondary level in several Metropolitan Toronto boards of education (see e.g. Wright & Tsuji, 1984) can be analysed as a function of institutionalized racism in the educational system. There is usually no intent to discriminate on the part of educators; however, their interactions with minority students are mediated by a system of unquestioned assumptions that reflect the values and priorities of the dominant middle-class culture. It is in these interactions that minority students are educationally disabled. A concrete example will illustrate the subtle but devastating ways in which institutionalized racism can manifest itself in the well-intentioned interactions between educators and minority students.

An example of institutionalized racism in practice

The following psychological assessment was one of more than 400 assessments of ESL, students carried out in a western Canadian city which were analysed by Cummins (1984a). It illustrates the assumptions that school psychologists and teachers frequently make about issues such as the appropriateness of standardized tests for minority students and the consequences of bilingualism for students' development.

Maria (not the child's real name) was referred for psychological assessment by her grade 1 teacher, who noted that she had difficulty in all aspects of learning. She was given both speech and hearing and psychological assessments. The former assessment found that all structures and functions pertaining to speech were within normal limits and hearing was also normal. The findings were summarized as follows: 'Maria comes from an Italian home where Italian is spoken mainly. However, language skills appeared to be within normal limits for English.'

The psychologist's conclusions, however, were very different. On the Wechsler Preschool and Primary Scale of Intelligence (WPPSI), Maria obtained a Verbal IQ of 89 and a Performance IQ of 99. In other words, non-verbal abilities were virtually at the average level while verbal abilities were 11 points below the mean, a surprisingly good score given the clear cultural biases of the test and the fact that the child had been learning English in a school context for little more than a year. The report to Maria's teacher read as follows:

> Maria tended to be very slow to respond to questions, particularly if she were unsure of the answers. Her spoken English was a little hard to understand, which is probably due to poor English models at home (speech is within normal limits). Italian is spoken almost exclusively at home and this will be further complicated by the coming arrival of an aunt and grandmother from Italy.
>
> There is little doubt that Maria is a child of low average ability whose school progress is impeded by lack of practice in English. Encourage Maria's oral participation as much as possible, and try to involve her in extra-curricular activities where she will be with her English-speaking peers.

Despite the fact that the speech assessment revealed no deficiencies in Maria's spoken English, the psychologist has no hesitation ('There is little doubt ...') in attributing Maria's academic problems to the use of Italian at home. The implicit message to the teacher (and parents) is clear: Maria's communication in L1 with parents and relatives detracts from her school performance, and the aim of the school programme should be to expose Maria to as much L2 as possible in order to compensate for these deficient linguistic and cultural background experiences.

How does this assessment (which was not atypical of the sample) represent institutional racism in action? First, the psychologist, despite being undoubtedly well-intentioned, lacks the knowledge base required to assess the child's academic potential. This is illustrated by the fact that an extremely culturally biased test, such as the verbal scale of the WPPSI, is administered and an IQ score reported, by the failure to distinguish between conversational and academic aspects of L2 proficiency among ESL students, and by the assumption that use of L1 in the home is contributing to the child's academic difficulties. A large body of research shows that this is not the case (see Cummins, 1984a).

Second, an implicit Anglo-conformity orientation is evident in the lack of sensitivity to the fact that the child's cultural background and linguistic talents differ significantly from those upon whom the test was normed; the institutionalized racism is manifested not only in the lack of knowledge but in the total lack of awareness on the part of the psychologist (and presumably the institutions that trained her or him) that there are any knowledge gaps. The psychologist is not conscious that the child's culturally specific experiences might have any implications for the administration or interpretation of the test; there is also no hesitation in drawing inferences about the negative effects of L1 use in the home nor in making recommendations about language use in school despite the fact that the psychologist has probably had no training whatsoever on issues related to bilingualism. In short, the institutional structure within which the psychological assessment takes place (e.g. with respect to policy/legal requirements and training/

certification programmes) orients the psychologist to locate the cause of the academic problem within the minority child herself. This has the effect of screening from critical scrutiny a variety of other possible contributors to the child's difficulty, e.g. the educational experiences to which the child has been exposed (see Coles, 1978). Because the psychologist is equipped only with psycho-educational assessment tools, the child's difficulty is assumed to be psycho-educational in nature. The psychologists' training has resulted in a tunnel vision that is out of focus with respect to the experiential realities of the children being assessed.

A related way in which the example above illustrates institutional racism in practice relates to the fact that the psychologist's professional credibility depends on providing a satisfactory interpretation of the child's difficulty and making reasonable placement or intervention recommendations; to admit that the assessment reveals nothing about causes of the minority child's academic difficulties would jeopardize the status and credibility of the psychologist. Thus, at the level of both individuals and institutions (e.g. university departments that train teachers, psychologists and administrators) there tends to be a denial of any lack of expertise or need for significant change in training and/or certification programmes. This denial process is illustrated by the refusal of many psychologists even to try any alternative assessment procedures for minority students other than the culturally and linguistically biased tests which they have become 'experts' in administering. Minority children become the victims of professional 'credibility'.

How do these subtle, unintentional forms of institutional racism victimize minority children? This issue is discussed in more detail later but the potential consequences can be illustrated with reference to the case of Maria. As a result of the assessment, there is an increased likelihood that Maria will be reprimanded for any use of Italian with other Italian students in school, thereby promoting feelings of shame in her own cultural background. It is also probable that the child's parents will be advised to use English rather than Italian at home.[2] If parents adhere to this advice, then they are likely not only to *really* expose the child to poor models of English, but also to reduce the quality and quantity of communication between adults and children in the home since they are likely to be much less comfortable in English than Italian. The importance of adult–child home interaction for future academic achievement has been demonstrated repeatedly (e.g. Wells, 1986) and thus, the advice to switch to English in the home has the potential to exert serious negative effects on children's development. Furthermore, it is likely to drive an emotional wedge between children and parents (including the recently arrived aunt and grandmother who will know no English) since parents may feel that communication of affection and warmth in Italian will reduce the child's future academic prospects.[3]

In summary, the example of Maria illustrates how students can become educationally disabled as a direct result of their interactions with well-intentioned educators. These interactions are mediated by the role definitions of educators which are moulded by a variety of influences; for example, the broader policy and legal structure within which they operate, the institutional structure within which they have been trained, and the school and school board structures (e.g. principal–teacher, administrator–principal relationships) that determine priorities for action on a day-to-day basis. All of these factors must be taken into account in analysing the operation and effects of institutionalized racism.

The dimensions of institutionalized racism in schools

A clear distinction exists between racism that is overt and intentional compared with the more subtle forms of institutionalized racism that are not associated with overtly racist attitudes. Within this latter category we can distinguish two major dimensions: first, the knowledge or informational dimension and second, the attitudinal dimension that reflects the extent of educators' acceptance of and openness to other cultural groups. Educators can be grouped along an 'informed–misinformed' continuum with respect to the first dimension[4] and along an 'intercultural–Anglo-conformity' dimension with respect to the second.

Thus, as illustrated in Figure 1, anti-racist education requires educators who are both informed with respect to the available research regarding minority students and who are also characterized by an intercultural orientation with respect to the desirability of promoting *all* students' linguistic and personal talents and reinforcing their cultural identity. An intercultural orientation also implies building on students' experiences in the classroom (or in the assessment situation) and sharing of these experiences among students from different cultural groups. Institutionalized racism is manifested in educator–student inter-actions that reflect either misinformation or an Anglo-conformity orientation or both. It is important to emphasize that an Anglo-conformity orientation is revealed in educators' actions (such as the psychological assessment of Maria above) rather than in their overtly expressed attitudes.

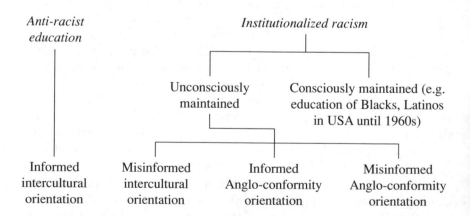

Figure 1 Dimensions of anti-racist education and institutionalized racism

The informational and attitudinal dimensions are clearly not independent since educators with an intercultural orientation will tend to seek out the information required to promote minority students' personal and academic development fully while those with an Anglo-conformity orientation will tend to deny that their knowledge base is in any way inadequate and reject any information that challenges their sociopolitical attitudes.

However, some educators may accept research information (e.g. regarding the benefits of bilingualism) but override the programmatic (and interactional) implications of this information because of their strong Anglo-conformity orientation.[5] Others may be genuinely intercultural in their orientation but lack important information; for example, they may truly believe that using two languages in the home 'confuses' bilingual children and consequently advise parents to switch to English. In other words, the resulting interactions are still disabling for minority students (and are manifestations of institutionalized racism) despite the educator's genuine intercultural orientation. However, if this misinformation persists despite ample opportunity to correct it, then one might suspect that the apparent intercultural orientation is simply a façade. A genuine commitment to empowering minority students implies acceptance of the educator's *ethical responsibility* to become informed with respect both to causes of minority students' academic difficulties and strategies for helping students overcome these difficulties.

A theoretical framework for analysing these issues and for planning educational intervention with respect to minority students is presented in the next section.

A Theoretical Framework for Intervention

The framework presented in Figure 2 is adapted from Cummins (1986) in order to reflect issues that are particularly relevant to implementation of anti-racist education policies in the Canadian context. A considerable amount of data shows that power and status relations between minority and majority groups exert a major influence on school performance (Cummins, 1984a; Ogbu, 1978). Minority groups that tend to experience academic difficulty (e.g. Finns in Sweden, Hispanic, Black and Native American groups in the USA, Franco-Ontarian, Black and Native American groups in the USA, Franco-Ontarian, Black and Native groups in Canada) appear to have developed an insecurity and ambivalence about the value of their own cultural identity as a result of their interactions with the dominant group. A central proposition of the theoretical framework is that minority students are disempowered educationally in very much the same way that their communities are disempowered by interactions with societal institutions. The converse of this is that minority students will succeed educationally to the extent that the patterns of interaction in school reverse those that prevail in society at large. In short, minority students are 'empowered' or 'disabled' as a direct result of their interactions with educators

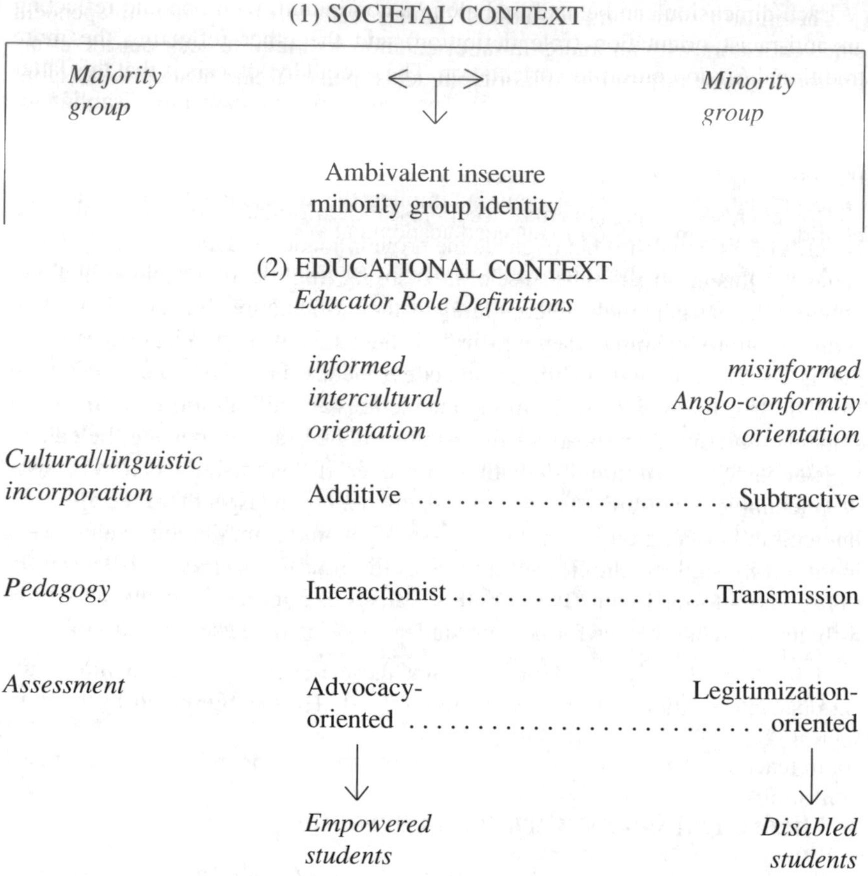

(1) SOCIETAL CONTEXT

Majority *group*	⟵ ⟶ ↓	*Minority* *group*
	Ambivalent insecure minority group identity	

(2) EDUCATIONAL CONTEXT
Educator Role Definitions

	informed *intercultural* *orientation*	*misinformed* *Anglo-conformity* *orientation*
Cultural/linguistic *incorporation*	Additive . . . . Subtractive	
Pedagogy	Interactionist . . . . Transmission	
Assessment	Advocacy-oriented	Legitimization-oriented
	↓	↓
	Empowered *students*	*Disabled* *students*

Figure 2 Empowerment of minority students: a framework for intervention

in schools. These interactions are mediated by the implicit or explicit role definitions that educators assume in relation to four institutional characteristics of schools. These characteristics reflect the extent to which:

(1) Minority students' language and culture are incorporated into the school programme.

(2) Minority community participation is encouraged as an integral component of children's education;

(3) The pedagogy promotes intrinsic motivation on the part of students to use language actively in order to generate their own knowledge; and

(4) Professionals involved in assessment become advocates for minority students by focusing primarily on the ways in which students' academic difficulty is a function of interactions within the school context rather than legitimizing the location of the 'problem' within students.

Each dimension can be analysed along a continuum, with one end reflecting an anti-racist orientation (role definition) and the other reflecting the more traditional Anglo-conformity orientation. The overall hypothesis is that this latter orientation will tend to result in the personal and/or academic disabling of minority students while anti-racist orientations (as operationally defined with respect to the framework) will result in minority student empowerment, a concept that, in the present context, implies the development of the ability, confidence and motivation to succeed academically.[6]

At least three of the dimensions analysed (cultural/linguistic incorporation, community participation, and assessment) are integral to most statements of 'multicultural education' policy. Although policy with respect to linguistic (as compared with cultural) incorporation has tended to be vague and ambivalent, the linguistic component is regarded as central to the present framework on the grounds that a multicultural education policy which ignores linguistic diversity is vacuous and there is considerable research evidence showing the importance of the linguistic component for minority students' academic achievement. The inclusion of 'pedagogy' as a central dimension of a framework for analysing anti-racist education may appear unusual; its relevance, however, derives from the fact that genuine incorporation of students' experiences (cultures) into the school programme requires that educators abandon pedagogical assumptions which focus primarily on transmission of pre-determined knowledge and skills.

The question to be posed in considering these dimensions is to what extent educational policy-makers, administrators, psychologists, principals and class-room teachers in Ontario have actually adopted anti-racist as opposed to Anglo-conformity role definitions.

Cultural/linguistic incorporation

Considerable research data suggest that for minority groups who experience disproportionate levels of academic failure, the extent to which students' language and culture are incorporated into the school programme constitutes a significant predictor of academic success (for example, Campos & Keatinge, this volume*; Cummins, 1983). In programmes where minority students' L1 skills are strongly reinforced, their school success appears to reflect both the more solid cognitive/academic foundation developed through intensive L1 instruction and also the reinforcement of their cultural identity (see Skutnabb-Kangas, 1984).

With respect to the incorporation of minority students' language and culture, educators' role definitions can be characterized along an 'additive–subtractive' dimension (see Lambert, 1975 for a discussion of additive and subtractive bilingualism). Educators who see their role as adding a second language and cultural affiliation to students' repertoire are likely to empower students more than those who see their role as replacing or subtracting students' primary language and culture in the process of assimilating them to the dominant culture. In addition to the personal and future employment advantages of proficiency in two or more languages, there is considerable evidence that subtle educational advantages result from continued development of both languages among bilingual students. Enhanced metalinguistic development, for example, is frequently found in association with additive bilingualism (e.g. Hakuta & Diaz, 1985).

When we examine the Ontario situation, we find considerable evidence of ambivalence at a policy level towards full educational incorporation of minority languages and cultures. More than 90,000 students receive heritage language instruction through the provincial government's heritage language programme (two and a half hours per week of instruction outside the regular five-hour school day), and the rhetoric which rationalizes this programme clearly acknowledges the validity of an additive orientation. However, one can question the adequacy of two and a half hours of instruction to achieve the goal of active bilingualism. The ambivalence of policy-makers with respect to promotion of minority languages is also evident in the marginal status which the heritage languages programme has had during the first decade of its existence (1977–87). The programme has not been legitimized as an important component of children's education in that it can only be offered outside the normal five-hour school day. Also, in contrast to western Canada, it is still illegal to offer bilingual programmes (e.g. 50% heritage language, 50% English) in Ontario schools.[7]

When we move to the level of school boards we find most boards responding to community requests for the heritage language programme; however, in at least one case (Scarborough) the board has refused to implement the programme despite strong and prolonged community pressure.

At the level of the school itself, we find generally little enthusiasm among principals and regular programme teachers for incorporation of heritage language programmes within an extended school day. In the Metropolitan Separate School Board (MSSB), the programme for Italian, Portuguese and Ukrainian has been integrated for almost a decade with relatively little controversy (but see Berryman, 1986) but in the Toronto Board the attempt to integrate the programme into an extended school day was strongly resisted by regular school staff. Much of the resistance was fuelled by the perception among teachers that they had not been adequately consulted by the board, but there was also a strong feeling among many teachers that the heritage language programme had little educational merit and would disrupt the teaching of the core curriculum. In some situations, ethnocultural community groups reported that teachers had explicitly communicated these beliefs to students in class. Parents still frequently report that teachers and other educators advise them to use English rather than their mother tongue in the home on the grounds that children's school progress is impeded by lack of exposure to English.

In short, with respect to cultural/linguistic incorporation, an institutional structure has been created in the province whose aim is to further students' appreciation of diverse cultures and to provide opportunities for language maintenance and acquisition. However, this structure falls short of recognizing heritage language learning as fully educationally legitimate and there is little evidence that a 'philosophy of multiculturalism' does actually permeate the curriculum and policies of most schools in the province. The evidence that exists (e.g. Samuda, 1979) suggests that the rhetoric of 'multicultural education' at a policy level is reflected to a much lesser extent in the actual interactions between educators and students. These interactions appear as likely to convey 'subtractive' messages to minority students with respect to their language and culture as they are to encourage language development and cultural reinforcement. In other words, Anglo-conformity is alive and well at a classroom level in many schools despite the lip-service paid to vague principles of multicultural education.

It is also worth noting that, in contrast to the United States, there has been very little discussion of the relevance of bilingual education programmes to promoting the academic achievement of minority students who are 'at risk' educationally. The heritage language programme is seen as an 'enrichment' opportunity rather than as an intervention designed to reinforce students' conceptual foundation (see Cummins, 1983). There are some exceptions, for example the L1 tutoring programme implemented for Spanish-speaking students in North York, but generally intervention for minority students 'at risk' does not go beyond the regular English language remediation programmes. There has been virtually no use made of heritage language instructors for either L1 assessment or remediation for minority students.

Community participation

It has been argued (Cummins, 1986) that minority students will be empowered in the school context to the extent that the communities themselves are empowered through their interactions with the school. When educators involve minority parents as partners in their children's education, parents appear to develop a sense of efficacy that communicates itself to children with positive academic consequences (see, for example, the 'Haringey Project' in Britain (Tizard *et al.,* 1982) and Ada, this volume, Chapter 9*).

The teacher role definitions associated with community participation can be characterized along a *collaborative–exclusionary* dimension. Teachers operating at the collaborative end of the continuum actively encourage minority parents to participate in promoting their children's academic progress both in the home and through involvement in classroom activities (see Ada, this volume*). A collaborative orientation may require a willingness on the part of the teacher to work closely with mother tongue teachers or aides in order to communicate effectively and in a non-condescending way with minority parents. Teachers with an exclusionary orientation, on the other hand, tend to regard teaching as *their* job and are likely to view collaboration with minority parents as either irrelevant or actually detrimental to children's progress. Often parents are viewed as part of the problem since they interact through their L1 with their children at home.

From the perspective of many teachers, parents' demands to have their languages taught within the school system further illustrates how misguided parents are with respect to what is good educationally for their children. From the parents' perspective, teachers' resistance to heritage languages represents an attempt to exclude the community's values and priorities from the educational system and suggests to them that the rhetoric about the importance of community participation refers only to participation by the Anglo-Celtic community.

A number of larger school boards employ school–community liaison officers to increase the participation of minority communities in the education of their children. However, there is a potential conflict of interest for employees of school systems if they attempt to become advocates for ethnocultural communities. This conflict of interest derives from the fact that school–community liaison officers are still expected to represent the interests of the school system which may not be willing to acknowledge problems that exist and may have a vested interest in maintaining the status quo. Thus, alerting communities to their rights and/or interests may be regarded as stirring up trouble.

This can be illustrated with reference to the 1984–86 heritage language controversy in the Toronto Board of Education[8] where the School–Community Relations (SCR) department was active in attempting to communicate research results to ethnocultural communities about the value of heritage language development, and also played a role in encouraging community participation at consultation meetings held to discuss integration of the programme in particular schools. In many cases the message they were conveying to communities was the opposite to that which regular programme teachers were attempting to convey.[9] As a consequence, many trustees and teachers opposed to integration of heritage language teaching did not view the activities of the SCR department favourably. These trustees gained control of the Board in the autumn 1985 elections; the SCR department was subsequently disbanded and, in August 1986, the co-ordinator was relieved of his duties 'because of the unavailability of work' (*Role Call*, Volume 9, No. 1, November 1986: 8).

The policy issue that arises with respect to community participation is whether employees of school boards are the appropriate people to represent the educational interests of minority communities, since one cannot assume that the interests of communities will match the interests of the boards. For school board employees to support the interests of communities against those of the status quo is to risk job security and/or advancement.[10]

Pedagogy

Several investigators have suggested that the learning difficulties of minority students are often pedagogically induced in that children designated 'at risk' frequently receive intensive instruction that confines them to a passive role and induces a form of 'learned helplessness' (e.g. Beers & Beers, 1980; Coles, 1978; Cummins, 1984a). Instruction that empowers students, on the other hand, will aim to liberate students from dependence on instruction in the sense of encouraging them to become active generators of their own knowledge.

Two major orientations can be distinguished with respect to pedagogy. These differ in the extent to which the teacher retains exclusive control over classroom interaction as opposed to sharing some of this control with students. The dominant instructional model in most Western industrial societies has been termed a 'transmission' model (Barnes, 1976; Wells, 1982); this can be contrasted with a 'reciprocal interaction' model of pedagogy.

The basic premise of the transmission model is that the teacher's task is to impart knowledge or skills that s/he possesses to students who do not yet have these skills. This implies that the teacher initiates and controls the interaction, constantly orienting it towards the achievement of instructional objectives.

It has been argued that a transmission model of teaching contravenes central principles of language and literacy acquisition and that a model allowing for reciprocal interaction between teachers and students represents a more appropriate alternative (Cummins, 1984a; Wells, 1982). This 'reciprocal interaction' model incorporates proposals about the relation between language and learning made by a variety of investigators, most notably, in recent years, in the Bullock Report (1975), and by Barnes (1976), Lindfors (1980) and Wells (1982). Its applications with respect to the promotion of literacy conform closely to psycholinguistic approaches to reading (e.g. Goodman & Goodman, 1977; Holdaway, 1979; Smith, 1978) and to the recent emphasis on encouraging expressive writing from the earliest grades (e.g. Chomsky, 1981; Graves, 1983).

The Ministry of Education and most boards of education in Ontario endorse an interactionist emphasis at a policy level but in many programmes (particularly second language programmes such as core FSL, immersion, heritage language programmes) the actual practice is still very much transmission-oriented.

A central tenet of the reciprocal interaction model is that 'talking and writing are means to learning' (Bullock Report, 1975: 50). Its major characteristics in comparison with a transmission model are as follows:

- genuine dialogue between student and teacher in both oral and written modalities;
- guidance and facilitation rather than control of student learning by the teacher;
- encouragement of student–student talk in a collaborative learning context;
- encouragement of meaningful language use by students rather than correctness of surface forms;
- conscious integration of language use and development with all curricular content rather than teaching language and other content as isolated subjects;
- a focus on developing higher level cognitive skills rather than factual recall;
- task presentation that generates intrinsic rather than extrinsic motivation.

In short, pedagogical approaches that empower students encourage them to assume greater control over setting their own learning goals and to collaborate actively with each other in achieving these goals. The approaches reflect what cognitive psychologists such as Piaget and Vygotsky have emphasized about children's learning for more than half a century. Learning is viewed as an *active* process that is enhanced through *interaction*. The stress on action (Piaget) and interaction (Vygotsky) contrasts with behaviouristic pedagogical models that focus on passive and isolated reception of knowledge.

The relevance of these two pedagogical models for multicultural education derives from the fact that a genuine multicultural orientation is impossible within a transmission model of pedagogy. To be sure, content about other cultural groups can be transmitted but appreciation of other cultural groups can come about only through interaction where experiences are being shared. Transmission models entail the suppression of students' experiences and consequently do not allow for validation of minority students' experiences in the classroom. Ontario (particularly Metropolitan Toronto) has potentially the perfect learning environment for genuine multicultural education given the diversity of human resources in most classrooms and communities. However, these resources can be utilized only when educators have

- an additive orientation to students' culture and language such that these can be shared rather than suppressed in the classroom;
- an openness to collaborate with community resource persons who can provide insight to students about different cultural, religious and linguistic traditions; and
- a willingness to permit active use of written and oral language by students so that students can develop their literacy and other language skills in the process of sharing their experiences with peers and adults.

Assessment

Historically, in both Canada and the United States, psychological assessment has served to legitimize the educational disabling of minority students by locating the academic 'problem' within the student herself. This has had the effect of screening from critical scrutiny the subtractive nature of the school programme, the exclusionary orientation of teachers towards minority communities, and transmission models of teaching that inhibit students from active participation in learning.

This process is virtually inevitable when the conceptual base for the assessment process is purely psycho-educational. If the psychologist's task (or role definition) is to discover the causes of a minority student's academic difficulties and the only tools at her disposal are psychological tests (in either L1 or L2), then it is hardly surprising that the child's difficulties are attributed to psychological dysfunctions.

To what extent have multicultural education policies influenced assessment and placement of minority students in Ontario? Very little, it appears. The Ministry of Education commissioned a survey of policies and programmes with respect to testing, assessment, counselling and placement of minority students in the late 1970s (Samuda & Crawford, 1980). This report documented the fact that a large majority of school boards had no policies or special provision for assessment and placement of minority students.

It is disturbing to contrast the concern for issues of discriminatory assessment in the United States with the virtual absence of any sustained consideration of these issues in Ontario, with the exception of a few boards of education. One might have expected that the endorsement of multicultural education policies in Ontario would make policy-makers and psychologists highly sensitive to issues of educational equity but there is little evidence that this has been the case. Even in the larger urban school boards where assessment policies do exist, these policies frequently bear little relationship to the research data that exist on minority assessment issues.

Ethnocultural community groups have expressed concern about discrimina tory assessment and streaming of minority students into vocational programmes since the early 1970s. First, the Dante Aligheri Society raised these issues with the Toronto Board on behalf of Italian students and more recently Portuguese, Greek and Black parents have expressed similar concerns. In the late 1970s, several Boards of Education adopted policies of delaying formal educational and psychological assessment of minority students until they had been in Canada for at least two years. However, the figure of two years was based on *assumptions* about how long it took children to learn English rather than on any empirical data. The empirical data, in fact, suggest that a much longer period (at least five years on average) is required for immigrant students to catch up with native speakers in academic aspects of English, although they may acquire relatively fluent conversational skills in English within about two years (Cummins, 1984a).

During the late 1970s and early 1980s, Ontario phased in its special education bill (Bill 82), modelled on the US special education bill (Public Law 94-142) which required school boards to identify all exceptional students (e.g. gifted, learning disabled, etc.) and provide them with an education appropriate to their needs. In the United States, many studies had documented the effects of dis-criminatory assessment of minority students as illustrated by the massive over-representation of Hispanic and Black students in classes for the retarded. Litiga-tion in the early 1970s required school districts to take steps to correct these abuses and relatively strong non-discriminatory assessment provisions were built into special education legislation (Public Law 94-142). Specifically, students were required to be assessed in their primary language unless it was clearly not feasible to do so. Throughout the 1970s and 1980s, psychological and special education journals in the United States have printed numerous articles on issues related to assessment of minority students, and the new field of 'bilingual special education' was born.

In Canada, by contrast, there has been minimal discussion of issues concerned with discriminatory assessment among academics and policy-makers involved in special education, and the issue of non-discriminatory assessment has been virtually ignored in special education legislation (Bill 82) and in subsequent documentation.[11] Similarly, the issue of non-discriminatory assessment has scarcely been raised in mainstream Canadian academic journals during the past decade. No courses on issues such as bilingualism, cultural diversity, non-discriminatory assessment are required or even offered in university departments which train school psychologists and special educators. Certification examinations for psychologists similarly ignore the issue despite the fact that in cities such as Metropolitan Toronto, with close to half the school population coming from non-English-speaking backgrounds, as many as 75% of the students being assessed are likely to have been exposed in the home to a language or dialect other than standard English.

Discussion of questions dealing with non-discriminatory assessment in support documents dealing with Bill 82 is limited to vague cautions such as the following:

> Where a child's language is other than English or French, a reasonable delay in the language-based aspects of assessment should be considered.
>
> (1980: 5)

A more recent memorandum to school boards gives somewhat greater recognition to potential problems in assessing minority students:

> If the pupil's first language is other than English or French and/or the pupil lacks facility in either of these languages, consideration should be given to postponing the assessment, or, where possible, conducting the assessment in the child's first language.'
>
> (Policy/Program Memorandum No. 59, p. 2)

However, no suggestions are given as to what constitutes a 'reasonable' delay, nor are pitfalls associated with L1 assessment considered. There appears to have been no obvious response at a policy level to the findings of the Samuda & Crawford (1980) report showing that many school boards across the province fail to pay even lip-service to Ministry guidelines regarding the testing of minority students. Apart from a handful of school boards, there is little evidence of minority students' cultural and/or linguistic backgrounds being systematically taken into account in the identification and placement process. Similarly, although Bill 82 mandates parental participation in Identification, Placement and Review Committee (IPRC) meetings, there is little evidence of sustained consideration of how to ensure meaningful parental participation when parents do not speak fluent English and/or do not understand the purpose or consequences of placement decisions that are being made.[12]

In short, academics, policy-makers and, to some extent, administrators in school boards have tended to show little sensitivity to issues concerned with non-discriminatory assessment despite the evidence from the United States and Canada that typical psychological assessment procedures significantly under-estimate the academic potential of minority students. No specific training has been or is currently being provided for psychologists on issues related to bilingualism and minority language development despite considerable evidence that misconceptions about the effects of bilingual language use in the home and the learning of heritage languages at school are common among both psychologists and other educators (Cummins, 1984a). Institutionalized racism with respect to the assessment of minority students has remained virtually unchallenged at the levels of policy and legal provision, professional training and certification, and (with one or two exceptions) school board programmes.

The alternative role definition that is required to reverse the traditional 'legitimizing' function of assessment can be termed an 'advocacy' or 'delegitimization' role (see Mullard, 1985 for discussion of delegitimization strategies in anti-racist education). The psychologist's or special educator's task must be to 'delegitimize' the traditional function of psychological assessment in the educational disabling of minority students; in other words, they must be prepared to become advocates for the child in scrutinizing critically the social and educational context within which the child has developed.[13]

Implementation of strategies to reverse discriminatory assessment policies is likely to be complex since these policies are rooted in the very organization of school systems and in the conceptualization of entire fields, such as special education and school psychology, where the normative 'medical' model of scholastic dysfunction still predominates. Ortiz and Yates (1983), for example, reported that Hispanic students in Texas were over-represented in the 'learning disabilities' (LD) category by a factor of 300%. In other words, despite non-discriminatory assessment provisions, the structure preserved itself by a simple shift from an Educable Mentally Retarded (EMR) classification to a LD classification. In short, the data suggest that the structure within which psychological assessment takes place orients the psychologist to locate the cause of the academic problem within the minority student herself and policy changes alone are unlikely to alter this structure significantly.

Samuda (1979) reports a similar disjunction between policy and school practice in Ontario with respect to the educational assessment of minority students. A strong assimilationist element was evident among school principals, teachers and resource people, especially in Metropolitan Toronto:

> Statements by Chairpersons of school boards, the various Work Groups on Multiculturalism within Metro Toronto, all illustrate the fact that the thrust for reform has developed outside and apart from the schools. And, significantly, there exists a lag between the words of the politicians and the attitudes and practices of the teachers who are the principal instruments in

the assessment, placement, and educational treatment of the new Canadian. The one recurring and persistent need is for the re-education – the inservice training – of teachers, administrators, and consultants, to move from an ethnocentric stance to a clearer understanding of the basic intent and meaning of the Province's multicultural policy and what it means in terms of educational policy and practice. The central feature for change must be the teacher's attitude, the teacher's understanding and acceptance which can only come by implementing preservice and inservice teacher education programs ... (1979: 49)

Samuda goes on to emphasize the need 'to make drastic changes in the kind of training that takes place in the faculties of education throughout the province where there is scant evidence of any real change in perspective from that of the ethnocentric WASP middle-class pattern' (p. 49).

The types of change process that should operate at different levels of the educational hierarchy are examined in the next section.

Conceptualizing the Change Process in Anti-racist Education

In conceptualizing the change process in anti-racist education, it is necessary to specify: first, the levels or constituencies involved in effecting change; second, the specific areas where change is required; and third, the practical strategies for implementing change. The levels involved in effecting change are outlined in Figure 3.

Policy/Legal Structure

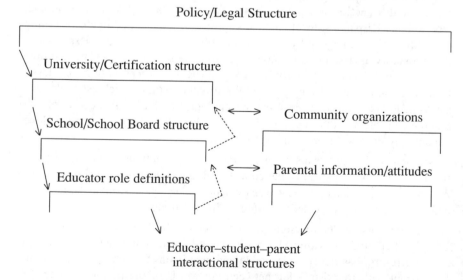

Figure 3 Change processes in anti-racist education

As discussed above, the most direct determinant of minority student outcomes is the type of interaction students experience with educators and their parents (or other significant adults). The role definitions of educators with respect to the dimensions discussed in Figure 2 (cultural/linguistic incorporation, community participation, pedagogy, and assessment) mediate their interactions with minority students and play a major role in empowering or, alternatively, disabling students. Thus, major changes in interactional structures that challenge the broader institutionalized racism *can* be effected by individual educators. However, the actions of individual educators are clearly influenced and constrained by the immediate school and school board context within which they operate as well as by both their training and the policy/legal context that exists within the society. For example, a teacher of Latino students in the United States may attempt to implement interactional pedagogy and strongly promote students' L1 academic skills but be reprimanded by the school principal who is concerned that the class is noisy (because there is a lot of language going on) and that there is too much Spanish being spoken. Similarly, change is less likely when there is no recognition of the need for change at the levels of policy and university training. The case of Bill 82 in Ontario, considered above, is a good example of how inadvertent institutionalized racism with respect to assessment of minority students was perpetuated by the failure of policy-makers and academics to acknowledge that there is even an issue here for educators to consider.

The relationships outlined in Figure 3 are two-way relationships; in other words, influence can be exerted upwards (e.g. from individual teachers to school/school board policy) as well as downwards. Also, no rigid hierarchy of influence is intended. For example, policy provisions can (and usually do) affect schools without going through the university structure. Also, individual teachers can take advantage of legal provisions to effect changes in school board policy, as described by Curtis (this volume). Parents and communities can also directly impact various levels of the educational hierarchy (see Honkala *et al.*, this volume, Chapter 10)*.

According to the framework developed above, change towards anti-racist education must focus on the ways in which structural economic/political factors are manifested both in the knowledge base and in the mind set or orientation of educators. These two are closely linked since information will frequently be ignored or denied by educators who are characterized by an Anglo-conformity orientation. These educators also tend to be reluctant to acknowledge that they hold Anglo-conformist views and may claim that they believe strongly in 'multiculturalism'.

Among the issues that educators and policy-makers should internalize as part of their knowledge base are the following:

- limitations of standardized tests;
- language/academic development among minority students;
- bilingualism in the home;

- bilingual/heritage language programmes;
- dialect differences;
- cognitive/cultural styles;
- parental involvement.

There is an ethical responsibility for educators at all levels of the educational hierarchy to ensure that *all* those interacting with or setting policy for minority students have internalized and are acting in ways consistent with this knowledge base. This applies not just to teachers but to principals, resource persons and administrators also.

However, although acquisition of the knowledge base is a necessary condition for anti-racist educational practice, it is not a sufficient condition. Also required is an intercultural orientation on the part of educators.

The task of changing basic attitudinal orientations is formidable and experience suggests that strong policy/legal provisions and incentives at the levels of Ministries of Education, universities and school boards are necessary. In addition, principals should make it clear that teachers with an Anglo-conformity orientation are out of place in their schools, and teachers should also communicate to other teachers that behavioural or attitudinal manifestations of institutionalized racism are unacceptable to them.

It would also be advisable to create an independent structure outside the school boards and the Ministry of Education to monitor the progress that boards are making towards implementation of anti-racist education. At a federal level in Canada, the auditor general and the Commissioner of Official Languages play such monitoring roles in the areas of government spending and national official language provisions.

Provision should also be made for 'community advocates', again independent of school boards, to provide input to parents (in their own languages) about their rights and to represent parents at times when crucial decisions are being made about their children's future (e.g. at student placement meetings following formal psychological assessment). It is essential that these community advocates be independent of school boards, since there is otherwise a conflict of interest when an employee of a school board potentially opposes school board policy or practice in advocating minority students' and parents' rights. The recent demise of the Toronto Board's School–Community Relations department discussed above illustrates the potential consequences of promoting informed parental participation in opposition to the wishes of some politicians and educators.

In conclusion, anti-racist educational initiatives are possible at all levels of the educational hierarchy, from the individual teacher or parent to government policy-makers. However, these initiatives are likely to be successful only when they represent a challenge to the societal power structure. Given the commitment by many people in society to maintain the dominant–dominated power relationships, we can predict that educational changes which threaten this power structure will be fiercely resisted. The fact that, in Ontario, up to this point multicultural education initiatives (with the exception of heritage language programmes which are outside the 'mainstream' of multicultural education) have met with little or no resistance is an indication of how little they threatened the educational basis of Anglo-conformity and, by the same token, how little they are likely to have empowered minority students. It remains to be seen to what extent the current anti-racist education initiatives being undertaken by the provincial government will challenge the roots of institutionalized racism in Ontario education.

Notes

* Reference to another part of the volume where this chapter was originally published (*Minority Education: From Shame to Struggle*).
1. 'Heritage language' is the most commonly used term in Canada to refer to mother tongue programmes. However, a variety of other terms (e.g. ancestral, ethnic, ethnic minority, modern, 'third' (after English and French), non-official (in contrast to the official languages)) have also been used, reflecting the confused status of the entire enterprise in many parts of Canada. See Skutnabb-Kangas, this volume, Chapter 1*, for a detailed discussion of the various ways in which the term 'mother tongue' has been used.
2. This is still an extremely common practice in North American schools.
3. See Rodriguez (1982) for an autobiographical account of the emotional schism brought about by teachers' advice to parents to switch from Spanish to English in the home.
4. In some cases 'disinformed' would be more accurate since the misinformation is promoted by political or social forces that are attempting to maintain the status quo with respect to dominant dominated group relations.
5. This appears to characterize many of those associated with the 'US English' movement in the United States who strongly promote better 'foreign' language programmes while arguing for the eradication of minority students' home languages.
6. Galtung's work, as discussed by Skutnabb-Kangas, this volume, Chapter 11*, is relevant to the analysis of minority student and community empowerment.
7. At the time of writing (February 1987) it appears possible that these restrictions may be lifted and heritage language instruction may be incorporated within the regular school day. A private member's bill (Bill 80) proposing incorporation of heritage language instruction within the regular school day has been endorsed by all three political parties. However, as in past debates on heritage language teaching in Ontario (see Cummins, 1984b), a strong backlash is likely. The tone of this backlash can be seen from the comments of one columnist (Judi McLeod, an ardent critic of heritage language programmes) who writes in a column entitled 'All Aboard for More Hogwash': '... I call the bill hogwash. The nauseating strategy of the lib-left will undoubtedly see any who speak against the heritage-language bill branded as racists and bigots. Yet educators keep telling us that one of the most pressing educational problems is the number of students graduating from high schools without an adequate grasp of English' (*Toronto Sun*, January 19, 1987: 18).
8. This controversy centred on the attempt by the Toronto Board to integrate the teaching of heritage languages within a school day extended by half an hour rather than outside regular school hours (e.g. after school or on Saturday). Regular programme teachers worked to rule for several months (e.g. refusing to participate in all extracurricular activities such as sports) and threatened full strike action to protest at what they saw as a decline in the quality of education and in their working conditions caused by the teaching of heritage languages during the extended day.
9. In an interview published in *Role Call* (Vol. 8, No. 3, April 1986), the Toronto Teachers' Federation monthly newspaper, Charlie Novogrodsky, the co-ordinator of

the SCR Department, described the conflict between the SCR Department and the teachers in terms of 'a classic confrontation between, on the one hand, a heartfelt community desire (in many hearts) to have their culture and language recognized as part of their regular school curriculum through an integrated program: that desire coming up against an equal desire, on the other hand, on the part of people who are closest to the work   teachers – to control the condition, including the time and scheduling under which they deliver their work. It is a classic community control versus professional control issue.'

10. The strike by Finnish parents in Rinkeby, Sweden (see Honkala *et al.*, this volume*) illustrates the importance of informed minority community groups to monitor actions by schools or school boards that might jeopardize their children's academic development.

11. This raises some disturbing questions; for example, was the issue of non-discriminatory assessment ignored because those who drafted Bill 82 were genuinely ignorant of the issue or because they considered it to be an unimportant or marginal issue? The first supposition is hardly credible since the issue was highlighted in most of the major academic journals in special education and school psychology during the previous decade; thus, it may be that the issue was simply an awkward question that was more convenient to ignore than to deal with. The lack of sensitivity among ethnocultural groups and opposition parties to the implications of the legislation for minority groups certainly facilitated this strategy. The Bill constitutes a prime example of how institutionalized racism can be perpetuated at a policy/legal level.

12. At the time of writing (February 1987) a comprehensive review of race relations policy in education is being conducted by the Ministry of Education in which serious consideration is being given to the manifestations of institutionalized racism in the educational system and strategies for eliminating it. Assessment of minority students is a major focus of this review.

13. It is worth noting that assessment and pedagogy are closely linked in that classroom teachers have considerable opportunities to observe children undertaking a variety of cognitive and academic tasks when the instruction is individualized and interactional. This information can and should play an important role in assessment/placement decisions. Within a transmission model, when the instructional tasks are teacher-imposed rather than expressive of children's own experience, then the instruction tends to mirror the biases of standardized tests and consequently provides much less opportunity for observation of children's capacities.

References

Abella, I. and Troper, H. (1983) *None is too Many*. Toronto: Lester & Orpen Dennys.

Anderson, S. E. and Fullan, M. (1984) *Policy Implementation Issues for Multicultural Education at the School Board Level*. Ottawa: Multiculturalism Canada.

Barnes, D. (1976) *From Communication to Curriculum*. Harmondsworth, Middlesex: Penguin.

Beers, C. S. and Beers, J. W. (1980) Early identification of learning disabilities: Facts and fallacies. *The Elementary School Journal* 81, 67–76.

Berryman, J. (1986) Implementation of Ontario's Heritage Languages Program: A case study of the extended school day model. Unpublished doctoral dissertation, OISE.

Bullock Report (1975) *A Language for Life*. Report of the committee of inquiry appointed by the Secretary of State for Education and Science under the chairmanship of Sir Alan Bullock. London: HMSO.

Chomsky, C. (1981) Write now, read later. In C. Cazden (ed.) *Language in Early Childhood Education* (2nd edn). Washington, DC: National Association for the Education of Young Children.

Coles, G. S. (1978) The learning disabilities test battery: Empirical and social issues. *Harvard Educational Review* 48, 313–40.

Cummins, J. (1983) *Heritage Language Education: A Literature Review.* Toronto: Ministry of Education, Ontario.

Cummins, J. (1984a) *Bilingualism and Special Education: Issues in Assessment and Pedagogy.* Clevedon: Multilingual Matters. Co-published in the United States by College Hill Press, San Diego.

Cummins, J. (1984b) Linguistic minorities and multicultural policy in Canada. In J. Edwards (ed.) *Linguistic Minorities, Policies and Pluralism.* London: Academic Press.

Cummins, J. (1986) Empowering minority students: A framework for intervention. *Harvard Educational Review* 56, 18–36.

Goodman, K. S. and Goodman, Y. M. (1977) Learning about psycholinguistic processes by analysing oral reading. *Harvard Educational Review* 47, 317–33.

Graves, D. (1983) *Writing: Children and Teachers at Work.* Exeter, NH: Heinemann.

Hakuta, K. and Diaz, R. M. (1985) The relationship between degree of bilingualism and cognitive ability: A critical discussion and some new longitudinal data. In K. E. Nelson (ed.) *Children's Language* (Vol. 5). Hillsdale, NJ: Erlbaum.

Harney, R. and Troper, H. (1975) *Immigrants: A Portrait of Urban Experience, 1890–1930.* Toronto: Van Nostrand Reinhold.

Holdaway, D. (1979) *Foundations of Literacy.* New York: Ashton Scholastic.

Lambert, W. E. (1975) Culture and language as factors in learning and education. In A. Wolfgang (ed.) *Education of Immigrant Students.* Toronto: OISE.

Lindfors, J. W. (1980) *Children's Language and Learning.* Englewood Cliffs, NJ: Prentice Hall.

Mullard, C. (1985) The social dynamic of migrant groups: From progressive to transformative policy in education. Paper presented at the OECD Conference on Educational Policies and the Minority Social Groups, Paris, January.

Ogbu, J. U. (1978) *Minority Education and Caste.* New York: Academic Press.

Ortiz, A. A. and Yates, J. R. (1983) Incidence of exceptionality among Hispanics: Implications for manpower planning. *NABE Journal* 7, 41–54.

Rodriguez, R. (1982) *Hunger of Memory.* Boston: David R. Godine.

Samuda, R. J. (1979) How are the schools of Ontario coping with a New Canadian population: A report of recent research findings. *TESL Talk* 11, 44–51.

Samuda, R. J. and Crawford, D. H. (1980) *Testing, Assessment, Counselling, and Placement of Ethnic Minority Students.* Toronto: Ministry of Education, Ontario.

Skutnabb-Kangas, T. (1984) *Bilingualism or Not: The Education of Minorities.* Clevedon: Multilingual Matters.

Smith, F. (1978) *Understanding Reading* (2nd edn). New York: Holt, Rinehart & Winston.

Tizard, J., Schofield, W. N. and Hewison, J. (1982) Collaboration between teachers and parents in assisting children's reading. *British Journal of Educational Psychology* 52, 1–15.

Troper, H. (1979) An uncertain past: Reflections on the history of multiculturalism. *TESL Talk* 10, 7–15.

Wells, G. (1982) Language, learning and the curriculum. In G. Wells, *Language, Learning and Education.* Bristol: Centre for the Study of Language and Communication, University of Bristol.

Wells, G. (1986) *The Meaning Makers: Children Learning Language and Using Language to Learn.* Portsmouth, NH: Heinemann.

Wright, E. N. and Tsuji, G. K. (1984) *The Grade Nine Student Survey: Fall 1983.* Toronto Board of Education, Research Report No. 174.

The Role and Use of Educational Theory in Formulating Language Policy

Although most politicians and policy-makers realize the necessity to pay lip-service to research in formulating educational policy and programs insofar as all initiatives must be justified as being 'in the best interests of children', it is not difficult to see that research and theory are coherently applied to policy only in situations where there is a relatively high degree of consensus in regard to both the societal and educational goals of the policy debates relating to language and education. Two of these debates are bilingual education programs in the United States and French immersion programs in Canada.

I shall argue that in both these cases, the sociological context of the debate, i.e. the power relations between dominant and subordinate groups in the society, plays a major role in determining the choice of issues to investigate, the conduct of the research, the interpretation of findings, and the relevance they assume for policy. In short, the relation between research, theory and policy can be understood only in the context of what Paulston (1980) terms a 'conflict' paradigm where group conflicts over values, resources, and power are explicitly taken into account.

The Relation Between Research, Theory and Policy

In the United States, controversy has raged for almost 20 years on appropriate ways of educating minority language children. Bilingual programs were mandated by the Office of Civil Rights in their interpretation of the Supreme Court's *Lau v. Nichols* decision in 1974, but there still exists no consensus regarding the effectiveness of such programs and many educators and policy-makers have expressed fears that bilingual education is 'unAmerican' and will balkanize the country.

A major reason why many policy-makers and educators in the United States regard the research basis for bilingual education as minimal or even non-existent is that they have failed to realize that data or 'facts' from bilingual programs

240

become interpretable for policy purposes only within the context of a coherent theory. It is the *theory* rather than the individual research findings that permits the generation of predictions about program outcomes under different condi- tions. Research findings themselves cannot be *directly* applied across contexts. For example, the fact that kindergarten and grade 1 Punjabi-background students in a bilingual program in Bradford, England, learned English just as successfully as a control group in a traditional English-only program (Rees, 1981) tells us very little about what might happen in the case of Greek-background students in Bradford or Hispanic students in the United States. Similarly, the findings of French immersion programs for majority students in Canada cannot be *directly* applied to policy-decisions regarding programs for minority students in the United States. Yet clearly the accumulation of research findings does have relevance for policy. This relevance is achieved by means of the integration of the findings within a coherent theory from which predictions regarding program outcomes under different conditions can be generated.

In short, although research findings cannot be applied directly across con- texts, theories are almost by definition applicable across contexts in that the validity of any theoretical principle is assessed precisely by how well it can account for the research findings in a variety of contexts. If a theory cannot account for a particular set of research findings, then it is an inadequate or incomplete theory.

Theory and the US Bilingual Education Policy Debate

Two opposing theoretical assumptions have dominated the US policy debate regarding the effectiveness of bilingual education in promoting minority students' academic achievement. These assumptions are essentially hypotheses regarding the causes of minority students' academic failure and each is associated with a particular form of educational intervention designed to reverse this failure. In support of transitional bilingual education where some initial instruction is given in students' first language (L1), it is argued that students cannot learn in a language they do not understand; thus, a home–school language switch will almost inevitably result in academic retardation unless initial content is taught through L1 while students are acquiring English. In other words, minority stu- dents' academic difficulties are attributed to a 'linguistic mismatch' between home and school.

The opposing argument is that if minority students are deficient in English, then they need as much exposure to English as possible. Students' academic difficulties are attributed to insufficient exposure to English in the home and environment. Thus, bilingual programs which reduce this exposure to English even further appear illogical and counterproductive in that they seem to imply that less exposure to English will lead to more English achievement. The following passage from a *New York Times* editorial (October 10, 1981) is typical:

> The Department of Education is analyzing new evidence that expensive bilingual education programs don't work ... Teaching non-English speaking children in their native language during much of their school day constructs a roadblock on their journey into English. A language is best learned through immersion in it, particularly by children ... Neither society nor its children will be well served if bilingualism continues to be used to keep thousands of children from quickly learning the one language needed to succeed in America.

Viewed as theoretical principles from which predictions regarding program outcomes can be derived, the 'linguistic mismatch' and 'insufficient exposure' hypotheses are each patently inadequate. The former is refuted by the French immersion data which clearly demonstrate that for English-background students in Canada a home–school language switch results in no academic retardation. The success of a considerable number of minority students under home–school language switch conditions similarly refutes the linguistic mismatch hypothesis.

The 'insufficient exposure' hypothesis fares no better. Virtually every bilingual program that has ever been evaluated (including French immersion programs) shows that students instructed through a minority language for all or part of the school day perform, over time, at least as well in the majority language (e.g. French in North America) as students instructed exclusively through the majority language.

The fact that two such patently inadequate theoretical assumptions have dominated the bilingual education policy debate in the United States illustrates the power of politics over logic. It also shows the necessity of integrating theory explicitly into the decision-making process. One possible decision-making sequence or 'flow-chart' with respect to bilingual education policy in different contexts is presented in the next section.

A Framework for Theoretically-based Decision-making in Educational Language Planning

Any language planning process will first identify a particular problem (e.g. underachievement of certain groups of minority students) and then focus upon solutions to this problem. These solutions will involve either explicit or implicit hypotheses about the causes of the problem (e.g. 'linguistic mismatch' or 'insufficient exposure' to the school language) followed by the identification of alternative goals and means to resolve the problem. An idealized (and undoubtedly over-simplified) sequence for this type of decision-making is presented in Figure 1.

1. Examine perceived problems
2. Generate hypotheses about causes in light of theory and research
3. Plan solutions to problems: identify goals and means
4. Implement interventions to resolve problem
5. Monitor (or initiate) research relevant to theory about causes of problem
6. Evaluate success or failure of intervention
7. Communicate intervention results to policy-makers, educators and public

Figure 1 Sequence for analysing language problems in education

The decision-making process can be illustrated by comparing the highly successful implementation of French immersion programs in Canada during the late 1960s and 1970s with the generally much less successful implementation of bilingual programs for linguistic minority students in the United States during the same period. In both situations the general perceived problem was similar, namely, lack of student proficiency in a socially-valued language (French in Canada and English in the United States). However, in Canada the 'clients' of immersion programs were members of the dominant group whereas bilingual programs in the United States were designed to remediate presumed deficiencies of subordinate groups.

With respect to causes of the problem, sociopolitical considerations have been largely ignored in the policy debates. However, as Paulston (1980) has frequently pointed out, the major causes of most language planning problems are sociopolitical in nature with psychoeducational and linguistic factors acting as intervening variables. By the same token, the effects of educational interventions aimed at resolving such problems can usually be understood only in terms of their interaction with sociopolitical factors. In other words, interventions based on linguistic or psychoeducational hypotheses in isolation from the context of inter-ethnic group relations will frequently fail to produce the predicted outcomes.

In the Canadian situation, the writings of the Montreal neurosurgeon Wilbur Penfield were influential. Penfield (1965) had speculated (partly on the basis of neuropsychological evidence) that there is an optimal prepubertal period for acquiring an L2 and our language learning capacity declines after this period; he also suggested that second languages should be taught by what he called 'the mother's method' by which he meant used as a medium of communication in the classroom to permit children to acquire their L2 in much the same way as they acquired their L1. It is not difficult to see how these hypotheses gave rise to early French immersion programs.

In the United States' situation as discussed previously, linguistic hypotheses ('linguistic mismatch' and 'insufficient exposure') have tended to dominate the debate regarding causes of linguistic minority students' underachievement. The linguistic mismatch hypothesis tends to give rise to 'quick-exit' transitional bilingual programs, whereas the insufficient exposure hypothesis justifies English-only programs, often with some English-as-a-second-language (ESL) instruction. It is at this point that the planning process begins to break down in the United States context since neither of these hypotheses is consistent with the research data. Thus, it is not surprising that programs implemented on the basis of these hypotheses have not been particularly successful.

At the third stage, the goals and means of immersion programs were clearly defined and non-problematic. They served the interests of the dominant group and there was general consensus regarding goals and means. This, however, was not the case with bilingual education in the United States. All parties agreed with the goal of improved English academic skills but many minority advocates also desired bilingual programs to further the development of a pluralistic society through an emphasis on native culture and language maintenance. This goal was vehemently resisted by many 'mainstream' educators and policy-makers. During the late 1970s, the suspicion grew that bilingual programs were in reality intended only to promote Hispanic political and economic goals (even Hispanic separatism following the Quebec model) under the guise of developing students' English language skills. Thus, lack of consensus on goals and means compounded difficulties created by questionable psychoeducational assumptions used to justify bilingual education.

Problems of implementation followed naturally from the confused psychoeducational rationale and disputed goals of bilingual education in the United States. An enormous variety of programs results, ranging from considerable use of L1 in the early grades to virtually no use of L1. Some programs appeared to work extremely well, others much less so. By contrast, immersion programs started off on a very small scale with the St. Lambert program in the Montreal area (Lambert & Tucker, 1972) and a team of researchers monitored the progress of students through the grades. No further implementation was carried out until the initial results of this evaluation were available.

In both the United States and Canadian contexts, a considerable amount of evaluative research was carried out to assess the effects of the bilingual programs. In the case of the immersion programs, the initial St. Lambert program was thoroughly evaluated over a period of seven years and students were also followed through high school and beyond. As the immersion program spread to other areas, large-scale evaluations were also carried out to assess the consistency of findings with those of the St. Lambert program (e.g. Swain & Lapkin, 1982). One of the reasons for this was continued doubts among educators and parents that children could spend so much instructional time through French with no negative consequences for their English academic skills. Although some problematic issues have emerged (Burns & Olson, 1981; Cummins, 1984), the weight of research evidence has overwhelmingly confirmed the initial St. Lambert findings. Over time, theoretical principles emerged which could account for the absence of negative effects on English academic skills (Lambert & Tucker, 1972; Cummins, 1984). For example, the 'interdependence principle' appears to account for the data from both French immersion programs and bilingual programs for minority students:

> To the extent that instruction in Lx is effective in promoting proficiency in Lx, transfer of this proficiency to Ly will occur provided there is adequate exposure to Ly (either in school or environment) and adequate motivation to learn Ly.

It is interesting to note that, with respect to the initial theoretical assumptions underlying immersion, the research has refuted Penfield's hypothesis of an optimal age for language learning in that students in late immersion programs (usually beginning at grade 7 – aged 12–13) also succeed very well. However, Penfield's notion of the 'mother's method' is entirely compatible with the current emphasis on interaction as a basis for language learning (see Cummins & Swain, 1986).

The story has been very different in the evaluations of bilingual programs in the United States. Much of the research carried out was poorly designed (Baker & de Kanter, 1981), in part because of the much more complicated sociopolitical and educational context. For example, students were frequently exited from bilingual programs at very early stages (e.g. after one year) with the result that if students continued to perform poorly in English academic skills it was unclear whether this was due to premature exit to an all-English program or to the lack of effectiveness of bilingual education. Evaluations also tended to be atheoretical in that theory-based predictions regarding outcomes were seldom generated and tested. Thus, evaluators attempted to assess the 'effectiveness' of bilingual education without any well-articulated hypotheses regarding how long it would take minority students to acquire age-appropriate levels of English academic skills and under what sociopolitical and instructional conditions (e.g. length and intensity of L1 instruction).

The overall conclusion of immersion program evaluations is that the pro grams have been a resounding success and this has been effectively communicated to policy-makers, parents and educators. The result has been a huge increase in parental demand for French immersion programs which now have an enrolment of about 200,000 students and are offered in every Canadian province. Sociopolitical and administrative problems have emerged as a result of the increased demand for immersion programs (e.g. concerns by minority franco-phones of increased competition for bilingual jobs, layoff of teachers who do not speak French, etc.). However, these problems have not significantly slowed the momentum of immersion.

By contrast, bilingual programs in the United States are perceived much more equivocably by policy-makers and educators. This perception was reinforced by the research review conducted by Baker and de Kanter (1981) which concluded that transitional bilingual programs overall were not much more successful than English-only programs in promoting minority students' achievement. This review reflects the major problems of transitional bilingual education in that it is almost completely atheoretical and consequently ignores the consistent patterns that do emerge in the research data regarding transfer or interdependence of cognitive academic skills across languages.

In summary, the importance of generating and evaluating predictions from a coherent theory has been emphasized as a central, but frequently neglected, aspect of rational policy-making. Research findings become meaningful only when interpreted within a coherent theoretical framework. The contrast between the general acceptance and application of immersion program findings in Canada compared to the lack of acceptance of similar findings supporting exactly the same theoretical principles in the case of bilingual education in the United States illustrates the importance of inter-group power relations in research interpretation. Immersion programs are implemented by and serve the interests of the dominant group in Canada whereas bilingual programs in the United States confer power and status (e.g. through jobs) on previously dominated minorities and serve the interests of minorities rather than those of the dominant group. The demographic changes occurring in the United States with respect to the huge increase in the Hispanic population add to the urgency felt by many within the dominant group to restrict as much as possible the expanding power base of the minorities. This has been done by emasculating bilingual programs as much as possible by reducing the use of L1 and denying the value of these programs regardless of the research pointing to the contrary.

Conclusion

The relationships between research, theory and policy have been illustrated with reference to current language/education planning situations in North American education. Two broad conclusions emerge: first, the central role of theory is minimally understood by many policy-makers. 'Theory' is frequently dismissed as idle speculation ('it's just theory') by policy-makers who fail to appreciate that 'facts' become interpretable only in the context of a coherent theory. For policy, theory is essentially the means for predicting outcomes under divergent conditions, and as such, is inseparable from the policy-making process. It has been shown in the case studies reviewed that policy-makers often operate with implicit theoretical assumptions that become immune from critical scrutiny as a result of the absence of a systematic process of validating/revising these theoretical assumptions in relation to research data.

The second general conclusion is that socio-political factors related to power and status relations between dominant and subordinate groups play a major role in the importance assigned to particular issues, the initiatives taken by policy-makers, the resources assigned to carry out research on particular topics, the conduct and interpretation of research, and the application of research to policy. There is no such thing as 'pure research' on issues that reflect the power conflicts within society. Both language and education have traditionally served to stratify societal groups along class and ethnic lines and, in the past, research has legitimized this stratification; for example, by attributing school failure to inherent deficiencies of the minorities themselves, such as genetic inferiority, bilingualism, and cultural deprivation (see Hakuta 1986, for a review). Given the societal commitment to preserve the power relations between dominant and subordinate groups, funded research will naturally tend to serve the interests of the dominant group, as documented above. Researchers (and policy-makers) concerned with contributing to societal equity are faced with the delicate task of persuading representatives of the dominant group to fund research whose results are likely to challenge the power of the dominant group. Strategies for achieving this goal merit further discussion.

References

Baker, K. A. and de Kanter, A. A. (1981) *Effectiveness of Bilingual Education: A Review of the Literature.* Washington, DC: Office of Planning and Budget, US Department of Education.

Burns, G. E. and Olson, P. (1981) *Implementation and Politics in French Immersion.* Toronto: Ontario Institute for Studies in Education.

Cummins, J. (1984) *Bilingualism and Special Education: Issues in Assessment and Pedagogy.* Clevedon: Multilingual Matters. Co-published in the United States by College Hill Press, San Diego.

Cummins, J. and Swain, M. (1986) *Bilingualism in Education: Issues in Theory, Research and Policy.* London: Longman.

Hakuta, K. (1986) *Mirror of Language: The Debate on Bilingualism.* New York: Basic Books.

Lambert, W. E. and Tucker, G. R. (1972) *Bilingual Education of Children: The St. Lambert Experiment.* Rowley, MA: Newbury House.

Paulston, C. B. (1980) *Bilingual Education: Theory and Research.* Rowley, MA: Newbury House.

Penfield, W. (1965) Conditioning the uncommitted cortex for language learning. *Brain* 88, 787–98.

Rees, O. (1981) *Mother Tongue and English Teaching Project.* Bradford College.

Swain, M. and Lapkin, S. (1982) *Evaluating Bilingual Education.* Clevedon: Multilingual Matters.

Section Three: The 1990s

The first article concerns heritage language teaching in Canada. Since the days when Jim Cummins first landed in Canada, there has been a dramatic increase both in ethnic and linguistic diversity in Canada and in the status given to bilingualism and biculturalism in that country. Since the mid-60s, the number of immersion schools has risen rapidly as has the volume of research on Canadian bilingualism. But while French–English bilingualism in Canada often receives support and encouragement, the immigrant languages (usually termed 'heritage languages' in Canada) are a more debated issue. A contentious issue has been whether heritage languages should be supported by a public school system. Given the presence of the indigenous Native Americans in Canada, discussions about the place of languages other than French and English in Canada have an indigenous as well as a French/English and immigrant dimension. The Canadian language mosaic is thus colorful but complex.

Jim Cummins has consistently assumed a 'pro-bilingualism for all' stance, and this first article provides his arguments to support such a position. In discussing heritage language teaching in Canadian schools, Cummins argues for linguistic and cultural diversity for all peoples without exception. All citizens should develop bilingual or multilingual abilities, both for individual and societal enrichment.

Empowerment through biliteracy has become a major theme in advocacy for language minority students in the US, particularly after California's Proposition 227 in 1998. Jim Cummins published a chapter on this very theme in a book on literacy and biliteracy for Spanish-speaking students. This second article in this section begins by a discussion of cultural and critical literacies, coercive and collaborative power relationships and how these dimensions are related in either depressing or raising academic achievement among minority language students in the United States. This article also provides a critical examination of United States opponents of bilingual education, in particular Linda Chavez and Rosalie Pedalino Porter. As a contrast, Cummins discusses the empirical support for bilingual education in the findings of the high-profile Ramírez Report of 1991.

The second half of the paper examines different forms of literacy (functional, cultural and critical), debates on literacy education in the United States and how different approaches to literacy relate to a transmission-oriented or collaborative/critical enquiry style in the classroom. Different approaches to literacy create a social control or a social transformation orientation in schools. With illustrations from the work of Alma Flor Ada, Cummins demonstrates how a critical literacy approach can be successfully enacted in the classroom.

The third article in this section is co-authored by Dennis Sayers. It examines the potential of global learning networks, particularly the Internet, in promoting intercultural literacy and critical thinking. The article shows how modern technology provides the means for collaborative critical enquiry, with students from different language and cultural backgrounds working together on issues of mutual interest. Rather than the early 20th century theme of 'bilingualism shuts doors', the authors show how bilingualism in students opens a pathway to wider experience, international understanding and interdependence. The hegemony of official knowledge in textbooks is compared with 'new technology' classroom approaches that break down hitherto impenetrable barriers of knowledge, understanding, attitudes, culture and language.

The fourth article is taken from a Jim Cummins book entitled *Negotiating Identities: Education for Empowerment in a Diverse Society* published by the California Association for Bilingual Education (1996). The ninth chapter in this book contains a sample of Jim Cummins' highly committed thinking. For him, the enemy faced by language minority children is often those involved in the politics of greed and exploitation. Society too frequently, he argues, works for coercive ends, promoting policies that increase economic differences between groups and lead to the marginalization of language minorities.

The chapter therefore argues passionately for a change in preparing students for the realities of the 21st century. Developing critical thinking and creative problem-solving skills in students should lead to transforming linguistic and social differences that are so ingrained in power elites in most nations.

The fifth article in this section elaborates on the themes of the fourth article, particularly examining how oppressive politics and educational preferences are so related. The article presents an overall theoretical formulation that combines power relationships, educator role definitions, and micro-interactions between educators and students. Jim Cummins reveals that choices in this formulation will either reinforce or transform relationships of power. The central theme is how coercive or collaborative relations of power both affect schooling, and are an outcome of schooling. Teachers and students operate within power relationships in wider society. The interactions between teachers and pupils can either reinforce or reverse such power relationships.

The final article in the book returns to a theme that has continuity from Jim Cummins' first paper through each decade to the present. He argues that individual research, meta-analysis of research and overviews of research will not usually lead to policy relevant conclusions. The relevance of research for policy-making occurs when research is mediated through theory. He argues that it is theory rather than research that permits predictions about program outcomes that can be applied across time and across different contexts. By critically examining recent meta-analyses and state-of-the-art reviews of research, he shows the limitations of policy formulations from these approaches. Instead, he advocates a three-stage Research–Theory–Policy approach and avoidance of the current two-stage Research–Policy preference.

The article concludes by providing brief answers to four central and continually-asked questions. (1) Does bilingual education work? (2) Does bilingual education work better than English-only instructional programs? (3) Will students suffer academically if they are introduced to reading in their second language? (4) Will greater amounts of English instruction result in greater English achievement?

The important and wide-ranging theoretical contribution of Jim Cummins becomes apparent when answers to such crucial and central questions are given. For example, the interdependence hypothesis and the thresholds theory have been supported by research and are valuable in providing answers to each question.

To conclude: in his first paper in 1973, Jim Cummins argued that theoretical formulation was almost absent in examining key issues in bilingualism and bilingual education. In three decades, he has provided central theories to fill that gap, with each theory delivering an answer to key questions raised by politicians, policy makers, practitioners and parents.

Heritage Language Teaching in Canadian Schools

The dramatic increase in ethnic and linguistic diversity in Canada's cities during the past 25 years has given rise to intense debate among virtually all sectors of society – policymakers, educators and the general public – about appropriate ways of educating students whose mother tongue is other than English or French. A major issue has been the extent to which the public school system should play a role in supporting the continued development of children's mother tongues (usually termed 'heritage languages' in Canada).[1] While ethnocultural communities have strongly pressed the case for the teaching of heritage languages within the public school system, these demands have outraged those who see heritage languages as having no place within the Canadian mainstream. I will first outline the demographic and political context within which the debate about heritage language teaching is taking place and then review the major issues of contention in the debate.

The Demographic Context

Approximately one-third of the Canadian population is of an ethnic origin other than Anglo/Celtic or French (termed 'ethnocultural' in this paper). This proportion is likely to rise significantly in view of dramatic increases in immigration levels in recent years. Immigrants to Canada numbered 84,302 in 1985 but have increased steadily during the past six years to a current (1991) projected level of 220,000, with projections of 250,000 annually from 1992 through to 1996. These increases have been implemented as part of the federal (Conservative) government strategy to combat the combined effects of low birth rates and a rapidly ageing population.

Within the schools of major urban centres, linguistic and cultural diversity have increased substantially in recent years. For example, in Toronto and Vancouver, more than half the school population comes from a non-English-speaking background. In Quebec, the large immigrant populations in some Montreal schools are seen by some politicians and commentators as a serious threat to the survival of the cultural integrity of the province (Cummins & Danesi, 1990). The demographic trends clearly indicate that cultural and linguistic diversity in urban schools will continue to increase. In other words, students from non-English-speaking (or, in Quebec, non-French-speaking) backgrounds will increasingly become the mainstream population in urban schools, a fact that has enormous implications for the education system at all levels. For example, to this point, teacher education programmes have taken relatively little account of the implications of diversity (Henley & Young, 1989) but this situation is likely to change as the needs of the field become more apparent.

The Policy Context

Federal policy with respect to heritage language teaching takes place within the context of Canada's national policy of multiculturalism, proclaimed by then-Prime Minister Trudeau in October 1971. One outcome of this policy was the commissioning of the *Non-Official Languages Study* (O'Bryan *et al.*, 1976) which found substantial support among ethnocultural communities across the country for heritage language teaching within the public school system. A parallel study, the *Majority Attitudes Study* (Berry *et al.*, 1977) found some lukewarm support for the policy of multiculturalism among anglophone and francophone Canadians but significant opposition to the use of public moneys to support the teaching of heritage languages.

Despite the ambivalence of many anglophone and francophone Canadians, the federal government initiated the Cultural Enrichment Program in 1977. This programme provided some very modest support (approximately 10% of the operating costs of supplementary schools, usually conducted on Saturday mornings) directly to ethnocultural communities for the teaching of heritage languages. This support was eliminated in 1990 (as part of a more general fiscal belt-tightening) but the federal government emphasized that it was simply changing priorities for heritage language support rather than diminishing its commitment to heritage languages. The major federal initiative in this area in recent years has been the establishment of the National Heritage Languages Institute in Edmonton, Alberta, which is expected to start operations in late 1991.

Because education is under provincial jurisdiction, the Canadian federal government cannot provide support directly to school systems for the teaching of heritage languages. Most provincial governments, however, operate programmes designed to encourage the teaching of heritage languages. The most extensive of these provincial programmes has been Ontario's *Heritage Language Program* (HLP). Announced in the spring of 1977 (shortly before a provincial election was called), the HLP provides funding to school systems for $2^1/_2$ hours per week of heritage language instruction. School systems are mandated to implement a programme in response to a request from community groups who can supply a minimum of 25 students interested in studying a particular language. Currently, more than 60 languages are taught to almost 100,000 students in the HLP. A central aspect of the HLP is that the instruction must take place outside the regular five-hour school day. This allows for three basic options, namely, at weekends, after the regular school day, or integrated into a school day extended by half-an-hour. This latter option has been highly controversial within the Toronto Board of Education, occasioning a teacher work-to-rule for several months during the early 1980s.

In Quebec, the *Programme d'Enseignement des Langues d'Origine* (PELO) was also introduced in 1977. This programme is established on generally similar lines to the Ontario HLP but on a considerably smaller scale. In 1989–90, 14 languages were taught to 5,886 students in the programme. The Quebec government initially took responsibility for the development of programmes of study and curriculum guides at the elementary level for Greek, Italian, Portuguese and Spanish. Subsequently, the Ministry delegated the responsibility to school boards who wished to offer courses in other languages. While it is possible for school boards to offer the language within the regular school day, this happens only rarely with most courses being offered for 30 minutes daily during the lunch break or before or after school.

Within the Prairie provinces of Manitoba, Saskatchewan and Alberta, provincial governments are generally very supportive of heritage language teaching, partly because of the relatively high proportion of the populations of these provinces that are of ethnocultural backgrounds and the fact that, unlike Ontario, there has been relatively little controversy surrounding the teaching of heritage languages. In these three provinces, bilingual programmes involving 50% of the instruction through a heritage language are in operation, although the numbers of students involved are relatively small. The two most common languages taught in these bilingual programmes are Ukrainian and German, although in Edmonton programmes involving Hebrew, Yiddish, Chinese (Mandarin), Arabic and Polish are also in operation. A variety of heritage languages are also taught as subjects within the school systems and by community groups with financial support from the provincial governments.

Controversial Issues

In contrast to bilingual programmes in the USA and some European countries which have been implemented primarily to remediate perceived problems in minority students' academic development, heritage language programmes in Canada share what Joshua Fishman (1976) has labelled an 'enrichment' rationale. The major goal is to promote proficiency in the heritage language, leading ultimately to bilingualism or trilingualism. By contrast, remedial or compensatory programmes may employ the heritage language as a temporary medium of instruction but the goal is usually monolingualism in the majority language.

In terms of the three orientations to language planning distinguished by Ruiz (1988), remedial programmes clearly fall into the 'language-as-problem' category (the problem being minority students' low academic achievement) whereas the Canadian heritage language programmes share aspects of the 'language-as-right' and 'language-as-resource' orientations. Ethnocultural communities have argued that government support for heritage language teaching is a right in view of federal and provincial multicultural policies and they have also emphasized that heritage languages represent both an individual and a national resource that entails considerable economic and diplomatic benefits for the country as a whole.

A survey of school boards carried out by the Canadian Education Association (1991: 47–48) indicated that 'satisfaction with the heritage languages programs runs high in almost every school board surveyed'. Among the advantage cited by teachers, parents and students were the following:

(a) positive attitude and pride in one's self and one's background;

(b) better integration of the child into school and society;

(c) increased acceptance and tolerance of other peoples and cultures;

(d) increased cognitive and affective development;

(e) facility in learning other languages;

(f) increased job opportunities;

(g) stronger links between parent and school;

(h) ability to meet community needs.

Disadvantages cited by boards of education were far fewer than advantages. According to the Canadian Education Association report, most boards mentioned primarily administrative difficulties connected to scheduling, classroom space, class size, etc., as well as shortages of appropriate teaching materials in the target language.

In support of some of the positive outcomes noted by boards of education, a considerable number of studies suggest that continued development of two languages, and the attainment of literacy in both, entail educational benefits for minority students (see Cummins & Danesi, 1990 for a review). A recent Canadian example (Swain & Lapkin, 1991) examined the influence of heritage language proficiency on the learning of additional languages. The study involved more than 300 grade 8 students in the Metropolitan Toronto Separate [Roman Catholic] School Board French–English bilingual programme. The programme starts at the grade 5 level and entails teaching 50% of the time through each language. Students also have the opportunity to study a heritage language outside regular school hours. Swain and Lapkin compared four groups of students on various measures of French proficiency: those who had no knowledge of a heritage language (HL); those with some knowledge but no literacy skills in the HL; those with HL literacy skills but who mentioned no active use of HL literacy; and finally those who understand and use the HL in the written mode. The first group had parents with higher educational and occupational status than the other three groups who did not differ in this regard.

Highly significant differences in favour of those students with HL literacy skills were found on both written and oral measures of French. There was also a trend for students from Romance language backgrounds to perform better in oral aspects of French but the differences between Romance and non-Romance language background students were not highly significant. The authors conclude that there is transfer of knowledge and learning processes across languages and development of first language literacy entails concrete benefits for students' acquisition of subsequent languages. In short, the research data suggest that there is considerable validity to the claim that promoting heritage language proficiency may enhance the educational development of the individual child. Multilingual skills are clearly also of potential benefit to the country as a whole in view of the increasing cross-cultural contact in both domestic and international spheres.

These probable benefits, however, are not significant enough to quell the considerable opposition to the use of 'taxpayers' money' for the teaching of heritage languages. This opposition was vehement in some parts of the country throughout the late 1970s and 1980s. The case for the opposition is succinctly put in a submission to the Toronto Board of Education in 1982 (cited in Johnson, 1982):

> Many people of diverse backgrounds fear balkanization of school communities, loss of time for core curriculum subjects, undue pressure on children, disruption in school programming and staffing, inadequate preparation for eventual employment, and indeed, a dramatic shift of direction in Canadian society.

The latter point appears to be at the heart of the debate. At issue are very different perspectives on the nature of Canadian society and how it should respond to demographic changes that are radically increasing the extent of linguistic and cultural diversity. While the dominant anglophone and francophone groups generally are strongly in favour of learning the other official language, they see few benefits to promoting heritage languages for themselves, for Canadian society as a whole, or for children from ethnocultural backgrounds. The educational focus for such children should be on acquiring English and becoming Canadian rather than on erecting linguistic and cultural barriers between them and their Canadian peers. In short, whereas advocates of heritage language teaching stress the value of bilingual and multilingual skills for the individual and society as a whole, opponents see heritage languages as socially divisive, excessively costly, and educationally retrograde in view of minority children's need to succeed academically in the school language.

What is being contested in the debate is the nature of Canadian identity and the perceived self-interest of different sectors of Canadian society. For almost 20 years, multicultural policies remained almost immune from sustained criticism, and in fact, have been viewed as an important component of the Canadian identity (Troper, 1979). During the 1970s and 1980s, it became commonplace for Canadian politicians (from parties of both the political left and right) to sing the praises of the Canadian 'mosaic' as opposed to the American 'melting pot'.

However, as diversity increases and traditional symbols of national identity are being modified to conform with the statutes of the Canadian Charter of Rights and Freedoms, the multiculturalism policy itself has come under critical scrutiny.[2] Policies with respect to heritage language teaching will clearly be affected by the outcomes of this broader debate. However, at this point, heritage language programmes in most provinces are beyond the experimental stage and are likely to remain relatively stable in view of the political pitfalls for any government that might want to significantly increase or reduce support.

Notes

1. The term 'heritage language' usually refers to all languages other than the aboriginal languages of First Nations peoples and the 'official' Canadian languages (English and French). A variety of other terms have been used in Canada to refer to heritage languages: for example, 'ethnic', 'minority', 'ancestral', 'third' and 'non-official' have all been used at different times and in different provinces. The term used in Quebec is 'langues d'origine'. The term 'community languages', commonly used in Australia, Britain and New Zealand, is rarely used in the Canadian context. A number of Canadian proponents of heritage language teaching have expressed misgivings about the term because 'heritage' connotes learning about past traditions rather than acquiring language skills that have significance for children's overall educational and personal development. In the Toronto Board of Education the term 'modern languages' is used partly in an attempt to defuse the strong emotional reactions that the term 'heritage languages' evokes.
2. Examples of the kind of issue that have been debated at a national level are the appropriateness of Christian prayers within public schools and the right of Sikhs within the Royal Canadian Mounted Police to wear turbans.

References

Berry, J. W., Kalin, R. and Taylor, D. M. (1977) *Multiculturalism and Ethnic Attitudes in Canada.* Ottawa: Ministry of Supply and Services Canada.

Canadian Education Association (1991) *Heritage Language Programs in Canadian School Boards.* Toronto: Canadian Education Association.

Cummins, J. and Danesi, M. (1990) *Heritage Languages: The Development and Denial of Canada's Linguistic Resources.* Toronto: Our Schools, Our Selves/Garamond.

Fishman, J. (1976) Bilingual education: What and why? In J. E. Alatis and K. Twaddell (eds) *English as a Second Language in Bilingual Education* (pp. 263–72). Washington, DC: TESOL.

Henley, R. and Young, J. (1989) Multicultural teacher education, Part 4: Revitalizing faculties of education. *Multiculturalism* 12 (3), 40–1.

Johnson, W. (1982) Creating a nation of tongues. *Toronto Globe and Mail,* 26 June.

O'Bryan, K. G., Reitz, J. and Kuplowska, O. (1976) *The Non-Official Languages Study.* Ottawa: Supply and Services Canada.

Ruiz, R. (1988) Orientations in language planning. In S. L. McKay and S. C. Wong (eds) *Language Diversity: Problem or Resource* (pp. 3–25). New York: Newbury House.

Swain, M. and Lapkin, S. (1991) Heritage language children in an English–French bilingual program. *Canadian Modern Language Review* 47 (4), 635–41.

Troper, H. (1979) An uncertain past: reflections on the history of multiculturalism. *TESL Talk* 10 (3), 7–15.

Empowerment through Biliteracy

For more than 15 years, educators, policymakers, and researchers in the United States have known how to create educational contexts that will develop fluent bilingual and biliteracy abilities among *all* American students, including those from both bilingual and monolingual English home backgrounds (see, for example, Lindholm & Aclan, 1991). However, only a tiny fraction of American schools even aspire to promote biliteracy. Most, in fact, are deliberately structured to minimize the possibility of biliteracy even among students who come to school already bilingual. Schools continue the tradition of eradicating students' bilingualism under the guise of helping them learn English.

For most educators it is not possible even to think of biliteracy as an educational option in view of the fact that schools appear to face an increasingly uphill battle in their efforts to develop literacy in just one language. Since the publication in 1983 of *A Nation at Risk* (National Commission on Excellence in Education, 1983), politicians and media commentators have regularly linked the declining international competitiveness of American industry with the failure of the educational system to deliver an adequate 'product' to industry and business. There is a widespread perception that educational standards have been in decline for a number of years and, as a result, American business interests are placed in jeopardy in an increasingly competitive world economy. As expressed by *A Nation at Risk*: 'Our once unchallenged pre-eminence in commerce, industry, science and technological innovations is being overtaken by competitors throughout the world' (1983: 1). In view of the documented low levels of 'functional literacy' among the Latino/Latina population (e.g. Kirsch & Jungeblut, 1986) and their disproportionately high educational drop-out rates, development of adequate levels of literacy in English seems like a formidable task, let alone literacy in both English and Spanish.

The national concern about 'functional illiteracy' and low levels of educational achievement has given rise to major efforts at school reform in most US states. However, despite the fact that so-called 'minorities' are strongly over-represented among the low-achieving students, few of the prescriptions for school reform specifically address the causes of educational failure among such students (see, for example, Stedman, 1987). Even fewer contemplate bilingualism and biliteracy as part of the solution rather than as part of the problem.

I argue in this paper that biliteracy must become an essential component of educational reform efforts directed at underachieving Latino/Latina students. However, literacy or even biliteracy are insufficient as educational goals if they remain at the level of 'functional literacy'. The educational goals, and pedagogical processes to achieve those goals, must expand to include both *cultural* and *critical* literacies in addition to functional literacy. In other words, students must learn not only to 'read the word' but also to 'read the world' (Freire & Macedo, 1987). I argue that the public focus and apparent political commitment to improving the ability of students (and adults) to 'read the word' represents a facade that obscures an underlying societal structure dedicated to preventing students from 'reading the world'. This reality implies that educators who strive to create educational contexts within which culturally diverse students develop a sense of empowerment, through acquisition of cultural and critical literacy, are of necessity challenging the societal power structure. By 'power structure' I am referring to the division of status and resources in the society and also to the propaganda apparatus designed, in Chomsky's (1987) terms, to 'manufacture consent'. This propaganda apparatus is very much in evidence in the debate about bilingual education (Baker, 1992).

A further distinction relating to the societal power structure is useful to make at this point. Throughout the paper I distinguish between *coercive* and *collaborative* relations of power. Coercive relations of power refer to the exercise of power by a dominant group (or individual) to the detriment of a subordinated group (or individual). The assumption is that there is a fixed quantity of power that operates according to a balance effect; in other words, the more power one group has the less is left for other groups. Coercive relations of power have constituted the predominant mode of intergroup contact since the beginnings of human history at the level of both international and domestic relations.

Collaborative relations of power, on the other hand, operate on the assumption that power is not a fixed predetermined quantity but rather can be *generated* in interpersonal and intergroup relations, thereby becoming 'additive' rather than 'subtractive'. In other words, participants are *empowered* through collaboration so that each is more affirmed in her or his identity and has a greater sense of efficacy to change her or his life or social situation. Thus, power is created in the relationship and shared among participants. In educational contexts, cooperative learning activities and sister class networks are documented examples of the academic and personal benefits that accrue when coercive relations of power shift to collaborative relations of power (e.g. DeVillar & Faltis, 1991; Sayers, 1991).

A fundamental argument of the present chapter is that the root causes of academic failure among subordinated group students are to be found in the fact that the interactions between educators and students reflect and reinforce the broader societal pattern of coercive relations of power between dominant and subordinated groups. Reversal of this pattern requires that educators resist and challenge the operation of coercive relations of power and actively seek to establish collaborative relations of power both in the school and in the broader society.

The next section focuses on the issue of biliteracy and examines the public debate on bilingual education in light of the research data, particularly the recent large-scale study of different program options carried out by Ramírez *et al.*, (1991a). The goal is to demonstrate that biliteracy is a feasible educational outcome for all students and what requires explanation is the public discourse that vehemently denies this reality. I then shift from a focus on 'biliteracy' to the broader issue of literacy itself. I suggest that not only are schools dedicated to reducing bilinguals to monolinguals, they are also structured to constrict the possibilities for students' identity formation and to control the scope of their ability to think, or in Freire's terms, to read the world. Finally, drawing on Ada's (1988a, 1988b) work, I suggest an alternative pedagogical orientation designed to promote critical biliteracy and student empowerment.

The Public Debate on Bilingual Education

Theory underlying opposition to bilingual education

Opponents of bilingual education have consistently attempted to attribute the low literacy levels of the Latino/Latina population, and their consequent low social mobility, to the attempts by 'activist' educators to educate students in Spanish rather than in English (e.g. Chavez, 1991; Dunn, 1987; Porter, 1990). Bilingual education is thus seen as contributing not only to the impoverishment of Spanish speakers but also to the economic difficulties of the nation as a whole. Linda Chavez (1991) has presented a succinct account of this line of reasoning:

> Unlike previous groups of immigrants who were encouraged to learn English quickly, Hispanics today are officially urged to hold on to their native language and culture. Public schools, which once stressed assimilation, now preach ethnic diversity. Nationally, about two-thirds of first-grade students from Spanish-speaking homes are taught to read in Spanish, and three-quarters are taught grammar and vocabulary in Spanish as well. Some students spend as little as 20 or 30 minutes a day being given English-language instruction while the rest of their lessons are taught in Spanish. In some school districts, Hispanic students spend from three to six years in bilingual programs ...

> Despite this dramatic change in school curricula, there is little evidence that Hispanic students are benefiting academically from being taught in Spanish. Even the most optimistic appraisals of bilingual programs show that Spanish-speaking students who are taught in Spanish are no more likely to keep up in math or social studies than similar children who are put into intensive English programs in which all their lessons are taught in English. Overall, Hispanics still lag significantly behind other students in academic achievement ...

Like many social programs, bilingual education benefits primarily those who provide the services. Bilingual educators, unlike the clients they serve, are well educated, well organized, and politically effective. For more than 25 years, they have dominated public-policy debates on this issue, produced self-serving research and intimidated their opponents into silence ...

Those who think they can ignore the problem had better begin looking at the nation's changing demographics. The Hispanic population is already growing at a rate five times as great as the rest of the population. Hispanics now make up more than 10% of school children, and their proportion is likely to increase dramatically in the next few decades. Today's Hispanic students will be tomorrow's workers. We simply cannot afford to have millions of such persons ill-prepared to function in the language of this nation. (p. 11A)

Chavez here presents a distorted picture of the proportion of time that Latino/Latina students are instructed in Spanish (studies suggest that only between 10% and 25% of instruction in the early grades is typically presented in students' primary language [L1] [Tikunoff, 1983; Wong Fillmore & Valadez, 1986]). She also ignores the large-scale Ramírez report (considered below) released about a year prior to her article that points to superior academic prospects for students who received the most intensive and sustained Spanish instruction throughout elementary school. This report clearly refutes her implication that intensive English programs result in better English academic performance than bilingual programs that instruct students in both Spanish and English. Also, to claim that bilingual education advocates have dominated public-policy debates ignores the fact that the vast majority of media articles on the topic have been strongly opposed to bilingual education (Cummins, 1981a).

In short, Chavez's account can only be described as a deliberately dishonest piece of propaganda (see Baker, 1992) designed to raise the alarm not only in regard to the growth of the Latino/Latina population but, more importantly, about the possibility that they might be less subject to control through the educational process if they are taught in Spanish rather than in English.

Other opponents of bilingual education (e.g. Imhoff, 1990; Porter, 1990) have provided more detail in regard to the theoretical basis of their opposition. Three major propositions, which are in principle testable, will be highlighted:

(a) the claim that 'time on task' is the major variable underlying language learning and hence immersion in English is the most effective means to ensure the learning of English;

(b) the claim that under these conditions of immersion, language minority students will quickly (within 1–2 years) pick up sufficient English to survive academically without further special support; and

(c) the claim that English immersion should start as early as possible in the student's school career since younger children are better language learners than older children.

Rosalie Pedalino Porter (1990) clearly articulates the first and third principles in stating:

> My personal experience and professional investigations together impel me to conclude that the two overriding conditions that promote the best learning of a second language are (1) starting at an early age, say at five, and (2) having as much exposure and carefully planned instruction in the language as possible. Effective time on task – the amount of time spent learning – is, as educators know, the single greatest predictor of educational achievement; this is at least as true, if not more so, for low-socioeconomic-level, limited-English students. Children learn what they are taught, and if they are taught mainly in Spanish for several years, their Spanish-language skills will be far better than their English-language ones.
>
> (1990: 63–4)

Nathan Glazer (Glazer & Cummins, 1985) has articulated the second principle as follows:

> All our experience shows that the most extended and steady exposure to the spoken language is the best way of learning any language … How long? It depends. But one year of intensive immersion seems to be enough to permit most children to transfer to [regular] English-language classes.
>
> (1985: 48)

Many other examples of these positions could be cited based on both academic and media commentary (see Cummins, 1989). The opposition claims are in direct contrast to those made by academic advocates of bilingual education, as outlined below.

Theory proposed by bilingual education advocates

It is important to highlight that most bilingual education theorists have distanced themselves from the popular conception of the rationale for bilingual programs, namely the 'linguistic mismatch' hypothesis. This position suggests that a home–school language switch (or linguistic mismatch) inevitably leads to academic difficulties since children cannot learn through a language they do not understand. While this claim has been persuasive to many policymakers and educators (and underlies the quick-exit transitional focus of most US bilingual education), it is seriously flawed.

Academic advocates of bilingual education have consistently rejected compensatory (or transitional) bilingual programs and argued for enrichment (or two-way) bilingual programs that promote biliteracy for both minority and majority language children (e.g. Fishman, 1976; Lambert, 1975; Swain, 1979). Three central psycho-educational principles, supported by empirical research, underlie this emphasis on enrichment or late-exit bilingual education:

(a) continued development of both languages enhances children's educational and cognitive development (see Cummins, 1989; Lindholm & Zierlein, 1991);

(b) literacy-related abilities are interdependent across languages such that knowledge and skills acquired in one language are potentially available in the other (Cummins, 1991; Verhoeven, 1991);

(c) while conversational abilities may be acquired fairly rapidly in a second language, upwards of five years are usually required for second language learners to attain grade norms in academically-related aspects of the second language (Collier, 1987; Cummins, 1981b).

Together, these principles suggest that reinforcing children's conceptual base in their first language throughout elementary school (and beyond) will provide a foundation for long-term growth in English academic skills. The theory also suggests that we should not expect bilingual children to approach grade norms in English academic skills before the later grades of elementary school.

The extent to which the alternative positions on bilingual education are consistent with the findings of the Ramírez report (Ramírez *et al.*, 1991a) are considered in the next section.

Consistency of alternative positions with the findings of the Ramírez report

The Ramírez study compared the academic progress of several thousand Latino/Latina elementary school children in three program types in different parts of the United States:

(a) English 'immersion', involving almost exclusive use of English throughout elementary school;

(b) early-exit bilingual in which Spanish was used for about one-third of the time in kindergarten and first grade with a rapid phase-out thereafter; and

(c) late-exit bilingual that used primarily Spanish instruction in kindergarten, with English used for about one-third of the time in grades 1 and 2, half the time in grade 3, and about 60% of the time thereafter.

One of the three late-exit programs in the study (site G) was an exception to this pattern in that students were abruptly transitioned into primarily English instruction at the end of grade 2. In other words, this 'late-exit' program was similar in its implementation to early-exit. Students in the 'immersion' and early-exit programs were followed from kindergarten through grade 3 while those in the late-exit program were followed in two cohorts (K–3 and 3–6).

It was possible to directly compare the progress of children in the English immersion and early-exit bilingual programs but only indirect comparisons were possible between these programs and the late-exit program because these latter programs were offered in different districts and schools from the former. The comparison of immersion and early-exit programs showed that by grade 3 students were performing at comparable levels in English language and reading skills as well as in mathematics. Students in each of these program types progress academically at about the same rate as students in the general population but the gap between their performance and that of the general population remains large. In other words, they tend not to fall further behind academically between first grade and third grade but neither do they bridge the gap in any significant way.

Contrary to the expectations of many policymakers, students in the 'immersion strategy' program did not exit the program more quickly than students in the early-exit program. This suggests that immersion strategy programs are likely to be comparable in cost to bilingual programs.

While these results do not demonstrate the superiority of early-exit bilingual over English immersion, they clearly do refute the argument that there is a direct relation between the amount of time spent through English instruction and academic development in English. If the 'time-on-task' notion were valid, the early-exit bilingual students should have performed at a considerably lower level than the English immersion students, which they did not.

The 'time-on-task' notion suffers even further indignity from the late-exit bilingual program results. In contrast to students in the immersion and early-exit programs, the late-exit students in the two sites that continued primary language instruction for at least 40% of the time were catching up academically to students in the general population. This is despite the fact that these students received considerably less instruction in English than students in early-exit and immersion programs and proportionately more of their families came from the lowest income levels than was the case for students in the other two programs.

Differences were observed among the three late-exit sites with respect to mathematics, English language (i.e. skills such as punctuation, capitalization, etc.) and English reading; specifically, according to the report:

> As in mathematics and English language, it seems that those students in site E, who received the strongest opportunity to develop their primary language skills, realized a growth in their English reading skills that was greater than that of the norming population used in this study. If sustained, in time these students would be expected to catch up and approximate the average achievement level of this norming population.
>
> (Ramírez *et al.*, 1991b: 35)

By contrast, students in site G who were abruptly transitioned into almost all-English instruction in the early grades (in a similar fashion to early-exit students) seemed to lose ground in relation to the general population between grades 3 and 6 in mathematics, English language, and reading.

The report concludes that

> students who were provided with a substantial and consistent primary language development program learned mathematics, English language, and English reading skills as fast or faster than the norming population used in this study. As their growth in these academic skills is atypical of

disadvantaged youth, it provides support for the efficacy of primary language development in facilitating the acquisition of English language skills.
(1991: 36)

These findings are entirely consistent with the results of other enrichment and two-way bilingual programs (e.g. Lindholm & Aclan, 1991) and show clearly that there is no direct relationship between the instructional time spent through the medium of a majority language and academic achievement in that language. If anything, the bulk of the evidence suggests an inverse relation between exposure to English instruction and English achievement for Latino/Latina students in the United States.

The Ramírez report data directly refute the three theoretical positions upon which the opposition to bilingual education is based. First, if the 'task' is conceived as exposure to English, then there is an inverse relation between 'time on task' and English academic development; second, students immersed in English do not pick up sufficient English to transfer to a regular program any more rapidly than those in bilingual programs; and third, early intensive exposure to English appears to be less effective than a more gradual introduction to English academic skills while students' L1 conceptual base and cultural identity are being reinforced.

By contrast, the data are consistent with the theoretical positions advocated by supporters of enrichment bilingual education. First, the emerging bilingualism and biliteracy of the late exit students is clearly not impeding their English academic development in any way; on the contrary, since these students appear to have the best academic prospects in English there may be some enhancement of language processing abilities, as suggested in other research; second, operation of the interdependence or academic transfer principle is evident in the fact that less time through the medium of English appears to result in more academic prospects in English; and third, consistent with the data suggesting that upwards of five years is required for language minority students to approach grade norms in English language arts, students in the late-exit bilingual programs only begin to close the gap between themselves and the norming group in the later grades of elementary school.

In summary, it is clear that programs that attempt to develop biliteracy through sustained L1 instruction throughout elementary school have better prospects for reversing the pattern of school failure for culturally-diverse students than programs that focus only on development of English literacy (see Crawford, 1989; Cummins, 1989, for many other examples). I have suggested that the reasons for this are not only cognitive and academic in nature but relate also to the messages conveyed by the school to students about their cultural identity (Cummins, 1989; see also Ferdman, 1990).

The Ramírez report, however, suggests that other essential components required for students to develop a sense of empowerment are absent from all three program types. This is discussed in the next section.

Broader educational implications of the Ramírez report

One disturbing aspect of the findings of the Ramírez report is that the class-room environment in all three program types reflects transmission models of pedagogy, or what Paulo Freire (1983) has called a 'banking education'. As expressed in the report:

> Of major concern is that in over half of the interactions that teachers have with students, students do not produce any language as they are only listening or responding with non-verbal gestures or actions ... Of equal concern is that when students do respond, typically they provide only simple information recall statements. Rather than being provided with the opportunity to generate original statements, students are asked to provide simple discrete close-ended or patterned (i.e. expected) responses. This pattern of teacher/student interaction not only limits a student's oppor-tunity to create and manipulate language freely, but also limits the student's ability to engage in more complex learning (i.e. higher order thinking skills). In sum ... teachers in all three programs offer a passive language learning environment, limiting student opportunities to produce language and develop more complex language and thinking skills.
>
> (Ramírez *et al.*, 1991b: 8)

Efforts to reverse the pattern of Latino/Latina academic underachievement must examine not only the language of instruction but also the hidden curriculum being communicated to students through that instruction. While improving literacy levels has been a major goal of educational reform reports, few policy-makers have asked the question: 'What kinds of literacy and for what purposes?' This question has been answered by Sirotnik (1983), who points out that the typical American classroom contains

> a lot of teacher talk and a lot of student listening ... almost invariably closed and factual questions ... and predominantly total class instructional configurations around traditional activities – all in a virtually affectless environment. It is but a short inferential leap to suggest that we are implicitly teaching dependence upon authority, linear thinking, social apathy, passive involvement, and hands-off learning. (1983: 29)

In other words, transmission models of pedagogy that predominate in pro-grams for culturally diverse students aim to produce compliant consumers of information (and disinformation) rather than critical generators of knowledge; they also aim to produce passive individuals who accept current social condi-tions rather than act to transform patterns of social injustice.

The remainder of this article focuses on the development of literacy for empowerment. At this point it is sufficient to define empowerment as the collaborative creation of power whereby students and educators, through their interactions, develop a strong sense of personal and cultural identity and the critical thinking abilities to analyze their experience and take action to transform patterns of social injustice.

The Social Construction of Literacy

Criteria of literacy

While different theorists have distinguished a variety of forms of literacy, for present purposes it is sufficient to distinguish *functional, cultural* and *critical* literacies (Williams & Snipper, 1990). Functional literacy implies a level of reading and writing that enables people to function adequately in society and, as such, is relative to changing societal demands.

Cultural literacy emphasizes the need for shared experiences and points of reference within an interpretive community in order to adequately comprehend texts. In contrast to functional literacy where the emphasis is on *skills*, cultural literacy focuses on particular content or knowledge that is basic to meaningful text interpretation in particular cultural contexts. For example, many recent immigrants may lack the 'cultural literary' to fully interpret typical situation-comedy programs on American television just as many middle-class white adults may lack the 'cultural literacy' to interpret rap music.

Critical literacy, as expounded in Paulo Freire's work, focuses on the potential of written language as a tool that encourages people to analyze the division of power and resources in their society and work to transform discriminatory structures. For example, from the perspective of critical literacy, it is important to inquire who defines criteria of 'adequacy' with respect to functional and cultural literacies and what social purposes are achieved by such definitions.

Most public policy reports in both Canada and the United States focus only on 'functional literacy' and view it as a fixed inventory of skills operationally defined in terms of particular grade-level abilities in reading and writing. 'Functional literacy' is viewed as though it were an autonomous, culturally neutral phenomenon that can be assessed outside of particular contexts of application.

Ferdman (1990) defines cultural identity as the behaviors, beliefs, values, and norms that a person considers to define himself or herself socially as a member of a particular cultural group and the value placed on those features in relation to those of other groups. Therefore, particular literacy behaviors that affirm the individual's sense of cultural identity will be acquired more easily and with more personal involvement than those that serve to deny or devalue his or her cultural identity.

The social construction process involved in defining functional and cultural literacies must be critically examined. What constitutes 'adequate' functional literacy is determined by the dominant group in relation to the requirements of the system of production (i.e. the workplace). This is equally so today as it was at the time when it was illegal in the United States to teach slaves to read. From the perspective of the dominant group, critical literacy among workers or students is no more welcome today than it was in the era of slavery.

Similarly, the construct of 'cultural literacy' cannot be isolated from historical and current intergroup power relations in particular societies. What constitutes valued knowledge or 'cultural literacy' (in Hirsch's (1987) sense) in a particular society is socially constructed, and not surprisingly, the dominant group plays a greater role in the construction process than do subordinated groups. Hirsch's attempt to define 'cultural literacy' is an attempt to further privilege the knowledge and values of the dominant group and to institutionalize the exclusion of subordinated group identities from the mainstream of economic and cultural life.

This analysis suggests that in the case of subordinated groups, literacy or educational reform programs that focus only on functional literacy (or in schools, standardized test performance) to the neglect of cultural and critical literacy are unlikely to succeed. The causes of educational underachievement and 'illiteracy' among subordinated groups are rooted in the systematic devaluation of culture and denial of access to power and resources by the dominant group.

From this perspective it is possible to examine the ways in which the issues in the public debate on literacy have been framed to reinforce dominant group hegemony. I will consider the issues in this debate under three general categories: (a) the consequences for industry of alleged declining educational standards and literacy levels; (b) literacy instruction in school; and (c) literacy and subordinated group status.

The public debates on literacy

Worker literacy, education and 'competitiveness'

Many of the educational reform reports of the 1980s in the United States explicitly related the difficulties of American industry in competing against Asian countries to the inadequacies of the 'human resources' that American industry had to draw on, specifically the low levels of worker 'functional literacy'. The low literacy of workers was, in turn, attributed to the failures of American schools to transmit basic literacy and numeracy skills in an organized and sequential way.

The recommendations of *A Nation at Risk* (National Commission on Excellence in Education, 1983) and most subsequent reports have focused primarily on raising standards and graduation requirements, eliminating the 'curriculum smorgasbord' of 'soft' subjects in favor of a common core curriculum for all students and increasing the amount of time that students are expected to spend learning the 'basics'. The thrust is toward 'getting tough' with students and teachers in order to increase the rigor in curriculum materials and instruction.

It can be argued that this discourse of 'competitiveness' and 'functional illiteracy' serves to make workers and educators scapegoats for the failures of North American industry in the 1980s and 1990s (e.g. Barlett & Steele, 1992).

As Hodgkinson (1991) has suggested, the American educational reform move-ment diverts attention from the failure of government to allocate resources to the social infrastructure essential for healthy human development.

Some of the data presented by Hodgkinson (1991) are the following:

- 23% of preschool children (birth to age 5) in the United States live in poverty, the highest rate of any industrialized nation;

- About 350,000 children annually are born to mothers who were addicted to cocaine during pregnancy;

- The United States ranked 22nd in global rankings for infant mortality with a rate of 10 deaths per 1,000 live births (1988 statistics);

- The number of reports of child abuse or neglect received annually by child protection agencies tripled between 1976 and 1987 to 2.2 million;

- Young males in the United States are five times as likely to be murdered as are their counterparts in other nations;

- A black male in the United States was about five times as likely to be in prison as a black male in South Africa (1988 statistics);

- More than 80% of America's 1 million prisoners are high school dropouts and each prisoner costs taxpayers upwards of $20,000 a year.

Hodgkinson points out that while America's best students are on a par with the world's best, 'ours is undoubtedly the worst "bottom third" of any of the industrialized democracies'. He summarizes the situation as follows:

> About one-third of preschool children are destined for school failure because of poverty, neglect, sickness, handicapping conditions, and lack of adult protection and nurturance. There is no point in trying to teach hungry or sick children. (1991: 10)

It is clear that while the rhetoric of raising educational standards and combating 'functional illiteracy' flourishes, there is little interest in helping students and workers to make the transition from 'reading the word' to 'reading the world'. In other words, the focus on 'functional illiteracy' is intended to reinforce coercive relations of power in the society despite the increasingly apparent costs of this focus for the dominant group itself. As discussed in the next section, transmission models of instruction are essential to prevent the spread of cultural and critical literacies with their potentially 'disruptive' social consequences.

Literacy instruction in schools

It is clearly beyond the scope of this article to review even a fraction of the vast amount of documentation on this topic. However, the major trends that have emerged in the public debate about literacy instruction can be summarized as follows:

- A major culprit to emerge in the perceived decline of student literacy and numeracy is the alleged proliferation of 'progressive' 'child-centered' teaching methods and the unwillingness of educators to teach 'basic skills' and content in a direct no-nonsense fashion (see Stedman & Kaestle, 1985, 1987, for an analysis of this perspective)

- When applied to reading instruction, this issue manifests itself in the perception that schools have virtually abandoned systematic instruction in phonics in favor of 'whole language' methods that eschew direct instruction in the subskills of reading; since students are denied access to the building blocks of reading, it is not surprising (according to this view) that they don't learn to read very well (Adams, 1991).

- Although it has been less prominent in the public debate, a parallel argument is beginning to be heard against 'process' approaches to writing instruction; since process writing instruction is alleged to have abandoned direct systematic instruction of vocabulary, spelling, and grammar in favor of allowing students to 'discover' these aspects of literacy in the process of writing, it appears hardly surprising to critics of this approach that students have meager vocabularies and that their grammar and spelling are substandard.

- With respect to content instruction, there is a common perception (and some evidence (Ravitch & Finn, 1987)) that American students are profoundly ignorant of their own culture and history. This is usually attributed to the failure of American educators to transmit 'cultural literacy' (in Hirsch's (1987) sense) to students; in other words, students have not had the opportunity to learn the essential shared knowledge base necessary to participate effectively in American society. The inference drawn by both academic and media commentators is that educators should desist from their permissive and 'progressive' ways and start to *teach*.

The major point that I want to make in relation to these trends is that the current 'back-to-basics' focus in literacy instruction associated with the educational reform movement is not a neutral stance based on educational research but rather part of the same sociopolitical agenda designed to limit the extent to which 'reading the word' might lead students to 'read the world'. In other words, the goals of this conservative discourse are

(a) to promote sufficient 'functional literacy' to meet the needs of industry in an increasingly technological work environment;

(b) to promote 'cultural literacy' and cultural identities that are in harmony with the societal power structure so that what is in the best interests of the dominant group is accepted as also being in the best interests of subordinated groups;

(c) to limit the development of critical literacy so that students do not develop the ability to deconstruct disinformation and challenge structures of control and social injustice.

Transmission approaches to pedagogy represent an essential component of this agenda.

Shannon (1989) points to the fact that basal reading programs have dominated the teaching of reading for most of this century. More than 90% of elementary school teachers rely on teacher's guide books and basal readers during 90% of their instructional time. As Durkin (1987) points out, the terminology and marketing strategies used to sell basal reading programs have changed over the years to reflect current pedagogical fashions but the programs themselves have remained essentially the same. Shannon's analysis suggests that school systems require teachers to use the basal materials and teacher's guidebooks as a means of controlling the production of literacy 'outputs' which will be assessed by means of standardized achievement tests. Within this 'production management' model of reading instruction:

> Teachers teach students what, when, where, how, and why to use the skill listed as next in the basal scope and sequence ... Questions asked during practice should be factual, encourage choral response from the group, and be carefully sequenced to lead students successfully to the goal without diversion. (Shannon, 1989: 90)

As Shannon points out, the argument that such approaches to reading are more effective than whole language approaches that substitute children's literature and creative writing for basal readers and 'reading management systems' is ironic in view of the fact that whole language approaches are used almost universally in New Zealand, the most literate country in the world with very low rates of reading failure and minimal use of standardized tests. The predominance of teacher-controlled transmission of information has the effect of limiting the possibility of any kind of critical thinking on the part of either teachers or students.

In summary, the common thread that runs through the current public discourse about literacy in schools is the intense effort to exclude from pedagogical practices any collaborative quest for meaning on the part of teachers and students. The only meanings that are appropriate to 'discover' are those that have been prescribed and sanitized. This hierarchical control of the instructional process dictates the current pedagogical focus on passive reception rather than active exploration, the focus on out-of-context phonics rather than meaning, the focus on spelling and grammar rather than creative writing, and the focus on ingesting the 'cultural literacy' of the dominant group rather than developing a critical literacy grounded in students' personal and cultural experiences.

Literacy and subordinated group status

In view of the fact that subordinated groups experience disproportionate academic failure, one might have expected educational reform efforts to be predicated on a causal analysis of this phenomenon. However, in a somewhat ironic twist, the public discourse has shifted to absolve schools and society from responsibility for minority group underachievement; continuing the tradition of 'scientific' explanations of minority group school failure, commentators once again attribute school failure to minority students' own deficiencies (lack of academic effort), deficiencies of their families (parental apathy or inadequacy manifested in antisocial activity such as drug use, etc.) or, as discussed above, to cynical manipulation by minority group politicians (e.g. Hispanic 'activists' forcing schools to implement ineffective bilingual education programs that deny children access to English). Thus, when the public debate stays at a general level, schools are castigated for their failure to promote adequate literacy and academic 'excellence' and for their cavalier attitude to 'accountability'; however, when the underachievement of minority students is specifically discussed, the blame shifts from the schools to minority students and their communities themselves.

The long-term effects of coercive relations of power are evident in the educational performance of groups that have been subordinated in the wider society over generations. Several theorists (e.g. Cummins, 1989; Ogbu, 1978) have pointed to the fact that minority groups that fail academically tend to be characterized by a sense of ambivalence about the value of their cultural identity and powerlessness in relation to the dominant group. This is what Ogbu (1978) refers to as 'caste-like' status, and its educational effects are strikingly evident in many situations where formerly subjugated or colonized groups are still in a subordinated relationship to the dominant group.

Many students resist the process of subordination through 'disruptive' behavior, often culminating in dropping out of school (Fordham, 1990; Willis, 1977). Others modify their cultural identity by 'acting white' (Fordham, 1990) – often buying educational success at the expense of rejection by their peers and ambivalence about their identity. Still others are never given the opportunity in school to gain either academic confidence or pride in identity and, over time, internalize the negative attributions of the dominant group and live down to their teachers' expectations.

A central characteristic of colonial situations is that the dominant group uses its coercive power to define, and where necessary, confine. In other words, the dominant group defines the status and identity of the subordinated group and the subordinated group is expected to internalize this externally-imposed identity.

The phenomenon of 'internal colonies' is exemplified by the fact that the three groups in the United States context that experience the most pronounced educational difficulty (African American, Latino/Latina and Native American students) have each been subordinated for centuries by the dominant group. Similar patterns exist in Scandinavia where Finnish minority students in Sweden are reported to experience severe academic difficulties, a phenomenon not unrelated to the fact that Finland was colonized by Sweden for several hundred years (Skutnabb-Kangas, 1984).

This analysis has important implications for the promotion of literacy among subordinated groups. Approaches that focus only on technical skills of reading and writing (in either L1 or L2) are unlikely to be successful. If the root causes of educational failure and 'functional illiteracy' are associated with a collective sense of ambivalence in regard to the group's cultural identity, resulting from the internalization of dominant group attributions, then to be successful, literacy instruction must address these root causes.

In a similar vein, Stedman (1987) has pointed out that much of the effective schools literature fails to focus specifically on schools that achieved and maintained grade-level success with low-income students. His reanalysis of the literature from this perspective highlights two aspects of effective schools that are omitted from most other accounts. The first of these is a focus on *cultural pluralism*, specifically, effective schools reinforce the ethnic identity of their students. The second is a focus on *academically rich programs* in which students are actively engaged in learning through tasks that can be related to their own experience. Similarly, Lucas *et al.* (1990) emphasize a focus on *empowerment* as a central characteristic of high schools that were effective in educating Latino/ Latina students in California and Arizona.

The vigorous opposition to bilingual education in the media and by groups such as *US English* illustrates the reluctance by the dominant group to address the real causes of subordinated group underachievement. The institutionalization of bilingual education would provide access to jobs and upward mobility for members of subordinated groups. In addition, the valorization of minority languages and subordinated group identities in the interactions between educators and students would challenge the historically entrenched pattern of dominant/ subordinated group relations in the broader society. As I have argued elsewhere (Cummins, 1989), the perceived potential of bilingual education to threaten the societal power structure has given rise to a campaign of disinformation designed to prevent educators, parents and policymakers from 'reading the world'. Under the guise of helping minority students to 'read the word' (i.e. achieve academically in English), opponents of bilingual education have sought to mystify research findings so that subordinated groups will acquiesce in the perpetuation of educational structures (e.g. English-only instruction) that constrict the possibilities for students' personal and academic development.

To acknowledge that bilingualism is a valuable cultural and economic asset would effectively reverse the historical pattern of devaluation of identity. The internal logic of the 'international competitiveness' discourse might suggest that in an increasingly interdependent world, it is the monolingual/monocultural individual who is 'culturally illiterate' and ill-equipped to prosper economically in 'the new world order'. Two-way bilingual programs for both majority and minority students illustrate very well the obvious potential of transforming coercive relations of power into collaborative relations. These programs develop bilingualism and biliteracy for both groups and significantly amplify the possibilities for knowledge generation and identity formation. By contrast, the present coercive structures attempt to render both groups 'culturally illiterate' and deny minority students the possibility even of 'functional literacy' in either of their languages.

In summary, the public debates on literacy and educational underachievement are orchestrated to build public support (or in Chomsky's (1987) terms 'to manufacture consent') for educational structures that exert increased hierarchical control over the interactions between educators and students. The content of instruction is prepackaged, the options for gaining access to and interpreting information are predetermined, and the possibilities for critical thinking and transformative action are stifled. In addition, educational success and upward mobility for members of subordinated groups is extended only to those who bring their identities into conformity with dominant group prescriptions.

A framework for considering alternatives to the perpetuation of coercive relations of power in the educational system follows.

Challenging Coercive Relations of Power in the Educational System

Pedagogical and social assumptions underlying transmission and critical role definitions

The framework outlined in Figure 1 attempts to map the pedagogical and social assumptions that reflect particular forms of institutional and individual educator role definitions. Conservative approaches to education that are reflected in much of the current focus on 'educational reform' in North America tend to combine a transmission orientation to pedagogy with a social control orientation to curricular topics and student outcomes. The patterns of classroom interaction and their social implications are similar to Sirotnik's description cited above.

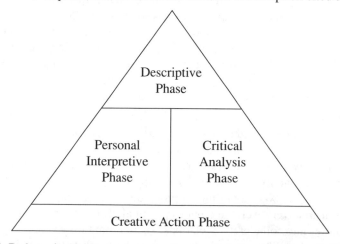

Figure 1 Pedagogical and social assumptions underlying educator role definitions

Within a transmission orientation, task analysis is typically used to break language down to its component parts (e.g. phonics, vocabulary, grammatical rules) and transmit these parts in isolation from each other. Knowledge is viewed as static or inert, to be internalized and reproduced when required. Approaches to learning associated with a transmission orientation reflect these views of language and knowledge in that learning is assumed to progress in a hierarchical manner from simple content to complex.

By contrast, within a collaborative critical inquiry orientation, educators encourage the development of student voice through critical reflection on experiential and social issues. Language and meaning are viewed as inseparable and knowledge is seen as a catalyst for further inquiry and action. This is consistent with a Vygotskian view of learning that emphasizes the centrality of the *zone of proximal development* (ZPD), where knowledge is generated through collaborative interaction and critical inquiry (Vygotsky, 1978). Expressed simply, the ZPD is the interpersonal space where minds meet and new understandings can arise through collaborative interaction and inquiry. Language use and inter-action in the classroom reflect and elaborate on students' experience and are focused on *generating* knowledge rather than on the transmission and con-sumption of socially sanitized information more typical of most North American classrooms.

The ZPD represents a useful metaphor for describing the dual process of collaborative generation of knowledge and reciprocal negotiation of identity. Educators whose role definition encompasses challenging institutional structures that reinforce social injustice and that restrict culturally diverse students' options for personal and academic development will attempt to create conditions for interaction that expand students' possibilities for identity formation and critical inquiry. Rather than constricting the ZPD so that students' voices are silenced, educators who adopt this type of role definition will attempt to initially constitute the ZPD in such a way that students' voices can be expressed, shared and ampli-fied within the interactional process. Under these conditions, the ZPD will then be co-constructed by students and educators as they script their own identities and that of the society they envisage.

With respect to social outcomes of schooling and ways of achieving these outcomes, conservative approaches aim to (re)produce compliant and uncritical students, and to this end, they ensure that all curricular content that might challenge the view of reality favored by the societal power structure is expunged. By contrast, critical educators are focused on creating conditions that open possibilities for student empowerment and transformation of oppressive social structures. Thus, they attempt to select curricular topics that relate directly to societal power relations and encourage students to analyze these topics/issues from multiple perspectives.[1]

As one example of the very different pedagogical implications of conser-vative versus critical approaches, consider the ways in which the issue of

Columbus's 'discovery' of America might be treated. Traditional curricula have celebrated Columbus as a hero whose arrival brought 'civilization' and 'salvation' to the indigenous populations. In fact, as Bigelow (1991) points out, few North American texts mention that Columbus initiated the slave trade and cut off the hands of any indigenous people who failed to bring him sufficient gold. The 'discovery' of America resulted within a few years in the genocide of the indigenous populations in the islands where Spanish rule was established. Critical educators would encourage students to explore the reality omitted from the sanitized accounts in traditional texts, critically inquire as to why the texts present the type of picture they do, and ask what are the parallels with current issues relating to power in our society. They would also explore the possibilities for taking action in relation to the issues raised through critical inquiry, as outlined by Bigelow (1991).

Integrating functional, cultural and critical literacies in the classroom

One framework that elaborates a critical literacy approach to the education of culturally diverse students is presented by Ada (1988a,b) on the basis of Paulo Freire's work. Ada's framework outlines how zones of proximal development can be created that encourage culturally diverse students to share and amplify their experience within a collaborative process of critical inquiry. She distinguishes four phases in what she terms 'the creative reading act'.[2] Each of the phases distinguished by Ada is characterized by an interactional process (either between the teacher and students or among peers) that progressively opens up possibilities for the articulation and amplification of student voices. The 'texts' that are the focus of the interaction can derive from any curricular area or from newspapers or current events. The process is equally applicable to students at any grade level. Ada (1988a) stresses that although the phases are discussed separately, 'in a creative reading act they may happen concurrently and be interwoven' (p. 103).

- *Descriptive Phase*
  In this phase the focus of interaction is on the information contained in the text. Typical questions at this level might be: Where, when, how did it happen? Who did it? Why? These are the type of questions for which answers can be found in the text itself. Ada points out that these are the usual reading comprehension questions and that 'a discussion that stays at this level suggests that reading is a passive, receptive, and in a sense, domesticating process' (1988a: 104). When the process is arrested at this level, the focus remains on internalization of inert information and/or the practice of 'reading skills' in an experiential and motivational vacuum. Instruction remains at a safe distance from any challenge to the societal power structure. This phase represents a focus on functional literacy isolated from both cultural and critical literacy.

- *Personal Interpretive Phase*

After the basic information in the text has been discussed, students are encouraged to relate it to their own experiences and feelings. Questions that might be asked by the teacher at this phase are: Have you ever seen (felt, experienced) something like this? Have you ever wanted something similar? How did what you read make you feel? Did you like it? Did it make you happy? Frighten you? What about your family?

Ada (1988a) points out that this process helps develop children's self-esteem by showing that their experiences and feelings are valued by the teacher and classmates. It also helps children understand that 'true learning occurs only when the information received is analyzed in the light of one's own experiences and emotions' (p. 104). An atmosphere of acceptance and trust in the classroom is a prerequisite for students (and teachers) to risk sharing their feelings, emotions and experiences. It is clear how this process of sharing and critically reflecting on their own and other students' experiences opens up identity options for culturally diverse students. These identity options are typically suppressed within a transmission approach to pedagogy where the interpretation of texts is non-negotiable and reflective of the dominant group's notions of cultural literacy. The personal interpretive phase deepens students' comprehension of the text or issues by grounding the knowledge in the personal and collective narratives that make up students' histories. It is also developing a genuine cultural literacy in that it is integrating students' own experiences with 'mainstream' curricular content.

- *Critical Analysis Phase*

After children have compared and contrasted what is presented in the text with their personal experiences, they are ready to engage in a more abstract process of critically analyzing the issues or problems that are raised in the text. This process involves drawing inferences and exploring what generalizations can be made. Appropriate questions might include: Is it valid? Always? When? Does it benefit everyone alike? Are there any alternatives to this situation? Would people of different cultures (or classes, or genders) have acted differently? How? Why? Ada emphasizes that school children of all ages can engage in this type of critical process, although the analysis will always reflect children's experiences and level of maturity. This phase further extends students' comprehension of the text or issues by encouraging them to examine both the internal logical coherence of the information or propositions and their consistency with other knowledge or perspectives. When students pursue guided research and critical reflection, they are clearly engaged in a process of knowledge generation; however, they are equally engaged in a process of self-definition; as they gain the power to think through issues that affect their lives, they simultaneously gain the power to resist external definitions of who they are and to deconstruct the socio-political purposes of such external definitions.

- *Creative Action Phase*

  This is a stage of translating the results of the previous phases into concrete action. The dialogue is oriented toward discovering what changes individuals can make to improve their lives or resolve the problem that has been presented. Let us suppose that students have been researching (in the local newspaper or in periodicals such as *National Geographic* and the *Greenpeace* magazines, etc.) problems relating to environmental pollution. After relating the issues to their own experience, critically analyzing causes and possible solutions, they might decide to write letters to congressional representatives, highlight the issue in their class/school newsletter in order to sensitize other students, write and circulate a petition in the neighborhood, write and perform a play that analyzes the issue, etc. Once again, this phase can be seen as extending the process of comprehension insofar as when we act to transform aspects of our social realities we gain a deeper understanding of those realities.

The processes described in Ada's framework are clearly compatible with Vygotskian approaches to learning. A context (or ZPD) is created in which students can voice their experience; meaningful and socially relevant content is integrated with active use of language in written and oral modalities; and students are challenged to use their developing language skills for higher-order thinking.

There is also a clear relationship with the *experience–text–relationship* (ETR) method (Au, 1979) insofar as each scheme focuses on relating culturally diverse students' experiences to the text. The ETR scheme makes the valid point that it is often useful to elicit students' experience prior to engaging in reading the text but it fails to highlight the importance of critical inquiry or creative action, which are central to Ada's scheme.

The representation of Ada's framework in Figure 2 highlights the fact that 'comprehension' is not an 'all-or-nothing' phenomenon; rather, it can take place at different levels and the process outlined by Ada represents phases in the progressive deepening of comprehension. This deepening of comprehension represents a progressive expansion of conceptual horizons. Thus, the more we process input or information, the more potential there is for deepening our understanding of the phenomena in question. The process of making input comprehensible is an active constructive process that can be facilitated or inhibited by those we are interacting with (or by characteristics of texts we are reading).

In short, we cannot understand messages without acting on them. Initially, the action is usually internalized (Piaget's cognitive operations) but external actions will also contribute to the process of understanding. At the tip of the pyramid in Figure 1 is the descriptive phase, in which students' comprehension of the text (or phenomenon) is quite limited in that they have processed or acted on the text only to the extent that they are capable of reproducing the basic information it contains. Minimal cognitive action is involved. If the process is arrested at this phase (as it is in most classrooms), the knowledge will remain inert rather than becoming a catalyst for further exploration.

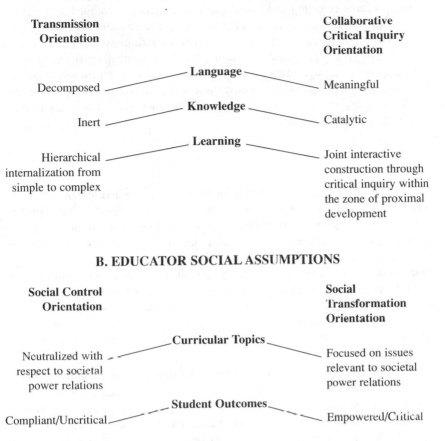

A. EDUCATOR PEDAGOGICAL ASSUMPTIONS

**Transmission
Orientation**

**Collaborative
Critical Inquiry
Orientation**

Language

Decomposed ——————— Meaningful

Knowledge

Inert ——————— Catalytic

Learning

Hierarchical
internalization from
simple to complex

Joint interactive
construction through
critical inquiry within
the zone of proximal
development

B. EDUCATOR SOCIAL ASSUMPTIONS

**Social Control
Orientation**

**Social
Transformation
Orientation**

Curricular Topics

Neutralized with
respect to societal
power relations

Focused on issues
relevant to societal
power relations

Student Outcomes

Compliant/Uncritical ——————— Empowered/Critical

Figure 2 Comprehensible input and critical literacy

The personal interpretive and critical analysis phases represent internalized
action on the text. While this internalized action can be carried out by individuals, the process will usually be enhanced when the action is collaboratively
constructed in the context of social interaction. The personal interpretive phase
deepens the individual's comprehension by grounding the knowledge in the
personal and collective narratives that make up our experience and history. The
critical analysis phase further extends the comprehension process by examining
both the internal logical coherence of the information or propositions and their
consistency with other knowledge or perspectives. Finally, the creative action
phase constitutes concrete action that aims to transform aspects of our social
realities. This external action to transform reality also serves to deepen our
comprehension of the issues.

With respect to expansion of possibilities for identity formation, culturally diverse students engaging in the critical literacy process outlined in Figure 2 have the possibility of actively voicing their own realities and their analyses of issues rather than being constricted to the identity definitions and constructions of 'truth' implicitly or explicitly transmitted in the prescribed curriculum. When classroom interaction progresses beyond the descriptive phase, students engage in a process of *self*-expression; in other words, by sharing and critically reflecting on their experience they collaboratively construct a ZPD that expands their options for identity formation.

Conclusion

I have argued that the construction of both knowledge and identity is jointly enacted by students and educators within the zone of proximal development. The ways in which educators define their roles with respect to culturally diverse students and communities will determine the extent to which they constrict the ZPD to limit students' possibilities for identity formation and knowledge generation or, alternatively, expand the ZPD to ground the curriculum in students' experiences such that a much broader range of possibilities for identity formation and knowledge generation are available to students. Educator role definitions reflect their vision of society, and implicated in that societal vision are their own identities and those of the students with whom they interact.

It is within this context that the debate on bilingual education must be understood. The history of the education of culturally diverse students in the United States and most other countries is a history of thinly disguised perpetuation of the coercive relations of power that operate in the wider society. The attempt to limit the framework of discourse so that promotion of biliteracy is not even considered as a policy response to the underachievement of Latino/Latina students illustrates the operation of coercive relations of power. Culturally diverse students are defined as deficient and confined to remedial programs that act to produce the deficits they were ostensibly intended to reverse. Empirical evidence that points to biliteracy as a feasible (and easily attainable) educational goal for culturally diverse students will either be distorted or ignored, as the quotation from Chavez (1991) cited at the beginning of this article makes clear. Maintenance of the lies of history and the facade of equity requires that bilingualism continue to be defined as part of the problem rather than as part of the solution.

Educators who aspire to challenge the operation of coercive relations of power in the school system must attempt to create conditions of collaborative empowerment. In other words, they must attempt to organize their interactions with students in such a way that power is generated and shared through those interactions. This involves becoming aware of, and actively working to change, the ways in which particular educational structures limit the opportunities that culturally diverse students might have for educational and social advancement. It also involves attempting to orchestrate the interactions with culturally diverse students in such a way that students' options for identity formation and critical inquiry are expanded rather than constricted. For Latino/Latina students, promotion of critical biliteracy is a necessary part of this empowerment process since, in the absence of critical biliteracy, they are unable to read either the word or the world in their two cultures.

Notes

1. Within the continua sketched in Figure 1, there are clearly many intermediate positions. For example, 'whole language' approaches highlight the importance of meaningful language use and two-way interaction within the classroom; however, critical analysis of issues related to social justice tends not to be a focus of instruction in many 'whole language' classrooms and has not been strongly emphasized by most 'whole language' theorists (see Shannon, 1989). Thus, while 'whole language' approaches are quite compatible with the critical and social transformation orientations sketched in Figure 1, in practice they sometimes remain at the level of uncritical celebration of individual narratives and neglect issues of power and social justice (see Delpit, 1988, for a critique of whole language approaches applied to inner-city African American children).

2. I have slightly modified the labels given by Ada for the four phases in order to try and highlight certain aspects of the process. Although presented here in a linear format, the phases should not be thought of as requiring a linear or sequential approach. In other words, the process of collaborative critical inquiry can begin at any of the four phases and be incorporated in any manner into the instructional process. For example, as suggested in the *experience text relationship* method elaborated by Au (1979) and her colleagues (e.g. Mason & Au, 1986), an experiential or personal interpretive phase in which the teacher elicits students' personal experiences relevant to the text or topic can precede the descriptive phase. Ada's scheme is not in any sense formulaic but should be reinvented by individual teachers according to their perceptions and circumstances. The essential components are that students' experience and critical inquiry constitute the curriculum as much as any 'text' since in the absence of students' experience and critical inquiry no text can become truly meaningful.

References

Ada, A. F. (1988a) Creative reading: A relevant methodology for language minority children. In L. M. Malave (ed.) *NABE '87. Theory, Research and Application: Selected Papers*. Buffalo: State University of New York.

Ada, A. F. (1988b) The Pájaro Valley experience: Working with Spanish-speaking parents to develop children's reading and writing skills in the home through the use of children's literature. In T. Skutnabb-Kangas and J. Cummins (eds) *Minority Education: From Shame to Struggle*. Clevedon: Multilingual Matters.

Adams, M. (1991) *Beginning to Read: Thinking and Learning about Print*. Champaign, IL: Center for the Study of Reading.

Au, K. H. (1979) Using the experience–text–relationship method with minority children. *Reading Teacher* 32, 677–9.

Baker, K. (1992) Comments on Suzanne Irujo's review of Rosalie Pedalino Porter's 'Forked tongue: The politics of bilingual education.' A reader reacts ... *TESOL Quarterly* 26, 397–405.

Barlett, D. L. and Steele, J. B. (1992) *America: What Went Wrong?* Kansas: Andrews & McMeel.

Bigelow, B. (1991) Discovering Columbus: Re-reading the past. *Our Schools, Our Selves* 3 (1), 22–38.

Chavez, L. (1991) Let's move beyond bilingual education. *USA Today*, December 30.

Chomsky, N. (1987) The manufacture of consent. In J. Peck (ed.) *The Chomsky Reader* (pp. 121–36). New York: Pantheon Books.

Collier, V. P. (1987) Age and rate of acquisition of second language for academic purposes. *TESOL Quarterly* 21, 617–41.

Crawford, J. (1989) *Bilingual Education: History, Politics, Theory and Practice.* Trenton, NJ: Crane Publishing.

Cummins, J. (1991) Interdependence of first- and second-language proficiency in bilingual children. In E. Bialystok (ed.) *Language Processing in Bilingual Children* (pp. 70–89). Cambridge: Cambridge University Press.

Cummins, J. (1989) *Empowering Minority Students.* Sacramento: California Association for Bilingual Education.

Cummins, J. (1981a) The public image of bilingual education. Report submitted to the Ford Foundation.

Cummins, J. (1981b) Age on arrival and immigrant second language learning in Canada: A reassessment. *Applied Linguistics* 2, 132–49.

Delpit, L. (1988) The silenced dialogue: Power and pedagogy in educating other people's children. *Harvard Educational Review* 58, 280–98.

DeVillar, R. A. and Faltis, C. J. (1991) *Computers and Cultural Diversity: Restructuring for School Success.* Albany: SUNY Press.

Dunn, L. (1987) *Bilingual Hispanic Children on the US Mainland: A Review of Research on their Cognitive, Linguistic, and Scholastic Development.* Circle Pines, MN: American Guidance Service.

Durkin, D. (1987) Influences on basal reader programs. *Elementary School Journal* 87, 331–41.

Ferdman, B. (1990) Literacy and cultural identity. *Harvard Educational Review* 60 (2), 181–204.

Fishman, J. (1976) Bilingual education: What and why? In J. E. Alatis and K. Twaddell (eds) *English as a Second Language in Bilingual Education* (pp. 263–71). Washington, DC: TESOL.

Fordham, S. (1990) Racelessness as a factor in black students' school success: Pragmatic strategy or pyrrhic victory? In N. M. Hidalgo, C. L. McDowell and E. V. Siddle (eds) *Facing Racism in Education.* Reprint series No. 21. *Harvard Educational Review* 232–62.

Freire, P. (1983) Banking education. In H. Giroux and D. Purpel (eds) *The Hidden Curriculum and Moral Education: Deception or Discovery?* Berkeley, CA: McCutcheon.

Freire, P. and Macedo, D. (1987) *Literacy: Reading the Word and the World.* South Hadley, MA: Bergin & Garvey.

Glazer, N. and Cummins, J. (1985). Viewpoints on bilingual education. *Equity and Choice* 2, 47–52.

Hirsch, E. D., Jr (1987) *Cultural Literacy: What Every American Needs to Know.* Boston: Houghton Mifflin.

Hodgkinson, H. (1991) Reform versus reality. *Phi Delta Kappan*, September, 9–16.

Imhoff, G. (1990) The position of US English on bilingual education. In C. B. Cazden and C. E. Snow (eds) *English Plus: Issues in Bilingual Education* (pp. 48–61). The Annals of the American Academy of Political and Social Science, March.

Kirsch, I. S. and Jungeblut, A. (1986) *Literacy: Profiles of America's Young Adults.* Princeton, NJ: Educational Testing Service.

Lambert, W. E. (1975) Culture and language as factors in learning and education. In A. Wolfgang (ed.) *Education of Immigrant Students* (pp. 55–83). Toronto: OISE.

Lindholm, K. J. and Aclan, Z. (1991) Bilingual proficiency as a bridge to academic achievement: Results from bilingual/immersion programs. *Journal of Education* 173 (2), 99–113.

Lucas, T, Henze, R. and Donato, R. (1990) Promoting the success of Latino language-minority students: An exploratory study of six high schools. *Harvard Educational Review* 60, 315–40.

Mason, J. M. and Au, K. H. (1986) *Reading Instruction for Today*. Glenview, IL: Scott, Foresman and Company.

National Commission on Excellence in Education (1983) *A Nation at Risk: The Imperative for Educational Reform*. Washington, DC: US Government Printing Office.

Ogbu, J. (1978) *Minority Education and Caste*. New York: Academic Press.

Porter, R. P. (1990). *Forked Tongue: The Politics of Bilingual Education*. New York: Basic Books.

Ramírez, J. D., Pasta, D. J., Yuen, S. D., Billings, D. K. and Ramey, D. R. (1991a) *Longitudinal Study of Structured English Immersion Strategy, Early-exit and Late-exit Transitional Bilingual Education Programs for Language-minority Children* (Vols 1–2). US Department of Education Report, Contract No. 300-87-0156. San Mateo, CA: Aguirre International.

Ramírez, J. D., Yuen, S. D. and Ramey, D. R. (1991b). *Executive Summary, Final Report: Longitudinal Study of Structured English Immersion Strategy, Early-exit and Late-exit Transitional Bilingual Education Programs for Language-minority Children*. Contract No. 300-87-0156. Submitted to the US Department of Education. San Mateo, CA: Aguirre International.

Ravitch, D. and Finn, C. E. (1987) *What Do our 17-year-olds Know? A Report on the First National Assessment of History and Literature*. New York: Harper & Row.

Sayers, D. (1991) Cross cultural exchanges between students from the same culture: A portrait of an emerging relationship mediated by technology. *Canadian Modern Language Review* 47, 678–96.

Shannon, P. (1989) *Broken Promises: Reading Instruction in 20th Century America*. South Hadley, MA: Bergin & Garvey.

Sirotnik, K. A. (1983) What you see is what you get – consistency, persistency, and mediocrity in classrooms. *Harvard Educational Review* 53, 16–31.

Skutnabb-Kangas, T. (1984). *Bilingualism or Not: The Education of Minorities*. Clevedon: Multilingual Matters.

Stedman, L. C. (1987) It's time we changed the effective schools formula. *Phi Delta Kappan* 69, 215–24.

Stedman, L. C. and Kaestle, C. F. (1987) Literacy and reading performance in the United States from 1800 to the present. *Reading Research Quarterly* 22, 8–46.

Stedman, L. C. and Kaestle, C. F. (1985) The test score decline is over: Now what? *Phi Delta Kappan* 67, 204–10.

Swain, M. (1979) Bilingual education: Research and its implications. In C. A. Yorio, K. Perkins and J. Schachter (eds) *On TESOL '79: The Learner in Focus*. Washington, DC: TESOL.

Tikunoff, W. J. (1983) *An Emerging Description of Successful Bilingual Instruction: An Executive Summary of Part 1 of the SBIF Descriptive Study*. San Francisco: Far West Laboratory.

Verhoeven, L. (1991) Acquisition of biliteracy. *AILA Review* 8, 61–74.

Vygotsky, L. S. (1978) *Mind in Society: The Development of Higher Psychological Processes*. In M. Cole, V. John-Steiner, S. Scibner and E. Souberman (eds). Cambridge, MA: Harvard University Press.

Williams, J. D. and Snipper, G. C. (1990) *Literacy and Bilingualism*. White Plains, NY: Longman.

Willis, P. (1977) *Learning to Labor. How Working Class Kids get Working Class Jobs*. Lexington, MA: D. C. Heath.

Wong Fillmore, L. (in collaboration with C. Valadez) (1986) Teaching bilingual learners. In M. Wittrock (ed.) *Handbook of Research on Teaching* (3rd edn). New York: Macmillan.

Multicultural Education and Technology: Promise and Pitfalls

It is common to observe that 'change is the only constant' to highlight the rapidity of technological change that characterizes the Information Age in which we are now immersed. The implications of these technological changes for education are hotly debated in many countries. In this paper we wish to address one aspect of this debate: the implications of technology for multicultural education.

We will draw from the analysis in our book *Brave New Schools: Challenging Cultural Illiteracy through Global Learning Networks* (Cummins & Sayers, 1995) in which we examine the potential of global learning networks, operating for example through the Internet, to promote intercultural literacy and critical thinking. We suggest that E. D. Hirsch's (1987) call for schools to develop students' *cultural literacy* represents a regression to monocultural myopia and is part of the renewed discourse of intellectualized xenophobia that has escalated in the United States and elsewhere during the past decade. In order to prepare students for the changing cultural, economic/scientific and existential realities of the 21st century, schools must adopt a pedagogy of *collaborative critical inquiry* that draws on the linguistic and cultural resources that students bring to school to analyze critically the social conditions and power structures that affect their lives and the world around them. We argue that technology can contribute significantly to this form of pedagogy through its power to link distant classrooms for purposes of collaborative projects focused on issues of mutual concern.

In order to contextualize the issues, we will briefly review the ongoing debates in the United States context on (a) cultural diversity and multiculturalism and (b) technology and education. Then we will outline the cultural, economic/scientific, and existential changes that will determine the nature of the society that our students will graduate into and presumably should define the directions for current educational reforms. Finally, we will examine the potential role of computer-mediated learning networks to promote the kind of multicultural awareness and critical literacy and that our society desperately needs if democracy is to survive as anything more than a meaningless ritual.

The Culture Wars

During the past decade, the alleged dangers of cultural diversity have been highlighted by academics concerned that the rapid growth of diversity endangers the coherence and unity of the United States. These authors have articulated a form of intellectualized xenophobia intended to alert the general public to the infiltration of the 'other' into the heart and soul of American institutions. Cultural diversity has become the enemy within, far more potent and insidious in its threat than any external enemy. Most influential was E. D. Hirsch's (1987) *Cultural Literacy: What Every American Needs to Know* which argued that the fabric of nationhood depended on a set of common knowledge, understandings, and values shared by the populace. Multilingualism and multiculturalism represented a threat to cultural literacy and, by extension, nationhood:

> In America, the reality is that we have not yet properly achieved *mono* literacy, much less multiliteracy ... Linguistic pluralism would make sense for us only on the questionable assumption that our civil peace and national effectiveness could survive multilingualism. But, in fact, multilingualism enormously increases cultural fragmentation, civil antagonism, illiteracy, and economic–technological ineffectualness. (1987: 92)

Hirsch's 'cultural literacy' represented a call to strengthen the national immune system so that it could successfully resist the debilitating influence of cultural diversity. Only when the national identity has been fortified and secured through 'cultural literacy' should contact with the 'other' be contemplated, and even then educators should keep diversity at a distance, always vigilant against its potent destructive power.

It is in this context that we can understand statements such as the following from Arthur Schlesinger Jr. (1991) in his book *The Disuniting of America*:

> In recent years the combination of the ethnicity cult with a flood of immigration from Spanish-speaking countries has given bilingualism new impetus ... Alas, bilingualism has not worked out as planned: rather the contrary. Testimony is mixed, but indications are that bilingual education retards rather than expedites the movement of Hispanic children into the English-speaking world and that it promotes segregation rather than it does integration. Bilingualism shuts doors. It nourishes self-ghettoization, and ghettoization nourishes racial antagonism ... Using some language other than English dooms people to second-class citizenship in American society ... Monolingual education opens doors to the larger world ... institutionalized bilingualism remains another source of the fragmentation of America, another threat to the dream of 'one people'. (1991: 108–9)

The claims that 'bilingualism shuts doors' and 'monolingual education opens doors to the wider world', are laughable if viewed in isolation, particularly in the context of current global interdependence and the frequently expressed needs of American business for multilingual 'human resources'. Schlesinger's comments become interpretable only in the context of a societal discourse that is profoundly disquieted by the fact that the sounds of the 'other' have now become audible and the hues of the American social landscape have darkened noticeably.

This discourse of diversity as 'the enemy within' has fueled the anti-immigrant sentiment of California's Proposition 187 and the movement to make English the official language of the United States. It is also broadcast into classrooms in ways that affect (and are intended to affect) the interactions between educators and culturally diverse students. With xenophobic rhetoric swirling all around the classroom, educators are required to challenge this discourse and the power structure it represents if they are to create a climate of respect, trust, and belonging in their interactions with culturally diverse students.

Perspectives that promote multicultural awareness (e.g. Darder, 1991; Delpit, 1992; Gates, 1992; Gay, 1995; Nieto, 1996; among many others) tend to occupy the much more limited public space of educational textbooks and periodicals, leaving the newspaper editorials and syndicated columns largely unopposed in preaching to the general public about the dangers of diversity. The media rarely, if ever, bring their readers' attention to the contradiction between the fear of diversity at home and the documented need of American business negotiating in the international marketplace for greater cultural awareness and linguistic competence.

The Promise and Threat of Technology

Business leaders and politicians tend to see the effective use of technology as one of the major means for improving education. Some go further in suggesting that the private sector is better positioned than the public school system to use technology effectively. They argue for the privatization of education as a means of boosting student outcomes while simultaneously generating profits for private investors. Technologically based instructional delivery will require fewer expensive humans, thereby realizing profits based on the same per-pupil expenditure as conventional schooling. In Douglas Noble's words: 'Corporate leaders view schools as the last major labor-intensive industry ripe for colonization and modernization. Public schools, finally, represent for them an expensive public monopoly overcome by bureaucratic inefficiency and abysmal productivity' (1994: 65).

By contrast, progressive educators (e.g. Apple, 1993; Olson, 1987, and many others) have tended to be highly suspicious of computers and technology in general. Canadian educators, Maud Barlow and Heather-Jane Robertson, for example, express their concerns about what they term the 'disinformation highway' as follows:

> To reach young people, as consumers, as future workers, as the social architects of tomorrow, business is looking to the powerful medium-of-choice for kids, high technology. Information is increasingly delivered not by books and teacher lectures but by computers and telecommunications (which are less easily regulated to reflect the consensus standards set by boards, parents, and governments). Technology is becoming the way to bypass the system and go directly to students with a message. While this is as true for environmentalists, labor groups, and others trying to persuade young people to their view, no other sector will have as much financial access as corporations to ride the highway into the schools.
>
> (1994: 89–90)

We share the concerns of many critics of the regime of technology. However, the dismissal of technology in general, and of the 'information superhighway' in particular by many progressive educators ignores the fact that it is here to stay and will play a determining role in the life of every student who graduates in the next millennium. The same critics who dismiss the educational potential of technology as a 'corporate plot' have no hesitation using the print medium (books, journals, etc.) to publicize their views and theories despite the fact that the publishing industry is likewise controlled by and largely serves the interests of the corporate sector. Rather than abandoning the field to narrow corporate interests, it seems imperative to us to articulate how powerful a teaching and learning medium the information highway can be when aligned with a pedagogy of collaborative critical inquiry.

The Changing Realities of the 21st Century

In *Brave New Schools* we argue that the changing cultural, economic/scientific, and existential realities that we are currently experiencing highlight the importance of promoting students' capacity for collaborative critical inquiry into social issues of immediate relevance to their lives. Briefly stated, the *cultural* changes are reflected in dramatically increased population mobility brought about by both economic crises and political conflicts in many parts of the world. To illustrate, in the United States the Asian American population is expected to quadruple by 2038 (to 32 million) while Latinos will account for more than 40% of population growth over the next 60 years and become the nation's largest minority group by 2013. African Americans will double in number by the year 2050.

These changing cultural realities have immense relevance to educational restructuring. Increased diversity at home and globalization internationally highlight the importance of promoting intercultural understanding and additional language competence in schools. Bilingual and multilingual individuals are essential to maintaining cohesion within our societies and cooperation between social groups and nations. They are also likely to be more attractive to employers faced with providing service to a culturally and linguistically diverse clientele in societal institutions (hospitals, seniors' homes, airports, schools, etc.) as well as to those engaged in international trade. As Australian historian Robert Hughes (1993) has expressed it: 'In the world that is coming, if you can't navigate difference, you've had it' (p. 100).

The *economic and scientific changes* are reflected in the explosion of information that individuals, communities, governments and business are dealing with on a daily basis. Both within the workplace and in our daily lives, we are increasingly required to get access to information and reduce it to manageable proportions through critical analysis of what is relevant and what is not. We must then be able to use the information for problem-solving in collaboration with others in the domestic and international arenas who will likely be from different cultural, racial, religious and linguistic backgrounds.

The clear implication for any school that aspires to prepare students for anything beyond low-level service employment is that students must be given the opportunity for collaborative critical inquiry within the classroom. Unfortunately, large-scale classroom data from the United States (e.g. Goodlad, 1984; Ramírez, 1992) suggest that most schools are still locked into traditional schooling patterns that emphasize transmission of information and skills rather than the generation of knowledge through critical inquiry.

By *existential realities,* we are referring to the increasing sense of fragility that characterizes our relationship to both our physical and social environment. A perusal of virtually any North American newspaper will quickly show the prominence of issues related to poverty, crime, racism, diversity of all kinds, environmental deterioration, global conflict, famine, etc.

Despite these changed existential realities, many schools appear dedicated to insulating students from awareness of social issues in domestic and global arenas rather than communicating a sense of urgency in regard to understanding and acting on them. In most schools across the continent, the curriculum has been sanitized such that students rarely have the opportunity to discuss critically, write about, or act upon issues that directly affect the society they will form. Issues such as racism, environmental pollution, genetic engineering and the causes of poverty are regarded as too sensitive for fragile and impressionable young minds. Still less do students have the opportunity to cooperate with others from different cultural and/or linguistic groups in exploring resolutions to these issues.

A major reason why schools try to maintain a facade of innocence in relation to social and environmental issues is that such issues invariably implicate power relations in the domestic and international arenas. Promoting a critical awareness of how power is wielded at home and abroad is not a task that society expects educators to undertake. In fact, renewed demands for a core curriculum and for imposition of 'cultural literacy' can be interpreted as a way of controlling the information that students can access so as to minimize the possibility of deviant thoughts.

It is hardly surprising that issues related to how power is wielded and consent is manufactured in our society are on the taboo list of what is appropriate to explore in schools. However, there are major financial and social costs associated with this attempt to limit critical literacy. Students whose communities have been marginalized will increasingly perceive the omission of these fundamental issues as dishonest and hypocritical, and this will reinforce their resistance to achievement under the current rules of the game. The continued exclusion of culturally diverse students from the learning process at school is pushing us toward a society where everyone loses because every dropout carries an expensive price tag for the entire society. By contrast, a focus on critical inquiry, in a collaborative and supportive context, will encourage students to engage in learning in ways that promote future productive engagement in their societies. The research, critical thinking and creative problem-solving skills that this form of education entails will position students well for full participation in the economic and social realities of their global community.

In summary, an analysis of the changing cultural, economic/scientific and existential realities highlights the importance of collaborative critical inquiry as the core pedagogical orientation required for schools to prepare students for both economic and democratic participation. Why is this form of pedagogy so rare in our schools in comparison to traditional transmission-oriented pedagogy?

Despite its obvious relevance to the economic and democratic health of our societies, collaborative critical inquiry is not encouraged in most educational systems for the simple reason that critical literacy reduces the effectiveness of indoctrination and disinformation. James Moffett (1989) has expressed clearly our ambivalence in regard to critical literacy and multicultural education, both of which permit alternative cultural and social perspectives to be considered:

> Literacy is dangerous and has always been so regarded. It naturally breaks down barriers of time, space, and culture. It threatens one's original identity by broadening it through vicarious experiencing and the incorporation of somebody *else's* hearth and ethos. So we feel profoundly ambiguous about literacy. Looking at it as a means of transmitting our culture to our children, we give it priority in education, but recognizing the threat of its backfiring we make it so tiresome and personally unrewarding that youngsters won't want to do it on their own, which is of course when it becomes dangerous ... The net effect of this ambivalence is to give literacy with one hand and take it back with the other, in keeping with our contradictory wish for youngsters to learn to think but only about what we already have in mind for them. (1989: 85)

How can participation in computer-mediated learning networks contribute to the promotion of critical literacy and multicultural awareness?

Promoting Critical Literacy and Multicultural Awareness through Global Learning Networks

Sister class exchanges through global learning networks are by no means a new phenomenon. The French educator Célestin Freinet originated interscholastic exchanges in 1924 using the printing press to 'publish' students' writings and exchange them and 'cultural packages' with distant classes. By the time of Freinet's death in 1966, the Modern School Movement, which he founded, involved 10,000 schools in 33 countries. These schools carried out collaborative projects using the regular postal service to exchange materials and maintain contact.

Although computer and telecommunications technology dramatically facilitate interscholastic exchanges, the basic pedagogical underpinnings of global learning networks are no different than those implemented by Freinet many years ago using much less sophisticated technology. Students involved in both historical and current learning networks engage in collaborative critical inquiry and creative problem-solving. The issues they focus on have social as well as curricular relevance. Learning takes place in the context of shared projects jointly elaborated by participants in the network rather than from textbooks. Students at the present time also have access to the enormous range of informational resources available through the Internet and World Wide Web.

There are currently a significant number of national and international networks that promote student exchange and inquiry into issues of both social and academic relevance (Cummins & Sayers, 1995). As one example, the multilingual *Orillas* project links students in the United States, Puerto Rico, Mexico, Canada and Argentina on a regular basis (Sayers, 1994; Sayers & Brown, 1987). Within this network, sister classes engage in two kinds of exchanges:

(a) monthly culture packages of maps, photos, audeo and videotapes, schoolwork and local memorabilia; and

(b) collaborative projects planned jointly by teachers in different sites that involve interdependent, cooperative activity in small groups at both sites.

These collaborative projects fall into several categories:

(1) shared student publications (e.g. newsletters);

(2) comparative/contrastive investigations (e.g. surveys of each community regarding topical social issues such as pollution);

(3) folklore compendiums and oral histories (e.g. collections of proverbs, children's rhymes and riddles, songs, etc.);

(4) cultural explorations (e.g. students in the sister classes alternately playing the roles of anthropologist and cultural informant in order to explore each other's culture).

The common element of all networking projects that focus on social and cultural inquiry is the emergence of a community of learning that thrives on incorporating alternative perspectives in its search for understanding. Such networks potentially challenge the 'cultural literacy' of socially approved interpretations of historical and current events by virtue of their incorporation of alternative perspectives on these events. These alternative perspectives derive from both the sister classes and the use of a much wider range of sources for research inquiry than just the traditional textbook. Critical literacy rather than cultural literacy is the goal. For example, the *Kids from Kanata* project links urban and rural First Nations (Native) students (and teachers) with non-Native students (and teachers) across Canada to explore and share the experience of living in Canada from very different geographic and cultural backgrounds. Students and teachers participating in this network undoubtedly have far greater opportunity to develop an understanding of the roots of First Nations protests in recent years than students who are not involved in this kind of exchange.

At the heart of *Brave New Schools* are eight portraits that we present in Chapter 2 of teachers, parents and students who are engaged in various global learning networks. These projects address a variety of issues that have immediate social relevance; for example:

- the impact of war and ethnic conflict on children and adults who have become refugees;
- understanding the different cultural realities experienced by deaf and hearing children from different countries;
- confronting inter-ethnic conflict between Latino and African American students;
- promoting intergenerational learning among children, adults and extended families;
- exploration and critical analysis of proverbs from different cultures;
- researching the Holocaust and other genocides as a way of furthering an end to intolerance;
- promotion of global awareness through collaboration in raising money to build village wells in Nicaragua;
- publication of an international students' magazine, *The Contemporary*, that focuses on controversial issues of global importance.

In the third portrait, we describe a long-distance collaboration initiated by a Spanish-speaking bilingual teacher from San Francisco and her African-American colleague. The two teachers together sought ways to confront the growing inter-ethnic prejudice in their school between newly-arrived Latino children of Mexican heritage and the African-American students. To do so, they established a 'distance team-teaching' partnership with a bilingual teacher in New York City who worked with Spanish-speaking students from the Caribbean.

Their rationale, according to Kristin Brown of *Orillas*, who helped locate a suitable partner class to work with in confronting intergroup prejudice, was straightforward:

> Since the partner classes in New York would include Spanish-speaking Latino students of African descent, we would be linking San Francisco's Latino students with faraway colleagues who in many ways were like them – students who spoke the same mother tongue and shared the experience of learning English as a second language – but whose physical attributes and pride in their African heritage more closely resembled their African-American schoolmates. In this way we hoped to provide a bridge between the African Americans and the Latinos who saw one another everyday at school but whose interactions were distorted by fears and deep-seated prejudice. (Cummins & Sayers, 1995: 36)

The two classes in San Francisco and their New York colleagues shared videos and other projects for a year, including an exchange of folkgames from Mexican, Caribbean and African-American cultures.

How do these interchanges work to reduce prejudice among these children? Research suggests these attitudes change through a process similar to the way in which cooperative learning works to reduce prejudice (Sayers, 1994). As Gordon Allport (1954) first proposed in his classic *The Nature of Prejudice,* dramatic reductions in prejudice can occur when children from different ethnic and racial backgrounds work interdependently in small groups. At a local level, cooperative learning helps break down barriers between 'ingroups' and 'outgroups' as a result of positive interdependence in achieving a common goal. In the same way, global learning networks can promote significant changes in attitude when two distant classes work cooperatively.

Was prejudice reduced as the San Francisco teachers hoped? There were definite signs it was. The parents of two African-American students in San Francisco *demanded* that their children be allowed to learn Spanish by studying with the children in the bilingual education class. Also, for the first time ever, Latina girls have joined the Girl Scout troop, originally organized by African-American and European-American mothers at the school. Who were the new recruits? Every single girl in the bilingual class that worked on the global learning project.

As a context for dialogue, intercultural learning networks provide an opportunity to find a voice, to have a say and to be heard in terms of learning goals shared with another distant group whose voices are equally valued. Above all, it is a dialogue about finding common ground for working with distant partners, about negotiating a joint site for meaning construction and the definition of identity. It is about jointly posing a significant problem of mutual interest to be investigated locally; about deciding on a basis for comparison of what is being learned; about discovering and refining comparable tools of study; and about sharing and comparing the outcomes of parallel locally-based studies and helping one another transform learning into action. It is about developing a working knowledge of what it means to 'think globally and act locally'.

Conclusion

We have argued that computer and telecommunications technology has the potential to act as a catalyst for the development of both intercultural understanding and critical literacy. The emergence of electronic communities of learning potentially threatens the hegemony of 'official knowledge', as encapsulated in textbooks, because it is much more difficult to pre-script and neutralize the content of communication across cultural and national boundaries. Only issues that relate directly to students' lives and to the world around them are likely to sustain long-term meaningful collaborative projects. In short, global learning networks represent a powerful tool to deconstruct the sanitized curriculum that most students still experience within the classroom and to prepare students to function within the cultural, economic/scientific and existential realities of the 21st century.

References

Allport, G. (1954) *The Nature of Prejudice*. Reading, MA: Addison-Wesley.

Apple, M. (1993) *Official Knowledge: Democratic Education in a Conservative Age*. New York: Routledge.

Barlow, M. and Robertson, H. (1994) *Class Warfare: The Assault on Canada's Schools*. Toronto: Key Porter Books.

Cummins, J. and Sayers, D. (1995). *Brave New Schools: Challenging Cultural Illiteracy through Global Learning Networks*. New York: St. Martin's Press.

Darder, A. (1991) *Culture and Power in the Classroom: A Critical Foundation for Bicultural Education*. New York: Bergin & Garvey.

Delpit, L. D. (1992) Education in a multicultural society: Our future's greatest challenge. *Journal of Negro Education* 61, 237–49.

Gates, H. L., Jr (1992) *Loose Canons: Notes on the Culture Wars*. New York: Oxford University Press.

Gay, G. (1995) Bridging multicultural theory and practice. *Multicultural Education* 3 (1), 4–9.

Goodlad, J. I. (1984) *A Place Called School: Prospects for the Future*. New York: McGraw Hill.

Hirsch, E. D., Jr (1987) *Cultural Literacy: What Every American Needs to Know*. Boston, MA: Houghton Mifflin.

Hughes, R. (1993) *Culture of Complaint: A Passionate Look into the Ailing Heart of America*. New York: Warner Books.

Moffett, J. (1989) Censorship and spiritual education. *English Education* 21, 70–87.

Nieto, S. (1996) *Affirming Diversity: The Sociopolitical Context of Multicultural Education* (2nd edn). New York: Longman.

Noble, D. (1994) The regime of technology in education. *Our Schools, Our Selves* 5 (3), 49–72.

Olson, P. (1987) Who computes? In D. W. Livingstone (ed.) *Critical Pedagogy and Cultural Power* (pp. 179–204). South Hadley, MΛ: Bergin & Garvey.

Ramírez, J. D. (1992) Executive summary. *Bilingual Research Journal* 16, 1–62.

Sayers, D. (1994) Bilingual team teaching partnerships over long distances: A technology-mediated context for intra-group language attitude change. In C. Faltis, R. DeVillar and J. Cummins (eds) *Cultural Diversity in Schools: From Rhetoric to Practice* (pp. 299–331). Albany, NY: State University of New York Press.

Sayers, D. and Brown, K. (1987) Bilingual education and telecommunications: A perfect fit. *The Computing Teacher* 17, 23–4.

Schlesinger, A., Jr (1991) *The Disuniting of America*. New York: W. W. Norton.

Babel Babble: Reframing the Discourse of Diversity

> Literacy is dangerous and has always been so regarded. It naturally breaks down barriers of time, space, and culture. It threatens one's original identity by broadening it through vicarious experiencing and the incorporation of somebody *else's* hearth and ethos. So we feel profoundly ambiguous about literacy. Looking at it as a means of transmitting our culture to our children, we give it priority in education, but recognizing the threat of its backfiring we make it so tiresome and personally unrewarding that youngsters won't want to do it on their own, which is of course when it becomes dangerous ... The net effect of this ambivalence is to give literacy with one hand and take it back with the other, in keeping with our contradictory wish for youngsters to learn to think but only about what we already have in mind for them. (James Moffett, 1989: 85)

Genuine critical literacy threatens established systems of privilege and resource distribution because it reduces the potency of indoctrination and disinformation. Critical literacy enables us to read between the lines, to look skeptically at apparently benign and plausible surface structures, to analyze claims in relation to empirical data, and to question whose interests are served by particular forms of communication.

Many social, cultural and religious institutions throughout the world tend to be wary of both critical literacy and cultural diversity because they bring other perspectives into mind. At issue is the question of whether being willing to look at current issues and historical events from the perspective of the Other will undermine or enrich our original perceptions. North American academics and policy-makers who argue stridently against multicultural and bilingual education view cultural diversity as the enemy within and want to minimize what they see as its destructive effects on the collective psyche of the nation. They want to ensure that students remain within predetermined cultural and intellectual boundaries. They want to retain control of what can be thought as a means of ensuring the smooth functioning of a democratic society in the service of the current power structure. Their dilemma, of course, is that the economic and diplomatic realities of our interdependent global society in the 21st century demand enormous critical literacy and problem-solving abilities and the constant crossing of cultural and linguistic boundaries.

In this chapter, I suggest that the enemy within is neither cultural diversity nor critical literacy but a politics of greed and exploitation that is willing to jeopardize not only the lives of individual children but also the coherence of entire societies for its own coercive ends. Core notions that define our societies, such as 'liberty and justice for all', have given way to policies that are promoting increased economic polarization and marginalization. The chapter analyzes how coercive relations of power operate to manufacture consent for programs and policies that are not for 'the common good' nor in the best interests of the society as a whole. The scapegoating of immigrants and cultural diversity since the late 1980s has reignited *Us versus Them* divisions and fears in order to obscure and distract attention from the increasingly obvious redistribution of wealth in North American societies. Indoctrination and disinformation are the tools whereby consent is manufactured for this process.

How can disinformation be identified? As outlined in the previous chapter*, disinformation is achieved by distorting empirical data, limiting the framework of discourse and ignoring logical contradictions (Chomsky, 1987). It can be identified by examining the empirical data. In the debate on the merits or otherwise of bilingual education, the evidence for disinformation is very clear. For example, on the surface, the claim that bilingual children need English-only instruction to maximize time-on-task appears plausible and well-intentioned. But when this claim is analyzed against the empirical data, it immediately falls apart. There is no evidence in the United States or elsewhere that less instructional time through the majority language reduces students' achievement in that language. If bilingual education were harmful, why would elite groups around the world demand it for their children? At this point, there is overwhelming evidence that the best prospects for academic enrichment of all children are provided in programs, such as two-way bilingual immersion programs, that aim to develop biliteracy rather than just literacy in one language.

Similarly, claims that 'bilingualism shuts doors' (Schlesinger) or 'causes personal problems for the individual and society' (Gingrich) are belied by the glossy full-page Berlitz advertisements for language courses that have been in virtually every airline magazine I have read during the past five years. The alleged problems of bilingualism for society are also belied by the fact that 'the Central Intelligence Agency now has difficulty meeting its needs for critical language skills, even in commonly taught languages such as Spanish' (The Stanford Working Group on Federal Programs for Limited-English-Proficient Students, 1993: 12). A more appropriate inference from the data would be that American society suffers from a lack of bilingualism rather than an excess. Despite the enormous potential linguistic resources of the United States, the situation has changed little since The President's Commission on Foreign Language and International Studies pointed out that 'Americans' scandalous incompetence in foreign languages' 'diminishes our capabilities in diplomacy, in foreign trade, and in citizen comprehension of the world in which we live and compete' (1980: 12).

A process of disinformation is also evident in the attempt to invoke Canadian French immersion programs as research support for English-only immersion in the United States. The extraordinary ignorance of these programs shown by many academics who oppose bilingual education (e.g. the claim that no more than five empirical studies of French immersion have been carried out and four of these involved low-income children) is matched only by their arrogance in posing as experts without having read even a fraction of the relevant research. If not an attempt at disinformation, how can we explain arguments for monolingual English-only education based on the success of bilingual programs, whose goal is bilingualism and biliteracy, and which are taught by bilingual teachers?

I suggested in the previous chapter* that these patently flawed arguments serve to reinforce a coercive power structure that historically has denied subordinated communities full access to societal resources. In this chapter, I try to place the xenophobic discourse against cultural diversity into the larger context of which it is a part. I argue that the scapegoating of immigrants and the demonization of bilingual education is part of an exercise to divert public attention away from the massive transfer of wealth from middle-class and poor to the rich that took place in the United States during the 1980s and continues to this day. I also suggest that coercive relations of power have reached a point of diminishing returns, even for those socially advantaged groups whose interests they are intended to serve. The fiscal and social costs of maintaining the current structure of privilege and resource distribution far outstrip the costs that would be involved in shifting to more collaborative relations of power.

Why should educators care about this larger social reality? How is it relevant to the task of teaching English and academic skills to bilingual students?

In the first place, we all have a vested interest in the future of our society, with respect to both its economic health and social cohesion. Our incomes and quality of life (and those of our children and grandchildren) are very much tied to how effectively our society functions and the extent to which our educational systems give students a stake in contributing to their society. If they don't develop the abilities and interest to participate productively in the social and economic life of their society, the chances are that they will drain resources from their society. If schools continue to fail in their attempts to educate students whose communities have been subordinated economically and socially for generations, everyone in society will pay the price. I have argued in this volume* that the source of this educational failure is a coercive power structure that is reflected, often inadvertently, in many schools and other societal institutions. Thus, educators who aspire to create contexts of empowerment with their students as the only route to educational success, must understand how disempowerment has all too frequently been created within our classrooms.

Secondly, as educators, we have considerable power to affect change in the lives of those we interact with. As Poplin and Weeres (1992) point out in the quotation that opens this volume, students respond very positively when they sense that their teachers care about them and want to connect with them as people. For teachers, their best experiences were also when they connected with students and were able to help them in concrete ways. These human relationships that form the core of successful schooling determine the social and economic horizon that students see when they look beyond the school.

Our interactions with students in the classroom embody an image of the society they will graduate into and the kind of contributions they are being enabled to make within this society. As educators we are faced with choices and constraints with respect to what and how we teach, the nature of our personal goals in teaching, and the kind of aspirations we have for the students we teach. Classroom interactions collectively shape both our students' future possibilities and those of our society. Thus, understanding the forces that influence the interactional choices we make in our classrooms and thinking critically about the constraints that are imposed on those choices is central to how we define our roles in our schools and the society beyond the school.

Because all sectors of our society have strong vested interests in what happens in schools, claims and counter-claims in the media about appropriate directions for education are broadcast loudly into classrooms. Although invariably phrased in terms of what is in the best interests of children, these claims and counter-claims also embody social agendas; they reflect alternative visions of society. The discourse on either side of these debates is intended to mold schools into conformity with particular social, cultural or religious images.

Educators are committed to helping children learn. However, their choices with respect to issues of language, culture, pedagogy and parent involvement also reflect the societal discourses that swirl around their classrooms in relation to these issues. If educators are to achieve their goal of helping children learn, it is imperative to analyze critically the societal discourses that are vying for their allegiance. To what extent are different claims supported by verifiable data? Whose interests do these claims serve? What forms of instruction are in the best interests of children and serve the common good of our society? What kinds of knowledge, skills, and values will best serve students as they graduate into the 21st century? Is this the kind of education I would want for my own child?

In the sections that follow, I present my own perspectives on these issues and elaborate the kind of education that I would want for my own children. These perspectives are part of a discourse that values cultural diversity, critical thinking and social justice. They represent an explicit vision of a society founded on principles of collaborative relations of power, as articulated in Chapter 1*. The claim is that the common good of society will be better served by educators and by educational systems that are oriented explicitly to challenging coercive relations of power.

As with any other set of discoursal claims, these arguments should be analyzed critically by readers. Are the data presented convincing? If not, where are the gaps or inaccuracies? Whose interests do these arguments serve? Ultimately, individual educators must define their roles and make their own choices about their instructional and social goals in the classroom. However, making well-informed choices should be an explicit process that takes account of the empirical data and critically examines alternative perspectives. Only through this form of critical analysis will educators challenge the structures in schools and society that serve to disempower them as much as their students.

Graduating into the 21st Century

Public schools serve the societies that fund them and they aim to graduate students with the knowledge, skills and values that will contribute most effectively to their societies. In an era of rapid and intense change, it is often difficult to predict the kinds of 'human resources' our societies will need in the future. However, some patterns are beginning to emerge and their implications for education are immense. In the sections below, I describe the changing cultural, economic/scientific and existential realities that should be reflected in classroom interactions if they are to prepare students to contribute effectively to their societies in the 21st century.[1]

Cultural realities

Schools intent on preparing students for the realities of the 21st century must take account of the fact that cultural diversity is the norm in both the domestic and international arenas.[2] Around the world we see unprecedented population mobility and intercultural contact resulting from factors such as economic migration, displacement caused by military conflicts and famine, as well as technological advances in transportation and communication. Increased intercultural contact within industrialized countries as a result of decades of migration is matched by growing intercultural contact between countries, reflecting increased global economic and political interdependence.

This escalation of intercultural contact, both domestically and internationally, has major implications for our schools. In the first place, it suggests that the transmission of cultural myopia in schools is a recipe for social disaster. The prophets of doom who warn about the infiltration of the Other in the guise of multicultural curricula and bilingual education have closed their eyes to the urgent need for school programs that promote sensitivity to, and understanding of, diverse cultural perspectives. If we are to learn anything from the racial and ethnic tensions in North American cities and the brutal armed conflicts abroad that have characterized the 1990s, surely it is that our schools have a crucial role to play in helping us live and grow together in our global village. Educators concerned with preparing students for life in the 21st century must educate them for global citizenship. The potential to achieve this goal is obviously greater in a classroom context where cultural diversity is seen as a resource rather than in one where it is either suppressed or ignored.

In the second place, if we take seriously the concerns about the competitiveness of American business in an increasingly interdependent global economy, highlighted by Reagan/Bush era educational reformers, then it is the monolingual/monocultural graduate who is 'culturally illiterate' and ill-equipped to prosper in the global economy. Students who grow up and are educated in a monocultural cocoon risk becoming social misfits, totally unprepared for the worlds of work or play in the 21st century. Hirsch got it wrong: students require not just cultural literacy, but intercultural literacy (Cummins & Sayers, 1995). A recent survey of eight major US-based multinational corporations reported that they are placing added value on college graduates with bilingual skills. These corporations are especially interested in less commonly taught languages such as Chinese, Japanese and Russian.[3] In short, bilingual and multilingual individuals are likely to be more attractive to employers involved in international trade as well as those faced with providing service to a linguistically diverse clientele in societal institutions (hospitals, seniors' homes, airports, schools, etc.).

It doesn't take a genius to see that nurturing the linguistic and cultural resources of the nation is simply good common sense in light of the cultural realities of the 21st century. Even minimal investment in bilingual programs for both majority and minority students and a focus on infusing multicultural awareness across the curriculum can contribute significantly both to the nation's economic competitiveness and to its ability to collaborate internationally in resolving global problems. Australian historian and *Time* magazine's Art critic, Robert Hughes, expressed it well in his best selling book *Culture of Complaint*.

> To learn other languages, to deal with other customs and creeds from direct experience of them and with a degree of humility: these are self-evidently good, as cultural provincialism is not ... In Australia, no Utopia but a less truculent immigrant society than this one, intelligent multiculturalism works to everyone's social advantage, and the conservative crisis-talk about creating a 'cultural tower of Babel' and so forth is seen as obsolete alarmism of a fairly low order ... In the world that is coming, if you can't navigate difference, you've had it. (1993: 88–100)

Economic/scientific realities

As discussed above, national economies are increasingly implicated in the global economy. A product may be conceived in one country, designed in another, manufactured in yet another, and then marketed and sold throughout the world. The capacity to communicate across cultural and linguistic boundaries is crucial to business success in this environment, as is access to and ability to manipulate information. Thus, the competitiveness of a business or a country in the global marketplace depends on its human resources: the knowledge, learning, information and intelligence possessed by its people; what Secretary of Labor in the

Clinton administration, Robert Reich (1991), has called *symbolic analysis skills*. These include abstract higher-order thinking, critical inquiry, and collaboration – defined as the capacity to engage in active communication and dialogue to get a variety of perspectives and to create consensus when necessary.

Even for relatively unskilled jobs in the fast-growing service sector, where high levels of literacy are not required for adequate job performance, employers have raised educational standards for applicants. This trend appears to be related to the perception that the 'trainability' of workers is essential for businesses to adapt in a flexible manner to a rapidly changing economic environment.

In short, many workers today employ literacy skills in the workplace that are far beyond what their parents needed. In a context where information is doubling every five years or so, employers are looking for workers who know how to get access to current information, who can think critically about what information is relevant and what is not, and who know how to collaborate creatively in problem-solving activities across cultural, linguistic and racial boundaries. What few work-places need are workers whose heads are full of inert and soon-to-be-obsolete information.

Two implications for education are clear. First, passive internalization of inert content, which, as noted earlier, research suggests is still a common mode of learning in many North American classrooms (e.g. Goodlad, 1984; Ramírez, 1992), does not promote the kind of active intelligence that the changing economy increasingly requires in the work force. To address the economic needs of the societies that fund them, schools must promote students' capacities for colla-borative critical inquiry.

Second, the failure of schools to educate all students carries enormous eco-nomic (and social) costs. If students do not graduate from school with the symbolic analysis skills to contribute productively to the economy, then they are likely to be excluded from the economy. Individuals who are excluded from the economy don't just fade away and disappear. They frequently end up on welfare or in jail. There is a huge correlation between dropping out of school and ending up in prison – more than 80% of prisoners in US prisons are high school drop-outs, each costing taxpayers a minimum of $20,000 a year to contain, much more than it would have cost to educate them (Hodgkinson, 1991). The US incar-cerates its population at a rate far higher than any other industrialized country (e.g. ten times that of the Netherlands and six times that of Australia) and this pattern has escalated dramatically in recent years at enormous cost to taxpayers. Natriello *et al.* (1990) in their aptly titled book *Schooling Disadvantaged Chil-dren: Racing Against Catastrophe* estimated conservatively that the cost to the nation of the dropout problem is approximately $50 billion in foregone lifetime earnings alone: 'Also associated with this cost are forgone government tax revenues, greater welfare expenditure, poorer physical and mental health of our nation's citizens, and greater costs of crime ...' (p. 43). As one example of the returns on educational investment, it has been estimated that every dollar spent on Head Start programs will save $7 in reduced need for special education, welfare, incarceration and so on (Schweinhart *et al.*, 1986).

In short, compared to the alternatives, education is one of society's most cost-effective investments. To push low-income culturally diverse students out of school at current levels in urban centers across the nation is financially absurd (not to mention socially unjust in the extreme). Thus, to address the economic realities of the 21st century, schools must look rationally at which programs for culturally diverse students are most likely to succeed in developing high levels of literacy. To exclude from consideration genuine bilingual and multicultural programs, whose success has been demonstrated repeatedly, purely on the ideological grounds that they are 'un-American' is irrational and simply panders to the neurotic paranoia of the patriotically-correct (to borrow Robert Hughes' phrase).

Existential realities

By 'existential realities', I am referring to the increasing sense of fragility that characterizes our relationship to both our physical and social environment. For example, a perusal of virtually any newspaper anywhere in the world will quickly show the extent of environmental deterioration and the enormity of the global ecological problems that our generation has created for our children's generation to resolve. Similarly, the 'new world order' of peaceful co-existence that seemed at hand with the end of the Cold War has been overtaken by eruptions of brutal conflicts around the world. Violence in our schools and streets signal the enormous pressures just beneath the surface of our social fabric. Increased incarceration responds to symptoms rather than to underlying causes and consequently has done little to curb crime. In fact, it has probably contributed to crime since it drains dollars from schools and other social programs.

Despite these changed existential realities, many schools appear dedicated to insulating students from awareness of social issues rather than communicating a sense of urgency in regard to understanding and acting on them. In most schools across the continent, the curriculum has been sanitized such that students rarely have the opportunity to discuss critically, write about, or act upon issues that directly affect the society they will form. Issues such as racism, environmental pollution, genetic engineering, and the causes of poverty are regarded as too sensitive for fragile and impressionable young minds. Still less do students have the opportunity to cooperate with others from different cultural and/or linguistic groups in exploring resolutions to these issues.

A major reason why schools try to maintain a facade of innocence in relation to social and environmental issues is that such issues invariably implicate power relations in the domestic and international arenas. Promoting a critical awareness of how power is wielded at home and abroad is not a task that society expects educators to undertake. In fact, renewed demands for a core curriculum and for imposition of 'cultural literacy' can be interpreted as a way of controlling the information that students can access so as to minimize the possibility of deviant thoughts. As Donaldo Macedo (1993, 1994) argues, in the shadows of the list of facts that every American should know is the list of facts that every American must be *discouraged* from knowing. Prominent among these is the history of imperialism and colonialism of Western powers from 1492 to the present (see, for example, *Rethinking Schools*, 1991).

In short, this analysis suggests that issues related to the organization of society, specifically the division of resources and power, be taken off the taboo list of what is appropriate to explore in school. Students whose communities have been marginalized will increasingly perceive the omission of these fundamental issues as dishonest and hypocritical, and this will reinforce their resistance to achievement under the current rules of the game. By contrast, a focus on critical inquiry, in a collaborative and supportive context, will encourage students to engage in learning in ways that will promote future productive engagement in their societies. The research, critical thinking and creative problem-solving skills that this form of education entails will position students well for full participation in the economic and social realities of their global community. By contrast, excluding students from the learning process at school is pushing us toward a society where everyone loses because every dropout carries an expensive price tag for the entire society.

This analysis of the cultural, economic/scientific and existential realities that students will graduate into in the 21st century suggests that priorities for our schools should be:

- Promoting bilingual or multilingual skills and intercultural sensitivity among all students;

- Promoting not just basic functional literacy but critical literacy that would include capacities for abstract higher-order thinking and collaborative problem-solving; in other words, collaborative critical inquiry should be the predominant learning focus in our schools;

- Creatively exploring ways to help all students graduate with high academic achievement; since subordinated group students are massively over-represented among dropouts and low-achievers, this essentially means restructuring schools to challenge and reverse the causes of subordinated group underachievement;

- Promoting an awareness of, and concern for, the common good in our societies; this will entail collaborative critical inquiry into domestic and international social justice issues related to the distribution of resources, status and power in our societies.

These educational directions represent direct inferences from an analysis of clearly observable social trends. Why is that so few schools across the North American continent are actively pursuing these directions? Why is it that even suggesting directions such as these is likely to be castigated as 'radical'? Why do so many working- and middle-class Americans feel such frustration and anger about issues such as immigration and diversity (as illustrated in the overwhelming support for Proposition 187 in California)?

To answer these questions we need to examine some data about how the power structure operates to deflect challenges and minimize dissent.

Coercive Relations of Power in Action

The polarization of income

Consider some of the data outlined in *Philadelphia Inquirer* reporters Donald Barlett and James Steele's (1992) book *America: What Went Wrong?* Chapter 1 of their book is entitled 'Dismantling the Middle Class' and the statistics show clearly how this has been achieved:

- In 1989, the top 4% in income earned as much as the bottom 51%. Thirty years earlier, in 1959, the top 4% earned as much as the bottom 35% – a 16 point difference. According to Barlett and Steele 'The wage and salary structure of American business, encouraged by federal tax policies, is pushing the nation toward a two-class society' (p. ix).

- During the 1980s, salaries of people earning $20,000 to $50,000 increased by 44% while salaries for those earning $200,000 to $1 million increased by 697%; if you were fortunate enough to earn more than $1 million, the icing on the cake was that you received a whopping salary increase of 2,184%! In Barlett and Steele's terms: 'Viewed more broadly, the total wages of all people who earned less than $50,000 a year – 85% of all Americans – increased an average of just 2% a year over those ten years. At the same time, the total wages of all millionaires shot up 243% a year' (p. 4).

- As a result of the Tax Reform Act of 1986 those earning up to $50,000 saw tax cuts of between 6% and 16% while those earning more than $500,000 saw tax cuts of between 31% and 34%. This represented an average 1989 tax savings per return of $300 for those earning $20,000 to $30,000 compared to an average savings of $281,033 for those earning $1 million or more.

- During the 1950s the corporate share of US income tax collected was 39% compared to 61% for individuals; in the 1980s the corporate share had dropped to 17% while individuals' share rose to 83%.

- The percentage of workers receiving fully paid health insurance fell from 75% to 48% between 1982 and 1989.

Barlett and Steele argue that as a result of the way the rules of the game have been rigged 'the already rich are richer than ever; there has been an explosion in overnight new rich; life for the working class is deteriorating, and those at the bottom are trapped' (p. 2). They summarize the data as follows:

Indeed the growth of the middle class – one of the underpinnings of demo-cracy in this country – has been reversed. By government action. Taken as a whole, these are the results of the rules that govern the game:

- They have created a tax system that is firmly weighted against the middle class.

- They have enabled companies to trim or cancel health-care and pension benefits for employees.

- They have granted subsidies to businesses that create low-wage jobs that are eroding living standards.

- They have undermined longtime stable businesses and communities.

- They have rewarded companies that transfer jobs abroad and eliminate jobs in this country.

- They have placed home ownership out of reach of a growing number of Americans and made the financing of a college education impossible without incurring a hefty debt.

Look upon it as the dismantling of the middle class. And understand that, barring some unexpected intervention by the federal government, the worst is yet to come. For we are in the midst of the largest transfer of wealth in the nation's history. (pp. 2–3)

Noam Chomsky (1995) is even more blunt in his assessment of the causes of crime and violence in American society. He points to the fact that 'we're the only industrial nation that doesn't have some sort of guaranteed health insurance … Despite being the richest society we have twice the poverty rate of any other industrialized nation, and much higher rates of incarceration' (pp. 128–129). In pointing to the powerful state protection for the rich (illustrated in Barlett and Steele's data), he suggests that:

The United States has, from its origins, been a highly protectionist society with very high tariffs and massive subsidies for the rich. It's a huge welfare state for the rich, and society ends up being very polarized. Despite the New Deal, and the Great Society measures in the 1960s, which attempted to move the United States toward the social contracts of the other indus-trialized nations, we still have the highest social and economic inequality, and such polarization is increasing very sharply. These factors – high polarization, a welfare state for the rich, and marginalization of parts of the population – have their effects. One effect is a lot of crime. (1995: 129)

One of the major sources of subsidies for the rich is the Pentagon, which is why, according to Chomsky, it hasn't declined substantially with the end of the Cold War. In fact the US is still spending almost as much on the military as the rest of the world combined.[4] In addition to the Pentagon, Chomsky highlights straight welfare payments to the rich in the form of home mortgage tax rebates, about 80% of which go to people with incomes over $50,000 (who represent just

15% of the population, according to Barlett and Steele). He justifies labelling these welfare payments on the grounds that 'it's exactly the same if I don't give the government $100 or if the government does give me $100' (p. 131). Another example of social welfare for the rich is business expenses as tax write-offs which far outweigh welfare payments to the poor.

In summary, the economic hardship that many middle-class people are feeling has come from the transfer of resources from middle-class and poor families to the wealthy. This combined with the Savings and Loan bailout of hundreds of billions of dollars and the obscene level of military expenditures during the 1980s and 1990s has resulted in hard times for ordinary people. They feel angry about it and want to blame someone.

Finding scapegoats

The escalation of rhetoric against immigration, bilingual education and cultural diversity in general is a convenient way of accomplishing two goals: First, it directs people's anger against a potential threat to the established power structure. The projected rapid growth of minority populations, particularly Spanish-speakers, is a source of concern; if these groups retain some cultural and linguistic distinctiveness, it is feared that they may be less subject to persuasion (control) than other Americans. If they were ever to exercise their right to vote in substantial numbers then, in columnist James Reston's view, they might 'not only influence but hold the decisive margin in state and local elections' (*The Journal*, Milwaukee, WI, February 5, 1981). In order to prevent this catastrophic scenario, it is imperative to reverse the infiltration of alien languages and cultures into American institutions as rapidly as possible.[5]

Second, directing people's anger against immigrants, bilingual educators, welfare mothers, single parent families, and the like, serves to divert attention from the massive transfer of wealth from middle-class and poor to the rich. It very effectively obscures the real operation of the power structure. Once again, Chomsky lucidly identifies how this scapegoating process works:

> The building up of scapegoats and fear is standard. If you're stomping on people's faces, you don't want them to notice that; you want them to be afraid of somebody else – Jews, homosexuals, welfare queens, immigrants, whoever it is. That's how Hitler got to power, and in fact he became the most popular leader in German history. People are scared, they're upset, the world isn't working, and they don't like the way things are. You don't want people to look at the actual source of power, that's much too dangerous, so therefore, you need to have them blame or be frightened of someone else. (1995: 134)

Resolving contradictions

The roots of the contradictions identified earlier become more intelligible in light of this analysis of coercive relations of power. To reiterate the contradictions:

- Our societies urgently need more people with fluent bilingual skills, yet we demonize bilingual education, the only program capable of delivering bilingualism and biliteracy.

- Our economy increasingly requires people with symbolic analysis skills who are capable of collaborative critical inquiry, but we still insist that schools 'get back to basics' (as though they ever left).

- In order to increase economic performance and decrease the escalating costs of incarceration, we need to enable more low-income young people to graduate from high school with the possibility of more than a below-the-poverty-line job; only in this way will they have a stake in contributing to our society; yet we resist the kind of educational reforms that would promote contexts of empowerment for low-income students, preferring instead to warehouse them indefinitely in prisons built at enormous cost to the taxpayer.

- Finally, our society desperately needs to restore some sense of coherence and community to its people, founded on notions such as social justice and the common good; yet, any attempt to desanitize the curriculum and look at historical and current issues of social justice from multiple perspectives is still vehemently resisted.

The reason our school systems are discouraged or prevented from pursuing these directions that respond rationally to the changing social realities of the 21st century is that, in one way or another, these directions potentially threaten the coercive power structure that manufactures consent for grossly inequitable resource distribution in our societies. If bilingualism or intercultural literacy were encouraged, it would legitimate the presence of the Other within societal institutions; if critical literacy were encouraged, it might undermine the process of manufacturing consent through indoctrination and disinformation; if we seriously contemplated reversing underachievement among low-income inner city youth, it would require 'an investment in education comparable to what has been spent on building a high-tech military machine' (Wirth, 1993: 365) – in other words, a significant transfer of wealth from the rich to the poor. Finally, it is virtually unthinkable in most societies around the world to invite educators to desanitize the curriculum and examine the ways in which power has been, and is, wielded for coercive ends.[6]

To what extent can educators, operating within these constraints, realistically create contexts of empowerment that would challenge the impact of coercive relations of power on themselves and their students? Chomsky is pessimistic:

It's just not going to be allowed, because it's too subversive. You can teach students to think for themselves in the sciences because you want people to be independent and creative, otherwise you don't have science. But science and engineering students are not encouraged to be critical in terms of the political and social implications of their work. In most other fields you want students to be obedient and submissive, and that starts from childhood. Now teachers can try, and do break out of that, but, they will surely find if they go too far, that as soon as it gets noticed there'll be pressures to stop them. (1995: 141)

I am somewhat more optimistic than Chomsky about what educators, individually and collectively, can achieve. This is elaborated in the final section.

Towards Collaborative Relations of Power in the Classroom

In the dismal scenario sketched above, there are two beacons of hope. One is the fact that power structures are not monolithic. There are many individuals and institutions within North American societies that are committed to challenging inequality and exploitation. In fact, at one level, the United States has committed itself to educational equity more vigorously than most other Western nations. Since the mid-1960s considerable resources have been expended on research to try to understand the causes of school failure and on intervention aimed at reversing a legacy of educational exclusion. This public commitment has been matched by the enormous dedication of many educators who go far beyond their job descriptions to promote contexts of empowerment in their classrooms. However, as documented above, at another level, a very different process is operating that attempts to neutralize potential challenges to the coercive power structure.

A reason for some optimism at this point is that the operation of coercive relations of power has reached a point of diminishing returns. The contradictions are becoming more obvious. Fiscal deficits are unlikely to be reduced when more police are required to combat crime and more prisons are being built to contain undereducated young people; business is unlikely to thrive when fewer people have the disposable income to buy its products; and so on. I am optimistic enough to believe that, in the coming years, coercive power structures will become visible to a greater number of people, thereby providing more scope for educational and other institutions to pursue an agenda of social justice and collaborative empowerment.

A second source of optimism lies in the power that schools, communities and individual educators have to create contexts of empowerment even under unfavorable conditions.[7] Scattered throughout this volume are examples of this process. School systems are increasingly showing an interest in two-way bilingual immersion programs that explicitly, and very successfully, challenge the *Us versus Them* ideology promoted by groups such as US English. Periodicals such as *Rethinking Schools* create a community of inquiry among educators that counteracts processes of indoctrination and disinformation. In many cases, culturally diverse communities themselves are mobilizing to demand respectful and high quality education for their children.[8]

As emphasized throughout this volume, individual educators are never powerless, although they frequently work in conditions that are oppressive both for them and their students (see, for example, Kozol, 1991). While they rarely have complete freedom, educators do have choices in the way they structure the micro-interactions in the classroom. They do determine for themselves the social and educational goals they want to achieve with their students. They are responsible for the role definitions they adopt in relation to culturally diverse students and communities. Even in the context of English-only instruction, educators have options in their orientation to students' language and culture, in the forms of parent and community participation they encourage, and in the way they implement pedagogy and assessment.

In short, through their practice and their interactions with students, educators define their own identities. Students, likewise, go through a process of defining their identities in interaction with their teachers, peers, and parents. This process of negotiating identities can never be controlled from the outside, although it will certainly be influenced by many forces. Thus, educators individually and collectively, have the potential to work towards the creation of contexts of empowerment. Within these interactional spaces where identities are negotiated, students and educators together can generate power that challenges structures of injustice in small but significant ways. Each student who graduates into the 21st century with well-developed critical literacy skills, intercultural sensitivity, and an informed commitment to the ideals of 'liberty and justice for all', enshrined in the American constitution, represents a challenge to coercive relations of power.

When classroom interactions are fueled by collaborative relations of power, students gain access to ways of navigating difference that our domestic and international communities are sadly lacking at the present time. Bilingual students who feel a sense of belonging in their classroom learning community are more likely to feel 'at home' in their society upon graduation and to contribute actively to building that society. Schools that have brought issues related to cultural and linguistic diversity from the periphery to the center of their mission are more likely to prepare students to thrive in the interdependent global society in which they will live. The goal for all of us as educators is to strive to make our classrooms and schools microcosms of the kind of caring society that we would like our own children and grandchildren to inherit. I strongly believe that this is an attainable goal.

Notes

* Reference to another part of the volume where this chapter was originally published *(Negotiating Identities: Education for Empowerment in a Diverse Society)*.
1. The analysis presented here is elaborated in more detail in Cummins and Sayers (1995). The analysis in the chapter as a whole elaborates on a keynote presentation I gave at the 1995 California Association for Bilingual Education conference in Anaheim entitled *Resisting Xenophobia: Proposition 187 and its Aftermath*.
2. Increased linguistic and cultural diversity is a phenomenon affecting many countries in addition to the United States. In Canada, for example, more than 50% of the student population in Toronto and Vancouver have a first language other than English. In the

Netherlands, 40% of students in Amsterdam schools are of non-Dutch origin and in the country as a whole close to 20% of the population will be of non-Dutch origin by the year 2000.

In the United States, immigrants' share of total population growth has increased significantly from 11% between 1960 and 1970 to 39% between 1980 and 1990. Latinos/ Latinas will account for more than 40% of population growth over the next 60 years and become the nation's largest minority in the year 2013. The Asian American population is expected to increase from 8 million in 1992 to 16 million by 2009, 24 million by 2024 and 32 million by 2038. African Americans are expected to double in number by the year 2050. At current growth rates, the US foreign-born population will probably exceed 10% by the year 2000 (*Hispanic Link Weekly Report*, 1995, Vol. 13, No. 31).

Consistent with these projected growth trends, the proportion of culturally diverse students is rapidly increasing in US urban centers. To illustrate, the National Coalition of Advocates for Students (1988) estimated that by the year 2001, minority enrollment levels will range from 70% to 96% in the nation's 15 largest school systems. In California, so-called minority groups (e.g. Latinos/Latinas, African Americans, Asian Americans) already represent a greater proportion of the school population than students from the so-called majority group. By the year 2030, half of all the children in the state are projected to be of Latino/Latina background while Euro-Americans will compose 60% of the elderly population, a reality that historian Paul Kennedy terms 'a troublesome mismatch' that raises the prospect of 'a massive contest over welfare and entitlement priorities between predominantly Caucasian retirees and predominantly nonwhite children, mothers and unemployed, each with its vocal advocacy organizations' (p. 313).

3. National Clearinghouse for Bilingual Education Internet Newsline, 23 May, 1995. The report entitled *What Employers Expect of College Graduates: International Knowledge and Second Language Skills* can be obtained (free) from the US Department of Education, OERI, 555 New Jersey Ave, NW, Washington, DC 20208. Tel. 800/424-1616.

4. Macedo (1994) reminds readers of the fraud rampant in the military–industrial complex during the 1980s as illustrated in the Pentagon paying $700 for a toilet seat and $350 for a screwdriver. He also illustrates the process of social welfare for the rich with current examples such as a $220 million subsidy paid to bail out McDonnell Douglas in 1990 and military action abroad to protect the interests of US corporations. Among the examples he cites are the following:

   • In 1954 the CIA spent millions of dollars to organize the overthrow of the elected president of Guatemala to save the properties of the United Fruit Company.
   • In 1973 the US government spent millions of dollars in concert with IT&T Corporation to overthrow the elected socialist leader of Chile, Salvador Allende.
   • The average tax rate for the top twelve American military contractors, who made $19 billion in profits in 1981, 1982 and 1983, was 1.5%. Middle-class Americans paid 15%. (1994: 93)

   Along the same lines, Chomsky (1995) points out that Newt Gingrich's congressional district, a very wealthy suburb of Atlanta, 'gets more federal subsidies – taxpayers' money – than any suburban county in the country, outside the federal system itself ... The biggest employer in his district happens to be Lockheed. Well, what's Lockheed? That's a publicly subsidized corporation. Lockheed wouldn't exist for five minutes if it wasn't for the public subsidy under the pretext of defense, but that's just a joke. The United States hasn't faced a threat probably since the War of 1812. Certainly there's no threat now' (129–30).

5. The debate on Proposition 187, intended to eliminate all services to undocumented immigrants, unleashed a lot of pent-up anti-immigrant emotion in California during 1994. In a presentation to the California Association for Bilingual Education conference in February 1995, I tried to draw out some of the lessons of this debate as follows:

Proposition 187 represents a turning point in the social history of California and probably in the social history of all of North America. Obviously those who support it intend for it to be a turning point – a first step in reclaiming the nation, reversing direction after 30 years of increasing multicultural fragmentation, increasing crime, increasing economic difficulty – all the social ills of the nation are symbolized within this proposition and the culprit for these social ills has been identified. The cause of the fear and the loathing embodied in this proposition is all around us in everything that we as bilingual educators collectively represent. Proposition 187 expresses the fear of diversity, the fear of difference, the fear of the Other, the fear of strangers – xenophobia.

It is also intended as a statement of identity – a statement of national unity, a statement of who the landlords of this country are and who are the tenants; a warning to the tenants that their lease is close to expiring and if they don't lower their voices, withdraw their demands, become silent and invisible, they will be evicted without ceremony.

Proposition 187 is about power, who has it and who intends to keep it. It is about intimidation and it is about racism and we must recognize these realities if we are to fight against it.

However, if we are to fight it effectively we must understand it better than I think we do. It is not enough to dismiss it as racist because certainly a large proportion of those who supported it do not see themselves as racist and are not racist in the usual sense of the term. If we are to reverse this process and work towards a saner more tolerant society, we must communicate and dialogue with many of those who currently see diversity as a threat. In fact, we must join forces with them to articulate a vision of our society where there is cooperation rather than competition across cultural boundaries, where cultural difference enriches the whole rather than scatters the parts. We have to find those areas where different cultural groups have common vested interests and join forces to achieve these common goals …

The general public, largely white- and blue-collar working people have bought into the message that diversity threatens their way of life. They believe the disinformation that has been transmitted about the costs of immigration, about immigrants taking jobs from residents, about students not learning any English in schools because of bilingual education, about multicultural advocates dismantling the history of this country. These people are afraid not only because of the increase in diversity but also because the media have skillfully associated diversity with increases in crime and economic hardship. Willie Horton may have stopped revolving in the prison door, but George Bush's message lives on: the Other is out there and he's waiting to get you.

Let's look at the realities:

Immigration. *Business Week* (July 13, 1992) reports that at least 11 million immigrants are working and from their earnings of $240 billion are paying more than $90 billion annually in taxes, a great deal more than the $5 billion they are estimated to receive in public assistance. In fact, despite their difficult economic situation as new arrivals, only 8.8% of immigrants receive public assistance, compared with 7.9% of the general population. Furthermore, the average immigrant family pays $2,500 more in tax dollars annually than they receive in public services (*New York Times*, June 27, 1993, p. A1). The American Council on Civil Liberties (ACLU) has also summarized data regarding the economic impact of immigration; among the information it compiled is the following:

• In a 1990 American Immigration Institute Survey of prominent economists, four out of five said that immigrants had a favorable impact on economic growth. None said that immigrants had an adverse impact on economic growth.

• According to a *Los Angeles Times* analysis summarizing the best available research, 'Immigrants contribute mightily to the economy, by paying billions in annual taxes, by filling low-wage jobs that keep domestic industry competitive, and by spurring investment and job-creation, revitalizing once-decaying communities. Many social scientists conclude that the newcomers, rather than drain government treasuries, contribute overall far more than they utilize in services.' (January 6, 1992).

- Studies by the Rand Corporation, the University of Maryland, the Council of Economic Advisors, the National Research Council and the Urban Institute all show that immigrants do not have a negative effect on the earnings and employment opportunities of native-born Americans. A 1989 Department of Labor study found that neither US workers in complementary jobs, nor most minority workers, appear to be adversely affected by immigration (ACLU, Department of Public Education, June 10, 1994).

6. In response to a question about how greed and the pursuit of profit are infused in the histories of the US and other countries, Chomsky discussed how the educational system works to make certain thoughts 'unthinkable:'

Well, [the teaching of history is] a little better than it used to be, but not much. Much of history is just wiped out. We just went through a war in Central America in which hundreds of thousands of people were slaughtered, and countries destroyed – huge terror. US operations were condemned by the World Court as international terrorism. It's nevertheless described in this country as an effort to bring democracy to Central America. How do they get away with that? If you have a deeply indoctrinated educated sector, as we do, you're not going to get any dissent there, and among the general population who may not be so deeply indoctrinated, they're marginal. They're supposed to be afraid of welfare mothers and people coming to attack us, and they're busy watching football games and so on, so it doesn't matter what they think. And that's pretty much the way the educational system and the media work. (1995: 139)

7. A more elaborated account of the collaborative creation of power (empowerment), and its opposite, can be found in Norwegian peace researcher Johan Galtung's (1980) description of what he calls *autonomy*:

Autonomy is here seen as power-over-oneself so as to be able to withstand what others might have of power-over-others. I use the distinction between ideological, remunerative and punitive power, depending on whether the influence is based on internal, positive external, or negative external sanctions. Autonomy then is the degree of 'inoculation' against these forms of power. These forms of power, exerted by means of ideas, carrots and sticks, can work only if the power receiver really receives the pressure, which presupposes a certain degree of submissiveness, dependency and fear, respectively. Their antidotes are self-respect, self-sufficiency and fearlessness ... 'self-respect' can be defined as 'confidence in one's own ideas and ability to set one's own goals', 'self-sufficiency' as the 'possibility of pursuing them with one's own means', and 'fearlessness' as 'the possibility of persisting despite threats of destruction ...'

The opposite [of autonomy] is penetration, meaning that the outside has penetrated into one's self to the extent of creating submissiveness to ideas, dependency on 'goods' from the outside, and fear of the outside in terms of 'bads'. (1980: 58–9)

8. For example, when the Foundation Center preschools were defunded by the California State Department in June 1995, parents in several centers refused to cooperate with the state until they themselves were granted the contract to operate the center.

References

Barlett, D. L. and Steele, J. B. (1992) *America: What Went Wrong?* Kansas: Andrews & McMeel.

Chomsky, N. (1987) The manufacture of consent. In J. Peck (ed.) *The Chomsky Reader* (pp. 121–36). New York: Pantheon Books.

Chomsky, N. (1995) A dialogue with Noam Chomsky. *Harvard Educational Review* 65, 127–44.

Cummins, J. and Sayers, D. (1995) *Brave New Schools: Challenging Cultural Illiteracy through Global Learning Networks*. New York: St Martin's Press.

Galtung, J. (1980) *The True Worlds: A Transnational Perspective*. New York: The Free Press.

Goodlad, J. I. (1984) *A Place Called School: Prospects for the Future*. New York: McGraw Hill.

Hodgkinson, H. (1991) Reform versus reality. *Phi Delta Kappan* 73 (September), 9–16.

Hughes, R. (1993) *Culture of Complaint: A Passionate Look into the Ailing Heart of America*. New York: Warner Books.

Kozol, J. (1991) *Savage Inequalities: Children in America's Schools*. New York: Crown Publishers.

Macedo, D. P. (1993) Literacy for stupidification: The pedagogy of big lies. *Harvard Educational Review* 63, 183–207.

Macedo, D. P. (1994) *Literacies of Power: What Americans are not Allowed to Know*. Boulder, CO: Westview Press.

Moffett, J. (1989) Censorship and spiritual education. *English Education* 21, 70–87.

National Coalition of Advocates for Students (1988) *New Voices: Immigrant Students in US Public Schools*. Boston: National Coalition of Advocates for Students.

Natriello, G., McDill, E. L. and Pallas, A. M. (1990) *Schooling Disadvantaged Children: Racing Against Catastrophe*. New York: Teachers College Press.

Poplin, M. and Weeres, J. (1992) *Voices from the Inside: A Report on Schooling from Inside the Classroom*. Claremont, CA: The Institute for Education in Transformation at the Claremont Graduate School.

Ramírez, J. D. (1992) Executive summary. *Bilingual Research Journal* 16, 1–62.

Reich, R. (1991) *The Work of Nations: Preparing Ourselves for 21st Century Capitalism*. New York: Knopf.

Rethinking Schools (1991) *Rethinking Columbus: Teaching about the 500th Anniversary of Columbus's Arrival in North America*. Madison, WI: Rethinking Schools Ltd.

Schweinhart, L. J., Weikart, D. P. and Larney, M. B. (1986) Consequences of three preschool curriculum models through age 15. *Early Childhood Research Quarterly* 1, 15–45.

Stanford Working Group (1993) *Federal Education Programs for Limited-English-proficient Students: A Blueprint for the Second Generation*. Stanford, CA: Report of the Stanford Working Group, Stanford University.

The President's Commission on Foreign Language and International Studies (1980) A critique of US capability. A report to the President from the President's Commission on Foreign Language and International Studies. *The Modern Language Journal* 64, 9–57.

Wirth, A. G. (1993) Education and work: The choices we face. *Phi Delta Kappan* (January) 360–66.

Cultural and Linguistic Diversity in Education: A Mainstream Issue?

Introduction

Issues related to equity and education have been fiercely debated in many countries during the past 30 years. In different contexts and at different times proponents of assimilationist, multicultural and anti-racist orientations to diversity have all proclaimed 'equity' as their primary consideration. At a more specifically linguistic level, the benefits for English language learners (ELL) of various forms of bilingual education, mother tongue support, English immersion, mainstream English-as-a-second-language (ESL) and withdrawal ESL support have all been argued.

For the most part these debates have taken place outside the realm of mainstream education reform efforts, accurately reflecting their perceived status as 'sideshow' events, footnotes to more serious concerns. In the UK for example, the National Curriculum documents contain few references to these issues. Similarly, in most European Union countries, pilot projects addressing issues of diversity produced few tangible changes in overall educational structures. Reid and Reich (1992), in their overview of 15 pilot projects implemented between 1986 and 1991, suggested that, for a large majority, mother tongue teaching remained a marginal activity, minority communities were not systematically involved in the development and planning of school subject content, teaching of the majority language tended to be 'naively assimilatory' or was seen as 'culturally neutral' (p. 241) and structural changes in educational provision were not a concern to the educational authorities. Similarly, although educational provision for ELL pupils in Canada and the USA is debated hotly, as documented below, it is rarely viewed as a central component of mainstream educational reform. For example, a major study of 73 Californian schools that were in the process of restructuring revealed a silence about issues of culture and identity and 'heavy barriers to bringing diversity and equity issues into the school's plans to better serve their students' (Olsen *et al.*, 1994: 31).

This marginalization of diversity issues is particularly surprising in view of the fact that in many of the larger cities of both Canada and the USA, so-called

315

'minority' pupils in fact constitute the majority student population. In the schools of metropolitan Toronto, for example, about 60% of the pupils come from homes where a language other than English or a non-standard form of English is usually spoken. Furthermore, in both Canada and the USA, certain groups of culturally diverse pupils are massively over-represented in school failure rates, the reversal of which is one of the major purposes of school restructuring.

In the present paper, I present a theoretical framework for analysing educational provision for culturally and linguistically diverse pupils. The framework attempts to link the interactions between educators and pupils in the school and classroom context (henceforth *micro-interactions*) with the relations of power that operate in the wider society between dominant and subordinated groups (henceforth *macro-interactions*). It focuses on the ways in which learning in school is intertwined with processes of identity negotiation between educators and pupils and argues that in culturally and linguistically diverse contexts the negotiation of identity always either reinforces or challenges patterns of coercive relations of power in the wider society. From this perspective, the marginalisation of issues related to diversity in educational reform initiatives is a reflection of persistent patterns of coercive relations of power in the wider society.

Power, Identity and Learning

Concerns about national identity are clearly implicated in the on-going debates in many countries about issues of racism, immigration and language. An illustrative statement that probably still reflects majority sentiment in many English speaking countries comes from a speaker at the 1913 Presbyterian Pre-Assembly Congress in Toronto (quoted by Harney & Troper, 1975: 110):

> The problem is simply this: take all the different nationalities, German, French, Italian, Russian and all the others that are sending their surplus into Canada: mix them with the Anglo-Saxon stock and produce a uniform race wherein the Anglo-Saxon peculiarities shall prevail.

The fear that diversity might undermine national identity is no less apparent in US historian Arthur Schlesinger Jr's more recent warning about the dangers of bilingual education (1991: 108–9):

> Bilingualism shuts doors. It nourishes self-ghettoization, and ghettoization nourishes racial antagonism ... Using some language other than English dooms people to second-class citizenship in American society ... Monolingual education opens doors to the larger world ... institutionalized bilingualism remains another source of the fragmentation of America, another threat to the dream of one people.

There is no hint in Schlesinger's diatribe against diversity that racism in the wider society, rather than bilingualism *per se*, might constitute a more reasonable explanation of why 'using some language other than English dooms people to second-class citizenship in American society'. A common element in the warnings about diversity in countries around the world is that they invariably problematise the culture, attitudes and language use of the subordinated group, which is expected to become invisible and inaudible either through assimilation or exclusion. Diversity becomes a problem only when subordinated groups refuse to accept their preordained status and demand 'rights'.

This process reflects the operation of coercive relations of power which can be defined as the exercise of power by a dominant group (or individual or country) to the detriment of a subordinated group (or individual or country). Coercive relations of power are reflected in and shaped through the use of language or discourse and usually involve a definitional process that legitimises the inferior or deviant status accorded to the subordinated group (or individual or country). In other words, the dominant group defines the subordinated group as inferior (or evil), thereby automatically defining itself as superior (or virtuous).

No classroom or school is immune from the influence of the coercive power relations that characterize societal debates about diversity and national identity. On a moment-to-moment basis educators, in their interactions with culturally and linguistically diverse pupils, sketch their ideological stance in relation to issues of diversity, identity and power. The science and practice of pedagogy is never neutral in relation to these issues in spite of its frequent self-portrayal as innocent and focused only on 'learning outcomes'.

To illustrate, let us look at historical and current practice in this area, particularly with respect to pupil language choice in school. The ways in which coercive power is used to convey a message about national and individual identity is very clear in the Welsh and Kenyan examples below, but it is also evident in the apparently more benign contemporary US example recounted by Elsa Auerbach (1995).

The 'Welsh not' came into existence after the 1870 Education Act in Britain as a means of eradicating the Welsh language. Any child heard speaking Welsh in school had a heavy wooden placard attached to rope placed over his or her shoulders. The placard reached to the child's shins and would bump them when the child walked. If that child heard another child speaking Welsh, he or she could transfer the 'Welsh not' to the other child. The child carrying this placard at the end of the day was beaten (Evans, 1978). Richard Llewellyn gives an account of this type of punishment in his autobiographical novel *How Green Was My Valley*:

> I heard crying in the infants' school as though a child had fallen and the voice came nearer and fell flat upon the air as a small girl came through the door and walked a couple of steps towards us ... About her neck a piece of new cord, and from the cord, a board that hung to her shins and cut her as

she walked. Chalked on the board, in the fist of Mr Elijah-Jones-Sessions, I must not speak Welsh in school ... And the board dragged her down, for she was small, and the cord rasped the flesh on her neck, and there were marks upon her shins where the edge of the board had cut.

(Llewellyn, 1968, p. 267)

Interestingly, Ngũgĩ wa Thiong'o (1986) gives a very similar account from the Kenyan context:

Thus, one of the most humiliating experiences was to be caught speaking Gikuyu in the vicinity of the school. The culprit was given corporal punishment – three to five strokes of the cane on bare buttocks – or was made to carry a metal plate around the neck with inscriptions such as I AM STUPID or I AM A DONKEY. Sometimes the culprits were fined money they could hardly afford. (1986: 11)

Irrelevant examples from the past? Well, compare them with the following account in which the surface structure of identity negotiation is certainly more benign but the deep structure is quite similar. In discussing how power dynamics enter into the ESL classroom, Auerbach highlights the 'commonsense' axiomatic view that only English is an acceptable medium of communication:

Teachers devise elaborate games, signals, and penalty systems to enforce the use of English only. For example, an article in a recent issue of the *TESOL Newsletter* (June, 1990) extols the virtues of *fining* students for committing 'crimes' against the teacher's first language, including the crime of using their first language; the teacher told students, 'This is an English-only classroom. If you speak Spanish or Cantonese or Mandarin or Vietnamese or Thai or Russian or Farsi, you pay me 25 cents. I can be rich'. (1995: 25)

In these three examples, we see educators defining their roles in ways that entail assumptions both about the relevance and status of English and the students' first language (L1) in the school and wider society and about the negative effects of students' L1 on their acquisition of English. Schlesinger's refrain that 'bilingualism shuts doors' is alive and well in many of the classrooms to which subordinated group pupils are consigned. The message is not just about bilingualism and language learning as linguistic and educational phenomena; more fundamentally it is a message about what kinds of identity are acceptable in the classroom and society. For subordinated group pupils, the price of admission into the teaching–learning relationship, and access to opportunity within the wider society, is frequently renunciation of self.

In some cases, students successfully cast off their old skins and become who they are expected to be; others are either not given that option or decide to reject it, frequently withdrawing mentally and finding identity and affirmation on the streets rather than in the classroom. In both cases, the costs can be high, as illustrated by this account from Antti Jalava (1988) of his reaction to the rejection of his Finnish identity that he experienced in Swedish schools:

> When the idea had eaten itself deeply enough into my soul that it was despicable to be a Finn, I began to feel ashamed of my origins ... A Swede was what I had to become, and that meant I could not continue to be a Finn. Everything I had held dear and self-evident had to be destroyed ... My mother tongue was worthless – this I realized at last; on the contrary it made me the butt of abuse and ridicule. So down with the Finnish language! I spat on myself, gradually committed internal suicide. (1988: 164)

Similar themes emerge in accounts of the experience of African American pupils in the USA and Afro-Caribbean pupils in Britain. Ladson-Billings (1995), for example, points out: 'The problem that African American students face is the constant devaluation of their culture both in school and in the larger society' (p. 485). Fordham's research (1990: 259) similarly highlighted the fact that '... within the school structure, Black adolescents consciously and unconsciously sense that they have to give up aspects of their identities and their indigenous cultural system in order to achieve success as defined in dominant-group terms'. In the British context, Morgan (1996) has argued that '... children of African-Caribbean heritage in Britain are caught up between two cultures, one of which they see devalued and the other with which they do not fully identify but which is seen as superior by society' (p. 39).

In short, educators' interactions with pupils reflect the ways they have defined their own roles or identities as educators. Role definitions refer to the mindset of expectations, assumptions and goals that educators bring to the task of educating culturally diverse students. These role definitions determine the way educators view pupils' possibilities and the messages they communicate to pupils with regard to the contributions they can make to their societies. Thus, educators are constantly sketching a triangular set of images in their interactions with pupils:

- an image of their own identities as educators;

- an image of the identity options that are being highlighted for pupils; consider, for example, the contrasting messages conveyed to pupils in classrooms focused on critical inquiry compared with classrooms focused on passive internalization of information;

- an image of the society into which pupils will graduate and to which they are being prepared to contribute.

In societies characterised historically by racism and the operation of various forms of class- and gender-based discrimination, educators' role definitions, and the interactions with pupils to which these role definitions give rise, can never be viewed as independent of power relations. The micro-interactions between educators and pupils will tend to reflect, in varying degrees, the macro-interactions between dominant and subordinated groups in the wider society.

Individual educators, however, are by no means powerless; they have many opportunities within the school to challenge the operation of the societal power structure. Specifically, they can become advocates for the promotion of pupils' linguistic talents, they can pursue partnerships with culturally diverse parents and communities to bridge the gap between home and school cultures and they can implement pedagogical approaches that develop forms of critical literacy that enable pupils to resist devaluation and 'take control of their own lives', as Alex McLeod (1986) has expressed it. When educators define their roles in terms of promoting social justice and equality of opportunity, their interactions with culturally diverse pupils are more likely to embody a transformative potential that challenges coercive relations of power as they are manifested in the school context.

Educational structures also reflect societal power structures. These structures include the organisation of schooling in a broad sense that includes policies, programmes, curriculum and assessment. This organisation is established to achieve the goals of education as defined primarily by the dominant group in the society. Among the structures that might systematically discriminate against culturally and linguistically diverse pupils are the following:

- ability grouping and streaming practices that deny pupils in low-ability groups access to quality instruction (Oakes, 1985);

- the use of culturally and linguistically biased IQ tests to give culturally diverse pupils a one-way ticket to special education or low-track programmes (see Cummins, 1984);

- teacher education institutions that until recently have treated issues related to culturally diverse pupils as marginal and that have sent new teachers into the classroom with minimal information regarding patterns of language and social development among such pupils and few pedagogical strategies for helping pupils learn;

- a curriculum that reflects only the experiences and values of middle-class English-speaking pupils and effectively suppresses the experiences and values of culturally diverse pupils;

- the absence from most schools of professionals capable of communicating in the languages of culturally diverse pupils and their parents; such professionals could assist in functions such as L1 instruction, L1 assessment for purposes of placement and intervention and parent/school liaison;

- criteria for promotion to positions of responsibility (e.g. headteachers) that take no account of the individual's experience with or potential for leadership in the education of culturally diverse pupils.

These educational structures constitute a frame that sets limits on the kinds of micro-interactions that are likely to occur between educators and pupils.

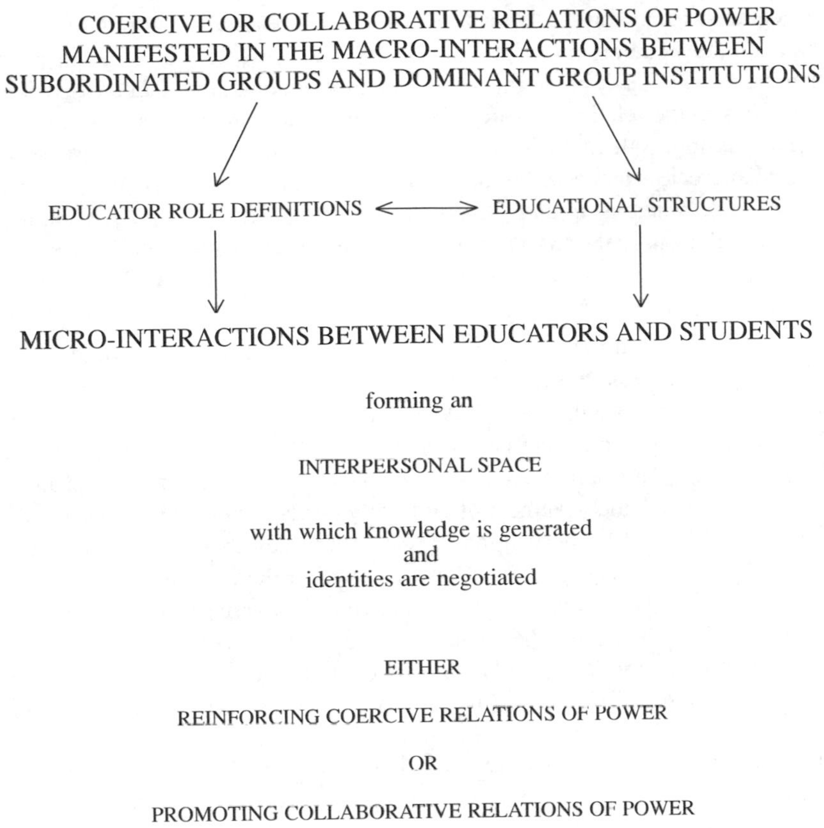

COERCIVE OR COLLABORATIVE RELATIONS OF POWER
MANIFESTED IN THE MACRO-INTERACTIONS BETWEEN
SUBORDINATED GROUPS AND DOMINANT GROUP INSTITUTIONS

EDUCATOR ROLE DEFINITIONS ⟷ EDUCATIONAL STRUCTURES

MICRO-INTERACTIONS BETWEEN EDUCATORS AND STUDENTS

forming an

INTERPERSONAL SPACE

with which knowledge is generated
and
identities are negotiated

EITHER

REINFORCING COERCIVE RELATIONS OF POWER

OR

PROMOTING COLLABORATIVE RELATIONS OF POWER

Figure 1

As expressed in Figure 1, educational structures combine with educator role definitions to determine the micro-interactions between educators, pupils and communities. These micro-interactions form an interpersonal or an interactional space within which the acquisition of knowledge and formation of identity is negotiated. Power is created and shared within this interpersonal space where minds and identities meet. As such, the micro-interactions constitute the most immediate determinant of student academic success or failure.

These micro-interactions between educators, pupils and communities are never neutral; in varying degrees, they either reinforce coercive relations of power or promote collaborative relations of power. In the former case, they contribute to the disempowerment of culturally diverse pupils and communities; in the latter case, the micro-interactions constitute a process of empowerment that enables educators, pupils and communities to challenge the operation of coercive power structures.

In contrast to coercive relations of power, collaborative relations of power operate on the assumption that power is not a fixed pre-determined quantity, but rather can be *generated* in interpersonal and intergroup relations. In other words, participants in the relationship are *empowered* through their collaboration such that each is more affirmed in her or his identity and has a greater sense of efficacy to create change in his or her life or social situation. Thus, power is created in the relationship and shared among participants. The power relationship is *additive* rather than *subtractive*. Power is *created with* others, rather than being *imposed on* or *exercised over* others. Within this framework, *empowerment* can be defined as *the collaborative creation of power.*

Expressed differently, the ways in which identities are negotiated in the interpersonal spaces created in educator–pupil interactions plays a major role in the extent to which pupils will engage academically. Affirmation of the identities of subordinated group pupils necessarily entails a challenge to the societal process of subordination. This perspective suggests that programme interventions aimed at reversing the underachievement of culturally diverse pupils will be successful to the extent that these interventions result in educator–pupil interactions that challenge patterns of coercive relations of power in the broader society. Thus, communicating to pupils that their bilingualism is a valuable asset both for them and their society challenges the societal discourse that proclaims 'bilingualism shuts doors'. Involving parents and minority communities as partners in a shared educational enterprise challenges the societal discourse that attributes pupils' academic difficulties to their cultural, linguistic or genetic backgrounds. Similarly, instruction that acknowledges and builds on pupils' prior experience and addresses issues that pupils see as relevant to their lives is much more likely to engage pupils academically than transmission-oriented instruction that effectively suppresses pupils' experience – what Paulo Freire (1983) termed a 'banking' education where teachers define their roles in terms of depositing information and skills in pupils' memory banks.

Conclusion

The framework outlined in the present paper focuses on how power relations operating in the broader society influence the interactions that occur between educators and pupils in the classroom. These interactions can be empowering or disempowering for both educators and pupils. Culturally diverse pupils are disempowered educationally in very much the same way that their communities have been disempowered historically in their interactions with societal institutions. The logical implication is that these pupils will succeed academically to the extent that the patterns of interaction in school reverse those that prevail in the society at large. In other words, in multicultural contexts characterized by unequal power relations among groups, a genuine commitment to helping all pupils succeed academically requires a willingness on the part of educators, individually and collectively, to challenge aspects of coercive power structures in the wider society.

Not surprisingly, few school systems are willing to commit themselves beyond a rhetorical level to challenging coercive relations of power in the wider society that funds them. By the same token, issues of power and its negotiation in society and schools seldom represent a significant component of teacher education courses. These issues are usually seen as even less relevant to the training of school psychologists and speech/language specialists, even in educational situations (such as metropolitan Toronto) where ELL students constitute the numerical 'mainstream'. One blatant illustration of the persistence of coercive power relations in the Canadian context is the fact that IQ tests that are culturally and linguistically biased in the extreme are still administered as a matter of course to virtually all candidates for special education, regardless of their linguistic and cultural background.

From the perspective of the present framework, the marginalisation of issues related to diversity in the pre-service preparation of educators and in the operation and policy making processes of schools is not a matter of neglect or innocent omission. It can only be understood as a function of coercive relations of power that continue to permeate our school systems. This coercive power structure is only reinforced by multicultural rhetoric that fails to address seriously either systemic structures that discriminate against culturally diverse pupils or the role definitions of educators *vis-a-vis* diversity issues.

When the task of educating ELL pupils is left to specialist ESL or bilingual teachers and no modifications are made in 'mainstream' educational structures to accommodate diversity, the interactions that pupils experience in 'mainstream' classrooms are unlikely to promote either academic growth or affirmation of pupil identity. Mainstream teachers are not prepared (in either sense of the word) to teach them. This unfortunate situation is exacerbated by teacher education colleges that continue to consign issues of diversity to the margins of concern. In the Canadian context, a large majority of Faculties of Education treat diversity and ESL issues as peripheral to their 'core' mandate of teacher education. In cities such as Toronto, this orientation amounts to preparing teachers to teach the pupil population that existed 30 years ago, rather than the one that exists today (Cummins & Cameron, 1994). It also has direct implications for the kind of interactions that these teachers will orchestrate with culturally diverse pupils in their classrooms. Inequities in pupil opportunities will be perpetuated as long as pre-service and in-service education of teachers focus on instructional techniques and strategies to the exclusion of issues of power relations and their intersection with processes of identity negotiation in classroom interactions.

How can educators, pupils and communities resist the operation of coercive relations of power in schools and society? Clearly, it is unrealistic to expect societal institutions to make visible their own hegemonic practices. Thus, resistance must originate with individuals and must focus initially on making visible the power relations that underlie the 'normal' organization of curricula and instruction. Fortunately, we are not short of documented accounts of educators, pupils and communities who have succeeded in doing just this (McLeod, 1986; Bigelow *et al.*, 1994; Frederickson, 1995; Cummins, 1996).

For educators, a starting point in thinking about genuine educational reform is to recognise that we do have choices in the way we structure the micro-interactions in our classrooms. While we operate under many constraints, we do determine for ourselves the social and educational goals we want to achieve with our pupils. We are responsible for the role definitions we adopt in relation to culturally diverse pupils and communities. We have the power to define our own identities in interaction with pupils and communities.

Within the interactional spaces where identities are negotiated, educators and pupils together can generate power that challenges structures of injustice in small but significant ways. Similarly, schools that succeed in bringing issues related to cultural and linguistic diversity from the periphery to the centre of their mission are much more likely to prepare pupils to thrive in the interdependent global society within which they will live. These schools will communicate to pupils and communities that their access to more than one culture and language is a resource that can enrich the entire school. This form of communication in itself challenges the racism and xenophobia that are all too common in societies around the world.

References

Auerbach, E. R. (1995) The politics of the ESL classroom: Issues of power in pedagogical choices. In J. W. Tollefson (ed.) *Power and Inequality in Language Education* (pp. 9–33). Cambridge: Cambridge University Press.

Bigelow, B., Christensen, L., Karp, S., Miner, B. and Peterson, B. (eds) (1994) *Rethinking our Classrooms: Teaching for Equity and Justice.* Milwaukee, WI: Rethinking Schools Ltd.

Cummins, J. (1984) *Bilingualism and Special Education: Issues in Assessment and Pedagogy.* Clevedon: Multilingual Matters.

Cummins, J. (1996) *Negotiating Identities: Education for Empowerment in a Diverse Society.* Los Angeles, CA: Association for Bilingual Education.

Cummins, J. and Cameron, L. (1994) The ESL student IS the mainstream: The marginalization of diversity in current Canadian educational debates. *English Quarterly* 26 (3), 30–3

Evans, E. (1978) Welsh (Cymraeg). In C. V. James (ed.) *The Older Mother Tongues of the United Kingdom.* London: Centre for Information on Language Teaching and Research.

Fordham, S. (1990) Racelessness as a factor in black students' school success: Pragmatic strategy or pyrrhic victory? In N. M. Hidalgo, C. L. McDowell and E. V. Siddle (eds) *Facing Racism in Education* (pp. 232–62). *Harvard Educational Review,* reprint series No. 21.

Frederickson, J. (ed.) (1995) *Reclaiming Our Voices: Bilingual Education, Critical Pedagogy and Praxis.* Ontario, CA: California Association for Bilingual Education.

Freire, P. (1983) Banking education. In H. Giroux and D. Purpel (eds) *The Hidden Curriculum and Moral Education: Deception or Discovery?* Berkeley, CA: McCutcheon.

Harney, R. and Troper, H. (1975) *Immigrants: A Portrait of Urban Experience 1890–1930.* Toronto: Van Nostrand Rheinhold.

Jalava, A. (1988) Nobody could see that I was a Finn. In T. Skutnabb-Kangas and J. Cummins (eds) *Minority Education: From Shame to Struggle* (pp. 161–6). Clevedon: Multilingual Matters.

Ladson-Billings, G. (1995) Toward a theory of culturally relevant pedagogy. *American Educational Research Journal* 32, 465–91.

Llewellyn, R. (1968) *How Green Was My Valley.* Toronto: Signet.

McLeod, A. (1986) Critical literacy: Taking control of our own lives. *Language Arts* 63 (1), 37–50.

Morgan, G. (1996) An investigation into the achievement of African-Caribbean pupils. *Multicultural Teaching* 14 (2), 37–40.

Ngũgĩ wa Thiong'o (1986) *Decolonising the Mind: The Politics of Language in African Literature.* London: James Curry.

Oakes, J. (1985) *Keeping Track: How Schools Structure Inequality.* New Haven: Yale University Press.

Olsen, L., Chang, H., De La Rosa Salazar, D., Leong, C., McCall Perez, Z., McClain, G. and Raffel, L. (1994) *The Unfinished Journey: Restructuring Schools in a Diverse Society.* San Fransisco, CA: California Tomorrow.

Reid, E. and Reich, H. (eds) (1992) *Breaking the Boundaries: Migrant Workers' Children in the EC.* Clevedon: Multilingual Matters.

Schlesinger, A., Jr (1991) *The Disuniting of America.* New York: W. W. Norton.

Alternative Paradigms in Bilingual Education Research: Does Theory Have a Place?

Interpretation of the voluminous research on bilingual education has been highly controversial among both academics and policymakers for more than 25 years. Clearly the political sensitivity of the issue has contributed to confusion about what the research is actually saying. A more fundamental cause of this confusion, however, is the extremely limited way in which educational researchers have examined the research, and in particular the quantitative research, on this issue. The dominant assumption among academic opponents and advocates of bilingual education has been that we can draw policy-relevant conclusions regarding the effectiveness of bilingual education only from 'methodologically acceptable studies'. Typically, these studies are program evaluations that involve treatment and control groups compared in such a way that outcome differences can be attributed to the treatment rather than to extraneous factors.

I argue that this approach represents an appropriate, but extremely limited, orientation to research in bilingual education. It is limited on two counts:

- It has proved virtually impossible to apply rigorous controls to comparisons between programs due to the myriad human, administrative and political influences that impact the implementation of programs over time;
- Underlying this approach is the assumption that there is a direct connection between research and policy: researchers will discover which program alternatives work best and policymakers will develop funding and implementation policies based on these findings. While this straightforward linkage between research and policy may work well in some spheres (e.g. opinion surveys), it seldom yields clear cut results in an area as multifaceted as educational research, where the treatment variable of interest (e.g. proportion of first language [L1] instruction) is intertwined and interacting with hundreds of other variables that will affect program outcomes.

As I document below, it is not surprising that this dominant research paradigm has yielded such paltry pickings for policy. The only thing that academic opponents and advocates of bilingual education seem to agree on with respect to the policy-related research is that it is of almost universally poor quality (August & Hakuta, 1997; Greene, 1998; Rossell & Baker, 1996).

I argue in this paper that 'poor quality' is in the eye of the beholder. Viewed through the lens of 'methodologically acceptable studies', it is possible to find fault with virtually all of the research studies, including many of those that survived the 'rigorous criteria' established by Greene (1998) and Rossell and Baker (1996). However, there is an enormous amount of relevant and interpretable research, both internationally and within the United States, that speaks directly to the bilingual education policy issues. I suggest that the policy issues have remained confused and contested at least partly because the bulk of the relevant research has been virtually ignored, both by advocates and opponents of bilingual education. The relevance of this research is not apparent within the dominant paradigm because the studies do not conform to the criteria of acceptability within this paradigm. However, when we examine this voluminous research from the perspective of an alternative paradigm, its relevance is immediately apparent.

The alternative paradigm claims that the relevance of research for policy is mediated through theory. In complex educational and other human organizational contexts, data or 'facts' become relevant for policy purposes only in the context of a coherent theory. It is the *theory* rather than the individual research findings that permits the generation of predictions about program outcomes under different conditions. Research findings themselves cannot be directly applied across contexts. For example, the fact that students in a Spanish–English bilingual program in New York City performed well academically in relation to grade norms (Beykont, 1994) tells us very little about whether a similar program might work with Mexican-American students in San Diego. Yet when certain patterns are replicated across a wide range of situations, the accumulation of consistent findings suggests that some stable underlying principle is at work. This principle can then be stated as a theoretical proposition or hypothesis from which predictions can be derived and tested.

In contrast to research findings, theories are almost by definition applicable across contexts. The validity of any theoretical principle is assessed precisely by how well it can account for the research findings in a variety of contexts. If a theory cannot account for a particular set of research findings, then it is an inadequate or incomplete theory. Thus, while no individual research finding can 'prove' a theory or confirm a hypothesis, any research finding can disconfirm or refute a theory or hypothesis. Thus, the criterion of validity for any hypothesis is extremely stringent: it must be consistent with *all* of the research data or at least be able to account for inconsistencies (e.g. poor implementation of a program).

In this paper, I label the former paradigm the 'Research–Policy' paradigm and the latter the 'Research–Theory–Policy' paradigm. In order to show the strengths and limitations of each, I examine how they have been employed in the bilingual education debate and the policy-relevant findings that each yields. I conclude that the former paradigm yields largely trivial information for policy purposes and perpetuates misconceptions regarding bilingual education that have persisted for almost 30 years. By contrast, the latter paradigm yields considerable information that has direct relevance to policy and addresses many of the most contentious issues in the bilingual education debate.

The Research–Policy Paradigm: Debunking the Mythology of 'Methodologically Acceptable Studies'

Both advocates and opponents of bilingual education have largely concurred on the conditions under which research in general and evaluation studies in particular can be considered 'methodologically acceptable'. For example, Greene (1998), whose interpretation of research is favorable to bilingual education, and Rossell and Baker (1996), whose conclusions are highly unfavorable to bilingual education, agreed on the appropriateness of the following criteria for designation of studies as 'methodologically acceptable':

(1) Studies had to compare students in bilingual programs to a control group of similar students;
(2) The design had to ensure that initial differences between treatment and control groups were controlled statistically or through random assignment;
(3) Results were to be based on standardized test scores in English;
(4) Differences between the scores of treatment and control groups were to be determined by means of appropriate statistical tests.

The approaches diverged on several additional points. Greene, for example, focused only on studies that had been carried out in the United States and which measured the effects of bilingual education after at least one year of the treatment, whereas Rossell and Baker included international research data in their review. Rossell and Baker also categorized programs according to pre-defined labels (structured immersion, transitional bilingual education, submersion, English-as-a-second-language (ESL)) whereas Greene adopted a more straightforward categorization of bilingual education as a program in which all students are taught using at least some of their native language. An additional difference was that Greene (like Willig, 1985) used meta-analysis to take into account effect sizes in individual studies whereas Rossell and Baker (like Baker & de Kanter, 1981) simply counted studies that were favorable or unfavorable to different treatments.

Using their respective criteria of 'methodologically acceptable' studies, Rossell and Baker rejected 228 studies and accepted 72, while Greene could find only 11 studies whose design permitted conclusions to be drawn.

August and Hakuta (1997) and their colleagues reviewed both the basic and policy-oriented research on schooling for language-minority children. Their review is comprehensive, balanced and useful for researchers and policymakers alike. It also offers very appropriate suggestions for improving the quality of program evaluations. However, it suffers from the same problematic orientation to research and policy as do the reviews by Greene (1998) and Rossell and Baker (1996). In interpreting both the basic research and program evaluations relevant to language learning and bilingual education, the authors pay only lip service to the role of theory in mediating the relevance of research for policy (Fitzgerald & Cummins, 1999). As a result, their conclusions are considerably weaker than they might have been and also considerably less useful for policy purposes.

I critique these three literature reviews below. Space does not permit a comprehensive review of these studies and thus my focus is directed towards identifying the limitations of the research paradigm these authors have adopted.

Greene's Meta-analysis

Greene reported that participation in a bilingual program over a period of two years made a difference of about one-fifth of a standard deviation in achievement. Thus, if a student in an English-only program performed at the 26th percentile at the end of those two years, the bilingual student would be at the 34th percentile. The problematic nature of this type of meta-analysis can be seen from examining some of the 11 studies included. One of the large-scale 'methodologically acceptable' studies included in the analysis (and in Rossell & Baker's review) was the American Institutes of Research (AIR) study (Danoff, 1978). This study aggregated a variety of programs labeled 'bilingual education' and compared them to non-bilingual programs, ignoring the fact that many bilingual programs are bilingual in name only or involve minimal amounts of L1 instruction by a non-trained paraprofessional (see, e.g. Gandara, 1997). In addition, as pointed out by August and Hakuta (1997) there was no clear demarcation between treatment and control groups:

> Nearly three-quarters of the experimental group had been in bilingual programs for two or more years, and the study measured their gains in the last few months. Additionally, about two-thirds of the children in the control group had previously been in a bilingual program; these children did not represent a control group in the usual sense of the term. Thus the AIR study did not compare bilingual education with no bilingual education. (1997: 140)

Krashen (1999a) has also pointed out that Greene's analysis included several 'methodologically acceptable' studies in which 'bilingual education' was either not described in any detail or involved minimal use of the L1 (e.g. use of bilingual paraprofessionals).

In short, Greene's meta-analysis makes no attempt to test the theoretical propositions underlying bilingual education or alternative English-only programs. The apparent rigor involved in reducing the extensive corpus of bilingual education data to 11 'methodologically acceptable' studies seems destined to end up in *rigor mortis* for this approach as the credibility of even these 11 studies is whittled away. However, this is not because most of the research is inadequate; the inadequacy is rather in the lens through which we are examining the research.

August and Hakuta's National Research Council Report

This report was intended to provide researchers and policymakers with a 'state-of-the-art' review of what basic and applied research could tell us about improving schooling for language-minority students. One might have expected to find clear and coherent answers to volatile policy-relevant questions such as:

- How long does it take English language learners (ELL) to catch up academically to their native English-speaking peers?
- Should reading instruction be provided initially through bilingual students' first language?
- What outcomes can be expected from different kinds of bilingual programs?
- How important is 'time-on-task', understood as the amount of instructional time spent through the target language, on second language academic development?

Although most of these questions are addressed to some extent in the report, the answers are at best tentative and not particularly helpful for policy purposes. This lack of incisiveness can be attributed to the focus on research in isolation from theory. Crucial theoretical issues such as the nature of language proficiency and its relationship to academic development are barely considered in the report. Similarly, the report fails to address the validity of the competing hypotheses that have been advanced to support either English-only programs (the 'time-on-task' or maximum exposure to English hypothesis (e.g. Porter, 1990)) or certain forms of bilingual programs (the 'linguistic interdependence' hypothesis (Cummins, 1981)).[1] Consequently, the first question listed above is barely considered in the report despite the fact that this has been a central issue to emerge in the context of Proposition 227 in California and the many policy debates leading up to this initiative.

Answers are given to some of the other questions; for example, the report states that '[t]he degree of children's native-language proficiency is a strong predictor of their English-language development' (p. 28). However, the authors fail to address what this finding means for policy. As I illustrate below, when this finding is integrated with theory in the form of the linguistic interdependence hypothesis, it provides an empirically testable basis for interpreting the outcomes of bilingual education programs in widely different sociolinguistic and sociopolitical contexts.

Similarly, the authors' treatment of the question of learning to read through a second language correctly identifies the major pattern of research findings but then lets the issue drop as though the findings were contradictory and few policy implications could be drawn:

> With respect to reading instruction in a second language, there is remarkably little directly relevant research. Clearly, one of the major intellectual stimuli to bilingual education programs has been the belief that initial reading instruction in a language not yet mastered orally to some reasonable level is too great a cognitive challenge for most learners. The evidence that better academic outcomes characterize immigrant children who have had two to three years of initial schooling (and presumably literacy instruction) in their native countries (Collier & Thomas, 1989; Skutnabb-Kangas, 1979) is consistent with the claim that children should first learn to read in a language they already speak. However, it is clear that many children first learn to read in a second language without serious negative consequences. (pp. 59–60)

By contrast, I would argue that there is a significant amount of directly relevant research. Reviews of this research from 25 years ago were able to conclude that the language of initial literacy instruction is not, in itself, a significant determinant of academic outcomes (Cummins, 1979; Engle, 1975; Wagner, 1998), although it may play a role as part of a much broader constellation of variables related to power relations and identity negotiation (Cummins, 1996).

Finally, overwhelming amounts of data on bilingual education programs internationally (e.g. Cummins & Corson, 1997) should have permitted the authors to state definitively that the major theoretical argument underlying the push for all-English programs is without merit. The 'time-on-task' (maximum exposure) hypothesis predicts that any form of bilingual education that reduces the amount of instructional time through the medium of English will result in academic difficulties in English. Or, as Rosalie Pedalino Porter (1990) has expressed it:

> The evidence of direct correlation between early, intensive second-language learning and high level of competence in the second language is inescapable, as is the on-task principle – that is, the more time spent learning a language, the better you do in it, all other factors being equal. (1990: 119)

As a theoretical proposition, this hypothesis is refuted by the outcomes of countless bilingual programs evaluated in countries around the globe which demonstrate that students suffer no adverse effects in their mastery of the majority language (English in North America) as a result of spending significant instructional time through the minority language (see Corson, 1993; Cummins, 1996, for reviews).

The policy implication is not that bilingual programs are necessarily 'effective', or will necessarily succeed better than alternative programs. Outcomes of any program will depend on a variety of implementation factors; rather, the data and associated theory show clearly that linguistic minority and linguistic majority students in well-implemented bilingual programs (of various types) will suffer no adverse consequences as a result of spending instructional time through both languages.

This type of clear policy-relevant conclusion is not forthcoming from the report, not because relevant data are lacking, but because the data are viewed through a very fuzzy lens. The authors' conclusion seems designed to provide policymakers on both sides of the bilingual education issue with what they want to hear:

> The beneficial effects of native-language instruction are clearly evident in programs that have been labeled 'bilingual education', but they also appear in some programs that are labeled 'immersion' (Gersten & Woodward, 1995). There also appear to be benefits of programs that are labeled 'structured immersion' (Baker & de Kanter, 1981; Rossell & Ross, 1986). (p. 147)

Theory is required to bring the data into focus. As I illustrate below, definitive answers could have been provided to many of the most contentious policy-related questions in the area of bilingual education had the authors articulated the major theoretical positions in the literature on bilingual education and examined the consistency of these positions with the available data.

Rossell and Baker (1996)

The outcomes of Rossell and Baker's review of the literature on the educational effectiveness of bilingual education are clearly stated in the abstract:

> The research evidence indicates that, on standardized achievement tests, transitional bilingual education (TBE) is *better* than regular classroom instruction in only 22% of the methodologically acceptable studies when the outcome is reading, 7% of the studies when the outcome is language, and 9% of the studies when the outcome is math. TBE is never better than structured immersion, a special program for limited English proficient children where the children are in a self-contained classroom composed solely of English learners, but the instruction is in English at a pace they can understand. (1996: 1)

Furthermore, the comparisons of reading scores between TBE and structured immersion showed that structured immersion was superior in 83% of cases and no differences were observed in 17%.

These conclusions, published in a reputable refereed journal, and apparently based on rigorous methodological criteria, would cause any policymaker to question the merits of transitional bilingual education.

Cracks appear very quickly, however, in the facade of objective rationality that this review of the literature projects. One problem is immediately obvious: when we look more closely at the research studies that supposedly demonstrated the superiority of 'structured immersion' over 'transitional bilingual education' it turns out that *90% of these studies are interpreted by their authors as support-ing the effectiveness of bilingual and even trilingual education.*

Seven of the ten studies that Rossell and Baker claim support structured immersion over TBE were studies of French immersion programs in Canada. Typically, in these programs English-speaking students are 'immersed' in French (their second language [L2]) in kindergarten and Grade 1 and English (L1) language arts are introduced in Grade 2. The proportion of English instruction increases to about 50% by Grades 4 or 5. The closest equivalent to the program in the United States is dual language immersion, which has repeatedly demonstrated its effectiveness for both majority and minority language students (e.g. Christian *et al.,* 1997; Dolson & Lindholm, 1995; Thomas & Collier, 1997). Note that, as in the US dual language programs, Canadian French immersion programs are bilingual programs, taught by bilingual teachers, and their goal is the development of bilingualism and biliteracy.

Even at the level of face validity, it seems incongruous that Rossell and Baker use the success of the Canadian French–English bilingual programs to argue for monolingual immersion programs taught largely by monolingual teachers with the goal of developing monolingualism. This is particularly the case since two of the seven programs they cite as evidence for monolingual structured immersion were actually *trilingual* programs involving instruction in French, English, and Hebrew (Genesee & Lambert, 1983; Genesee *et al.,* 1977).

In addition to these seven French immersion program evaluations, one of the ten studies (Malherbe, 1946) was an extremely large-scale study of Afrikaans–English bilingual education in South Africa involving 19,000 students. The other two were carried out in the United States (Gersten, 1985; Peña-Hughes & Solis, 1980).

The Peña-Hughes and Solis program (labelled 'structured immersion' by Rossell and Baker, 1996) involved an hour of Spanish language arts per day and was viewed as a form of bilingual education by the director of the program (Willig, 1981–1982). I would see the genuine promotion of L1 literacy in this program as indicating a much more adequate model of bilingual education than the quick-exit transitional bilingual program to which it was being compared. Gersten's (1985) study involved an extremely small number of Asian-origin students (12 immersion students in the first cohort and nine bilingual program students, and 16 and seven in the second cohort) and hardly constitutes an adequate sample upon which to base national policy.

Malherbe's (1946) study concluded that students instructed bilingually did at least as well in each language as students instructed monolingually, despite much less time through each language. He argues strongly for the *benefits* of bilingual education (however, see Krashen, 1999b, for a critique of the design of this study).

In short, Rossell and Baker's (1996) conclusions are immediately suspect as a result of the fact that they use the documented success of bilingual and trilingual programs to argue against bilingual education. There are many other problems with their literature review that bring the entire enterprise of basing policy decisions primarily on 'methodologically acceptable' treatment control group studies into question. Some of the problems are briefly outlined below (see also Cummins, 1999a; Dicker, 1996; Escamilla, 1996; Krashen, 1996).

The criteria for deciding which studies are 'methodologically acceptable' are unclear and are applied in an arbitrary manner. Krashen (1999b), for example, points out significant design problems with Malherbe's (1946) study and, as noted above, the AIR study confounds the experimental and control treatments since both groups experienced some (unknown) forms of bilingual education.

The labels assigned to different programs are arbitrary and applied in an inconsistent manner. For example, Rossell and Baker (1996) claim to compare French immersion (structured immersion) programs in Canada with 'transitional bilingual education'. There are no transitional bilingual education programs in Canada. The El Paso Independent School District (1987) program was labeled a 'Spanish–English dual immersion' program by Baker in 1992 and a 'structured English immersion' program by Baker in 1998, and a 'submersion' program by Rossell and Baker (1996 – Appendix C, p. 72). This program involved a 'native language cognitive development' component of 90 minutes a day at Grade 1, gradually reducing to 60 minutes a day by Grade 3 and 30 minutes a day by Grade 4 (Gersten & Woodward, 1995; Krashen, 1996).

Limiting the framework of discourse to exclude bilingual programs designed to promote bilingualism and biliteracy. An additional example of arbitrary labeling is their treatment of Legaretta's (1979) kindergarten study. Originally labeled a 'structured immersion' program by Baker and de Kanter (1981), this study demonstrated the superiority of a 50% Spanish, 50% English kindergarten program over both English-only and other bilingual program options with respect to students' learning of English. Rossell and Baker (1996) list this study as showing 'no difference' between TBE and submersion (English-only) treatments. Yet the program option that was significantly better than all others was neither TBE nor submersion! The consistently positive outcomes of this kind of 'Enriched Education' program (Beykont, 1994; Cloud *et al.*, 2000) are nowhere represented in Rossell and Baker's review. By limiting the framework of discourse to 'transitional bilingual education' versus varieties of English-only programs, they have excluded the type of dual-language program option endorsed by virtually all applied linguists and also by some academics who have been highly critical of bilingual education (Glenn & LaLyre, 1991; Porter, 1990). There appears, in fact, to be an emerging consensus among advocates and opponents of 'bilingual education' that dual language and other programs that aspire to bilingualism and biliteracy are effective in developing English academic skills among both linguistic minority and majority students (Cummins, 1999b).

Rossell and Baker's (1996) reporting of French immersion data is blatantly inaccurate. In response to critiques from Kathy Escamilla (1996) and Susan Dicker (1996) regarding the fact that French immersion programs are fully bilingual in both goals and implementation, Rossell (1996) pointed out:

> In the first two years, the program is one of total immersion, and evaluations conducted at that point are considered to be evaluations of 'structured immersion'. It is really not important that, in later years, the program becomes bilingual if the evaluation is being conducted while it is still and always has been a structured immersion program. (1996: 383)

The significance of this point is that the major empirical basis of Rossell and Baker's entire argument for structured English immersion rests, according to their own admission, on the performance in French of English-background students *in the first two years* of Canadian French immersion programs. They interpret this research as follows:

> Both the middle-class and working-class English-speaking students who were immersed in French in kindergarten and grade one were almost the equal of native French-speaking students until the curriculum became bilingual in grade two, at which point their French ability declined and continued to decline as English was increased. (Rossell & Baker, 1996: 22)

Rossell and Baker (1996) seem oblivious to the fact that at the end of Grade 1 French immersion students are still at very early stages in their acquisition of French. Despite good progress in learning French (particularly receptive skills) during the initial two years of the program, they are still far from native-like in virtually all aspects of proficiency – speaking, listening, reading and writing. Most Grade 1 and 2 French immersion students are still incapable of carrying on even an elementary conversation in French without major errors and insertions of English. Similarly, it is bizarre to claim, as Baker and Rossell do without even a citation to back it up, that the French proficiency of Grade 6 immersion students is more poorly developed than that of Grade 1 students, and to attribute this to the fact that L1 instruction has been incorporated in the program.

The research data show exactly the *opposite* pattern to that claimed by Rossell and Baker (1996). Lambert and Tucker (1972), for example, report highly significant differences between Grade 1 immersion and native French-speaking students on a variety of vocabulary, grammatical and expressive skills in French, despite the fact that no differences were found in some of the sub-skills of reading such as word discrimination. By the end of Grade 4, however, (after three years of English [L1] language arts instruction), the immersion students had caught up with the French controls in vocabulary knowledge and listening comprehension, although major differences still remained in speaking ability. Similarly, in the United States, the one large-scale 'methodologically acceptable' study that investigated this issue (Ramírez, 1992) found that early-grade students in 'structured immersion' were very far from grade norms in English even after four years of English-only immersion.

In summary, to claim that two years of immersion in French in kindergarten and Grade 1 results in almost native-like proficiency in French in a context where there is virtually no French exposure in the environment or in school outside the classroom flies in the face of a massive amount of research data. This can be verified by anyone who cares to step into any of the thousands of Grade 1 French immersion classrooms across Canada.

In conclusion, Rossell and Baker's (1996) literature review is characterized by inaccurate and arbitrary labeling of programs, inconsistent application of criteria for 'methodological acceptability', and highly inaccurate interpretation of the results of early French immersion programs. Ironically, the data they review (both methodologically 'acceptable' and 'unacceptable') do have considerable relevance for policy purposes, if the interpretive paradigm is changed.[2]

The Research–Theory–Policy Paradigm: Progressive Refinement of Theory to Explain and Predict Phenomena

In most scientific disciplines, knowledge is generated not by evaluating the effects of particular treatments under strictly controlled conditions but by observing phenomena, forming hypotheses to account for the observed phenomena, testing these hypotheses against additional data, and gradually refining the hypotheses into more comprehensive theories that have broader explanatory and predictive power. Take just one example: meteorology or climatology – the understanding and prediction of weather patterns. What scientists do to generate knowledge in this discipline (and many others) is to observe phenomena (e.g. the conditions under which hurricanes appear) and build up theoretical models that attempt to predict these phenomena. With further observations they test and refine their predictive models. There is no control group, for obvious reasons, yet theory-based predictions are constantly being tested and refined.

In the same way, I would suggest that a much wider body of research data is both theoretically and policy relevant than typical reviews in the area of bilingual education have suggested. For example, case studies of particular programs or evaluations that assess student progress in relation to grade norms are potentially theoretically relevant. They become relevant for theory and policy when their outcomes are assessed in relation to the predictions derived from particular hypotheses or theoretical frameworks. The process is as follows:

(1) Establish that the phenomenon is genuine and not an artifact of measurement or observational procedures (e.g. data collection errors).
(2) Once the phenomenon has been established as genuine, ask what theoretical constructs can potentially account for the data.
(3) The third stage involves examining hypotheses in relation to additional data (e.g. designing research to test the hypotheses explicitly). As noted above, it takes only one contrary finding to refute a theoretical proposition or cause it to be modified.

(4) The final stage involves continual refinement of hypotheses and increasing integration into broader theoretical frameworks capable of more comprehensive explanations and accurate predictions.

There is nothing new in any of this. It reflects, for example, the process whereby we came to understand the movement of the planets and countless other scientific phenomena. Why then has this process not been applied in the recent policy-oriented literature reviews relating to bilingual education? Had this process been applied, a much clearer picture of the research findings and their implications would have emerged. The three literature reviews outlined above would have been able to communicate to policymakers and the general public the following answers to at least some of their central questions:

- In response to the relatively unsophisticated question, 'Does bilingual education work?' the research shows clearly that successful bilingual education programs have been implemented in countries around the world for both linguistic minority and majority students and exactly the same patterns are observed in well-implemented programs: students do not lose out in their development of academic skills in the majority language despite spending a considerable amount of instructional time learning through the minority language. This pattern is demonstrated in the vast majority of the 300 studies listed by Rossell and Baker (1996) as well as in the broader reviews of literature undertaken by August and Hakuta (1997) and Cummins and Corson (1997). These data are consistent with predictions derived from the interdependence hypothesis, which suggests that this theoretical construct can be used as a predictive tool by policymakers.

- In response to the question, 'Does bilingual education work better than English-only instructional programs?' no definitive answers can be given until the term 'bilingual education' is defined more precisely. The trend in much of the data is that programs that aspire to develop bilingualism and biliteracy (Enriched Education programs) show much better outcomes than English-only or quick-exit transitional bilingual programs that do not aspire to develop bilingualism and biliteracy. Specific hypotheses (e.g. regarding the positive effects of bilingualism on cognitive and linguistic functioning) and more comprehensive theoretical frameworks (e.g. Cummins, 1996; Lucas et al., 1990; Ovando & Collier, 1998) have been advanced that are consistent with this trend for Enriched Education programs to show highly positive outcomes. However, considerably more research is required to refine these frameworks to take account of the multiple interactions that occur among variables that contribute to bilingual students' academic success.

- In response to the question, 'Will students suffer academically if they are introduced to reading in their second language?' the research indicates that the language of initial introduction of reading is not, in itself, a determinant of academic outcomes. The linguistic mismatch hypothesis therefore has no credibility, as was evident in the 1970s (Engle, 1975; Cummins, 1979).

In response to the question, 'Will greater amounts of English instruction (time-on-task) result in greater English achievement?' the answer is simply, no. The research data overwhelmingly fails to show any positive relationship between the amount of English instruction in a program and student outcomes.

In arguing for the theoretical and policy relevance of research findings that report student outcomes in relation to grade norms without direct control group comparisons, I am not suggesting that individual studies in isolation provide any definitive information. Rather, the findings of individual evaluations or research studies represent phenomena that require explanation. Specific conditions in any particular context may have contributed to program outcomes such that similar findings are not observed in contexts where these conditions are absent. What we can state is that a particular set of findings is consistent or inconsistent with hypothesis X. However, before much credibility can be placed in the general relevance of hypothesis X, it is necessary to assess its consistency with a much wider set of findings in contexts where a variety of other unique conditions may be present. If the predictions that derive from hypothesis X are confirmed across these diverse contexts, then the credibility of hypothesis X increases significantly despite the fact that control group comparisons may not have been carried out.

Let us take a hypothetical example. Suppose that dual language or two-way bilingual immersion programs (which usually have between 50% and 90% minority language instruction in the early grades) were to show consistently the pattern that most of those that have been evaluated to this date apparently do show: by the end of elementary school, students from majority language backgrounds develop high levels of biliteracy skills at no cost to their English (L1) academic development; students from minority language backgrounds by Grade 6 show above average L1 literacy development and come close to grade norms in English (L2) academic skills. Let us suppose, hypothetically, that we have 100 such programs demonstrating this pattern from around the United States and the few programs that do not demonstrate this pattern can be shown to have been poorly implemented or not to have followed the prescribed model in some important respects.

Do these 100 programs demonstrating a consistent pattern of achievement in relation to grade norms tell us anything that is policy relevant? Rossell and Baker would say no – these studies are not 'methodologically acceptable' because control groups were not used and results are reported only in relation to grade norms.

I have argued, by contrast, that such a pattern is directly relevant to policy because it permits us to test certain theoretical predictions against the research data. Thus, the hypothetical pattern described for both minority and majority students is clearly inconsistent with the 'time-on-task' hypothesis because students instructed through the minority language for significant parts of the school day suffered no adverse effects in English language academic development.

These data would also refute the linguistic mismatch hypothesis since majority language students whose initial literacy instruction was through Spanish experienced no long-term difficulty in either English or Spanish literacy skills. This pattern of data, however, would be consistent with the interdependence hypothesis, which predicts that instruction through a minority language will result in no adverse consequences for academic development in the majority language.

In conclusion, the alternative Research–Theory–Policy paradigm conforms more closely to typical scientific procedures than the virtual elimination of theoretical considerations in the Research–Policy paradigm that has dominated the recent bilingual education policy debate. Not surprisingly, it also yields information for policy that is much more interpretable and useful. Experimental and quasi-experimental research is an appropriate approach to inquiry but by itself is limited in its ability to answer the major policy-related questions in the education of linguistic minority students, as the inadequacies of the three literature reviews analyzed above illustrate.

Notes

1. The interdependence principle has been stated as follows (Cummins, 1981: 29):
   > To the extent that instruction in Lx is effective in promoting proficiency in Lx, transfer of this proficiency to Ly will occur provided there is adequate exposure to Ly (either in school or environment) and adequate motivation to learn Ly.

2. Rossell and Baker (1996) do acknowledge the existence of the interdependence hypothesis but they distort it beyond recognition, attributing to me a 'facilitation theory' (a label which I have never used), which predicts that minority students taught through their L1 should always perform better in English than students taught exclusively through English regardless of the conditions or sociocultural context. This is a very different prediction than that which derives from the interdependence hypothesis, which is that the transfer of conceptual and linguistic knowledge across languages can compensate for the significantly reduced instructional time through the majority language (see Cummins, 1999).

References

August, D. and Hakuta, K. (1997) *Improving Schooling for Language Minority Children: A Research Agenda*. Washington, DC: National Academy Press.

Baker, K. (1992) Review of *Forked Tongue. Bilingual Basics,* Winter/Spring, pp. 6–7.

Baker, K. (1998) Structured English immersion: Breakthrough in teaching limited-English-proficient students. *Phi Delta Kappan* 80, 199–204.

Baker, K. A. and de Kanter, A. A. (1981) *Effectiveness of Bilingual Education: A Review of the Literature*. Washington, DC: US Department of Education.

Beykont, Z. F. (1994) Academic progress of a nondominant group: A longitudinal study of Puerto Ricans in New York City's late-exit bilingual programs. Unpublished doctoral dissertation, Harvard University.

Christian, D., Montone, C. L., Lindholm, K. J. and Carranza, I. (1997) *Profiles in Two-way Immersion Education*. Washington, DC: Center for Applied Linguistics and Delta Systems.

Cloud, N., Genesee, F. and Hamayan, E. (2000) *Dual Language Instruction: A Handbook for Enriched Education*. Boston: Heinle & Heinle.

Collier, V. P. and Thomas, W. P. (1989) How quickly can immigrants become proficient in school English? *Journal of Educational Issues of Language Minority Students* 5, 26–38.

Corson, D. (1993) *Language, Minority Education and Gender: Linking Social Justice and Power.* Clevedon: Multilingual Matters.

Cummins, J. (1979) Linguistic interdependence and the educational development of bilingual children. *Review of Educational Research* 49, 222–51.

Cummins, J. (1981) The role of primary language development in promoting educational success for language minority students. In California State Department of Education (ed.) *Schooling and Language Minority Students: A Theoretical Framework* (pp. 3–49). Los Angeles: National Dissemination and Assessment Center.

Cummins, J. (1996) *Negotiating Identities: Education for Empowerment in a Diverse Society.* Los Angeles: California Association for Bilingual Education.

Cummins, J. (1999a) Beyond adversarial discourse: Searching for common ground in the education of bilingual students. In I. A. Heath and C. J. Serrano (eds) *Annual Editions: Teaching English as a Second Language* (pp. 204–24). Guildford, CT: Dushkin/McGraw-Hill.

Cummins, J. (1999b) The ethics of double-think: Language rights and the bilingual education debate. *TESOL Journal* 8 (3), 13–17.

Cummins, J. and Corson, D. (eds) (1997) *Bilingual Education.* Dordrecht, The Netherlands: Kluwer Academic Publishers.

Danoff, M. N. (1978) *Evaluation of the Impact of ESEA Title VII Spanish–English Bilingual Education Programs.* Technical Report. Washington, DC: American Institutes for Research.

Dicker, S. (1996) RTE Forum: Letters from readers. *Research in the Teaching of English* 30 (1), 373–6.

Dolson, D. and Lindholm, K. (1995) World class education for children in California: A comparison of the two-way bilingual immersion and European Schools model. In T. Skutnabb-Kangas (ed.) *Multilingualism for All* (pp. 69–102). Lisse, The Netherlands: Swets & Zeitlinger.

El Paso Independent School District (1987) *Interim Report of the Five-year Bilingual Education Pilot 1986–87 School Year.* El Paso, TX: Office for Research and Evaluation.

Engle, P. (1975) The use of the vernacular language in education. *Bilingual Education* (Series No. 2). Washington, DC: Center for Applied Linguistics.

Escamilla, K. (1996) RTE Forum: Letters from readers. *Research in the Teaching of English* 30 (1), 371–3.

Fitzgerald, J. and Cummins, J. (1999) Bridging disciplines to critique a national research agenda for language-minority children's schooling. *Reading Research Quarterly* 34 (3), 378–90.

Gandara, P. (1997) *Review of Research on Instruction of Limited English Proficient Students.* Davis, CA: University of California Linguistic Minority Research Institute Education Policy Center.

Genesee, F. and Lambert, W. (1983) Trilingual education for majority-language children. *Child Development* 54, 105–14.

Genesee, F., Lambert, W. and Tucker, G. (1977) *An Experiment in Trilingual Education.* Montreal: McGill University.

Gersten, R. (1985) Structured immersion for language minority students: Results of a longitudinal evaluation. *Educational Evaluation and Policy Analysis* 7, 187–96.

Gersten, R. and Woodward, J. (1995) A longitudinal study of transitional and immersion bilingual education programs in one district. *The Elementary School Journal* 95 (3), 223–39.

Glenn, C. L. and LaLyre, I. (1991) Integrated bilingual education in the USA. In K. Jaspaert and S. Kroon (eds) *Ethnic Minority Languages and Education* (pp. 37–55). Amsterdam, The Netherlands: Swets & Zeitlinger.

Greene, J. (1998) *A Meta-analysis of the Effectiveness of Bilingual Education*. Claremont, CA: Tomas Rivera Policy Institute.

Krashen, S. D. (1996) *Under Attack: The Case against Bilingual Education*. Culver City, CA: Language Education Associates.

Krashen, S. D. (1999a) *Condemned Without a Trial: Bogus Arguments against Bilingual Education*. Portsmouth, NH: Heinemann.

Krashen, S. D. (1999b) Why Malherhe (1946) is NOT evidence against bilingual education. Manuscript submitted for publication.

Lambert, W. E. and Tucker, G. R. (1972) *Bilingual Education of Children: The St. Lambert Experiment*. Rowley, MA: Newbury House.

Legaretta, D. (1979) The effects of program models on language acquisition by Spanish speaking children. *TESOL Quarterly* 13, 521–34.

Lucas, T., Henze, R. and Donato, R. (1990) Promoting the success of Latino language-minority students: An exploratory study of six high schools. *Harvard Educational Review* 60, 315–40.

Malherbe, E. G. (1946) *The Bilingual School*. Johannesburg: Bilingual School Association.

Ovando, C. J. and Collier, V. P. (1998) *Bilingual and ESL Classrooms: Teaching in Multicultural Contexts*. Boston: McGraw-Hill.

Peña-Hughes, E. and Solis, J. (1980) ABCs. Unpublished report. McAllen, TX: McAllen Independent School District.

Porter, R. P. (1990) *Forked Tongue: The Politics of Bilingual Education*. New York: Basic Books.

Ramírez, J. D. (1992) Executive summary. *Bilingual Research Journal* 16, 1–62.

Rossell, C. H. (1996) RTE Forum: Letters from readers. *Research in the Teaching of English* 30, 376–85.

Rossell, C. H. and Baker, K. (1996) The effectiveness of bilingual education. *Research in the Teaching of English* 30, 7–74.

Rossell, C. H. and Ross, J. M. (1986) The social science evidence on bilingual education. *Journal of Law and Education* 15 (4), 385–419.

Skutnabb-Kangas, T. (1979) *Language in the Process of Cultural Assimilation and Structural Incorporation of Linguistic Minorities*. Arlington, VA: National Clearinghouse for Bilingual Education.

Thomas, W. P. and Collier, V. P. (1997) *School Effectiveness for Language-minority Students*. Washington, DC: National Clearinghouse for Bilingual Education.

Wagner, D. A. (1998) Putting second language first: Language and literacy learning in Morocco. In L. Verhoeven and A. Y. Durgunoglu (eds) *Literacy Development in a Multilingual Context: Cross-cultural Perspectives* (pp. 169–84). Mahwah, NJ: Lawrence Erlbaum Associates.

Willig, A. C. (1981/1982) The effectiveness of bilingual education: Review of a report. *NABE Journal* 6, 1–19.

Willig, A. C. (1985) A meta-analysis of selected studies on the effectiveness of bilingual education. *Review of Educational Research* 55 (3), 269–317.

Curriculum Vitac

Name: James Patrick Cummins

Rank: Full Professor

Status: Tenured

Member of Graduate Faculty: Full

Date of Preparation: May 2001

Degrees:

Ph.D	University of Alberta, Educational Psychology, 1974.
Diploma	Applied Psychology (Postgraduate one-year program, second class, honours, grade one), The National University of Ireland, 1971.
BA	Psychology, National University of Ireland (first class honours), 1970.

Employment History:

1996–present	Professor, Modern Language Centre, Department of Curriculum, Teaching and Learning, OISE/UT.
1989–1996	Professor, Modern Language Centre, Department of Curriculum, OISE.
1992–1993	Head, Modern Language Centre, Department of Curriculum, OISE
1983–1989	Associate Professor, Modern Language Centre, Department of Curriculum, OISE.
1981–1983	Assistant Professor, Modern Language Centre, Department of Curriculum, OISE.
1980–1981	Associated Instructor, Department of Curriculum, OISE.
1978–1980	Visiting Professor, Modern Language Centre, Department of Curriculum, OISE.
1976–1978	Research Associate, Centre for the Study of Mental Retardation, The University of Alberta.
1974–1976	Research Associate, Educational Research Centre, St. Patrick's College, Dublin 9.

Honours

2000 Article selected for Harvard Education Review (HER) Classics Series (12 articles published in the HER between 1931 and 2000 selected by the journal editors for the importance of their contribution to education); article selected: Cummins, J. (1986) Empowering minority students: A framework for intervention. *Harvard Educational Review* 56, 18–36.

1997 Doctorate in Humane Letters (honorary).
Bank Street College of Education, New York, May.

1992 Los Angeles County Bilingual Directors Association Award.

1990 English-Speaking Union's Duke of Edinburgh English Language Book Competition (highly commended) *The Development of Second Language Proficiency.* (B. Harley, P. Allen, J. Cummins and M. Swain (eds), Cambridge University Press, 1990).

1979 International Reading Association, Albert J. Harris Award for best paper on detection and remediation of reading disability (J. Cummins and J. P. Das, Cognitive processing and reading difficulties: A framework for research. *Alberta Journal of Educational Research* 1977, 23, 245–56).

Scholarly and Professional Activities

Editorial/Advisory Board Memberships:

Journals:
Skolio ke zoi (School and Life) (2000–)
The International Journal of Educational Policy, Research and Practice (2000–)
Glossikos Hypologistes (1999–)
Journal of Postcolonial Education (1999–)
Educational Researcher (1999–)
Asia Pacific Journal of Language in Education (1998–)
Language Learning and Technology (1997–2000)
Language, Speech, and Hearing Services in Schools (1997–2000)
Indian Journal of Applied Linguistics (1978–1980)
International Education Journal (1984–1986)
International Journal of Applied Semiotics (1997–)
International Journal of Bilingual Education and Bilingualism (1997–)
Bilingual Research Journal (1991–)
Canadian Modern Language Review (Advisory Committee 1990–)
College ESL (1990–)
Journal of Multilingual and Multicultural Development (1980–)
Language Culture and Curriculum (1987–)
NABE Journal (1980–1984)
Our Schools, Our Selves (1988–)
TESOL Quarterly (1990–1994)

Monograph Series:
OISE Monograph Series on 'Language and Literacy' (Series editors: J. Cummins, S. Lapkin and M. Swain) (1980–1990)

Newsletter:
Heritage Language Bulletin (1984–1986)

Appointments to Commissions/Boards of Directors/Adjudication/Advisory Committees:

Advisory Editorial Board, Swets & Zeitlinger Publishers, *Multilingualism and Linguistic Diversity* book series (1999–).
Advisory Committee for Centre for Education and Training project: *Providing New Media Solutions for Foreign-Trained Immigrant Professionals in the Pharmaceutical Industry* (1999–2001).
Advisory Board, Dushkin/McGraw-Hill, Annual Editions, Teaching English as a Second Language (1998–).
Panel of Judges, 1999 Outstanding Dissertation Competition, National Association for Bilingual Education, 1998.
Advisory Board, Su Lin Foundation on Global Education (1996–).
Language Advisory Board, Scholastic Publishers (1992–1994).
Multiculturalism Canada Adjudication Committee on Heritage Language Innovative Projects (1992).
Multicultural History Society of Ontario Encyclopedia Project Board of Advisors (1991–1998) (The Peoples of Canada: An Encyclopedia for the Country).

Member of the Scientific Board, University Language Teaching Resource Unit, University of Toronto (1991–).

Ontario Ministry of Education Heritage Language Program Resource Guide Advisory Committee (1989).

The Board of Directors, International Centre for Ethnic Studies, Sri Lanka (1988).

Organization for Economic Cooperation and Development (OECD) (1985–1991) (Member of Expert Team for Case Studies project, *Education and Cultural and Linguistic Pluralism*, Centre for Educational Research and Innovation, OECD).

Study/Lecture Tours:

Lecture Series on Bilingualism, Technology, and Literacy, The University of the Aegean, Rhodes, Greece, May 1997, May 1998, June 2000, March/April 2001.

Lecture Series on Language Learning and Bilingualism at the invitation of the Sophia Institute for International Communication, Sophia University, Tokyo, Japan, December 1990 (published as a monograph in *Sophia Linguistica* 29, 1991).

Study/Lecture tour of Maori bilingual programs and New Settler education programs at invitation of New Zealand Department of Education (February 1989).

Lecture Series/Consultancy to the Basque Government on development and evaluation of Basque/Spanish bilingual education programs (1986–1987).

Since 1980, I have presented, on average, 12–15 keynote/invited plenary presentations and more than 40 workshops annually to educators on topics related to language learning, bilingual education, English as a second language, multicultural education, special education, technology and education, and educational reform. In addition to North America, keynote/plenary presentations have been given in Australia, New Zealand, Hong Kong, United Kingdom, The Netherlands, Netherlands Antilles (Curacao), Aruba, Mexico, Italy, Japan, Spain (Catalonia and the Basque Country), France, Ireland, Finland, Sweden, Denmark, Norway, Greece, and Switzerland.

Publications

Career Totals	
Books Authored	13
Books Edited	8
Chapters in Books	104
Articles in Refereed Journals	88
Book Forewords/Afterwords	18
Book Reviews	19
Technical Reports	22
Other Publications (e.g. newsletter articles)	27

Academic Books Authored

Cummins, J. (2000) *Language, Power, and Pedagogy: Bilingual Children in the Crossfire*. Clevedon: Multilingual Matters.

Cummins, J. (1999) *Taftotites ypo Diapragmatefsi (Negotiating Identities)* (Greek edn). Athens: Gutenberg. (ISBN: 960-01-0797-1)

Cummins, J. (1996) *Negotiating Identities: Education for Empowerment in a Diverse Society*. Los Angeles: California Association for Bilingual Education. (ISBN: 1-889094-00-5)

Cummins, J. and Sayers, D. (1995/1997) *Brave New Schools: Challenging Cultural Illiteracy through Global Learning Networks*. New York: St. Martin's Press. (ISBN: 0-7744-0430-2)

Cummins, J. (1991) *Language Learning and Bilingualism*. Tokyo: Sophia University (Sophia Linguistica Monograph, 29). (ISSN 0287-5357)

Cummins, J. and Danesi, M. (1990) *Heritage Languages: The Development and Denial of Canada's Linguistic Resources*. Toronto: Our Schools/Our Selves and Garamond Press. (ISBN: 0-921908-05-9 (Our Schools/Our Selves); 0-920059-69-4 (Garamond))

Samuda, R. J., Kong, S. L., Cummins, J., Lewis, J. and Pascal-Leone, J. (1989) *Assessment and Placement of Minority Students*. Toronto: C. J. Hofgrefe and ISSP. (ISBN: 0-88937-024-9 (hb); 0-92113-01-3 (pb))

Cummins, J. (1989) *Empowering Minority Students*. Sacramento: California Association for Bilingual Education.

Cummins, J. and Swain, M. (1986) *Bilingualism in Education: Aspects of Theory, Research and Policy*. London: Longman. (ISBN: 0-582-55380-6)

Cummins, J. (1984) *Bilingualism and Special Education: Issues in Assessment and Pedagogy*. Clevedon: Multilingual Matters (co-published in USA by College-Hill Press). (ISBN: 0-905028-14-7 (hb); 0-905028-13-9 (pb))

Cummins, J. (1983) *Heritage Language Education: A Literature Review*. Toronto: Ministry of Education.

Cummins, J. (1981) *Effects of French Language Experience at Kindergarten Level on Academic Progress in French Immersion Programs*. Toronto: Ministry of Education.

Cummins, J. (1981) *Bilingualism and Minority Language Children*. Toronto: Ontario Institute for Studies in Education.

Edited Academic Books/Journal Special Issues

Cummins, J. and Corson, D. (eds) (1997) *Bilingual Education* (Vol. 5) *Encyclopedia of Language and Education*. Dordrecht, The Netherlands: Kluwer Academic Publishers. (ISBN: 0-7923-4806-0)

DeVillar, R. A., Faltis, C. J. and Cummins, J. (eds) (1994) *Cultural Diversity in Schools: From Rhetoric to Practice*. Albany: SUNY Press. (ISBN: 0-7914-1673-9 (hb); 0-7914-1674-7 (pbk))

Cummins, J. (ed.) (1994) *Multilingual/Multicultural Education*. Special issue of *English Quarterly* 26 (3). Montreal: Canadian Council of Teachers of English and Language Arts.

Cummins, J. (ed.) (1991) *Heritage Languages*. Special issue of *Canadian Modern Language Review* 47 (4).

Harley, B., Allen, P., Cummins, J. and Swain, M. (eds) (1990) *The Development of Second Language Proficiency*. Cambridge: Cambridge University Press. (ISBN: 0-521-38410-9 (hb); 0-521-38795-7 (pb))

Skutnabb-Kangas, T. and Cummins, J. (eds) (1988) *Minority Education: From Shame to Struggle*. Clevedon: Multilingual Matters.

Cummins, J. (ed.) (1987) *Heritage Languages in Canada: Research Perspectives*. Ottawa: Multiculturalism Canada. French version published as *Les Langues Ancestrales au Canada: Perspectives de Recherche*.

Cummins, J. (ed.) (1983) *Heritage Language Education: Issues and Directions*. Ottawa: Multiculturalism Canada. (ISBN: 0-662-12426-X)

Chapters in Books

Cummins, J. (in press) BICS and CALP: Origins and rationale for the distinction. In C. B. Paulston and G. R. Tucker (eds) *Sociolinguistics: The Essential Readings*. London: Blackwell.

Cummins, J. (in press) Rights and responsibilities of educators of bilingual–bicultural children. In L. D. Soto (ed.) *Making a Difference in the Lives of Bilingual–Bicultural Learners*. New York: Peter Lang Publishers.

Cummins, J. (2001) Assessment options for bilingual learners. In J. V. Tinajero and S. Hurley (eds) *Literacy Aassessment of Bilingual Learners* (pp. 115–29). Boston: Allyn & Bacon.

Cummins, J. (2000) BICS and CALP. In M. Byram (ed.) *Encyclopedia of Language Teaching and Learning* (pp. 76–9). London: Routledge.

Cummins, J. (2000) 'This place nurtures my spirit': Creating contexts of empowerment in linguistically-diverse schools. In R. Phillipson (ed.) *Rights to Language: Equity, Power and Education* (pp. 249–58). Mawah, NJ: Lawrence Erlbaum Associates.

Cummins, J. (2000) Putting language proficiency in its place: Responding to critiques of the conversational/academic language distinction. In J. Cenoz and U. Jessner (eds) *English in Europe: The Acquisition of a Third Language* (pp. 54–83). Clevedon: Multilingual Matters.

Cummins, J. and Sayers, D. (2000) Families and communities learning together: Becoming literate, confronting prejudice. In Z. F. Beykont (ed.) *Lifting Every Voice: Pedagogy and Politics of Bilingualism* (pp. 113–37). Cambridge: Harvard Education Publishing Group.

Cummins, J. (1999) Biliteracy, empowerment, and transformative pedagogy. In J. V. Tinajero and R. A. DeVillar (eds) *The Power of Two Languages: 2000* (pp. 9–19). New York: McGraw-Hill.

Cummins, J. (1999) Beyond adversarial discourse: Searching for common ground in the education of bilingual students. In C. J. Ovando and P. McLaren (eds) *The Politics of Multiculturalism and Bilingual Education: Students and Teachers caught in the Crossfire* (pp. 126–47). Boston: McGraw-Hill.

Cummins, J. (1999) Beyond adversarial discourse: Searching for common ground in the education of bilingual students. In I. A. Heath and C. J. Serrano (eds) *Annual Editions: Teaching English as a Second Language 99/00* (pp. 204–24). Guildford, CT: Dushkin/McGraw-Hill.

Cummins, J. (1998) Semilingualism. In J. L. Mey (ed.) *Concise Encyclopedia of Pragmatics* (pp. 3812–14). Oxford: Elsevier Science.

Cummins, J. (1998) Language issues and educational change. In A. Hargreaves, A. Lieberman, M. Fullan and D. Hopkins (eds) *International Handbook of Educational Change* (pp. 440–59). Dordrecht, The Netherlands: Kluwer Academic Publishers.

Brown, K., Cummins, J., Figueroa, E. and Sayers, D. (1998) Global learning networks: Gaining perspective on our lives with distance. In E. Lee, D. Menkart and M. Okazawa-Rey (eds) *Beyond Heroes and Holidays: A Practical Guide to K-12 Anti-racist, Multicultural Education and Staff Development* (pp. 334–54). Washington, DC: Network of Educators on the Americas.

Cummins, J. (1998) Bilingual education and English immersion: The Ramírez report in theoretical perspective. In I. A. Heath and C. J. Serrano (eds) *Annual Editions: Teaching English as a Second Language 98/99* (pp. 231–6). Guildford, CT: Dushkin/McGraw-Hill.

Cummins, J. (1998) The teaching of international languages. In J. Edwards (ed.) *Language in Canada*. Cambridge: Cambridge University Press.

Cummins, J. (1997) Introduction. In J. Cummins and D. Corson (eds) *Bilingual Education*. Vol. 5: *International Encyclopedia of Language and Education* (pp. xi–xiv). Dordrecht: Kluwer Academic Publishers.

Cummins, J. (1997) Educational attainment of minority students: A framework for intervention based on the constructs of identity and empowerment. In A. Sjogren (ed.) *Language and Environment* (pp. 89–101). Stockholm: Mangkulturellt Centrum.

Cummins, J. (1997) Echoes from the past: Stepping stones towards a personal critical literacy. In C. P. Casanave and S. R. Schecter (eds) *On Becoming a Language Educator* (pp. 57–68). Lawrence Erlbaum Associates.

Cummins, J. (1996) L'education multilingue aux Etats-Unis d'Amerique et au Canada. In P. H. Nelde (ed.) *Contact Linguistics: An International Handbook of Contemporary Research* (Vol. 1) (pp. 473–82). Berlin: Walter de Gruyter.

Cummins, J. (1996) L'educazione bilingue: ricerca ed elaborazione teoreica. In P. E. Balboni (ed.) *Educazione Bilingue* (pp. 11–22). Perugia: Edizioni Guerra.

Cummins, J. (1996) Empowering minority students: A framework for intervention. In T. Beauboeuf-Lafontant and D. Smith Augustine (eds) *Facing Racism in Education* (2nd edn). Reprint Series No. 28, *Harvard Educational Review* (pp. 349–68). Cambridge, MA: Harvard Educational Review.

Cummins, J. (1995) Canadian French immersion programs: A comparison with Swedish immersion programs in Finland. In M. Buss and C. Lauren (eds) *Language Immersion: Teaching and Second Language Acquisition. From Canada to Europe* (pp. 7–20). Tutkimuksia No. 192. Vaasa: Univesity of Vaasa.

Cummins, J. (1995) Power and pedagogy in the education of language minority students. In J. Frederickson (ed.) *Reclaiming our Voices*. Ontario, CA: California Association for Bilingual Education.

Cummins, J. (1995) The European schools model in relation to French immersion programs in Canada. In T. Skutnabb-Kangas (ed.) *Multilingualism for All* (pp. 159–68). Amsterdam/Lisse: Swets & Zeitlinger.

Cummins, J. (1995) Discursive power in educational policy and practice for culturally-diverse students. In D. Corson (ed.) *Discourse and Power in Educational Organizations* (pp. 191–209). Cresskill, NJ: Hampton Press.

Cummins, J. (1995) Underachievement among minority students. In D. B. Durkin (ed.) *Language Issues: Readings for Teachers*. New York: Longman.

Cummins, J. (1995) Heritage language teaching in Canadian schools. In O. Garcia and C. Baker (eds) *Policy and Practices in Bilingual Education: A Reader*. Clevedon: Multilingual Matters.

Cummins, J. (1994) Primary language instruction and the education of language minority students. In C. Leyba (ed.) *Schooling and Language Minority Students* (2nd edn). Los Angeles: Evaluation, Dissemination and Assessment Center.

Cummins, J. (1994) Forging identities in the preschool: Competing discourses and their relationship to research. In K. de Bot, K. Jaspaert and S. Kroon (eds) *Maintenance and Loss of Minority Languages*. Amsterdam/Lisse: Swets & Zeitlinger.

Cummins, J. (1994) The discourse of disinformation: The debate on bilingual education and language rights in the United States. In R. Phillipson and T. Skutnabb-Kangas (eds) *Linguistic Human Rights*. Berlin: Mouton de Gruyter.

Cummins, J. (1994) Semilingualism. In R. R. Asher (ed.) *International Encyclopedia of Language and Linguistics* (2nd edn) (pp. 3812–4). Oxford: Elsevier Science.

Cummins, J. (1994) From coercion to collaborative relations of power in the teaching of literacy. In B. M. Ferdman, R-M. Weber and A. Ramírez (eds) *Literacy across Languages and Cultures* (pp. 295–331). Albany: SUNY Press.

Cummins, J. (1994) The acquisition of English as a second language. In R. Pritchard and K. Spangenberg-Urbschat (eds) *Kids Come in all Languages* (pp. 36–62). Newark, DE: International Reading Association.

Cummins, J. (1994) Heritage language learning and teaching. In J. W. Berry and J. A. Laponce (eds) *Ethnicity and Culture in Canada: The Research Landscape* (pp. 435–56). Toronto: University of Toronto Press.

Cummins, J. (1994) The socioacademic achievement model in the context of coercive and collaborative relations of power. In R. A. DeVillar, C. J. Faltis and J. Cummins (eds) *Cultural Diversity in Schools: From Rhetoric to Practice* (pp. 363–92). Albany: SUNY Press.

Cummins, J. (1994) Knowledge, power and identity in teaching English as a second language. In F. Genesee (ed.) *Educating Second Language Children: The Whole Child, the Whole Curriculum, the Whole Community* (pp. 33–58). Cambridge: Cambridge University Press.

Cummins, J. (1993) Bilingualism and second language learning. In W. Grabe (ed.) *Annual Review of Applied Linguistics* (pp. 51–70). Cambridge: Cambridge University Press.

Cummins, J. (1992) Bilingual education. In W. Bright (ed.) *International Encyclopedia of Linguistics*. New York: Oxford University Press.

Cummins, J. (1992) Empowerment through biliteracy. In J. V. Tinajero and A. F. Ada (eds) *The Power of Two Languages: Literacy and Biliteracy for Spanish-speaking Students* (pp. 1–17). New York: McGraw-Hill.

Allen, P., Cummins, J., Harley, B. and Swain, M. (1992) Restoring the balance: A response to Hammerly. In S. Rehorick and V. Edwards (eds) *French Immersion: Process, Product & Perspectives* (pp. 314–21). Welland, Ontario: The Canadian Modern Language Review.

Cummins, J. (1992) The empowerment of Indian students. In J. Reyhner (ed.) *Teaching American Indian Students*. The University of Oklahoma Press.

Cummins, J. (1992) Language proficiency, bilingualism, and academic achievement. In P. A. Richard-Amato and M. A. Snow (eds) *The Multicultural Classroom: Readings for Content-area Teachers* (pp. 16–26). New York: Longman.

Cummins, J. (1991) Interdependence of first- and second-language proficiency in bilingual children. In E. Bialystok (ed.) *Language Processing in Bilingual Children* (pp. 70–89). Cambridge: Cambridge University Press.

Bialystok, E. and Cummins, J. (1991) Language, cognition, and education of bilingual children. In E. Bialystok (ed.) *Language Processing in Bilingual Children* (pp. 222–32). Cambridge: Cambridge University Press.

Cummins, J. (1991) Empowering minority students: A framework for intervention. In M. Minami and B. P. Kennedy (eds) *Language Issues in Literacy and Bilingual/ Multicultural Education* (pp. 372–90). Reprint Series No. 22, Harvard Educational Review. Cambridge, MA: Harvard Educational Review.

Cummins, J. (1991) The politics of paranoia: Reflections on the bilingual education debate. In O. Garcia (ed.) *Bilingual Education. Focusschrift in Honor of Joshua A. Fishman on the Occasion of his 65th Birthday* (Vol. I) (pp. 183–99). Amsterdam/ Phildadelphia: John Benjamins Publishing Co.

Cummins, J. (1991) Language development and academic learning. In L. Malavé and G. Duquette (eds) *Language, Culture and Cognition* (pp. 161–75). Clevedon: Multilingual Matters.

Cummins, J. and Sayers, D. (1990) Education 2001: Learning networks and educational reform. In C. J. Faltis and R. A. DeVillar (eds) *Language Minority Students and Computers* (pp. 1–30). New York: The Haworth Press.

Harley, B., Cummins, J., Swain, M. and Allen, P. (1990) The nature of language proficiency. In B. Harley, P. Allen, J. Cummins and M. Swain (eds) *The Development of Second Language Proficiency* (pp. 7–25). Cambridge: Cambridge University Press.

Allen, P., Swain, M., Harley, B. and Cummins, J. (1990) Aspects of classroom treatment: Toward a more comprehensive view of second language education. In B. Harley, P. Allen, J. Cummins and M. Swain (eds) *The Development of Second Language Proficiency* (pp. 57–81). Cambridge: Cambridge University Press.

Cummins, J., Harley, B., Swain, M. and Allen, P. (1990) Social and individual factors in the development of bilingual proficiency. In B. Harley, P. Allen, J. Cummins and M. Swain (eds) *The Development of Second Language Proficiency* (pp. 119–33). Cambridge: Cambridge University Press.

Cummins, J. (1990) Multilingual/multicultural education: Evaluation of underlying theoretical constructs and consequences for curriculum development. In P. Vedder (ed.) *Fundamental Studies in Educational Research* (pp. 141–74). Amsterdam: Swets & Zeitlinger.

Cummins, J. (1990) Heritage language teaching and the ESL student: Fact and friction. In J. Esling (ed.) *Multicultural Education and Policy: ESL in the 1990s* (pp. 3–17). Toronto: OISE Press.

Cummins, J. (1990) Empowering minority students: A framework for intervention. In N. M. Hidalgo, C. L. McDowell and E. V. Siddle (eds) *Facing Racism in Education* (pp. 50–68). Reprint Series No. 21, *Harvard Educational Review*. Cambridge, MA: Harvard Educational Review.

Cummins, J. (1989) The sanitized curriculum: Educational disempowerment in a nation at risk. In D. M. Johnson and D. H. Roen (eds) *Richness in Writing: Empowering ESL Students* (pp. 19–38). New York: Longman.

Cummins, J. (1989) Bilingual special education. In T. Husen and T. N. Postlethwaite (eds) *The International Encyclopedia of Education: Research and Studies* (Supplementary Vol. One) (pp. 104–7). Oxford: Pergamon Press.

Cummins, J. (1989) Institutionalized racism and assessment of minority children: A comparison of policies and programs in the United States and Canada. In R. J. Samuda, S. L. Kong, J. Cummins, J. Lewis and J. Pascal-Leone (eds) *Assessment and Placement of Minority Students*. Toronto: C. J. Hofgrefe/ISSP.

Cummins, J. (1989) Heritage language acquisition and bilingualism: Principles and pedagogy. In G. C. Arthur, V. Cecchetto and M. Danesi (eds) *Current Issues in Second Language Research and Methodology: Applications to Italian as a Second Language* (pp. 22–30). Ottawa: Canadian Society for Italian Studies.

Cummins, J. (1988) Empowering Indian students: What teachers and parents can do. In J. Reyhner (ed.) *Teaching the Indian Child* (2nd edn) (pp. 301–7). Billings, MT: Eastern Montana College.

Cummins, J. (1988) From multicultural to anti-racist education: An analysis of programs and policies in Ontario. In T. Skutnabb-Kangas and J. Cummins (eds) *Minority Education: From Shame to Struggle* (pp. 127–57). Clevedon: Multilingual Matters.

Cummins, J. (1988) Mother tongue maintenance in Canada: From politics to pedagogy. In V. S. Lee (ed.) *Language Teaching and Learning: Canada and Italy* (pp. 75–86). Rome: Canadian Academic Centre in Italy.

Cummins, J. (1988) Language planning in education in multilingual settings. In V. Bickley (ed.) *Languages in Education in a Bi-lingual or Multi-lingual Setting* (pp. 262–74). Hong Kong: Institute of Language in Education.

Cummins, J. (1988) Language proficiency, bilingualism and academic achievement. In P. Richard-Amato (ed.) *Making it Happen: Interaction in the Second Language Classroom: From Theory to Practice* (pp. 382–95). New York: Longman.

Cummins, J. and Nichols McNeeley, S. (1987) Language development, academic learning and empowering minority students. In S. H. Fradd and W. J. Tikunoff (eds) *Bilingual Education and Bilingual Special Education: A Guide for Administrators* (pp. 75–94). San Diego: College-Hill Press.

Cummins, J. (1987) Immersion programs: Current issues and future directions. In L. L. Stewin and S. J. McCann (eds) *Contemporary Educational Issues: The Canadian Mosaic* (pp. 192–206). Toronto: Copp Clark.

Cummins, J. (1987) Theory and policy in bilingual education. In Centre for Educational Research and Innovation (ed.) *Multicultural Education* (pp. 303–30). Paris: OECD.

Cummins, J. (1987) Educational linguistics and its sociological context in heritage language research. In J. Cummins (ed.) *Heritage Languages in Canada: Research Perspectives* (pp. 45–62). Ottawa: Multiculturalism Canada.

Cummins, J. (1987) Bilingualism, language proficiency and metalinguistic development. In P. Homel, M. Palif and D. Aaronson (eds) *Childhood Bilingualism: Aspects of Linguistic, Cognitive, and Social Development* (pp. 57–74). Hillsdale, NJ: Lawrence Erlbaum Associates.

Cummins, J. (1987) Second language acquisition within bilingual education programs. In L. Beebe (ed.) *Second Language Acquisition* (pp. 145–66). Rowley, MA: Newbury House.

Cummins, J. (1986) Psychological assessment of minority students: Out of context, out of focus, out of control. In A. C. Willig and H. F. Greenberg (eds) *Bilingualism and Learning Disabilities: Policy and Practice for Teachers and Administrators*. New York: American Library Publishing Co.

Cummins, J. (1986) Theory and policy in bilingual education. In Institute for Ethnic Studies (ed.) *Education in Multicultural Societies: Treatises and Documents* (pp. 281–308) Ljubljana: Institute for Ethnic Studies.

Cummins, J. and Bountrogianni, M. (1985) Assessment of minority children. In TV Ontario (ed.) *Educating the Special Child* (pp. 40–3). Toronto: TV Ontario.

Cummins, J. and Genesee, F. (1985) Bilingual education programmes in Wales and Canada. In C. J. Dodson (ed.) *Bilingual Education: Evaluation, Assessment and Methodology* (pp. 37–50). Cardiff: University of Wales Press.

Cummins, J. (1985) The construct of language proficiency in bilingual education. In J. E. Alatis and J. J. Staczek (eds) *Perspectives on Bilingualism and Bilingual Education* (pp. 209–31). Washington, DC: Georgetown University Press. Reprinted in A. R. Contreras, C. Iacon and J. G. Valtierra (eds) *Bilingual Education*. Phi Delta Kappa Hot Topics Series (pp. 105–28). Bloomington, IN: Phi Delta Kappa, 1988.

Cummins, J. (1985) Language and Canadian multiculturalism: Research and politics. In M. Lupul (ed.) *OSVITA: Ukrainian Bilingual Education* (pp. 77–92). Edmonton: University of Alberta.

Cummins, J. (1985) Future directions for Ukrainian-language education. In M. Lupul (ed.) *OSVITA: Ukrainian Bilingual Education* (pp. 261–8). Edmonton: University of Alberta.

Cummins, J. and Troper, H. (1985) Multiculturalism and language policy in Canada. In J. Cobarrubias and J-D. Gendron (eds) *Language Policy, Language Rights and Legislation in Canada* (pp. 16–27). Quebec: CIRB Université Laval.

Cummins, J. (1984) Linguistic minorities and multicultural policy in Canada. In J. R. Edwards (ed.) *Linguistic Minorities, Policies and Pluralism* (pp. 81–106). London: Academic Press.

Cummins, J. (1984) Implications of bilingual proficiency for the education of minority language students. In P. Allen and M. Swain (eds) *Language Issues and Education Policies* (pp. 21–34). Oxford: Pergamon Press. ELT Documents 119.

Cummins, J. (1984) Bilingualism and cognitive functioning. In S. Shapson and V. D'Oyley (eds) *Bilingual and Multicultural Education: Canadian Perspectives* (pp. 55–70). Clevedon: Multilingual Matters.

Cummins, J. (1984) The minority language child. In S. Shapson and V. D'Oyley (eds) *Bilingual and Multicultural Education: Canadian Perspectives* (pp. 71–92). Clevedon: Multilingual Matters.

Cummins, J. (1984) Minority students and learning difficulties: Issues in assessment and placement. In M. Paradis and Y. Lebrun (eds) *Early Bilingualism and Child Development* (pp. 47–68). Lisse: Swets & Zeitlinger.

Cummins, J. (1984) Wanted: A theoretical framework for relating language proficiency to academic achievement among bilingual students. In C. Rivera (ed.) *Language Proficiency and Academic Achievement* (pp. 2–19). Clevedon: Multilingual Matters.

Cummins, J. (1984) Language proficiency and academic achievement revisited: A response. In C. Rivera (ed.) *Language Proficiency and Academic Achievement* (pp. 71–6). Clevedon: Multilingual Matters.

Cummins, J., Swain, M., Nakajima, K., Handscombe, J., Green, D. and Tran, C. (1984) Linguistic interdependence among Japanese and Vietnamese immigrant students. In C. Rivera (ed.) *Communicative Competence Approaches to Language Proficiency Assessment: Research and Application* (pp. 60–81). Clevedon: Multilingual Matters.

Cummins, J. (1984) Heritage language and Canadian school programs. In J. R. Mallea and J. C. Young (eds) *Cultural Diversity and Schooling in Canada: Issues and Innovation* (pp. 477–500). Carleton Library Series, Oxford University Press.

Lapkin, S. and Cummins, J. (1983) Canadian French immersion education: Current administrative arrangements and instructional practices. In California State Department of Education (ed.) *Studies on Immersion Education: A Collection for U.S. Educators* (pp. 58–86). Sacramento: California State Department of Education.

Cummins, J. (1983) Understanding language acquisition and bilingualism. In *Another Window on the World.* Cardiff: Harlech Television.

Cummins, J. (1983) Psychological assessment of minority language students. In R. J. Samuda, J. W. Berry and M. Laferriere (eds) *Multicultural Education in Canada* (pp. 238–49). Toronto: Allyn and Bacon.

Cummins, J. (1983) Language proficiency and academic achievement. In J. W. Oller (ed.) *Issues in Language Testing Research* (pp. 108–30). Rowley, MA: Newbury House.

Cummins, J. (1983) Mother tongue development as educational enrichment: Research findings. In J. Cummins (ed.) *Heritage Language Education: Issues and Directions* (pp. 40–3). Ottawa: Multiculturalism Canada.

Cummins, J. (1983) Functional language proficiency in context: Classroom participation as an interactive process. In W. Tikunoff (ed.) *Significant Bilingual Instructional Features Study: Compatibility of the SBIF Features with other Research on Instruction for LEP Students* (pp. 109–31). San Francisco: Far West Laboratory.

Swain, M. and Cummins, J. (1982) Bilingualism, cognitive functioning and education. In V. Kinsella (ed.) *Surveys 1: Eight State-of-the-art Articles on Key Areas in Language Teaching* (pp. 23–37). Cambridge: Cambridge University Press.

Cummins, J. and Das, J. P. (1982) Language processing and reading disability. In K. D. Gadow and I. Bialer (eds) *Advances in Learning and Behavioral Disabilities* (pp. 3–21). Greenwich, CT: JAI Press.

Cummins, J. (1982) Die Schwellenniveau und die Interdependenz-Hypothese: Erklarungen zum Erfolg Zweispracher Erzichung. In J. Swift (ed.) *Bilinguale und Multikulturelle Erziehung* (pp. 34–43). Wurzberg: Konigshausen and Neumann.

Cummins, J. (1981) The role of primary language development in promoting educational success for language minority students. In California State Department of Education (ed.) *Schooling and Language Minority Students: A Theoretical Framework* (pp. 3–49). Los Angeles: National Dissemination and Assessment Center.

Cummins, J. and Abdollel, A. (1981) Bilingualism and educational adjustment of immigrant children: A case study of Lebanese families in Ontario. In L. Eitinger and D. Schwarz (eds) *Strangers in the World: Problems of Dislocation, Migration and Refugee Status* (pp. 147–60). Berne: Hans Huber.

Cummins, J. (1981) Biliteracy, language proficiency, and educational programs. In J. R. Edwards (ed.) *The Social Psychology of Reading* (pp. 131–46). Silver Spring: Institute of Modern Languages.

Cummins, J. (1981) North American research and experience in the education of minority language children. In Council of Europe (ed.) *The Education of Migrant Workers' Children.* Stuttgart: Hogrefe International Inc.

Cummins, J. (1980) The construct of language proficiency in bilingual education. In J. E. Alatis (ed.) *Georgetown University Round Table on Languages and Linguistics.* Washington, DC: Georgetown University Press.

Stern, H. H. and Cummins, J. (1980) Language teaching/learning research: A Canadian perspective on status and directions. In J. Phillips (ed.) *Action for the '80s: A Political, Professional and Public Program for Foreign Language Education* (pp. 195–248). ACTFL Foreign Language Education Series.

Cummins, J. (1980) Issues in psychological assessment of minority language children. In R. F. Jarman and J. P. Das (eds) *Issues in Developmental Disabilities* (pp. 50–70). Wisconsin: University Microfilms International.

Cummins, J. (1979) Language functions and cognitive processing. In J. P. Das, J. Kirby and R. F. Jarman (eds) *Simultaneous and Successive Processing* (pp. 175–85). New York: Academic Press.

Cummins, J. (1978) Metalinguistic development of children in bilingual education programs: Data from Irish and Canadian (Ukrainian–English) programs. In M. Paradis (ed.) *Aspects of Bilingualism* (pp. 127–38). Columbia, SC: Hornbeam Press.

Cummins, J. (1977) Psycholinguistic evidence. In *Bilingual Education: Current Perspectives*. Vol. 4: *Education* (pp. 78–89). Arlington, VA: Center for Applied Linguistics.

Cummins, J. (1977) A comparison of reading skills in Irish and English medium schools. In V. Greaney (ed.) *Studies in Reading* (pp. 128–34). Dublin: Educational Co. of Ireland. Reprinted in *Oideas* 1982, 26, 21–6.

Cummins, J. and Gulutsan, M. (1974) Some effects of bilingualism on cognitive functioning. In S. T. Carey (ed.) *Bilingualism and Education* (pp. 129–36). Edmonton: University of Alberta Press.

Articles in Refereed Journals

Cummins, J. (in press) Negotiating intercultural identities in the multilingual classroom. *CATESOL Journal*.

Cummins, J. (2001) Instructional conditions for trilingual development. *International Journal of Bilingual Education and Bilingualism* 4 (1), 61–75.

Cummins, J. (2001) Tosprogede borns modersmal: Hvad er vigtigt I deres uddannelse? (Bilingual children's mother tongue: Why is it important for education?). *Sprogforum* (February) No. 19 (Denmark).

Cummins, J. (2000) Academic language learning, transformative pedagogy and information technology: Towards a critical balance. *TESOL Quarterly* 34 (3), 537–48.

Cummins, J. (1999) The ethics of doublethink: Language rights and the bilingual education debate. *TESOL Journal* 8 (3), 13–17.

Cummins, J. (1999) Alternative paradigms in bilingual education research: Does theory have a place? *Educational Researcher* 28 (7), 26–32.

Fitzgerald, J. and Cummins, J. (1999) Bridging disciplines to critique a national research agenda for language-minority children's schooling. *Reading Research Quarterly* 34 (3), 378–90.

Cummins, J. (1998) Using text as input for computer-supported language learning. *Computer-assisted English Language Learning Journal* 9 (1), 3–10.

Cummins, J. (1998) e-Lective language learning: Design of a computer-assisted text-based ESL/EFL learning system. *TESOL Journal* (Spring) 18–21.

Cummins, J. (1998) Review essay: Bilingual education in the United States: Power, pedagogy, and possibility. *The Review of Education/Pedagogy/Cultural Studies* 20 (3), 255–70.

Cummins, J. (1997) Cultural and linguistic diversity in education: A mainstream issue? *Educational Review* 49 (2), 99–107.

Cummins, J. (1997) Minority status and schooling in Canada. *Anthropology and Education Quarterly* 28 (3), 411–30.

Cummins, J. (1996) Negotiating identities in the classroom and society. *Multicultural Teaching* 15 (1), 47–50.

Cummins, J. and Sayers, D. (Spring, 1995) Multicultural education and technology: Promise and pitfalls. *Multicultural Education* 4–11.

Cummins, J. (1994) Lies we live by: National identity and social justice. *International Journal of the Sociology of Language* 110, 145–55.

Cummins, J. (1994) Introduction. *English Quarterly* 26 (3), 3–4.

Cummins, J. and Cameron, L. (1994) The ESL student IS the mainstream: The marginalization of diversity in current Canadian educational debates. *English Quarterly* 26 (3), 30–3.

Cummins, J. (1993) Ideological assumptions in the teaching of English as a Second Language. *Revue de l'ACLA/Journal of the CAAL* 15 (2), 37–50.

Cummins, J. (1992) L'educazione bilingue: ricerca e elaborazione teorica. *Il Quadrante Scolastico* (Dicembre) 55, 54–69.

Cummins, J. (1992) Bilingual education and English immersion: The Ramírez report in theoretical perspective. *Bilingual Research Journal* 16, 91–104.

Cummins, J. (1992) Heritage language teaching in Canadian schools. *Journal of Curriculum Studies* 24, 281–6.

Cummins, J. (1991) The development of bilingual proficiency from home to school: A longitudinal study of Portuguese-speaking children. *Journal of Education* 173, 85–98.

Cummins, J. (1991) Conversational and academic language proficiency in bilingual contexts. *AILA Review* 8, 75–89.

Cummins, J. (1991) Introduction. *The Canadian Modern Language Review* 47, 601–5.

Cummins, J. (1991) Forked tongue: The politics of bilingual education: A critique. *The Canadian Modern Language Review* 47, 786–93.

Cummins, J. (1991) Preventing pedagogically-induced learning difficulties among indigenous students. *Journal of Navajo Education* 8 (3), 3–9.

Cummins, J. and Sayers, D. (1990) Education 2001: Learning networks and educational reform. *Computers in the Schools* 7, 1–29.

Cummins, J. (1990) Dalla citta al villaggio globale: Il microcomputer come catalizzatore per un apprendimento collaborativo e lo scambio culturale. *Le Lingue nell'Educazione* 2, 2–9. (Translation of *Language, Culture, and Curriculum* 1988 article.)

Cummins, J. (1990) Empowering minority students: An analysis of the bilingual education debate. *Estudios Fronterizos* 8, 15–35.

Cummins, J. (1990) When a learner attempts to become literate in a second language, what is he or she attempting? *TESL Talk* 20 (1), 7–10.

Allen, P, Cummins, J, Harley, B and Swain, M (1989) Restoring the balance: A response to Hammerly. *Canadian Modern Language Review* 45 (4), 770–6.

Cummins, J. (1989) A theoretical framework for bilingual special education. *Exceptional Children* 56, 111–9.

Cummins, J. (1989) Language and literacy acquisition in bilingual contexts. *Journal of Multilingual and Multicultural Education* 10, 17–31.

Cummins, J. (1989) De la ciudad aislada a la aldea global: el microordenador como catalizador del aprendizaje cooperativo y del intercambio cultural. *Communicacion, Lenguaje y Educacion* 1, 57–70. (Translation of *Language, Culture and Curriculum* 1988 article).

Cummins, J. (1988) Teachers are not miracle workers: Lloyd Dunn's call for Hispanic activism. *Hispanic Journal of Behavioral Sciences* 10, 263–72.

Cummins, J. (1988) Lingue materne nella scuola elementare: recerche e esperienze canadesi. *Scuola e Lingue Moderne* 26, 249–54.

Cummins, J. (1988) From the inner city to the global village: The microcomputer as a catalyst for collaborative learning and cultural interchange. *Language, Culture and Curriculum* 1, 1–14.

Cummins, J. (1988) The role and use of educational theory in formulating language policy. *TESL Canada Journal* 5, 11–19.

Cummins, J. (1987) Psychological assessment in multicultural school systems. *Canadian Journal for Exceptional Children* 3, 115–7.

Cummins, J. (1986) Empowering minority students: A framework for intervention. *Harvard Educational Review* 56, 18–36.

Cummins, J. (1986) Bilingual education and anti-racist education. *Interracial Books for Children Bulletin* 17, 9–12.

Cummins, J. (1986) Psychological assessment of minority students: Out of context, out of focus, out of control. *Journal of Reading, Writing and Learning Disabilities International* 2, 9–20.

Cummins, J. (1986) Cultures in contact: Using classroom microcomputers for cultural interchange and reinforcement. *TESL Canada Journal* 3, 13–31.

Cummins, J. and Glazer, N. (1985) Viewpoints on bilingual education. *Equity and Choice* 3, 47–52.

Carey, S. and Cummins, J. (1984) Communication skills in immersion programs. *Alberta Journal of Educational Research* 30, 270–83.

Cummins, J. (1984) Heritage language education: fact and friction. *Orbit* 15, 3–6.

Cummins, J. (1983) Interdependencia linguistica y desarrolo educativo de los ninos bilingues. *Infancia y Aprendizaje* 21, 37–61. (Translation of *Review of Educational Research*, 1979, article).

Cummins, J. (1983) Bilingualism and special education: Program and pedagogical issues. *Learning Disability Quarterly* 6, 373–86.

Cummins, J. (1983) Language proficiency, biliteracy and French immersion. *Canadian Journal of Education* 8, 117–38.

Carey, S. and Cummins, J. (1983) Achievement, behavioral correlates and teachers' perceptions of Francophone and Anglophone immersion students. *Alberta Journal of Educational Research* 8, 117–38.

Cummins, J. and Swain, M. (1983) Analysis by rhetoric: Reading the text or the reader's own projections? A reply to Edelsky *et al. Applied Linguistics* 4, 23–41.

Cummins, J. (1982) Through the looking glass: What really happens in an immersion classroom? *Interchange* 13, 40–4.

Cummins, J. (1981) Four misconceptions about language proficiency in bilingual education. *NABE Journal* 5, 31-45.

Cummins, J. (1981) Age on arrival and immigrant second language learning in Canada. A reassessment. *Applied Linguistics* 2, 132–49.

Beaudoin, M., Cummins, J., Dunlop, H., Genesee, F. and Obadia, A. (1981) Bilingual education: A comparison of Welsh and Canadian experiences. *Canadian Modern Language Review* 37, 498–509.

Cummins, J. (1981) Empirical and theoretical underpinnings of bilingual education. *Journal of Education* 163, 16–29.

Cummins, J. (1981) Educational success for Canadian minority language children: The role of mother tongue development. *Canadian Journal of Italian Studies* 4, 299–315.

Cummins, J. and Das, J. P. (1981) Cognitive processing, academic achievement, and WISC-R performance in EMR children. *Journal of Consulting and Clinical Psychology* 48, 777–9.

Cummins, J. (1980) Ancestral language maintenance: The roles of home and school. *Multiculturalism* 4, 23–7.

Cummins, J. (1980) The entry and exit fallacy in bilingual education. *NABE Journal* 4, 25–60.

Cummins, J. (1980) The cross-lingual dimensions of language proficiency: Implications for bilingual education and the optimal age issue. *TESOL Quarterly* 14, 175–87.

Cummins, J. (1980) Bilingualism and the ESL student. *TESL Talk* 11, 8–13.

Cummins, J. (1980) Psychological assessment of immigrant children: Logic or intuition? *Journal of Multilingual and Multicultural Development* 1, 97–111.

Cummins, J. (1980) The language and culture issue in the education of minority group children. *Interchange* 10, 72–88.

Cummins, J. (1979) Linguistic interdependence and the educational development of bilingual children. *Review of Educational Research* 49, 222–51. (Reprinted in the National Dissemination and Assessment Center, Bilingual Education Paper Series, September, 1979.)

Das, J. P., Kirby, J. R., Jarman, R. F. and Cummins, J. (1979) Simultaneous and successive processes, language, and mental abilities. *Canadian Psychological Review* 20, 1–11.

Cummins, J. and Mulcahy, R. (1979) Simultaneous and successive processing and narrative speech. *Canadian Journal of Behavioural Science* 11, 64–71.

Cummins, J. (1979) Bilingualism and educational development in anglophone and minority francophone groups in Canada. *Interchange* 9, 40–51.

Cummins, J. (1979) Should the child who is experiencing difficulties in early immersion be switched to the regular English program? A reinterpretation of Trites' data. *Canadian Modern Language Review* 36, 139–43.

Swain, M. and Cummins, J. (1979) Bilingualism, cognitive functioning and education. *Language Teaching and Linguistic Abstracts* 12, 4–18.

Cummins, J. (1979) Cognitive/academic language proficiency, linguistic interdependence, the optimum age question and some other matters. *Working Papers on Bilingualism* No. 19, 197–205.

Cummins, J. (1978) Immersion programmes: The Irish experience. *International Review of Education* 24, 273–82.

Cummins, J. and Das, J. P. (1978) Academic performance and cognitive processes in EMR children. *American Journal of Mental Deficiency* 83, 197–99.

Cummins, J. and Das, J. P. (1978) Simultaneous and successive syntheses and linguistic processes. *International Journal of Psychology* 13, 129–138.

Cummins, J. and Abdollel, A. (1978) Bibliographic focus: Adjustment of immigrant children in bilingual situations. *Indian Journal of Applied Linguistics* 4, 80–5.

Cummins, J. (1978) The cognitive development of bilingual children: A review of recent research. *Indian Journal of Applied Linguistics* 4, 75–99.

Cummins, J. (1978) Bilingualism and the development of metalinguistic awareness. *Journal of Cross-cultural Psychology* 9, 131–49.

Cummins, J. (1978) The cognitive development of children in immersion programs. *The Canadian Modern Language Review* 34, 855–983.

Cummins, J. (1978) Language and children's ability to evaluate contradictions and tautologies. A critique of Osherson and Markman's findings. *Child Development* 49, 895–7.

Cummins, J. and R. Mulcahy (1978) Orientation to language in Ukrainian–English bilinguals. *Child Development* 49, 479–82.

Cummins, J. (1978) Educational implications of mother tongue maintenance for minority language groups. *Canadian Modern Language Review* 34, 395–416.

Cummins, J. and Das, J.P. (1977) Cognitive processing and reading difficulties. *Alberta Journal of Educational Research* 23, 245–56.

Cummins, J. (1977) Immersion education in Ireland: A critical review of Macnamara's findings. *Working Papers on Bilingualism* No. 13, 121–9.

Cummins, J. (1977) Delaying native language reading instruction in immersion programs: A cautionary note. *Canadian Modern Language Review* 34, 46–49.

Cummins, J. (1977) Cognitive factors associated with the attainment of intermediate levels of bilingual skills. *Modern Language Journal* 61, 3–12.

Cummins, J. (1976) The cognitive basis of the Uznadze illusion. *International Journal of Psychology* 11, 89–100.

Cummins, J. (1976) The influence of bilingualism on cognitive growth: A synthesis of research findings and explanatory hypotheses. *Working Papers on Bilingualism* No. 9, 1–43.

Cummins, J. and Gulutsan, M. (1975) Set, objectification and second language learning. *International Journal of Psychology* 10, 91–100.

Cummins, J. and Gulutsan, M. (1974) Bilingual education and cognition. *The Alberta Journal of Educational Research* 20, 259–69.

Cummins, J. (1974) Bilingual cognition: A reply to Neufeld. *Working Papers on Bilingualism* No. 4, 99–106.

Cummins, J. (1973) A theoretical perspective on the relationship between bilingualism and thought. *Working Papers on Bilingualism* No. 1, 1–9.

Papers in Conference Proceedings

Cummins, J. (in press) Psychological and cognitive bases of bilingual education. In *Proceedings of the International Congress Llengua, Societat I Ensenyament* held at Alacant, Spain, November 2000.

Cummins, J. (2000) e-Lective language learning: Design of a computer-assisted text-based ESL/EFL learning system. In G. Thill (ed.) *Sustainable Development in the Islands and the Roles of Research and Higher Education* (Vol. 2) (pp. 41–6). Proceedings of the Congress, Rhodes, Greece, 30/4–4/5/1998. Bruxelles: Prelude.

Cummins, J. (1998) Immersion education for the millennium: What have we learned from 30 years of research on second language immersion? In M. R. Childs and R. M. Bostwick (eds) *Learning through Two Languages: Research and Practice. Second Katoh Gakuen International Symposium on Immersion and Bilingual Education* (pp. 34–47). Katoh Gakuen, Japan.

Cummins, J. (1998) How can we maximize students' learning in a content-based foreign language program? In M. R. Childs and R. M. Bostwick (eds) *Learning through Two Languages: Research and Practice. Second Katoh Gakuen International Symposium on Immersion and Bilingual Education* (pp. 83–86). Katoh Gakuen, Japan.

Cummins, J. (1996) Aspectes psicolinguistics de l'educacio plurilingue. In *Ier Congrés de L'Escola Valenciana* (pp. 31–40). Valencia: Federacio Escola Valenciana.

Cummins, J. (1992) Significant developments in bilingual education. In Proceedings/ Memoria: First annual conference on 'Books in Spanish for Young Readers'. October, 1991 (pp. 5–16). San Marcos, CA: Center for the Study of Books in Spanish for Children and Adolescents.

Book Forewords and Afterwords

Cummins, J. (in press) Foreword. In A. M. Y. Lin and E. Y. F. Man *L1 and/or L2 as Medium of Instruction? International and Hong Kong Perspectives*.

Cummins, J. (2000) Foreword. In R. D. González and I. Melis (eds) *Language Ideologies: Critical Perspectives on the Official English Movement* (pp. ix–xx). Urbana, IL: National Council of Teachers of English.

Cummins, J. (2000) Foreword. In E. Ariza, C. A. Morales-Jones, N. Yahya and H. Zainnudin *Why TESOL? The Changing Face of America. Theories and Issues in Teaching English as a Second Language for K-12 Teachers* (pp. ix–xi). Dubuque, IA: Kendall/Hunt Publishing Company.

Cummins, J. (1999) Foreword. In N. Cloud, F. Genesee and E. Hamayan *Dual-language Instruction: A Handbook for Enriched Education* (pp. xi–xii). Boston: Heinle & Heinle.

Cummins, J. (2000) Foreword. In S. Nieto *Affirming Diversity: The Sociopolitical Context of Multicultural Education* (3rd edn) (pp. xv–xvii). New York: Longman.

Cummins, J. (1998) Foreword. In C. J. Ovando and V. P. Collier *Bilingual and ESL Classrooms: Teaching in Multicultural Contexts* (pp. ix–xi). Boston: McGraw-Hill.

Cummins, J. (1998) Foreword. In V. Edwards *The Power of Babel: Teaching and Learning in Multilingual Classrooms* (p. v). Stoke-on-Trent: Trentham Books.

Cummins, J. (1998) Foreword. In M. E. Brisk *Bilingual Education: From Compensatory to Quality Education* (pp. vii–ix). Mahwah, NJ: Lawrence Erlbaum Associates.

Cummins, J. (1998) Foreword. In E. Coelho *Teaching and Learning in Multicultural Schools*. Clevedon: Multilingual Matters.

Cummins, J. (1996) Foreword. In J. M. O'Malley and L.V. Pierce *Authentic Assessment for English Language Learners* (pp. iii–v). White Plains, NY: Addison Wesley.

Cummins, J. (1996) Foreword. In S. Nieto *Affirming Diversity: The Sociopolitical Context of Multicultural Education* (2nd edn) (pp. xv–xvii). New York: Longman.

Cummins, J. (1996) Preface. In J. M. Lopes and M. de Sao Pedro Lopes (eds) *Uma Longa Viagem: Historia da Emigracao Portuguesa para o Canada* (pp. iv–vi). Toronto: OISE Press.

Cummins, J. (1994) Afterword. In S. Paloma McCaleb *Building Communities of Learners* (pp. 195–99). New York: St. Martin's Press.

Cummins, J. (1992) Foreword. In S. Nieto *Affirming Diversity: The Sociopolitical Context of Multicultural Education* (pp. xvii–xix). New York: Longman.

Cummins, J. (1992) Foreword. In B. Harry *Cultural Diversity, Families, and the Special Education System: Communication and Empowerment* (pp. vii–ix). New York: Teachers College Press.

Cummins, J. (1991) Foreword. In R. A. DeVillar and C. Faltis *Computers and Cultural Diversity: Restructuring for School Success* (pp. vii–ix). Albany: SUNY Press.

Cummins, J. (1989) Foreword. In J. Sierra and I. Olazircgi *EIFE 2: Influence of Factors on the Learning of Basque: Study of the Models A, B, and D in Fifth Year Basque General Education* (pp. 15–17) Gasteiz: Central Publications Service of the Basque Government.

Cummins, J. (1988) Foreword. In M. W. O Murchú and H. O Murchú (eds) *Aspects of Bilingual Education: The Italian and Irish Experience*. Dublin: Bord Na Gaeilge.

Book Reviews

Cummins, J. and Tompkins, J. (2001). Review of S. Nieto (1999) *The Light in their Eyes: Creating Multicultural Learning Communities*. New York: Teachers College Press. *TESOL Quarterly* 35 (1), 200 1.

Cummins, J. (2000) Review of E. Thompson (ed.) *'The Emigrant's Guide to North America'* by Robert McDougall. *Canadian Ethnic Studies* 23 (2), 144–5.

Cummins, J. (2000) Review of S. D. Krashen *'Condemned Without a Trial: Bogus Arguments Against Bilingual Education'* and K. D. Samway and D. McKeon *'Myths and Realities: Best Practices for Language Minority Students'*. *Journal of Multilingual and Multicultural Development* 21 (2), 181–3.

Cummins, J. (2000) Review of J. A. Fishman (ed.) *Handbook of Language and Ethnic Identity*. Oxford: Oxford University Press, 1999. *Journal of Sociolinguistics* 4 (4), 117–20.

Cummins, J. (1998) Review of Mace-Matluck, B., Alexander-Kasparik, R. and Queen, R. (1998) *Through the Golden Door: Educational Approaches for Immigrant Adolescents with Limited Schooling*. McHenry, IL: Delta Systems and Center for Applied Linguistics. *Bilingual Research Journal* 22 (1), 83–6 (appeared in 2000).

Cummins, J. (1997) Review of J. Edwards *'Multilingualism'*. *Canadian Ethnic Studies*.

Cummins, J. (1996, May) Review of H. Baetens Beardsmore (ed.) *'European Models of Bilingual Education'*. *Comparative Education Review* 40 (2), 212–5.

Cummins, J. (1995) Review of E. Reid and H. Reich (eds) *'Breaking the Boundaries: Migrant Workers' Children in the EC'*. *Language and Education*.

Cummins, J. (1992) Review of A. G. Reynolds (ed.) *'Bilingualism, Multiculturalism, and Second Language Learning: The McGill Conference in Honour of Wallace E. Lambert'*. *Canadian Journal of Experimental Psychology* 47 (3).

Cummins, J. (1991) Review of Canadian Education Association *'Heritage Language Programs in Canadian School Boards'*. *Our Schools Our Selves* 3 (3), 170–3.

Cummins, J. (1990) Review of M. Ashworth *'Blessed with Bilingual Brains: Education of Immigrant Children with English as a Second Language'*. TESL Canada Journal 7, 103–6.
Cummins, J. (1989) Review of Hamers, J. F. and Blanc, M. H. A. *'Bilinguality and Bilingualism'*. Language and Education 3, 213–6.
Cummins, J. (1988) Review of P. O'Riagain (ed.) *'Language Planning in Ireland'*. Language, Culture and Curriculum 1, 303–8.
Cummins, J. (1988) Review of K. Hakuta *'Mirror of Language: The Debate on Bilingualism'*. Studies in Second Language Acquisition 10, 74–5.
Cummins, J. (1988) Review of B. McLaughlin *'Second Language Acquisition in Childhood'* (2nd edn) (Vol. 1). Contemporary Psychology.
Cummins, J. (1985) Review of A. Tosi *'Immigration and Bilingual Education'*. Journal of Multilingual and Multicultural Development 6, 515–9.
Cummins, J. (1980) Review of H. Giles (ed.) *'Language, Ethnicity and Intergroup Processes'*. Language in Society 9.
Cummins, J. (1978) Review of A. Simoes (ed.) *'The Bilingual Child'*. International Review of Education 24, 427.
Cummins, J. (1978) Review of M. Cole *et al.* *'The Cultural Context of Learning and Thinking'*. The Economic and Social Review 4, 605.

Technical Writings
Tests
Munoz, A., Cummins, J., Alvarado, C. G. and Ruef, M. L. (1998) *The Bilingual Verbal Ability Tests*. Itasca, IL: Riverside Publishing.

Curriculum Programs
Cummins, J. (co-author) (2000) *Lectura Scott Foresman*. Glenview, IL: Scott Foresman.
Cummins, J. (ESL consulting author). (2000). *Reading 2000*. Glenview, IL: Scott Foresman.
Cummins, J. (co-author) (2000) *Adding English: ESL Teacher's Guide. Grades 1, 2, 3* (3 volumes). Ancilliary material for *Reading 2000*. Glenview, IL: Scott Foresman.
Cummins, J. (consulting author) (2000) *Ciencias*. Scott Foresman.
Cummins, J. (ESL consulting author) (1999) *The Literacy Place Teacher's Guide (Grades 4, 5, 6)*. Toronto: Scholastic Canada.
Chamot, A. U., Cummins, J., Kessler, C., O'Malley, J. M. and Wong Fillmore, L. (1996) *Scott Foresman ESL: Accelerating English Language Learning*. Glenview, IL: Scott Foresman Addison Wesley.
Ada, A. F., Chamot, A. U., Cummins, J., Ewy, C., Kessler, C. and O'Malley, J. M. (consulting authors) (1995) *Parade*. Glenview IL: Scott Foresman Publishers.

Reports
Cummins, J. (1999) Medium of instruction in schools: The case of Canada and the United States. Paper prepared for the Regional Report on Medium of Instruction in Schools, Hong Kong Standing Committee on Language Education and Research, April 1999.
Cummins, J. (1999) The construct of general language proficiency: Theoretical foundations, assessment, and articulation to the Canadian language benchmarks. Prepared for the Canadian Language Benchmarks Assessment Project, Peel Board of Education, March.
Cummins, J. (1998) Options for accommodation and exemptions for ESL students. Report prepared for the Education Quality and Accountability Office, Toronto, Ontario.
Cummins, J. (1994) The role of language maintenance and literacy development in promoting academic achievement in a multicultural society. A report prepared for the Ontario Royal Commission on Learning.
Cumming, A., Hart, D., Corson, D. and Cummins, J. (1993) Provisions and demands for ESL, ESD, and ALF programs in Ontario schools. Report submitted to the Ontario Ministry of Education and Training, December, 1993.

Cummins, J. (1992) Interpretations of Calgary RCSSD #1 Literacy Immersion Project Year 3 data. Report submitted to the Calgary RCSSB #1.

Cummins, J. (1990) Assessment and placement of minority students: Identification and analysis of significant initiatives and policy options in Ontario. Unpublished research report, OISE.

Cummins, J. and Lam, M. (1989) The classroom microcomputer as a catalyst for interactive/experiential pedagogy. Unpublished research report, OISE.

Cummins, J. and Aguiar, M. (1988) Conference report: National conference on heritage language teacher training. Final report submitted to the Multiculturalism sector, Secretary of State, March.

Harley, B., Allen, P., Cummins, J. and Swain, M. (1987) The development of bilingual proficiency (Vols I, II, III). Final report submitted to the SSHRC, April.

Cummins, J. (1987) The National Heritage Language Resource Unit. Final report submitted to the Multiculturalism Sector, Secretary of State, March.

Harley, B., Allen, P., Cummins, J. and Swain, M. (1983) The development of bilingual proficiency. Second year report submitted to the SSHRC, June.

Cummins, J. (1984) Evaluation of the Calgary French School. Report submitted to the Board of Directors, Calgary French School, September.

Cummins, J. (1983) Policy report: Language and literacy learning in bilingual instruction. Austin, TX: Southwest Educational Development Laboratory.

Cummins, J., Swain, M., Nakajima, K., Handscombe, J., Green, D. and Tran, C. (1983) Linguistic interdependence among Japanese and Vietnamese immigrant students. Washington, DC: National Clearinghouse for Bilingual Education.

Cummins, J. (1982) Interdependence and cultural ambivalence: Regarding the pedagogical rationale for bilingual education. Rosslyn, VI: National Clearinghouse for Bilingual Education. (Occasional publication).

Cummins, J. and Green, D. (1982) Early identification of learning difficulties among bilingual children: A pilot study. Research report submitted to the North York Board of Education.

Lapkin, S. and Cummins, J. (1981) Evaluation of the Frontenac-Lennox and Addington Roman Catholic Separate School Board Grades Five and Six bilingual program, Year 2, OISE.

Cummins, J. (1980) Psychological assessment of immigrant students. Research report. (ED 206 153)

Lapkin, S. and Cummins, J. (1980) Evaluation of the Frontenac-Lennox and Addington Roman Catholic Separate School Board Grade Five bilingual program, Year 1, OISE.

Carey, S. T. and Cummins, J. (1978) English and French achievement of Grade 5 children from English, French and mixed French-English home backgrounds attending the Edmonton Separate School System English–French bilingual program. Report submitted to the Edmonton Separate School System.

Madaus, G., Kellaghan, T., Rakow, E., King, D., Cummins, J. and Polit, D. (1975) A study of the sensitivity of measures of school effectiveness. Report submitted to the Carnegie Corporation, New York, 1975.

Other Publications

Cummins, J. (2000) BICS and CALP: Clarifying the distinction. *ED 438 551.*

Cummins, J. (1999) Linguistic enrichment in dual-language Spanish/English programs. *Leadership Letters: Issues and Trends in Bilingual Education.* Glenview, IL: Scott Foresman.

Cummins, J. (1999, June) Research, ethics, and public discourse: The debate on bilingual education. *AAHE Bulletin* 51 (10), 3–5.

Watson, C. and Cummins, J. (1999, March) Some things to know about children acquiring two languages. *WigWag* 3–5.

Cummins, J. (1998) Rossell and Baker: Their case for the effectiveness of bilingual education. *Currents in Literacy* 1 (2), pp. 10, 11 & 31. (Also appeared in *California Association for Bilingual Education Newsletter* 21 (3), pp. 10, 33–4).

Cummins, J. (1996) Official English on the Brink. *The Clarion: Newsletter of the European Second Language Association* 2 (1), 27–8.

Cummins, J. (1996) *Accelerating English Language Learning*. Glenview, IL: Scott Foresman Publishers.

Cummins, J. and Danesi, M. (1995) Literacy and heritage language education: What does the research say? *Il Forneri* 9 (2), 70–83 (published in 1999).

Cummins, J. (1993) Underdompelingsprogramma's (2): Hjoeddeiske problemen en rjochtlinen foar de takomst. *De Pompebleden* 64 (2), April, 32–7.

Cummins, J. (1993) Underdompelingsprogramma's (1): Hjoeddeiske problemen en rjochtlinen foar de takomst. *De Pompebleden* 64 (1), February, 11–14.

Cummins, J. (1993) Negotiating identities in the ESL classroom. *Contact* 19 (1), 30–2.

Cummins, J. (1991) Heritage languages in Canadian schools: Fact and friction. *Lectures and Papers in Ethnicity* No. 6. Department of Sociology, University of Toronto.

Cummins, J. (1987) Bilingual education and politics. *The Education Digest* 53, 30–3. (Abridged from *Interracial Books for Children Bulletin* 1986.)

Cummins, J. (1986) Around the world in 80 seconds: Computer networks and language learning. *Heritage Language Bulletin* 1, 1–3.

Cummins, J. (1986) Computers stimulate real life language interaction. *Canadian Parents for French Newsletter* 35, 4.

Cummins, J. and Glazer, N. (1986) Viewpoints on bilingual education. *California School Boards Journal* 44, 10–13. (Abridged from *Equity and Choice* 2.)

Aguiar, M., Cummins, J., Fiorucci, S., Katsaiti, L. and Kruk, R. (1986) *The Write Way. Promoting Creative Writing in Heritage Languages*. Toronto: The National Heritage Language Resource Unit.

Cummins, J. (1985) Bilingualism and minority language children. *Manitoba Heritage Review* 2, 7–10.

Cummins, J. (1985) Bilingualism in the home. *Heritage Language Bulletin* 1, 10–11.

Cummins, J. (1982) Tests, achievement and bilingual students. *Focus* No. 9, 1–5.

Cummins, J. (1982) A test is a test are tests: Psychological tests and students for whom English is a second language. *Set: Research Information for Teachers* (New Zealand) No. 2, 1–4.

Cummins, J. (1982) A short summary and discussion of related research. In *Towards a Comprehensive Language Policy: The Final Report of the Work Group on Third Language Instruction*. Toronto Board of Education.

Cummins, J. (1981) Research findings from French immersion programs across Canada: A parent's guide. In BC Ministry of Education, *Early French Immersion: Teacher's Resource Book*. Victoria: Ministry of Education, British Columbia, 1981. Reprinted as CFP Special Report, *Canadian Parents for French Newsletter*, October, 1983.

Cummins, J. (1980) Mother-tongue maintenance for minority language children: Some common misconceptions. Translated into Korean, Vietnamese and Spanish and distributed by the California State Department of Education, 1980. (Reprinted in Inner London Education Authority, *Forum* No. 2, Spring 1984.)

Cummins, J. (1980) Det Forsta Spraket (The first language). *Invandrare och Minoriteter* (Sweden) 12–18.

Cummins, J. (1980) Report on Georgetown University Round Table. *SLANT* 58–65.

Cummins, J. (1977) The linguistic and cognitive development of retarded children: A review of recent research. *Mental Retardation Bulletin* 5, 9–29.

Cummins, J. (1976) Sensitivity to non-verbal communication as a factor in language learning. *Grazer Linguisitic Studien* No. 3.

Cummins, J. (1976) The Coleman Report ten years later. *Mental Retardation Bulletin* 4, 139–46.